EVERY DOG

THE ULTIMATE GUIDE
TO OVER 450 DOG BREEDS

NANCY HAJESKI

FIREFLY BOOKS

"The world would be a nicer place if everyone had the ability to love as unconditionally as a dog."

M.K. CLINTON

A FIREFLY BOOK

Published by Firefly Books Ltd. 2016
Copyright © 2016 Moseley Road Inc

First printing

Publisher Cataloging-in-Publication Data (U.S.)
A CIP record for this title is available from Library of Congress

Library and Archives Canada Cataloguing in Publication
A CIP record for this title is available from Library and Archives Canada

Published in the United States by
Firefly Books (U.S.) Inc.
P.O. Box 1338, Ellicott Station
Buffalo, New York 14205

Published in Canada by
Firefly Books Ltd.
50 Staples Avenue, Unit 1
Richmond Hill, Ontario L4B 0A7

All other correspondence (author inquiries, permissions) concerning the content of this book should be addressed to Moseley Road Inc., info@moseleyroad.com;
www.moseleyroad.com
President: Sean Moore
Designer: Adam Moore
Layout Designers: Tina Vaughan and Heather McCarry
Production Director: Adam Moore

Printed in China

With thanks to Duncan Youel and Philippa Baile OilOften.co.uk

EVERY DOG

CONTENTS

AT A GLANCE EXPLAINED

AT A GLANCE
The explanations below will help you understand the different topics in the breed characteristic charts.

EASE OF TRAINING
This refers to a dog's ability to respond to a verbal or physical prompt and master commands like "sit," "heel," "come," and "stay." (The average dog can recognize 165 words, the same as a two-year-old child, as well as hand signals and gestures.) These are the basic commands dogs should know, especially if you wish to ensure their safety off leash. Some breeds are adept at learning quickly, while other, more opportunistic, breeds may need rewards or games to comply.

AFFECTION
This is the level of emotional response your dog offers you and your family. Many breeds are effusive, returning loving responses to human overtures. Others can be aloof or independent, rarely seeking physical attention or displaying cuddling behavior; instead they show their affection by remaining nearby and staying highly attuned to their families. It helps to start with a puppy that has been raised in a home environment and knows how to bond with humans.

PLAYFULNESS
This measures your dog's desire for engaging in fun activities. It also indicates the amount of physical interaction your dog will expect you to supply. Some breeds can tire out a room full of toddlers; others are happy to lounge with you in front of the TV. Senior citizens or apartment dwellers probably don't want a breed that needs hours of play or exercise; conversely, activity-inclined adults or families with young children or teens won't want a canine couch potato. Certain breeds are also quite good at amusing themselves— gathering up their toys or patrolling squirrels from window to window. Be aware that there are some herding breeds that need assigned "jobs" . . . or they will end up herding your children and their friends.

GOOD WITH CHILDREN
Breeders use the term "soft" when describing certain gentle, amiable, forgiving breeds, and these are the ones that are especially good with children. Then again, the "nanny" breeds are not foolproof on an individual basis, while even hyper or dominant breeds can learn to live with and love kids. One potential indicator of temperament is to meet both parents of your puppy and gauge their interactions with children.

GOOD WITH OTHER DOGS

The breeds that are noted as tolerant of other dogs will generally accept them as housemates and will not show aggression toward them outside the home. Pack hunters, such as beagles or coonhounds, are known to enjoy the company of other dogs. Yet there are many variables that can affect how one dog sees another. Some dominant or territorial breeds can happily play with other dogs outdoors, but will not tolerate them in their home. If you choose to house multiple dogs of any breed that have not been raised together, introduce them slowly and carefully over a period of several days.

GROOMING REQUIRED

With certain breeds, grooming not only improves appearance but also helps to maintaining good health. The majority of long-haired breeds need multiple daily brushings to remove the undercoat and keep them snarl-free, whereas short-haired breeds usually require only a quick brushing and an occasional bath or ear cleaning. Curly-, wire- or broken-coated dogs, like poodles and terriers, need frequent trips to the groomer for trimming and shaping. Wrinkled breeds like the Chinese Shar Pei, or hairless breeds like the Peruvian Inca Orchid, are prone to skin ailments and may require prescription salves or lotions and the application of sun block. Obviously, the coats of show dogs, especially long-haired breeds such as the Lhasa Apso, Irish Setter, or Afghan Hound, require a much higher level of care than those of companion dogs.

DISCLAIMER

The traits and qualities listed here under "At A Glance" are based on kennel club guidelines, breeders' recommendations, and studies of various breeds. The behavior of different breeds, however, can also be affected by a puppy's experiences during its formative months, levels of training, and a variety of other factors. If you buy a dog from a reputable breeder, most of them will help you deal with any behavioral problems or replace the puppy if remedial measures do not work. Also, remember that puppies, just like human children, go through difficult stages, like the "terrible twos." As a wise owner it is up to you to whether these awkward phases and to understand that common misbehaviors—gnawing, chewing, crying, howling, growling, relieving themselves indoors—are rarely a sign of a bad puppy, but rather an indication that you and your new pet still need to work on communicating.

INTRODUCTION

THE NATURE OF A DOG

No other mammal—and certainly no domestic animal—has been transformed by human requirements (or their aesthetic whims) into such a broad range of shapes, sizes, and coat textures as the modern-day dog. The towering Irish Wolfhound and the diminutive Chihuahua are the exact same species, as are the narrow-skulled Borzoi and the blunt-faced English Bulldog. Ditto the speedy Whippet and the ambling, low-slung Basset Hound, as well as the long-haired Collie, the plush-coated Chow Chow, the wire-haired Border Terrier, the dreadlocked Komondor, and the virtually hairless Chinese Crested. And although most dogs were "engineered" to perform specific tasks—form following function—certain dogs were bred solely for a fashionable appearance or a pleasing nature. Hence, we find the dandification of the French Poodle, with a dense, curling coat that lends itself to stylish trims (based on traditional clips that were meant to protect this one-time sporting dog's organs in the field and water) and the rise of the endearing toy breeds, those favorites of royalty, which could easily be transported in one's coat pocket—or sleeve, in the case of the Pekingese.

The fact that canines are conspecific explains why vastly different breeds are able to mate and produce fertile offspring—called purebreds if both parents are the same breed, crossbreeds if the parents are two purebreds, and mongrels or mutts if one or both parents are crossbreeds.

THE EARLIEST CANIDS

Dogs evolved from small, early flesh-eating mammals known as *Creodonts*, which roamed the planet along with the dinosaurs. They, in turn, evolved into tree- and den-dwelling *Miacis*, roughly 54 to 38 million years ago, through *Cynodictus* (or possibly *Hesperocyon*) to a wolflike, bone-crushing carnivore known as *Tomarctus*. Twelve million years ago this early canid arose in North America and then spread to Eurasia. Two million years ago the foundation stock for modern carnivores evolved, including the canid family from which came foxes, wolves, jackals, hyenas, and dogs.

Most researchers agree that dogs were descended from the gray wolf of central Asia, *canis lupus*, and domesticated from 17,000 to 14,000 years ago. It is believed that their relationship with man first started with scavenging wolves picking over the remains of animal carcasses discarded near human camps. Perhaps a bold wolf puppy wandered into the camp itself and was fostered by the humans. Adopting the offspring of native species as pets is still common in many primitive cultures, indicating that wild babies were likely no strangers to early man. If that wolf pup grew into a trusting companion animal, it's not impossible to imagine it coursing—running down—game for its new family, or indicating to a group of hunters where prey might be hiding.

By the time of the first recorded histories,

dogs were already entrenched within human society. Yet they were not always welcome additions to the culture. Although they featured prominently in early Middle Eastern and Indian life and were venerated by the Egyptians, who considered them part of the family, dogs were believed to be unclean or impure by certain Jewish and Muslim sects and were forbidden entry in the home. In ancient China and Mesoamerica, dogs were both revered as messengers of the gods and also consumed as food and used for sacrifice—something of a mixed blessing.

RECLAIMING THE OUTCASTS

For centuries the term "pariah" dogs was given to any feral or free-ranging dogs that lived in and around human settlements and fed on their refuse. Today, many of these aboriginal or outcast dogs, such as the Canaan Dog of the Middle East, are now recognized as authentic breeds and are being selectively bred. Pariahs often display primitive features—yellow, rusty, or spotted coloring and a fox-like or wolf-like appearance: wedge-shaped head, almond eyes, pointed muzzle, erect ears, and long, curved tails.

Some studies indicate that breeds like the Carolina Dog, the Singing Dog of New Guinea, and the African Basenji descended from Dingoes—the feral Australian dogs whose ancestors were semi-domesticated dogs of East Asia. Other researchers believe the Dingo might be a species unto itself.

MAPPING CANINE GENES

One of the most exciting aspects of studying *canis lupus familiaris* is that genetic research is furnishing new, often controversial, details about its evolution. Although science generally accepted that dogs evolved from wolves, it was not until researchers were able to study the DNA of dogs that their true origins came to light. In a 2009 study, a team of scientists at the Royal Institute of Technology in Stockholm analyzed the mitochondrial DNA from the cell walls of dogs around the globe and found indications that dogs shared one lineage—that is, that all dogs sprang from one domestication event in one location. Subsequently, a major European DNA project called LUPA, which was formed to study the pathogenesis of diseases common to both humans and dogs, mapped the genes of a wide range of dog breeds, using SNP, simple nucleotide polymorphism, to establish a DNA fingerprint for each of 35 breeds. LUPA's analysis revealed that dogs had descended from wolves alone and that early humans had bred dogs independently in many locations around the world. Clearly, there is still a great deal to be uncovered on this front.

> "When the Man waked up he said, 'What is Wild Dog doing here?' And the Woman said, 'His name is not Wild Dog any more, but the First Friend, because he will be our friend for always and always and always.'"
>
> RUDYARD KIPLING

Canine genetic research has also revealed that only a few powerful genes lead to the vast diversity of dog shapes and sizes, whereas the unique appearance of human beings is created through the interaction of hundreds of different weak genes.

THE RIGHT DOG FOR THE JOB

The physical evolution of the domestic dog, from lupine lurker around campfires to the versatile "shape-shifting" companion we know today, was made possible by selective breeding by their early masters, who chose only dogs that displayed desired traits—a keen nose, swiftness of foot, or a docile temperament—for reproduction, with the hope that they would pass those traits on to their offspring.

The basic canine types that eventually developed fell into five skill categories: hunting, guarding, herding, working dogs, and companion dogs. Greyhounds, which are swift coursing sight hounds, were possibly the first "type" developed, with the Saluki, or Arabian Greyhound, being the first distinct "breed." Large, heavy-boned guardian dogs similar to the Mastiff and called Molossers, were the second type that evolved. Within these five categories, dogs were used in many capacities—as hunters they located, flushed, chased, took down, and retrieved game; as guardians they protected families and homes, merchants and businesses, farms and livestock, and soldiers and military encampments; as herders they directed and

drove livestock; and as workers they pulled carts or sleds and turned spits or industrial treadmills, sought out and rescued those lost on land or at sea; or performed in stage shows. As companion dogs they offered an affectionate and steady presence in the home, and often acted as a nanny to young children. Their roles have not changed much over the passing years. For instance, certain large, sturdy breeds are still used by law enforcement and the military as guard dogs and sentry dogs. Government agencies now also use dogs with a keen sense of smell to detect drugs and other contraband and to perform search and rescue missions.

In modern times a new category arose— service or assistance dogs, which are trained to lead the blind, "hear" for the deaf, and aid those who are disabled in other ways. Service dogs can be of almost any breed, and because they are allowed into public buildings and on public transport, they typically wear some kind of harness or vest to distinguish them. There are also therapy dogs that visit people in hospitals, retirement homes, nursing homes, and hospices, as well as comfort dogs that provide affection and emotional support to residents of areas that have suffered natural disasters or mass shooting attacks.

Most of the modern dog breeds we encounter today were developed during the last two hundred years. Unfortunately, some breeds have been altered to meet show ring standards that call for extreme traits, such as the blunt muzzle of the Boxer or the low rear stance of the German Shepherd. The current attitude among many dog aficionados is to move away from these physical extremes, which can affect the health of the animal as it matures.

While many breeds of the past, like the Alaunt, a massive hunting dog used for centuries to chase large game, or the crooked-legged little Turnspit Dog of the Tudor through Victorian eras, have been lost to us, some ancient breeds, like the African Basenji and the Mexican Xoloitzcuintli, still exist—and bear a close resemblance to ancestors that were immortalized on monuments and tombs.

A CHERISHED RELATIONSHIP

Regardless of their appearance or bloodlines, all domesticated dogs have an eons-long interdependence on humans. Those that gave up the thrill of the pack hunt and noisy revels beneath the moon for the more mundane comforts of the fireside—among them food and shelter—in return began to work for their new masters, turned their territorial aggression against any outside threat and hunting or herding, simply for the reward of an encouraging word.

At the same time, the early humans whom these dogs honored with their company understood they were getting the best of the bargain—dependable guardians and hunters who, over time, developed such a powerful bond with their new homo sapien "packs" that another plus factor entered the equation: love. And unconditional love, at that. Dogs not only served their humans, they soon came to venerate them, placing *their* needs foremost over their own and in some case dying for them. This level of canine worship resulted in an almost equally doting response from their owners—an appreciation of the dog far beyond its ability to perform its given job. As millennia passed, dogs were increasingly recognized as jolly, uplifting companions, and many left the fields to become valued household members. This was their new job, simply being cherished family pets.

While we may never know precisely what it is about these animals that allows them to steal our hearts at the same time they guard our homes, we do know that in their relatively short lifespans they affect us so deeply that the death of a companion dog grieves us on a level akin to the loss of a family member. There is surely something in our fragile human natures that craves the solid comfort and unspoken understanding that these remarkable creatures are capable of providing.

SIGHTHOUNDS & PARIAHS

Afghan Hound

Tazi / Da Kochyano Spay / Ogar Afgan / Barakzai Hound /
Eastern Greyhound / Persian Greyhound

AFGHANISTAN

Exercise required

Afghan Hound pup

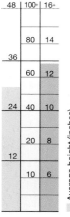

Common
Coat Colors

Common colors include red, cream, domino, blue, brindle, and black and tan.

In spite of their elegant appearance, Afghans were bred to hunt. They are aloof, haughty dogs around strangers, but can be loving, playful companions in the home. With their gorgeous, high-maintenance coats and their regal manner, these dogs could be considered the "super-models" of the canine world.

AT A GLANCE

Ease of training	■■ ■
Affection	■■ ■■
Playfulness	■■ ■
Good with children	■■ ■
Good with other dogs	■■ ■
Grooming required	■■ ■■ ■■

! Afghans' silky coats are extremely high maintenance.

+ Afghans are prone to cataracts and often suffer from the lung disease chylothorax. They can also be sensitive to anesthesia.

HISTORY

Afghan Hounds were originally employed as hunters and guardians in their native Afghanistan and their lineage pre-dates our modern breeds. Returning British army officers took sighthounds from Afghanistan, India, and Iran home with them in the early 1900s. The most famous dog, which set the breed standard, was Zardin, imported from India in 1907. In the 1920s, two types were imported to UK and formed the basis for breed development there. The Afghan arrived in the U.S. in 1922, with breeding kennels established on the East Coast. Zeppo Marx, youngest of the Marx brothers, famously imported two Afghans in 1931.

Africanis

African Dog / Bantu Dog / Hottentot Hunting Dog / Khoikhoi Dog
Tswana breed dog / Zulu Dog / Umbwa Wa Ki-Shenzi

SOUTH AFRICA

Exercise required
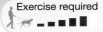

Africanis puppy

		48	100+	16+
			80	14
		36		
			60	12
		24	40	10
			20	8
		12		
			10	6

Average height (inches)
Average weight (pounds)
Average life expectancy (years)

Common
Coat Colors

The Africanis is an ancient Southern African dog with a friendly, though watchful, temperament. It is known for its physical strength, speed, and exceptional good health. This short-coated, medium-sized dog is well muscled, can be of any color, and occasionally shows a ridgeback.

✚ This breed's good health may be because over the years it has developed a natural resistance to disease and internal and external parasites.

! Reportedly, these dogs can become grumpy as they grow older.

AT A GLANCE

Ease of training	
Affection	
Playfulness	
Good with children	
Good with other dogs	
Grooming required	

HISTORY

Traditional African dogs arrived in Egypt around 4700 BCE from the Levant. The Egyptians bred them to be swift and slender, and they continued there for centuries in isolation, eventually migrating to southern Africa. As time passed, they likely bred with the dogs of traders or seafarers until the current type was achieved. Their Swahili name, *Umbwa Wa Ki-Shenzi,* means common or mongrel.

American Staghound

Staghound
AMERICA

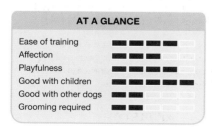

American
Staghound pup

Common
Coat Colors

Exercise required

48	100+	16+		
	80	14		
36				
	60	12		
24	40	10	Average height (inches)	Average life expectancy (years)
	20	8	Average weight (pounds)	
12				
	10	6		

AT A GLANCE

Ease of training	
Affection	
Playfulness	
Good with children	
Good with other dogs	
Grooming required	

➕ Due to its low percentage of body fat-to-muscle ratio, the Staghound is sensitive to anesthesia.

❗ Staghounds are very fast but are not hyperactive.

The American Staghound was originally created to hunt deer, wolves, and coyote, and still fills the role of a large animal hunter today. They resemble the Greyhound, but come in two coat varieties—smooth and rough, and are accepted in all coat colors. This breed is gentle, calm, and affectionate with children and makes a wonderful family dog, especially in rural environments with lots of open space. Staghounds may not be suitable for homes with smaller, furry pets, which they may see as prey. They are seldom territorial, so don't make the best watchdogs.

HISTORY

The American Staghound resulted from settlers crossing Scottish deerhounds and Greyhounds, and both are still occasionally introduced to enrich the breed. The modern version likely traces back to the 1800s; General George Armstrong Custer used them to hunt on the American plains.

Azawakh

Idi / Hanshee / Oska / Rawondu
Bareeru / Wulo

EGYPT

Exercise required

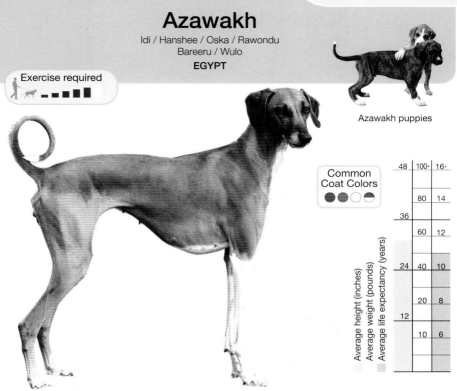

Azawakh puppies

Common
Coat Colors

	Average height (inches)	Average weight (pounds)	Average life expectancy (years)
	48	100+	16+
		80	14
	36		
		60	12
	24	40	10
		20	8
	12		
		10	6

Azawakhs are a graceful, elegant breed that were once used for hunting gazelles. They are aloof and haughty with strangers, but become very emotionally attached to their families. Their hunting instincts make them some danger to smaller animals; they will possibly give chase if they see them running.

AT A GLANCE

Ease of training	
Affection	
Playfulness	
Good with children	
Good with other dogs	
Grooming required	

 The dogs are very social and can be emotional.

✚ There is a small occurrence of adult-onset idiopathic epilepsy in the breed.

HISTORY

This breed originated from the pariah dogs of Sub-Saharan Africa—also called bush dogs or basenji—and it is also closely related to the Sloughi of the Maghreb. Despite morphological similarities, mitochondrial DNA evidence shows that it is only very distantly related to other sighthounds. They are relatively uncommon in Europe and North America, but there is a growing band of devotees.

Basenji

African Bush Dog / African Barkless Dog / Ango Angari / Congo Dog / aZande Dog

DEMOCRATIC REPUBLIC OF THE CONGO

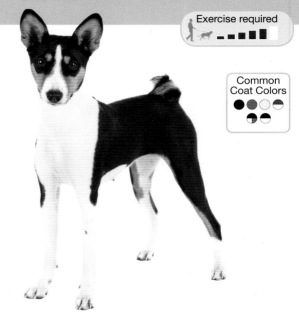

Exercise required

Basenji pup

Common Coat Colors

Average height (inches)
Average weight (pounds)
Average life expectancy (years)

48	100+	16+
	80	14
36		
	60	12
24	40	10
	20	8
12		
	10	6

This deer-like, primitive Central African breed was once used to track lions. These unique, playful dogs form strong bonds of loyalty with their owners and families. They are inquisitive and extremely playful, and are often noted for their excellent problem-solving abilities. Basenjis are called "barkless dogs," but they definitely do communicate—through a range of chortles, yodels, and barroos. They are also known for being very clean, almost odorless dogs—another primitive trait.

AT A GLANCE

Ease of training	▮▮▮▮▯
Affection	▮▮▮▮▯
Playfulness	▮▮▮▮▯
Good with children	▮▮▮▮▯
Good with other dogs	▮▮▯▯▯
Grooming required	▮▯▯▯▯

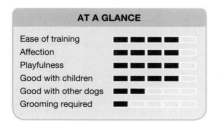

! The Basenji tends to become emotionally attached to a single human.

+ Basenjis are prone to Fanconi syndrome, a kidney ailment, and may suffer blindness from PRA (progressive retinal atrophy).

HISTORY

Recent genetic testing has revealed that these are among the oldest type dog in the world—likely descended from Asian wolf crosses—making them an important link to ancient canine history. Similar dogs are seen on many Egyptian stelae, sitting at the feet of royalty. Their name means "wild dog from the bush," as it was in the remote bushlands of Africa's Congo Basin that they developed their unique characteristics. The breed was not discovered by Europeans until the nineteenth century. Two dogs were exhibited at Crufts in London in 1895, but tragically both died from distemper. Basenjis arrived in the U.S. in 1937, and the AKC recognized them in 1944.

Borzoi

Barzoï / Russian Wolfhound / Russian Hunting Sighthound
Russkaya / Psovaya Borzaya / Psovoi

RUSSIA

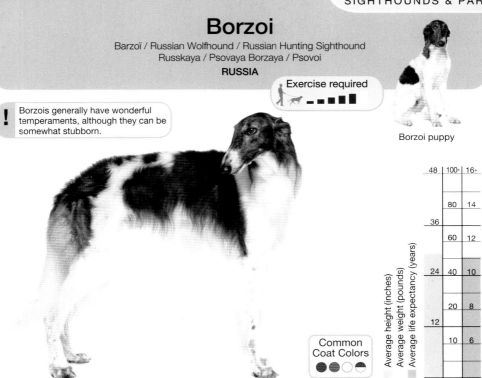

Exercise required

> ! Borzois generally have wonderful temperaments, although they can be somewhat stubborn.

Borzoi puppy

48	100+	16+
	80	14
36		
	60	12
24	40	10
	20	8
12		
	10	6

Average height (inches)
Average weight (pounds)
Average life expectancy (years)

Common Coat Colors

Slender, elegant Borzois can make wonderful companion animals, though as sighthounds, they retain a strong hunting instinct that can put smaller pets at risk. While outwardly lithe and graceful, they are also surprisingly strong and tenacious. These were wolf hunters, after all. Generally they have calm, friendly temperaments, though they can be stubborn and require competent, experienced owners.

AT A GLANCE

Ease of training	▬▬ ▬/▬
Affection	▬▬ ▬▬ ▬/
Playfulness	▬▬ ▬▬ ▬▬
Good with children	▬▬ ▬▬ ▬▬
Good with other dogs	▬▬ ▬▬
Grooming required	▬▬ ▬/▬

> ✚ The breed is known to be at a higher risk from mastocytoma (mast cell tumors) than the general dog population.

HISTORY

These elegant dogs, also known as Russian Wolfhounds, were originally bred for hunting wolves and hares in Russia. The breed is believed to have developed through cross-breeding ancient sighthounds, such as the Saluki, with heavier native Russian dogs. Some of the earliest references to "hare-coursing dogs" date back to the year 1260 at the court of the Grand Duke of Novgorod. There are also records of a special breeding station for these sighthounds at the Imperial Czar's kennels in Gatchina that date back to 1613. The breed was first imported to the United States in 1888, and was registered by the AKC in 1891. By this date, the breed had also become popular in the UK, due to the influence of Kathleen, Duchess of Newcastle, who had established a breeding kennel that produced a number of champion dogs.

19

Canaan Dog

ISRAEL

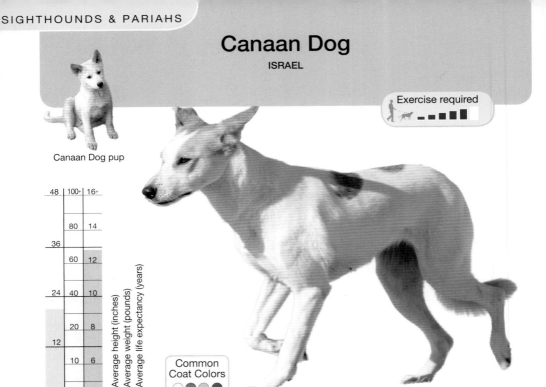

Exercise required

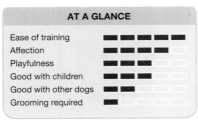

Canaan Dog pup

48	100+	16+
	80	14
36		
	60	12
24	40	10
	20	8
12		
	10	6

Average height (inches)
Average weight (pounds)
Average life expectancy (years)

Common Coat Colors

The Canaan Dog, a pariah dog of the Middle East, has been in existence for thousands of years—sometimes feral, sometimes domesticated. The modern Canaans share many qualities of other primitive dogs, including a strong survival instinct. They will bark at strangers, making them good watchdogs, but they are not aggressive. This breed is good with children, enjoys active family life, and excels at competitions like obedience, showmanship, agility, flyball, tracking, and herding.

AT A GLANCE

Ease of training	■ ■ ■ ■ ■
Affection	■ ■ ■ ■
Playfulness	■ ■ ■
Good with children	■ ■ ■
Good with other dogs	■ ■
Grooming required	■

+ Canaans are a hardy breed and don't suffer from any known hereditary health problems.

! Canaan Dogs are blessed with an endearing and responsive personality.

HISTORY

This early dog was used by the Israelites to guard their camps and herd their livestock. Excavations of an ancient dog cemetery in Ashkelon, Israel, unearthed 700 dog skeletons, all of them anatomically similar to the modern Canaan dog. Canaan Dogs were unknown in the West until 1934, when Austrian animal behaviorist Rudolphina Menzel began training them as guard dogs for the Israeli Defence Forces.

Carolina Dog

UNITED STATES

Exercise required

Carolina Dog puppy

		Average height (inches)	Average weight (pounds)	Average life expectancy (years)
	48		100+	16+
			80	14
	36			
			60	12
	24		40	10
			20	8
	12			
			10	6

Common Coat Colors

The Carolina Dog, a primitive breed of North America, is surprisingly similar to a small Dingo in appearance. It is well-muscled and powerful for its size, a free-running dog, showing strong movement with a lot of drive; it is also agile and able to turn instantly. The breed is known for its "fish-hook" tail, which is carried in various positions according to the mood of the dog, but is never slack or loose.

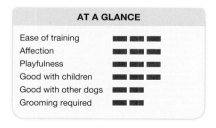

AT A GLANCE	
Ease of training	▅▅▅ ▅▅▅ ▅▅▅
Affection	▅▅▅ ▅▅▅ ▅▅▅
Playfulness	▅▅▅ ▅▅▅
Good with children	▅▅▅ ▅▅▅
Good with other dogs	▅▅▅ ▅▅
Grooming required	▅▅▅ ▅▅

! These active dogs are not recommended for apartment life.

➕ Generally healthy, the Carolina Dog should be taken for a daily long walk.

HISTORY

Carolina Dogs were originally Native American dogs and were the first domesticated canines of the Americas, thought to be direct descendants of the ancient pariah dogs that accompanied Asians across the Bering Strait land bridge 8,000 years ago. In the 1970s this same dog was discovered roaming wooded areas of the Deep South by Dr. I. Lehr Brisbin, Jr., a senior research ecologist at the University of Georgia's Savannah River Ecology Lab. It was he who named them. The remoteness of their home area allowed the dogs to develop naturally, with little influence from other breeds.

Chippiparai

Tamil Greyhound / Tamil Nadu
INDIA

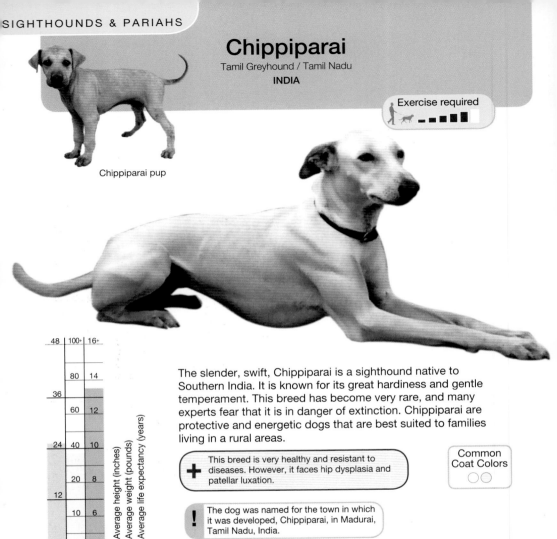

Chippiparai pup

Exercise required

The slender, swift, Chippiparai is a sighthound native to Southern India. It is known for its great hardiness and gentle temperament. This breed has become very rare, and many experts fear that it is in danger of extinction. Chippiparai are protective and energetic dogs that are best suited to families living in a rural areas.

Common Coat Colors

+ This breed is very healthy and resistant to diseases. However, it faces hip dysplasia and patellar luxation.

! The dog was named for the town in which it was developed, Chippiparai, in Madurai, Tamil Nadu, India.

Average height (inches)
Average weight (pounds)
Average life expectancy (years)

48	100+	16+
	80	14
36		
	60	12
24	40	10
	20	8
12		
	10	6

HISTORY

This breed is believed to be a descendant of the Saluki, one of the world's oldest pure-bred dogs. For many years Chippiparais were highly valued in Southern India for their incredible speed, and they were held only by those of the highest caste. Wealthy aristocrats in Tamil Nadu sent them into the field after deer, hare, and wild boar.

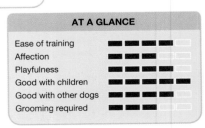

AT A GLANCE

Ease of training
Affection
Playfulness
Good with children
Good with other dogs
Grooming required

Cirneco dell'etna

Cirneco
ITALY

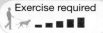

Exercise required

Cirneco dell'etna puppy

In spite of their lithe appearance, Cirneco dell'Etnas are rugged, hardy dogs, that originated near Mount Etna on the island of Sicily. They thrive in the hot, harsh climate of their home country, and have historically been used to hunt rabbits and other vermin. Today, although still used for hunting, these intelligent, energetic dogs are also happy to be companion animals, provided they get regular exercise.

Common Coat Colors

Average height (inches)	Average weight (pounds)	Average life expectancy (years)
48	100+	16+
	80	14
36		
	60	12
24	40	10
	20	8
12		
	10	6

! Attentive, keen to learn, and highly intelligent, this breed is more than a little mischievous!

+ Cirnechi are extremely hardy and free from inherited health problems.

AT A GLANCE

Ease of training	
Affection	
Playfulness	
Good with children	
Good with other dogs	
Grooming required	

HISTORY

This breed was named after Mount Etna, a volcanic mountain in Sicily, where Cirneco dell'Etnas were used to hunt rabbits. It is the smallest of the Mediterranean island hunting hounds, which also includes the Pharaoh and Ibizan Hounds. The breed was recognized by the United Kennel Club in 2006, but not recognized by the American Kennel Club until 2015.

23

Eastern Greyhound

Hortaya Borzaya / Chortaj

RUSSIA

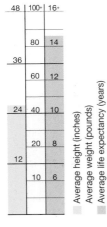

Eastern Greyhound pup

Common Coat Colors

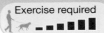

Exercise required

48	100+	16+
	80	14
36		
	60	12
24	40	10
	20	8
12		
	10	6

Average height (inches)
Average weight (pounds)
Average life expectancy (years)

This ancient sighthound is large, lean, robust with an elongated body. It is used by hunters for its speed and keen eyesight that can spot a moving object at a very far distance. Unusual for a sighthound, it has an excellent sense of smell. It is friendly, quiet, balanced and affectionate, and well suited to home life where there are no smaller pets.

AT A GLANCE

Ease of training	▬▬▬▬
Affection	▬▬▬
Playfulness	▬▬▬
Good with children	▬▬▬▬▬
Good with other dogs	▬▬▬
Grooming required	▬▬

 Breed-specific illnesses or hereditary diseases, such as hip dysplasia and elbow dysplasia, are so far unknown.

HISTORY

The Eastern Greyhound is a rare breed developed in the 15th to 17th century and indigenous to a region extending from modern Ukraine and south of Russia to western Kazakhstan. It was not known outside the USSR until that state's dissolution. It is recognized as a suitable pet, but can be very difficult to obtain outside Russia.

! It is never aggressive or fierce towards humans.

Galgo Español

Spanish Galgo / Spanish greyhound
SPAIN

Galgo Español puppy

Exercise required

Common Coat Colors

	48	100+	16+
		80	14
	36		
		60	12
	24	40	10
		20	8
	12		
		10	6

Average height (inches)
Average weight (pounds)
Average life expectancy (years)

The Galgo Español, or Spanish Greyhound, is an ancient breed that is not well known outside Spain. In their homeland they are still widely used for coursing and competing for the prestigious annual Copa de Su Majestad el Rey, or the King's Cup. Galgos are calm, quiet, and gentle in the home and many are surprisingly cat friendly, for sighthounds. They can sometimes be shy with strangers.

AT A GLANCE

Ease of training	▬▬ ▬▬ ▬▬
Affection	▬▬ ▬▬
Playfulness	▬▬ ▬▬ ▬▬
Good with children	▬▬ ▬▬ ▬▬
Good with other dogs	▬▬ ▬▬ ▬▬
Grooming required	▬▬

 Galgos have a very similar nature to Greyhounds.

Galgos are a fairly healthy breed, although they are sensitive to anaesthesia.

HISTORY

This is an ancient breed of dog that dates back at least to the early Middle Ages. At that time they were the province of nobility, and there were laws in effect at that time to punish anyone who killed or stole a Galgo. Linguistically, the Galgo is not only the "Spanish Greyhound" but also the "Spanish dog" — the name is probably derived from the Latin canis Gallicus or "dog from Gaul." The Galgo is also possibly the ancestor of the English Greyhound.

Greyhound

ENGLAND

Exercise required

Despite being bred for speed for many centuries, and excelling at their task, Greyhounds are also noted for their affectionate temperaments. They are akin to oversized "lap dogs," generally calm and quiet around the house, needing only short but vigorous bouts of exercise. They are loyal, friendly, and typically good with children. Although Greyhounds make excellent companions, some retain their instincts to hunt on sight, so small, furry pets, including other dogs, are not always safe around them.

Even with their reputation for speed, Greyhounds do not need extended periods of daily exercise. They are bred for sprinting rather than endurance and are happy to spend most of the day relaxing at home.

Greyhound pup

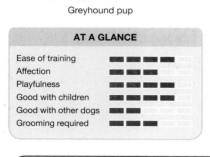

AT A GLANCE

Ease of training	■ ■ ■ ■
Affection	■ ■ ■
Playfulness	■ ■ ■ ■
Good with children	■ ■ ■ ■
Good with other dogs	■ ■
Grooming required	■ ■ ■

+ Normally very healthy dogs, Greyhounds can suffer from bone cancer, gastric torsion, poor teeth, and corns.

Common Coat Colors

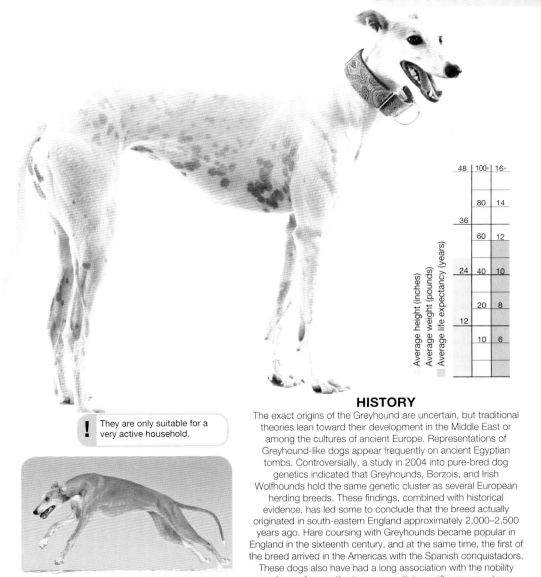

Average height (inches)	Average weight (pounds)	Average life expectancy (years)
48	100+	16+
	80	14
36		
	60	12
24	40	10
	20	8
12		
	10	6

! They are only suitable for a very active household.

The world's fastest dogs, Greyhounds have been bred for speed and can reach up to 45 mph over a short distance.

HISTORY

The exact origins of the Greyhound are uncertain, but traditional theories lean toward their development in the Middle East or among the cultures of ancient Europe. Representations of Greyhound-like dogs appear frequently on ancient Egyptian tombs. Controversially, a study in 2004 into pure-bred dog genetics indicated that Greyhounds, Borzois, and Irish Wolfhounds hold the same genetic cluster as several European herding breeds. These findings, combined with historical evidence, has led some to conclude that the breed actually originated in south-eastern England approximately 2,000–2,500 years ago. Hare coursing with Greyhounds became popular in England in the sixteenth century, and at the same time, the first of the breed arrived in the Americas with the Spanish conquistadors. These dogs also have had a long association with the nobility and were frequently given as prestigious gifts among rulers; Greyhound were usually kept separate from other hunting dogs and given preferential treatment. At the end of the nineteenth century, racing Greyhounds on a track became a popular sport and remains so today.

Ibizan Hound

Ibizan Warren Hound

IBIZA

Ibizan Hound pup

Common Coat Colors

Exercise required

48	100+	16+
	80	14
36		
	60	12
24	40	10
	20	8
12		
	10	6

Average height (inches) · Average weight (pounds) · Average life expectancy (years)

With their slender frames and large, upstanding ears, Ibizan Hounds are frequently described as "deer-like." They appear in two coat types—smooth and wire, although the latter can sometimes soften into long hair. These energetic dogs have an incredible jumping ability—they can clear a five-foot fence with ease—and an elegant springy trot. Prone to seeking attention, these engaging clowns are well suited to active households. They can be sensitive during training and do not "learn" from punishment.

AT A GLANCE

Ease of training	■■■
Affection	■■■■
Playfulness	■■■■
Good with children	■■■■
Good with other dogs	■■■■
Grooming required	■■■

 Minor health concerns for the breed include seizures and allergies.

! They have also been known to scale trees; worth considering before purchasing one!

HISTORY

The Ibizan Hound originated on the Mediterranean island of Eivissa and was popular in the Catalan-speaking areas of Spain and France for hunting rabbits and other small game. It was bred to be a fast dog that could hunt on all types of terrain, working by scent, sound and sight. Hunters run these dogs in mostly female packs, with perhaps a male or two, because the females are considered the better hunters. The breed was fully recognized by the American Kennel Club in 1978.

Indian Pariah Dog

Pye-dog

INDIA

Exercise required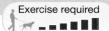

Common Coat Colors

Indian Pariah Dog puppy

	Average height (inches)	Average weight (pounds)	Average life expectancy (years)
	48	100+	16+
		80	14
	36		
		60	12
	24	40	10
		20	8
	12		
		10	6

One of the earliest primitive breeds, the Indian Pariah evolved in the outskirts of towns and villages, close to forests where tigers and leopards were common. As a result, this is a highly cautious breed that makes an excellent watchdog. They can also be territorial in defense of their pack or family. The term pariah can mean outcast, but in the canine sense it refers to a primitive class of dog that is not formally recognized or commercially bred.

AT A GLANCE

Ease of training	▬ ▬ ▬ ▬ ▬
Affection	▬ ▬ ▬
Playfulness	▬ ▬ ▬
Good with children	▬ ▬ ▬ ▬
Good with other dogs	▬ ▬ ▬ ▬
Grooming required	▬

 These dogs bark at the slightest provocation and can be noisy.

+ They have very few health concerns and thrive with minimal maintenance.

HISTORY

The Indian Pariah Dog (*Canis lupus familiaris*) is thought to trace back 15,000 years, making it one of the oldest canine lineages in the world. It is the aboriginal land-race, meaning naturally selected dog, of the Indian sub-continent, which includes India, Pakistan, Bangladesh, and Nepal. The modern-day Pariah Dog resembles the fossil remains of many early dogs from around the world, and may also be the progenitor of the Australian Dingo.

Irish Wolfhound

Cú Faoil

IRELAND

Exercise required

The tallest of the hound breeds, the Irish Wolfhound can be a real couch potato and loves nothing better than to lie around in the most comfortable spot. These dogs have superb temperaments, are calm when indoors, and are generally easygoing, making them excellent pets for people who can give them occasional space to roam.

+ This is a very healthy breed, but problems can include gastric torsion, bone cancer, heart problems, and hip or elbow dysplasia.

Irish Wolfhound pup

AT A GLANCE	
Ease of training	
Affection	
Playfulness	
Good with children	
Good with other dogs	
Grooming required	

Common Coat Colors

! Wolfhound puppies initially grow very quickly and will be large by six months of age.

30

Average height (inches)	Average weight (pounds)	Average life expectancy (years)
48	100+	16+
	80	14
36		
	60	12
24	40	10
	20	8
12		
	10	6

HISTORY

Irish Wolfhounds may have been brought to Ireland as far back as 7000 BCE; they were highly valued since Roman times as guardians, hunters, and companions. Despite their even temperaments, Irish Wolfhounds were known for being ferocious and fearless, and were used to hunt wolves and guard livestock. The coat of arms of early Irish kings bore an image of the Irish Wolfhound and the words "Gentle when stroked, fierce when provoked." Nearly extinct by the late 1800s, the breed was recreated from the few remaining specimens by Scotsman Captain George Augustus Graham.

Italian Greyhound

Iggy
ITALY

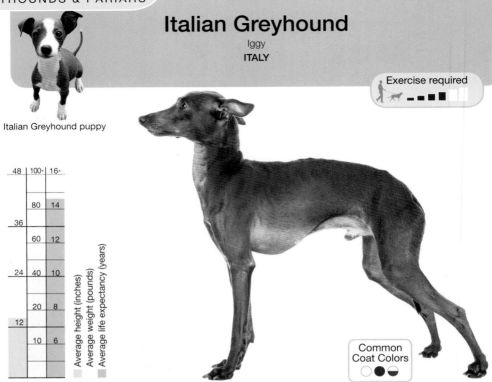

Italian Greyhound puppy

Exercise required

Average height (inches)
Average weight (pounds)
Average life expectancy (years)

48	100+	16+
	80	14
36		
	60	12
24	40	10
	20	8
12		
	10	6

Common Coat Colors

The Italian Greyhound, sometimes called an "Iggy," is the smallest of the sighthounds. The name comes from their popularity during Renaissance Italy. These are playful, lively little dogs that thrive on attention and they make charming companion animals for mature adults. They are not advised for families with children, however; these dogs are fragile and can be injured if handled too roughly.

AT A GLANCE

Ease of training	■■■■■
Affection	■■■■■
Playfulness	■■■■■
Good with children	■
Good with other dogs	■■■■
Grooming required	■

 Puppies need lots of attention, diversions, and moderate exercise, to prevent destructive behavior.

+ These dogs are typically healthy, but prone to teeth and gum problems, idiopathic epilepsy, hypothyroidism, and progressive retinol atrophy.

HISTORY

These svelte little dogs originated more than 2,000 years ago in the regions now known as Greece and Turkey; depictions on Egyptian tombs and from ancient Rome show petite Greyhound-like dogs that were the ancestors of the modern Italian Greyhound. Although they were undoubtedly bred as pets, the breed was likely also used in vermin control. By the sixteenth century they had made their way to England— and were also found in aristocratic homes throughout Europe.

Kanni

INDIA

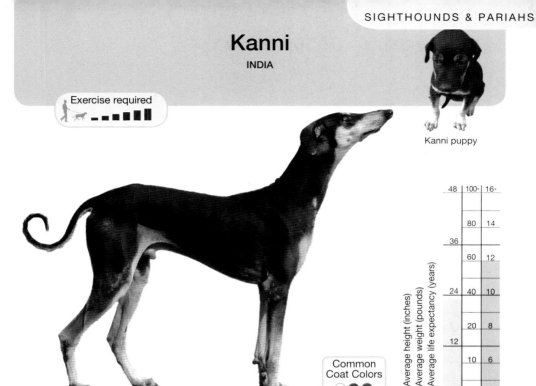

Kanni puppy

Exercise required

		48	100+	16+		
			80	14		
	36					
			60	12		
		24	40	10		
			20	8		
	12					
			10	6		

Average height (inches)
Average weight (pounds)
Average life expectancy (years)

Common Coat Colors

Like all sighthounds, Kannis are accomplished at hunting small game and deer, and are particularly fast and strong. These are agile, graceful dogs that resemble a slimmed-down, elongated Doberman Pinscher. They are often shy, but can be counted on to defend their homes and families. Kannis are also known as a silent breed that does not bark needlessly. At home with their families they are faithful and easy to train, but can be independent-minded.

AT A GLANCE

Ease of training	■■ ■■ ■■
Affection	■■ ■■ ■■
Playfulness	■■ ■■ ■■■
Good with children	■■ ■■ ■■
Good with other dogs	■■ ■■ ■■
Grooming required	■■ ■■ ■■

 They are only suitable for a very active household.

+ The breed is now extremely rare, and is on the verge of extinction.

HISTORY

This rare breed of sighthound was traditionally given as a gift by a bride to her groom as part of her dowry; kanni translates as "maiden" or "virgin" in the classical language Tamil. The dogs are still highly prized by families and still given as gifts, never bought or sold, and only if the recipient promises to take great care with the dog. They are fed a diet of milk and corn porridge, and only get meat once a week or so. Although this beloved breed is near extinction, no group has come forward to save it.

Magyar Agár

Hungarian Greyhound

HUNGARY

Magyar Agár pup

Exercise required

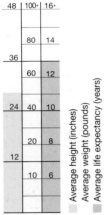

Average height (inches)
Average weight (pounds)
Average life expectancy (years)

Common Coat Colors

Although they resemble Greyhounds, Magyar Agárs are a distinct breed, with their own unique traits. A more fitting name would be Hungarian Gazehound. These dogs should be elegant but rugged, with a body longer than it is tall, and a relatively heavy bone structure. They should also be able to handle rough terrain and show stamina and endurance. In the home, these tireless hunters are affectionate and docile, well-behaved with children, other dogs, and, with proper introduction, even cats.

AT A GLANCE	
Ease of training	
Affection	
Playfulness	
Good with children	
Good with other dogs	
Grooming required	

+ This is generally a very healthy breed with no known medical issues.

HISTORY

The lineage of the Magyar Agár, also called the Hungarian Greyhound, stretches back more than 1,100 years. These dogs were first bred to accompany hunters on horseback and are; therefore, capable of traveling long distances at steady speeds. Traditionally, these sighthounds were owned by the nobility, although the working classes kept smaller versions of the dog, known as farm Agars or hare catchers, which unfortunately no longer exist.

! Although they are rare outside Europe, a few Magyar Agár live in the United States.

Mudhol Hound

Mudhol Dog / Caravan Hound
INDIA

Exercise required

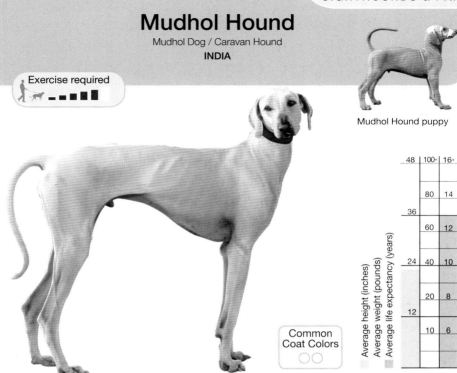

Mudhol Hound puppy

	Average height (inches)	Average weight (pounds)	Average life expectancy (years)
	48	100+	16+
		80	14
	36		
		60	12
	24	40	10
		20	8
	12		
		10	6

Common Coat Colors
○○

Few dogs are known by as many different names as the Mudhol Hound—the feathered variety is the Pashmi, the village dog is the Karwani. This Indian sighthound is above all a working dog, capable of bringing down anything from small game, likes hares; to larger game, like antelope. They are elegant, graceful, and courageous, hunting over taxing terrain that most dogs would find daunting. In the home they are loyal but can be aloof. Their two chief requirements are plenty of space and lots of exercise.

AT A GLANCE

Ease of training	▬ ▬ ▬ ▬
Affection	▬ ▬ ▬ ▬
Playfulness	▬ ▬ ▬ ▬
Good with children	▬ ▬ ▬
Good with other dogs	▬ ▬ ▬
Grooming required	▬

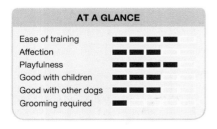

! Shrimant Rajesaheb Malojirao Ghorpade revived these dogs in the early 1900s.

+ The Mudhol Hound is generally healthy and does not have any specific health issues.

HISTORY

The Mudhol Hound is an ancient breed that was introduced to western India from central Asia and Arabia, making it a likely descendent of the Saluki or Tazi. It's possible they were brought to India by the Pathans, Afghans, Arabs, and Persians through the famous Kyber Pass. These dogs were known to travel with nomadic peoples and to follow their caravans from one place to another. The breed name comes from the town of Mudhol, where the dogs are popular.

35

New Guinea Singing Dog

Hallstrom dog

NEW GUINEA

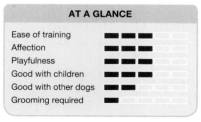

New Guinea Singing Dog pup

Common Coat Colors

Exercise required

48	100+	16+
	80	14
36		
	60	12
24	40	10
	20	8
12		
	10	6

Average height (inches) · Average weight (pounds) · Average life expectancy (years)

These "foxy"-looking reddish dogs once ran wild across New Guinea, although feral populations are now thought to be extinct. Even though experts disagree over whether they are a true wild dog, they are certainly an ancient and genetically pure breed that is related to the Australian Dingo. Their limbs and spines are quite flexible and their paws rotate enough to allow them to climb trees with thick bark. The name comes from their melodious howl, which sounds like singing; groups indulge in chorus howling.

AT A GLANCE

Ease of training	
Affection	
Playfulness	
Good with children	
Good with other dogs	
Grooming required	

! These shy dogs are gentle and friendly with people.

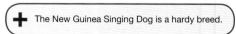 The New Guinea Singing Dog is a hardy breed.

HISTORY

The first specimen of this dog, taken on Mount Scratchley, was collected and described in 1897 by Charles Walter De Vis. Twentieth-century Australian philanthropist Sir Edward Hallstrom, who had set up a native animal study center in Nondugi, also studied the breed. When researchers determined that the New Guinea Singing Dog was a distinct species, it was named *Canis hallstromi*, in his honor. Today, the breed's greatest risk is hybridizing with other dogs.

Old Croatian Sighthound

Hrti

CROATIA

Old Croatian Sighthound
puppy

Exercise required

Average height (inches)	Average weight (pounds)	Average life expectancy (years)
48	100+	16+
	80	14
36	60	12
24	40	10
	20	8
12		
	10	6

**Common
Coat Colors**

The Old Croatian Sighthound, or Hrti, is a relative newcomer to Eastern Europe, with a number of sighthounds in its background. It displays typical greyhound conformation—rose ears, slender body, and a short coat that is predominately white with markings of black or dark brown, or with yellowish spotting. It is agile and fast, ideal for coursing small game or competing in racing trials.

AT A GLANCE	
Ease of training	▰ ▰ ▰
Affection	▰ ▰ ▰
Playfulness	▰ ▰ ▰
Good with children	▰ ▰ ▰
Good with other dogs	▰ ▰
Grooming required	▰ ▰ ▰

! They are only suitable for a
very active household.

+ The breed is known to be at a higher risk from
mastocytoma (mast cell tumours) than the
general population of dogs.

HISTORY

Descended form the Old Bosnian Greyhound, this breed's lineage also includes the Hungarian Greyhound, Posavac Hound, Istrian Hound, the Whippet, and the English Greyhound. The breed was almost exterminated by war when Croatia was still part of Yugoslavia. Researchers studied this dog's decline as an example of how the loss of aristocratic landowners—who hunted on horseback with their sighthounds—opened the way to yeoman hunters who followed their scent hounds on foot.

Peruvian Inca Orchid

Moonflower Dog
PERU

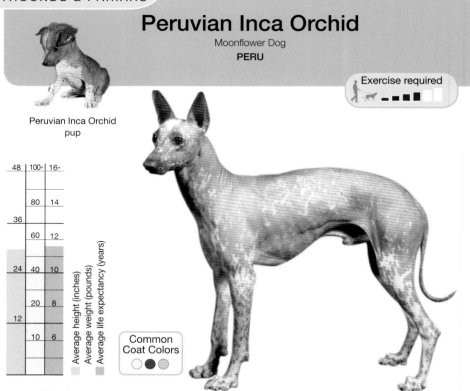

Peruvian Inca Orchid
pup

Exercise required

48	100+	16+
	80	14
36		
	60	12
24	40	10
	20	8
12		
	10	6

Average height (inches)
Average weight (pounds)
Average life expectancy (years)

Common
Coat Colors

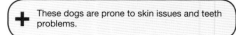

Often referred to as a "hairless" breed, these endearing little dogs have sparse patches of hair on the head, tail, and feet. Some puppies are born with a full coat, although the coated variety cannot be shown. They are exceptionally clean dogs, free from odor, and may be suitable for people with allergies. For the right person, the Peruvian Inca Orchid is an exotic treat, but its delicate skin does require special care. Affectionate with family members, they can be wary of newcomers.

AT A GLANCE

Ease of training	▬ ▬ ▬ ▬
Affection	▬ ▬ ▬
Playfulness	▬ ▬ ▬ ▬
Good with children	▬ ▬ ▬ ▬ ▬
Good with other dogs	▬ ▬ ▬ ▬
Grooming required	▬

! Peruvian Inca Orchids can get cold very easily.

+ These dogs are prone to skin issues and teeth problems.

HISTORY

When Spanish explorers first entered Peru in the early 1500s, they came upon this unique breed in the homes of the Inca nobility. The dog actually pre-dates this period—facsimiles of hairless dogs were found on ceramic vessels dated 750 AD, and they were kept as pets by pre-Incan cultures that lived along the coast. They were probably also eaten by some cultures, although the conquering Incas forbid it. Today in the U.S. the descendants of 13 Peruvians dogs are recognized by the AKC.

Pharaoh Hound

EGYPT

Pharaoh Hound puppy

Exercise required

48	100+	16+
	80	14
36		
	60	12
24	40	10
	20	8
12		
	10	6

Average height (inches)
Average weight (pounds)
Average life expectancy (years)

Common Coat Colors

The graceful, elegant Pharaoh Hound looks like the hunting dogs seen on many royal Egyptian tombs, hence the name. They have no link with that country, however, but they do resemble other sighthounds of the Mediterranean region, including the Sicilian Cirneco and the Portuguese Podengo. They typically hunt at night, when there are fewer distractions. When small prey goes to ground, this dog will leap into the air and land hard, trying to roust the animal from its hole.

AT A GLANCE

Ease of training	▬ ▬ ▬ ▬
Affection	▬ ▬ ▬
Playfulness	▬ ▬ ▬
Good with children	▬ ▬ ▬ ▬
Good with other dogs	▬ ▬ ▬
Grooming required	▬

! They are only suitable for a very active household.

+ The breed is known to be at a higher risk from mastocytoma (mast cell tumours) than the general population of dogs.

HISTORY

The Pharaoh Hound is likely an ancient breed, going back roughly 2,000 years. It the national dog of Malta, where it is used to course rabbits. Recent DNA testing has shown that these dogs have no link with ancient Egypt. The breed remained largely unknown in the West until a pair arrived in England in the 1920s. The first Pharaoh Hounds were imported into the U.S. in 1967 and the breed was officially recognized by the AKC.

Podenco Canario

Canary Islands Warren Hound

SPAIN

Exercise required

Podenco Canario pup

48	100+	16+
	80	14
36		
	60	12
24	40	10
	20	8
12		
	10	6

Average height (inches)
Average weight (pounds)
Average life expectancy (years)

Common Coat Colors

These sighthounds developed in isolation on the Canary Islands, where they were used for hunting the rabbits that overran the landscape. Although they are known for their durability and toughness, these dogs are also gentle and loyal pets, with a temperament similar to the Greyhound. Recognized by several minor registries, this dog is gaining interest from those looking for a unique breed.

AT A GLANCE

Ease of training	■■■ ■■
Affection	■■ ■■
Playfulness	■■ ■■ ■■
Good with children	■■ ■■
Good with other dogs	■■ ■■ ■■
Grooming required	■■ ■■

+ A very rare ovotesticular/testicular disorder has been seen in one dog of this breed; it results in dogs that are genetically females developing testes or ovotestes instead of ovaries.

! The breed standard calls for a "nervy, agitated" dog.

HISTORY

The Podenco Canario is an older breed found throughout the Canary Islands, off the coast of Morocco, where it still hunts rabbits in packs. The dogs were believed to have been brought over from Egypt and Africa by early settlers, including the Phoenicians, but DNA testing revealed they are no more primitive or ancient than other European hunting breed.

Polish Greyhound

Chart Polski
POLAND

Polish Greyhound
puppy

Exercise required

Average height (inches)	Average weight (pounds)	Average life expectancy (years)
48	100+	16+
	80	14
36		
	60	12
24	40	10
	20	8
12		
	10	6

Although it is very similar in appearance to the English Greyhound, the muscular Chart Polski is not descended from that breed. This dog is used primarily to hunt hare, fox, and deer, running down prey with its great speed. It has an insulating double coat during all seasons, and as the weather turns cold it grows a heavy undercoat to compensate for frigid Polish winters. In the home, these determined dogs need a firm hand and a lot of guidance. In the show ring, they are known for being real hams.

AT A GLANCE

Ease of training	■■ ■■ ■■ ■■
Affection	■■ ■■ ■■
Playfulness	■■ ■■ ■■
Good with children	■■ ■■ ■■ ■■ ■
Good with other dogs	■■ ■■ ■■ ■■
Grooming required	■■ ■■ ■■

 The Chart Polski is a very low-maintenance breed.

It appears that no health studies have been conducted on the Chart Polski.

HISTORY

The Chart Polski was developed before dog breeding records were kept, meaning that much of its history has been lost. It is known that this dog had a long association with Poland, where it has traditionally been a favorite of the Polish nobility, who used it on wolves. The breed has been mentioned in Polish literature since the thirteenth century. Today the dog is rarely seen in the U.S., even though it was recognized by the United Kennel Club in 1996.

Portuguese Podengo Pequeno

PORTUGAL

Exercise required

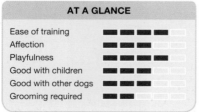

Podengo Pequeno pup

Average height (inches) | Average weight (pounds) | Average life expectancy (years)

48 | 100+ | 16+
36 | 80 | 14
| 60 | 12
24 | 40 | 10
| 20 | 8
12 | 10 | 6

Common Coat Colors

The smallest of the three Podengo varieties, this lively little firecracker was used to flush rabbits and control vermin, including on the ships of Portuguese seafarers. They rely on sight, scent, and hearing when trailing prey. The smooth coat is short and dense; the wire or rough coat is long and harsh, with a bearded muzzle. The approved colors are yellow or fawn. In the home, these dogs are active, amusing, affectionate companions that do well in many sports. They also make excellent watchdogs.

AT A GLANCE

Ease of training	■ ■ ■ ■
Affection	■ ■ ■ ■
Playfulness	■ ■ ■ ■ ■
Good with children	■ ■ ■
Good with other dogs	■ ■ ■
Grooming required	■ ■

+ This long-lived breed is generally healthy, but problems can include Legg-Calves-Perthes disease and luxating patella.

 This was originally a rustic breed used by farmers for pest control.

HISTORY

An ancient breed, Podengos trace their history back to at least to 1000 BCE, when they were taken to the Iberian Peninsula by Romans and Phoenician traders. They likely share their lineage with the Pharaoh Hound, Ibizan Hound, Cirneco dell'Etna, and Basenji. During the Age of Discovery, the Podengo Pequeno accompanied Portuguese explorers on their ships and earned their way by killing rats. A wire-coat Pequeno was first shown in the U.S. in 2001 in Boston.

Portuguese Podengo

PORTUGAL

Young Portuguese Podengo

Exercise required

Coat Colors

	48	100+	16+
		80	14
	36		
		60	12
	24	40	10
		20	8
	12		
		10	6

Average height (inches)
Average weight (pounds)
Average life expectancy (years)

Common Coat Colors

This hardy pack hunter developed in three sizes: large, medium, and small, each with two coat options—smooth and wire. The Grande was used on deer and wild boar, and the Medio was used for rabbits and flushing game; the Pequeno, which chased rabbits, is now recognized as a separate breed. These are clever dogs with a touch of mischief. Good with children, other animals, and livestock.

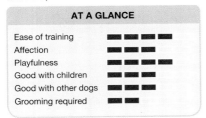

AT A GLANCE	
Ease of training	▬ ▬ ▬ ▬
Affection	▬ ▬ ▬
Playfulness	▬ ▬ ▬ ▬
Good with children	▬ ▬ ▬ ▬
Good with other dogs	▬ ▬ ▬ ▬
Grooming required	▬ ▬

 Legg-Calves-Perthes disease has been noted in the Podengo.

HISTORY

Podengos are an ancient hunting dog that can trace their history back to at least to 1000 BCE, when they arrived on the Iberian Peninsula with Romans and Phoenician traders. They share a heritage with the Pharaoh Hound, Ibizan Hound, Cirneco dell'Etna, and Basenji. Today, both the Grande and Medio are registered by the AKC as one breed in the hound group. These dogs are rarely seen outside Portugal, although there are a number of Medios in the U.S.

! The charming Medio has often been used in Hollywood films such as Dante's Peak.

43

Rampur Greyhound

Rampur Hound

INDIA

Exercise required

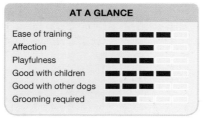

Rampur Greyhound
pup

Average height (inches)
Average weight (pounds)
Average life expectancy (years)

48	100+	16+
	80	14
36		
	60	12
24	40	10
	20	8
12		
	10	6

Common
Coat Colors
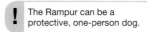

This substantial sighthound is a fairly recent addition to the group, developed in the early twentieth century to take down large predators, such as jackals, in the Rampur region of India. Built to cover great distances quickly, they are also dogs of remarkable endurance. Rampurs crave human companionship and do well with other dogs—two carousing Rampurs will intentionally butt into each other at high speeds. They also keep themselves as clean as cats inside the house.

AT A GLANCE

Ease of training	■■■ ■■■
Affection	■■■ ■■
Playfulness	■■■ ■■
Good with children	■■■ ■■■
Good with other dogs	■■■ ■■
Grooming required	■■■

 One of the most common problems in Rampur Hounds is bloating, caused by the sudden influx of gas and air in the stomach.

HISTORY

This breed orginated in the early 1900s during the reign of His Royal Highness Ahmed Ali Khan Bahadur, the Nawab of Rampur. His intent was to create a fierce and agile breed with the intent of hunting wild boar, a favoured pastime of the royals. He bred powerful, fierce Afghani Tazis with English Greyhounds to produce a fearless hunter that was not intimidated by large predators like jackals, lions, tigers, and coyotes in addition to wild boar.

! The Rampur can be a protective, one-person dog.

44

Saluki

Persian Greyhound
MIDDLE EAST

Saluki puppy

Exercise required

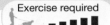

	Average height (inches)	Average weight (pounds)	Average life expectancy (years)
	48	100+	16+
		80	14
	36		
		60	12
	24	40	10
		20	8
	12		
		10	6

Common Coat Colors

These lithe sighthounds, with their slender frames and regal appearance, might look fragile but they are tough, resilient dogs with tremendous stamina and great speed. They are possibly the first dog selectively bred by early humans, somewhere in the Fertile Crescent. There are two types—smooth, with silky fur only on the legs, and feathered. They are reserved with strangers, independent, and easily bored—owners that furnish a lot of interaction, however, will be rewarded with great loyalty.

AT A GLANCE

Ease of training	▬ ▬ ▬ ▬
Affection	▬ ▬ ▬
Playfulness	▬ ▬ ▬ ▬
Good with children	▬ ▬ ▬
Good with other dogs	▬ ▬
Grooming required	▬ ▬ ▬

＋ Because of their low level of body fat, slender sighthounds such as the Saluki are often sensitive to anesthesia and certain other drugs.

! The name Saluki may come from ancient Sumerian, or from the old Yemeni.

HISTORY

Scientists speculate that Salukis descended from the earliest dogs and made their way throughout the Mediterranean region with their nomadic owners. Depictions of dogs resembling Salukis appear on Egyptian tombs dating to 2100 BCE. some 4,000 years ago. Legends maintains that returning Crusaders first brought them to Europe; they were frequently included in Renaissance paintings.

Scottish Deerhound

Highland deerhound
SCOTLAND

Scottish Deerhound
pup

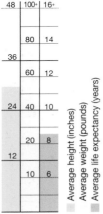

Average height (inches)
Average weight (pounds)
Average life expectancy (years)

Exercise required

Common
Coat Colors

Scottish Deerhounds are superbly designed to hunt fast animals for long periods over difficult terrain. They are in a sense the 4x4 vehicle of the dog world. Like many sighthounds, the Deerhound has a wonderful temperament—calm and affectionate in the home and happy to lie about on a couch for much of the day. Scottish Deerhounds are very large dogs, but for the right family, they make truly wonderful companions.

AT A GLANCE

Ease of training	
Affection	
Playfulness	
Good with children	
Good with other dogs	
Grooming required	

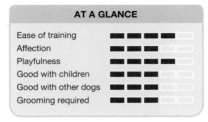

! In spite of their size, they don't make good guard dogs because of their loving natures.

+ Sighthounds, including Scottish Deerhounds, are sensitive to anesthesia and some other drugs.

HISTORY

These dogs have been known as Irish wolf-dogs, Scottish Greyhounds, Rough Greyhounds, and Highland deerhounds. It is possible they were used to hunt wolves and then re-purposed to hunt the great stags of the Highlands, but they were certainly used as far back as the sixteenth century to bring down deer. Sir Walter Scott was a fan of Deerhounds and featured one in his novel, The Talisman. A Deerhound also played Sirius Black as Padfoot in the Harry Potter films.

Silken Windhound

UNITED STATES

Silken Windhound puppy

Exercise required

		48	100+	16+
			80	14
		36		
			60	12
		24	40	10
			20	8
		12		
			10	6

Average height (inches)
Average weight (pounds)
Average life expectancy (years)

Common Coat Colors

Silken Windhounds are a recent breed, developed as a smaller version of the tall, elegant sighthounds. Like their larger cousins, they hunt by sight and are able to course game at high speeds. They are easy to train, but wither under harsh methods. At home, they love lounging on the couch with their humans. They are unsuitable as guard dogs due to their friendly natures. Like most sighthounds, Silkens excel at racing or lure coursing, as well as competing in flyball, agility, and obedience trials.

AT A GLANCE

Ease of training	■ ■ ■ ■
Affection	■ ■ ■
Playfulness	■ ■ ■ ■
Good with children	■ ■ ■ ■ ■
Good with other dogs	■ ■ ■ ■
Grooming required	■ ■ ■

 There have been some cases of cryptorchidism, umbilical hernia, and lotus syndrome.

! Silkens will work eagerly and form strong relationships with their owners.

HISTORY

The Silken Windhound was created by Francie Stull, a breeder of top show and performance Borzoi and Scottish Deerhounds. Utilizing her decades of experience with these hounds, she combined their best aspects with the bloodlines of some of the top Borzois and Whippets in America. The result was a small-to-medium size dog with all the admirable sighthound qualities—speed, endurance, and the desire to form a strong bond with humans.

Sloughi

Arabian Greyhound / Berber Greyhound
MOROCCO

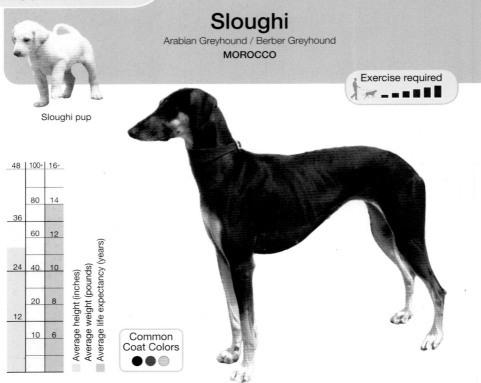

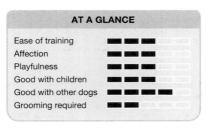

Sloughi pup

Exercise required

Average height (inches)
Average weight (pounds)
Average life expectancy (years)

| 48 | 100+ | 16+ |
| 80 | 14 |
| 36 |
60	12
24	40	10
20	8
12
10	6

Common Coat Colors

The elegant short-haired Sloughi was originally used for coursing and hunting small game in the deserts and mountains of North Africa. It still excels in this respect. It has long, flat muscles, as opposed to the brawny muscles of Greyhounds and Whippets, and a feather-light gait. These are sensitive, intelligent dogs that cannot be trained using punishment. They enjoy many activities—long walks, romping, and racing—and do well in most homes if provided with a variety of exercises.

AT A GLANCE

Ease of training	▦▦▦
Affection	▦▦▦
Playfulness	▦▦▦
Good with children	▦▦▦▦
Good with other dogs	▦▦▦▦
Grooming required	▦▦

+ Only a few genetic conditions have been noted in the breed, in particular progressive retinal atrophy (PRA).

! Despite the similar name, they are not related to Salukis.

HISTORY

These dogs probably originated in Ethiopia sometime around 3000 BCE; similar dogs appear on pot shards that date from that time. Fine specimens were likely presented as gifts to the Egyptian Pharaohs. DNA study indicates that this is a genetically unique population of sighthounds; its genetic sequences are shared by the Basenji, placing this breed firmly in Africa. Today it is found mainly in Morocco, Algeria, Tunisia, and Libya. It was recognized by the AKC in 2016.

Taigan

Kyrgyz Sighthound

KYRGYZSTAN

Exercise required

Common Coat Colors

Taigan puppy

Average height (inches)	Average weight (pounds)	Average life expectancy (years)
48	100+	16+
	80	14
36		
	60	12
24	40	10
	20	8
12		
	10	6

This sighthound has adapted to the extreme mountainous conditions in the Tian Shan range of its Central Asian homeland, where it hunts ibex, roe deer, wolf, fox and marmot. The Taigan is also used in conjunction with trained birds of prey. The medium-length coat is soft and slightly curly.

AT A GLANCE

Ease of training	▬▬ ▬▬ ▬▬
Affection	▬▬ ▬▬
Playfulness	▬▬ ▬▬ ▬▬
Good with children	▬▬ ▬▬ ▬▬ ▬▬ ▬▬
Good with other dogs	▬▬ ▬▬ ▬▬
Grooming required	▬▬ ▬▬

 This versatile breed hunts with all its senses, not just sight.

✚ The breed is known to be at a higher risk from mastocytoma (mast cell tumours) than the general population of dogs.

HISTORY

For thousands of years the Taigan of Kyrghz was a valued hunter for nomadic tribes that travelled from Siberia to Central Asia. Collective farming under the USSR replaced the nomadic life for many, but when Kyrghzstan became independent in 1991, some people again took up the nomadic life, and coursing the Taigan for game became a way of earning money. Meanwhile, the upper classes began to acquire this dog as a symbol of their national heritage.

Thai Ridgeback

TRD

THAILAND

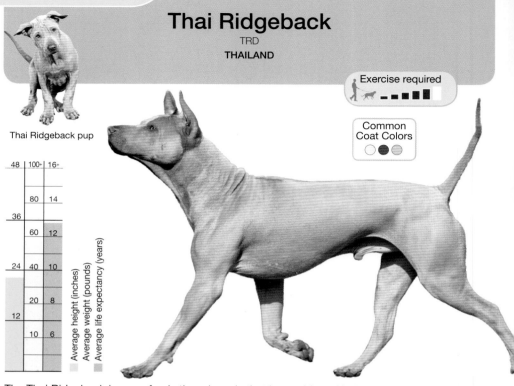

Exercise required

Common Coat Colors

Thai Ridgeback pup

Average height (inches)	Average weight (pounds)	Average life expectancy (years)
48	100+	16+
	80	14
36		
	60	12
24	40	10
	20	8
12		
	10	6

The Thai Ridgeback is one of only three breeds that has a ridge of hair running down its back in the opposite direction to the rest of the coat. The other two are the Rhodesian Ridgeback and the Phu Quoc Ridgeback of Vietnam. These muscular dogs are intelligent, and loyal, and can be protective of the home. They have no trouble relaxing around the house, but will require outlets for sudden bursts of energy. Because they can be independent-minded, they are not a good choice for the novice owner.

AT A GLANCE

Ease of training	▄▄▄▄▄
Affection	▄▄▄▄
Playfulness	▄▄▄▄▄
Good with children	▄▄▄▄
Good with other dogs	▄▄▄
Grooming required	▄▄

+ The Thai Ridgeback is a very healthy breed.

HISTORY

The Thai Ridgeback has been found in eastern Thailand since the Middle Ages, but its ancestors go back to early primitive dogs. It is considered an ancient land-race dog, that is, a breed that evolved naturally on its own. One genetic-based hypothesis is that both Thai Ridgebacks and Phu Quocs are descended from the Funan Ridgeback Dog, which originated over 1,000 years ago in the Funan Era. Thai Ridgebacks have only recently had a formal breed standard.

! Thai farmers know this breed as the "cart-following dog."

Xoloitzcuintli

Mexican Hairless
MEXICO

Exercise required

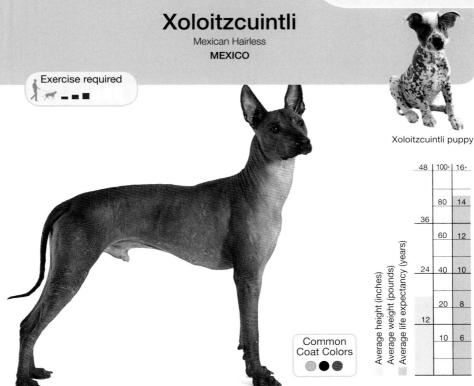

Xoloitzcuintli puppy

	Average height (inches)	Average weight (pounds)	Average life expectancy (years)
	48	100+	16+
		80	14
	36		
		60	12
	24	40	10
		20	8
	12		
		10	6

Common
Coat Colors

The virtually hairless Xolo comes in three sizes — small, medium and large —and in a coated form. All these varieties can appear in the same litter. Hairlessness in this breed is a dominant genetic mutation, but the hairless Xolo does have some fluff on the top of the head, the tip of the tail, and the toes. Xolos should exhibit a "primitive" temperament—intelligence, sensitivity, curiosity, high energy, and strong hunting and social instincts, and they are not emotionally mature until two years old.

AT A GLANCE	
Ease of training	▬ ▬ ▬ ▬
Affection	▬ ▬ ▬
Playfulness	▬ ▬ ▬ ▬
Good with children	▬ ▬
Good with other dogs	▬ ▬ ▬ ▬
Grooming required	▬ ▬ ▬

! The breed's name comes from two Nahuatl words meaning "god" and "dog."

+ The delicate-skinned Xolo needs protection from the sun and from extremely cold weather.

HISTORY

Once the sacred dogs of the Aztecs, Xolos possibly came to the Americas across the Bering Strait with nomadic tribes; genetic testing has shown they are related to several Old World breeds. In the modern era they were village dogs, without fanfare. Today the breed is considered a national treasure in Mexico, and was named Dog of the Year in 2010. Approximately 30,000 are known to exist worldwide.

Whippet

ENGLAND

Common
Coat Colors

Exercise required
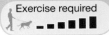

Whippets were bred to exterminate vermin. These charismatic and highly intelligent dogs make great companions and are suitable for homes with other pets and children as long as they get the right introduction, socialization, and supervision. Whippets are active dogs that thrive on interacting with their families; they make good agility dogs, love to go jogging with their owners, and are very obedient with correct and sensitive training. They are sight hounds, though, and will naturally chase small, furry things that move. One of the biggest causes of fatality in the breed is being hit by cars, so it is essential to provide a properly enclosed area for exercise.

As well as being adorable, Whippet puppies are really smart and learn quickly.

Whippet puppies

AT A GLANCE

Ease of training	▬ ▬ ▬ ▬
Affection	▬ ▬ ▬
Playfulness	▬ ▬ ▬
Good with children	▬ ▬ ▬ ▬ ▬
Good with other dogs	▬ ▬ ▬
Grooming required	▬ ▬ ▬

 Normally very healthy dogs, Whippets can suffer from bone cancer, gastric torsion, poor teeth, and corns.

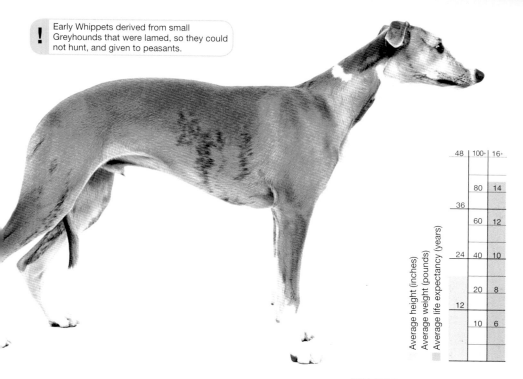

! Early Whippets derived from small Greyhounds that were lamed, so they could not hunt, and given to peasants.

Average height (inches)	Average weight (pounds)	Average life expectancy (years)
48	100+	16+
	80	14
36		
	60	12
24	40	10
	20	8
12		
	10	6

Whippets exercise often, but in energetic bursts, characteristically speeding around their owners in wide circles. Although they are built for speed, they also enjoy comfort and, after sufficient exercise, will happily curl up and sleep for much of the day.

HISTORY

The exact origin of the Whippet is unknown, although other small dogs of this type trace back to ancient times. The modern history of the Whippet begins in the nineteenth century in northern England, where the small, sporty dogs became popular with factory workers and miners for killing vermin and racing. Sometimes called "the poor man's Greyhound"—and Greyhounds were certainly used in their development—Whippets were cheaper and easier to keep, but just as much fun to race. Poachers also favored Whippets for catching their ill-gotten game, and could hide the dogs in their coats if necessary. An early blood sport was testing how many rabbits a Whippet could "snap up" in an enclosure; this led to the breed's nickname "snap dogs." During Whippet races, owners encouraged their dogs by waving pieces of rag, earning them the name "rag dogs." Whippets came to the United States with immigrants, particularly mill operators in the Massachusetts area, but the dog's popularity quickly spread to Baltimore, Maryland—home of the prestigious Green Spring Valley racing track. The American Kennel Club recognized the breed in 1888, but the Whippet was not accepted by the British Kennel Club until 1891.

SCENT HOUNDS

Alpine Dachsbracke

AUSTRIA

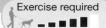
Exercise required

Alpine Dachsbracke
puppy

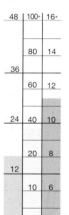

Average height (inches)	Average weight (pounds)	Average life expectancy (years)
48	100+	16+
	80	14
36		
	60	12
24	40	10
	20	8
12		
	10	6

Common
Coat Colors

The Alpine Dachsbracke is a small but sturdy scent hound used for tracking and shooting. These cheerful, bold dogs can make good companions if socialized early and are noted for getting along with children and other dogs. Their smooth, short coats are easy to maintain with a stiff brush.

AT A GLANCE

Ease of training	
Affection	
Playfulness	
Good with children	
Good with other dogs	
Grooming required	

! These dogs have great vitality and stamina and are bred with weather-resistant coats. A stiff bristled brush is your best bet for grooming.

 No known recurring issues, as the breed is relatively rare.

HISTORY

Believed to have developed in ancient times, in the mid-nineteenth century this breed was linked to the kennels of Austria's Crown Prince Rudolf. His gamekeepers kept Alpine Dachsbrackes (or their ancestors) and used the low-slung dogs for tracking wounded deer and scenting out hare and foxes. Crown Prince Rudolf is said to have taken some of his Dachsbrackes to hunt in Egypt and Turkey. They were first recognized in Austria in 1932.

American English Coonhound

English Coonhound / Redtick Coonhound

UNITED STATES

Exercise required

American English Coonhound puppy

Average height (inches)	Average weight (pounds)	Average life expectancy (years)
48	100+	16+
	80	14
36		
	60	12
24	40	10
	20	8
12		
	10	6

Common Coat Colors

These agile, fast, and enduring hounds possess an excellent voice, which they put to good use when tracking small furred game, and a racy body that allows them to speed over most terrain. This kind-natured breed can fit into most family life if given exercise, but they are happiest when hunting.

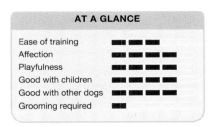

AT A GLANCE	
Ease of training	▬ ▬ ▬ ▬
Affection	▬ ▬ ▬ ▬ ▬
Playfulness	▬ ▬ ▬ ▬ ▬
Good with children	▬ ▬ ▬ ▬
Good with other dogs	▬ ▬ ▬ ▬
Grooming required	▬

! The American English Coonhound is an especially noisy dog, and may not be suitable for a home with nearby neighbors.

+ Can overheat during hunts in the summer.

HISTORY

Also known as the English Coonhound or the Redtick Coonhound, this breed traces back to the earliest English Foxhounds brought to the southern U.S. in the 1600s and 1700s—including by George Washington—and crossed with local types adapted to the harsher climate. Their offspring were sometimes known as Virginia Hounds. The current breed was recognized by the AKC in 2011.

American Foxhound

UNITED STATES

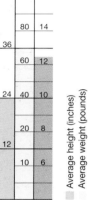

American Foxhound
puppy

Exercise required

48	100+	16+
	80	14
36		
	60	12
24	40	10
	20	8
12		
	10	6

Average height (inches)
Average weight (pounds)
Average life expectancy (years)

These large, rangy pack hounds enjoy a communal environment with other dogs, but American Foxhounds are also docile and sweet around humans—though they may act shy with strangers.

AT A GLANCE

Ease of training	■■■□□
Affection	■■■■□
Playfulness	■■■■□
Good with children	■■■■■
Good with other dogs	■■■■■
Grooming required	■□□□□

Common Coat Colors ○●●

! American Foxhounds perform four different types of work: they compete in field trials; slow-trailing hounds with good voices are used by hunters with guns; drag hounds follow an artificial scent; and packs of hounds kept by hunt clubs follow real foxes.

✚ This breed is generally very healthy, but hereditary problems can include hip dysplasia, deafness, and platelet abnormalities.

HISTORY

The American Foxhound traces to the seventeenth century and the efforts of Robert Brooke, a wealthy landowner who moved from England to Maryland, bringing his foxhounds with him. He established a huge estate and bred his hounds to have speed and endurance so they could cope with all the open spaces in his new home. Fox hunting was becoming increasingly popular in the United States, and many new hunt clubs were established. The racy American Foxhounds were ideal for this type of cross-country hunting, easily able to stay ahead of mounted riders. President George Washington was a keen hunter and bred hounds that were significant in the development of the American Foxhound. He wrote in his diaries that he wanted to create a "perfect pack of hounds" by mixing English Foxhounds with Irish, French, and German hounds to produce a stronger, faster type suitable for the rolling terrain of the Virginia countryside.

Ariegeois

Ariege Hound / Briquet du Midi
FRANCE

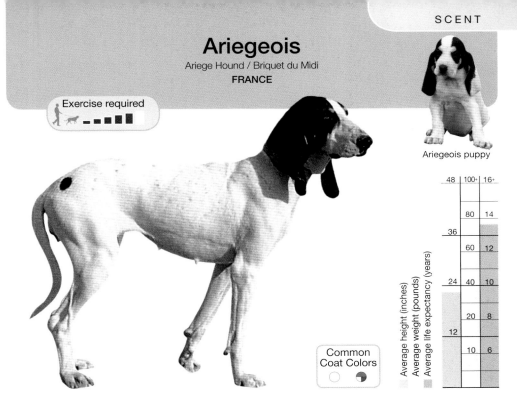

Ariegeois puppy

Exercise required

		48	100+	16+
			80	14
	36			
			60	12
Average height (inches)	Average weight (pounds)	Average life expectancy (years)		
		24	40	10
			20	8
	12			
			10	6

Common Coat Colors

The medium-sized Ariegeois is an affectionate and exceptionally loyal dog that originated in France, where they were bred to course large or small game or drive it toward waiting hunters. They are known for being good with strangers, making them a poor choice as a guard dog. Additionally, they were bred to work in large packs, so they exhibit low levels of aggression with other dogs. The Ariegeois is an affectionate, low-maintenance dog that would fit well into most households.

HISTORY

This relatively new breed is a member of the French scent hound family that developed in the early twentieth century, possibly 1912. It arose in the mid-Pyrennees region of southern France and was believed to be derived from crossing Grand Bleu de Gascogne and Grand Gascon Saintongeois hounds with local Briquet dogs. It is now also being bred in Italy, where hunters are finding it effective when used against wild boar.

AT A GLANCE

Ease of training	
Affection	
Playfulness	
Good with children	
Good with other dogs	
Grooming required	

They are vulnerable to ear infections because of the shape of their ears—long and drooping.

! This breed almost became extinct during World War II, but has made a full comeback and is now common in France.

59

Artois Hound
Chien d'Artois
FRANCE

Artois Hound pup

Exercise required

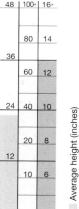

48	100+	16+
36	80	14
	60	12
24	40	10
	20	8
12		
	10	6

Average height (inches)
Average weight (pounds)
Average life expectancy (years)

Common Coat Colors

The Chien Artois is an energetic, brave, loyal breed that can be very willful. It requires an experienced and dominant owner. At home it is calm, affectionate and well balanced.

+ At risk for ear and nail infections.

! This is an ancestor of the Bassett Hound.

AT A GLANCE

Ease of training	
Affection	
Playfulness	
Good with children	
Good with other dogs	
Grooming required	

HISTORY

This is an ancient breed of scent hound whose history traces back to the nth century and the larger Grand Chien d'Artois from which it developed. The dogs were used for hunting in small packs, both on foot and to accompany hunters on horseback. They are mostly used on small game, but these brave hounds will also hunt wild boar, deer, and other large game. The breed was influenced by crossbreeding to gun-dog types in the nineteenth century and will occasionally point.

Austrian Black and Tan Hound

Brandlbracke
AUSTRIA

Exercise required

Common
Coat Colors

Young Austrian Black and Tan

The Austrian Black and Tan Hound is known for its keen sense of smell, lovely voice, and elegant running style. It has been used in the Austrian highlands to hunt hare and to track wounded game. The approved color is black with small fawn markings, especially above the eyes. Although they make good-natured pets, these dogs require a lot of room to run and do not do well in a city.

Average height (inches)	Average weight (pounds)	Average life expectancy (years)
	48	100+	16+
		80	14
36			
		60	12
	24	40	10
		20	8
12			
		10	6

 These hounds are called "four eyes" due to the fawn dots above their eyes.

✚ This breed is prone to cataracts and often suffers from the lung disease chylothorax. They can also be sensitive to anesthesia.

AT A GLANCE

Ease of training
Affection
Playfulness
Good with children
Good with other dogs
Grooming required

HISTORY

Thought to be the true descendant of the original Celtic Hounds, the Gaelic guardians decribed in Irish legends, there is no recorded history of the Austrian Black and Tan Hound until after the middle of the nineteenth century. These large dogs are not well-known outside their native land, but those who have worked with Black and Tans, consider them among the finest trackers and hunters.

Basset Artésien Normand

FRANCE

Exercise required

Common Coat Colors

48	100+	16+
	80	14
36		
	60	12
24	40	10
	20	8
12		
	10	6

Average height (inches)
Average weight (pounds)
Average life expectancy (years)

Basset Artésien
Normand pup

These cheerful dogs are full of character, with superb temperaments that make them good companions. They can be independent by nature, however, and possess deep, loud voices.

AT A GLANCE

Ease of training	■■ ▢▢▢▢
Affection	■■ ■■ ■■ ▢
Playfulness	■■ ■■ ■ ▢▢
Good with children	■■ ■■ ■ ▢▢
Good with other dogs	■■ ■■ ■ ▢▢
Grooming required	■■ ▢▢▢▢

! Some early Bassets had crooked front legs (Normand) and some had straight legs (Chien).

+ This breed may suffer from hip dysplasia, back problems, ruptured disks, and weight gain.

HISTORY

First documented as a breed in 1870, the Basset Artésien Normand was developed by Leon Verrier from the Artois Hound in the early twentieth century, based on Verrier's female Belette. The word basset means "low set," which is an apt description of these keen scent hounds that will hunt singly or in packs. They were bred as "walking" hounds, meant to precede a hunter on foot.

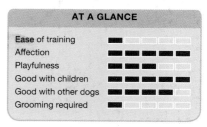

Basset Bleu de Gascogne

Blue Gascony Basset
FRANCE

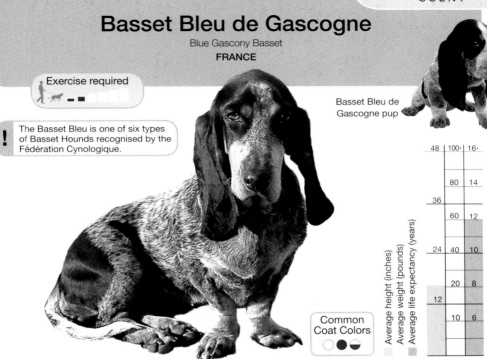

Exercise required

Basset Bleu de Gascogne pup

! The Basset Bleu is one of six types of Basset Hounds recognised by the Fédération Cynologique.

Average height (inches)	Average weight (pounds)	Average life expectancy (years)
48	100+	16+
	80	14
36		
	60	12
	24	40	10
	20	8
12		
	10	6

Common Coat Colors

Also known as the Blue Gascony Basset, this long-backed, short legged hound likely originated during the Middle Ages, when it was used to hunt hare, as well as wild boar and wolves. Perhaps the oldest French native breed, it is rarely seen outside its homeland. Yet it possesses the typical easy-going basset nature and makes a fine companion dog. It is recognized internationally by the Fédération Cynologique Internationale, in the UK by the Kennel Club, and by the United Kennel Club in the United States. The "bleu" of its name is a reference to its coat which has a ticked blue-gray appearance.

HISTORY

The Basset Bleu de Gascogne is directly descended from the old Grand Bleu de Gascogne and was recorded in fourteenth century paintings from Gascony, in southwest France. Its exact origin is debated; one theory is that it is a cross of the Grand Bleu with the Saintongeois Basset, another is that the Basset Bleu is a natural mutation of the Grand combined with selective breeding for shorter legs in order to slow down its speed. It nearly became extinct in the early nineteenth century, when hunting declined in popularity. The breed's re-establishment was attributed to Alain Bourbon.

AT A GLANCE

Ease of training	■■ ■■ ■■
Affection	■■ ■■ ■■ ■■
Playfulness	■■ ■■
Good with children	■■ ■■ ■■ ■■
Good with other dogs	■■ ■■ ■■
Grooming required	■■

+ The Basset Blue is known to suffer from very few hereditary health issues and are known to be one of the more robust pure breeds. However, they can be prone to ear problems.

Basset Fauve de Bretagne

FRANCE

Basset Fauve de Bretagne pup

Exercise required

Common Coat Colors

48	100+	16+
	80	14
36		
	60	12
24	40	10
	20	8
12		
	10	6

Average height (inches) · Average weight (pounds) · Average life expectancy (years)

These are brave, tenacious hounds with superb temperaments that, although it remains a rare breed, it is now finding increased popularity and can make wonderful family companions.

AT A GLANCE

Ease of training	███
Affection	████
Playfulness	███
Good with children	█████
Good with other dogs	█████
Grooming required	█

! These dogs get lonely when not around people, and prefer active, busy lives with lots of attention.

✚ Hardy, no known issues.

HISTORY

The Basset Fauve de Bretagne is believed to have developed from the old French Fauve hounds, of which there were four types, divided by coat color and texture. Today only one survives, the Griffon Fauve de Bretagne. The Basset Fauve de Bretagne was probably created by breeding the smallest Griffons together, although no records exist. By the nineteenth century, however, there were packs of the small, courageous hounds living throughout France. In the twentieth century, the Basset Fauve de Bretagne was influenced by Basset Griffon Vendéen to improve its hunting skills, and Red Standard Wire Haired Dachshund improved the color.

Basset Hound

FRANCE

Basset Hound puppy

Exercise required

Common Coat Colors

Average height (inches) | Average weight (pounds) | Average life expectancy (years)

48	100+	16+
	80	14
36		
	60	12
24	40	10
	20	8
12		
	10	6

These long-eared, low-slung dogs, along with their taller relatives, the Bloodhounds, are used for the slow pursuit of hare and for driving small game from dense undergrowth into open country where a hunter can sight them. They are typically used in packs, although they can work alone. Like other Basset breeds, they are sociable, warm-natured, and are now much-loved companion dogs.

AT A GLANCE

Ease of training	▰▰ ▰▰
Affection	▰▰ ▰▰ ▰▰ ▰▰
Playfulness	▰▰ ▰▰
Good with children	▰▰ ▰▰ ▰▰
Good with other dogs	▰▰ ▰▰ ▰▰ ▰▰
Grooming required	▰▰ ▰▰

! Basset Hounds are extremely sociable dogs and generally get along well with other dogs.

 Basset Hounds may develop bleeding disorders, bloat, elbow and hip dysplasia, glaucoma, and luxating patella.

HISTORY

The charismatic Basset Hound, among the most recognizable of all breeds, originated in France during the Middle Ages. They are believed to have developed from leggy hounds that were bred by monks at the Monastery of St. Hubert in Belgium. In the late seventh and early eighth centuries, Hubert supplied the aristocracy with hounds from his monastery. It is possible that the Basset arrived through genetic mutations of these large hounds resulting in a strain of short-legged dogs.

Bavarian Mountain Hound

Bayerischer Gebirgsschweißhund

GERMANY

Bavarian Mountain
Hound pup

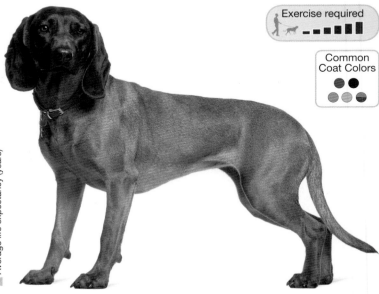

Exercise required

Common
Coat Colors

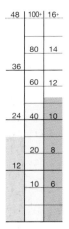

Average height (inches)	Average weight (pounds)	Average life expectancy (years)
48	100+	16+
	80	14
36		
	60	12
24	40	10
	20	8
12		
	10	6

The Bavarian Mountain Hound is one of Germany's preeminent hunting dogs, an outstanding tracking and trailing "bloodhound" breed that instinctively follows a blood trail, making them valuable for tracking large, wounded game. Their scenting ability is so acute, they can follow a "cold" trail that is several days old. In the home they are calm and poised, becoming very attached to their families.

AT A GLANCE

Ease of training	▰▰▰▰▱▱
Affection	▰▰▰▰▰
Playfulness	▰▰▰▱▱
Good with children	▰▰▰▱
Good with other dogs	▰▰▰▱
Grooming required	▰▱

! They don't make great guard dogs—
even though they mistrust strangers,
they avoid confrontations.

+ They are generally healthy with no known
hereditary health issues.

HISTORY

The Bavarian Mountain Hound, as its name suggests, was first bred and developed in the mountainous regions of Bavaria, Germany. Likely decsended from hunting dogs known as Bracken, these hounds were developed during the nineteenth century by crossing heavier Hanovarian Hounds with Red Mountain Hounds. The result was a lighter, more agile dog that would be able to work well as a leashed scenting hound that would single-mindedly track injured or wounded game—a necessity during the Middle Ages, when more primitve weaponry left many animals wounded but not dead.

Beagle-Harrier

FRANCE

Exercise required

Young Beagle-Harrier

Common Coat Colors

	Average height (inches)	Average weight (pounds)	Average life expectancy (years)
	48	100+	16+
	36	80	14
	24	60	12
	12	40	10
		20	8
		10	6

The Beagle-Harrier takes its name from two breeds: the smallish beagle and the leggier harrier. It is a medium-sized, tricolor dog, somewhere between the beagle and harrier in both height and weight. These lively dogs make good pets for homes with children or other animals. While they are calm and even tempered, like most hounds, beagle-harriers require a lot of exercise.

AT A GLANCE

Ease of training	
Affection	
Playfulness	
Good with children	
Good with other dogs	
Grooming required	

 The Beagle-Harrier is a hunting breed, so it needs a large space to run.

+ This breed is generally healthy, although there is some chance of hip dysplasia.

HISTORY

Although they may be quite a bit older, recognized Beagle-Harriers were bred in France in the nineteenth century by painter Baron Gerard. The Beagle-Harrier might be a mixture of the two breeds . . . or the link in the bloodlines where the two strains parted. The breed was recognized by the FCI in 1972. It is also recognized by the Continental Kennel Club. Unfortunately, the Beagle-Harrier is now rarely found in France or other parts of the world.

Beagle

ENGLAND

48	100+	16+
	80	14
36		
	60	12
24	40	10
	20	8
12		
	10	6

Average height (inches)
Average weight (pounds)
Average life expectancy (years)

The Beagle is a superb small hunting hound that has also become popular as a companion animal, particularly in the United States. Beagles have an engaging, lively, and often comical nature; they are highly entertaining, interactive, and affectionate. On the downside, and as is the case with most hound breeds, Beagles can be very noisy. They are suitable for urban living as long as their barking is managed and they are given plenty of exercise and diversions. Due to their pleasing temperament and compact size, Beagles are often used as therapy dogs, and also for bomb and drug detection.

Young Beagle

HISTORY

Accounts of small hounds used for tracking hare date back to Xenophon (c. 430–354 BCE) in Ancient Greece and his treatise *On Hunting*. The Romans probably took these small hounds along on their conquest of Europe, including into England, where the modern Beagle developed. Many written accounts of these small hound types indicate that various monarchs such as Edward II and Henry VII kept packs at the royal kennels. The term "beagle" was introduced in the fifteenth century by Edward, Second Duke of York, in his treatise *The Master of the Game*. Early in their history, Beagles were bred in different sizes including the Glove or Pocket Beagle, so called because it could fit into a gauntlet cuff or a saddle bag. Elizabeth I kept a pack of Pocket Beagles and had her portrait painted with one of them. In the United States, Beagles are divided into two height divisions: 13 inches and 15 inches. The American Kennel Club registered the first Beagle in 1885, and the National Beagle Club of America was established in 1888.

Exercise required

Common Coat Colors

+ Beagles are generally healthy, but hereditary problems can include hip dysplasia and intervertebral disk.

! Beagles are gregarious, pack-oriented dogs that are generally not happy to be left alone for extended periods.

Beagle pup

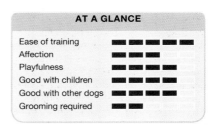

AT A GLANCE	
Ease of training	
Affection	
Playfulness	
Good with children	
Good with other dogs	
Grooming required	

Berner Laufhund

Schweizerischer Niederlaufhund / Swiss Bernese Hound

SWITZERLAND

Exercise required

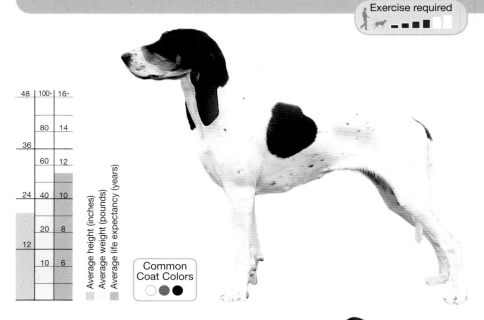

48	100+	16+
	80	14
36		
	60	12
24	40	10
	20	8
12		
	10	6

Average height (inches)
Average weight (pounds)
Average life expectancy (years)

Common Coat Colors

Originally used for hunting, the Bernese Hound is an enthusiastic companion for an active owner and will thrive in organized activities such as scenting trials. They prefer company, are good with children and adapt easily to home life.

Berner Laufhund pup

AT A GLANCE	
Ease of training	▰▰▰
Affection	▰▰▰
Playfulness	▰▰▰
Good with children	▰▰▰
Good with other dogs	▰▰▰▰
Grooming required	▰

✚ Generally healthy, chance of hip dysplasia.

HISTORY

By the nineteenth century, there were five varieties of the Swiss Hound, and in 1882 each got its own breed standard. By 1909 one of the five, the Thurgovie, had disappeared. In 1933 a revised single standard was applied to the four remaining hounds, (based largely on color). These are the Bernese Hound, Lucerne Hound, Schwyz Hound, and Jura Hound.

Billy
FRANCE

Exercise required

Common Coat Colors

48	100+	16+
	80	14
36		
	60	12
	24	40	10
	20	8
12		
	10	6

Average height (inches)
Average weight (pounds)
Average life expectancy (years)

The Billy is an elegant-looking hound, with a great turn of speed. It is known for its exceptional scenting abilities and its deep, sonorous bay in pursuit of large game. The Billy was based on several extinct French hound breeds such as the Montaimboeuf, Ceris, and Larye, and it has had a more recent introduction of Foxhound blood. It is an active dog not suited to small homes.

AT A GLANCE

Ease of training	▬
Affection	▬ ▬ ▬
Playfulness	▬ ▬
Good with children	▬ ▬ ▬
Good with other dogs	▬
Grooming required	▬

➕ At a risk for colds and bronchitis, due to their short and fine coat.

HISTORY

This rare French hound was developed during the nineteenth century, primarily by Monsieur Gaston Hublot du Rivault at his Chateau de Billy in Poitou. Only two hounds survived World War II, and they were bred back to the Poitevin, the Porcelaine and the Harrier to revive the breed.

Young Billy Hound

Black and Tan Coonhound

UNITED STATES

Exercise required

48	100+	16+
	80	14
36		
	60	12
24	40	10
	20	8
12		
	10	6

Average height (inches)
Average weight (pounds)
Average life expectancy (years)

Common
Coat Colors

Young Black and Tan Coonhound

Black and Tans have superb scenting abilities and can follow a "cold" trail—one that is several days old. They are excellent tracking and treeing dogs and, as their name suggests, are particularly suited to hunting raccoons.

AT A GLANCE

Ease of training	▄ ▄ ▄ ▄ ▄
Affection	▄ ▄ ▄
Playfulness	▄ ▄ ▄
Good with children	▄ ▄ ▄ ▄ ▄
Good with other dogs	▄ ▄ ▄
Grooming required	▄

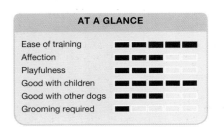

+ Hip dysplasia, cateracts.

! They have a strong tendency to wander, and need a proper fence to keep them in one area; an electric fence isn't likely to keep them from escaping.

HISTORY

The American Black and Tan Coonhound is a stylish-looking hound that traces back to the nineteenth century to the southern United States. They were developed primarily from American Foxhounds with the addition of Bloodhound, which gave rise to the Black and Tan's color; its long, pendent ears; and heavy frame.

Black Forest Hound

Slovenýsky Kopov / Slovakian Hound
SLOVAKIA

Exercise required

Black Forest
Hound puppy

	48	100+	16+
		80	14
	36		
		60	12
	24	40	10
		20	8
	12		
		10	6

Average height (inches)
Average weight (pounds)
Average life expectancy (years)

Common
Coat Colors

The Slovenský Kopov, also known as the Black Forest Hound in North America, is not widespread outside its homeland of Slovakia. This breed is a preeminent wild boar hunter, despite its relatively small size in comparison to its ferocious prey. These brawny dogs have a formidable reputation for endurance while trailing large predators, and will continue to work and hunt all day long, giving voice. These are loyal, affectionate, and independent hounds in the home, and because they can be wary of strangers, they make very good watchdogs.

AT A GLANCE

Ease of training	■■ ■■ ■
Affection	■■ ■■ ■■
Playfulness	■■ ■■ ■
Good with children	■■ ■■ ■■
Good with other dogs	■■ ■
Grooming required	■

+ This dog is generally healthy.

! These dogs need very little grooming, and can develop skin problems if bathed too frequently.

HISTORY

A well-known type of hunting dog since antiquity, today's Black Forest Hound was first recognized in the 1870s. The Brandlbracke (Austrian Black and Tan Hound), Chart Polski, and Magyar Agár (Hungarian Greyhound) were likely used in the breed's background. The etymology of the name seems to refer to the dog's color, not a specific location. The breed club was established in Bratislava in 1988.

Bloodhound

ENGLAND

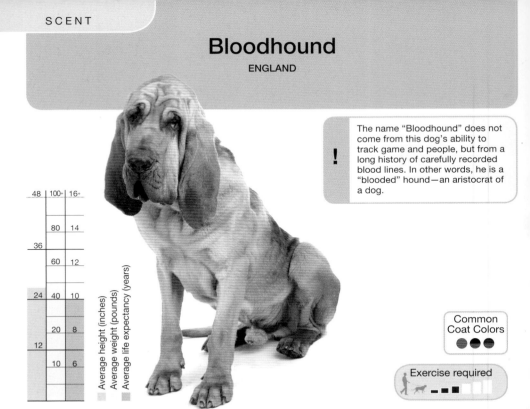

! The name "Bloodhound" does not come from this dog's ability to track game and people, but from a long history of carefully recorded blood lines. In other words, he is a "blooded" hound—an aristocrat of a dog.

Average height (inches)
Average weight (pounds)
Average life expectancy (years)

48	100+	16+
36	80	14
24	60	12
	40	10
12	20	8
	10	6

Common Coat Colors

Exercise required

The Bloodhound is one of the foremost trailing and tracking dogs in the world, with superlative scenting skills and the ability to track old trails over virtually any terrain—even occasionally across water. These dogs are used extensively by the police for tracking, as well as by search-and-rescue organizations. The breed's name is based on the dog's ability to follow a blood trail. Bloodhounds have exceptional temperaments: they are kind, gentle, and mostly good with children and other animals. However, they require lots of space, like to be with other dogs, have a tendency to bay loudly when excited, and can be difficult to obedience train. They are not, therefore, ideal for first-time dog owners.

HISTORY

Known as the Chien de Saint Hubert in most of continental Europe, the modern Bloodhound is generally believed to have developed from the ancient St. Hubert's Hound, which was bred by monks at the Monastery of St. Hubert in Belgium from the eighth century. These hounds were often sent to kings and aristocrats as gifts to curry favor for the monastery, and accordingly, word of their fine hunting skills spread throughout Europe. The dogs were taken to England early in their history, possibly by William the Conqueror, and were described in detail in 1570 by John Caius in his book Of Englishe Dogges. Bloodhounds were first specifically mentioned in the United States in 1619 at the Virginia Assembly when it was made illegal to sell them to Native Americans. Bloodhounds were accepted by the American Kennel Club in 1885, but numbers remained low until the twentieth century. The breed is now relatively well supported in the United States and England.

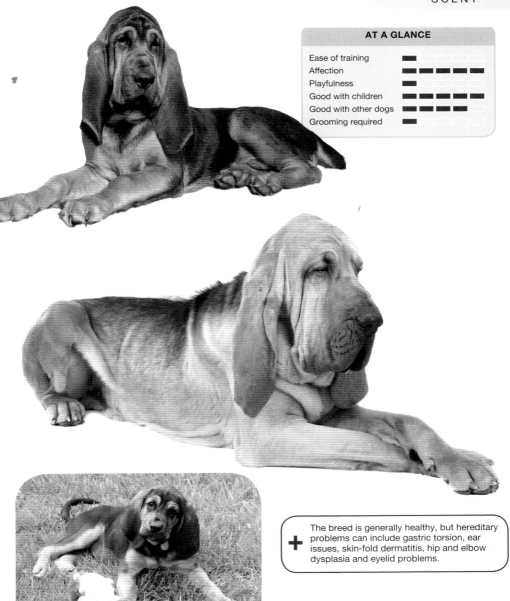

AT A GLANCE

Ease of training	▬
Affection	▬ ▬ ▬ ▬ ▬
Playfulness	▬
Good with children	▬ ▬ ▬ ▬
Good with other dogs	▬ ▬ ▬ ▬
Grooming required	▬

The breed is generally healthy, but hereditary problems can include gastric torsion, ear issues, skin-fold dermatitis, hip and elbow dysplasia and eyelid problems.

Bloodhound pup

75

Bluetick Coonhound

UNITED STATES

Young Bluetick
Coonhound

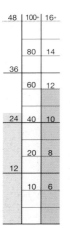

48	100+	16+
	80	14
36		
	60	12
24	40	10
	20	8
12		
	10	6

Average height (inches)
Average weight (pounds)
Average life expectancy (years)

Common
Coat Colors

Exercise required

Blueticks are noted for their loud, drawn-out bay that reaches different pitches depending on the stage of the hunt. They are bred for tracking and treeing game and will hunt a wide variety, including bobcats, mountain lions, bears, and, most commonly, raccoons.

AT A GLANCE

Ease of training	
Affection	
Playfulness	
Good with children	
Good with other dogs	
Grooming required	

! The Bluetick can be found in various forms of pop culture. Emmylou Harris mentions a Bluetick named Gideon in her song "Red Dirt Girl," the University of Tennessee mascot is a Bluetick Coonhound named Smokey, and a Bluetick stars in a commercial for Miracle Whip.

HISTORY

The Bluetick Coonhound was developed in the southern United States based on English Foxhounds bred to other hound types; the breed's distinctive coloring is attributed to the influence of French breeds like the Grand Bleu de Gascogne.

+ Bluetick Coonhounds are generally healthy, but a few have been diagnosed with hip dysplasia and lysosomal storage disease. They may also be prone to bloat.

Briquet Griffon Vendéen

FRANCE

Exercise required

Briquet Griffon
Vendéen puppy

		Average height (inches)	Average weight (pounds)	Average life expectancy (years)
		48	100+	16+
			80	14
		36		
			60	12
		24	40	10
			20	8
		12		
			10	6

**Common
Coat Colors**

A determined and tough hunter, the talented, tousled French Briquet will pick up a trail, hot or cold, in the pursuit of game. They make good family companions as long as they get plenty of exercise, but can be difficult to obedience train—they have strong opinions and don't like being told what to do.

AT A GLANCE

Ease of training	■■
Affection	■■ ■■ ■■ ■■
Playfulness	■■ ■■ ■■
Good with children	■■ ■■ ■■ ■■
Good with other dogs	■■ ■■ ■■
Grooming required	■■ ■■ ■■

! The Briquet Griffon Vendeen is the least well known of the four Griffon Vendeen breeds.

HISTORY

The word briquet translates as "medium-size dog," which is appropriate for a dog that was bred down from the larger Grand Griffon Vendéen. There are four Vendéen hounds: the two aforementioned, the Petit Basset Griffon Vendéen (the smallest), and the Grand Basset Griffon Vendéen. Developed prior to World War I, by World War II this breed almost disappeared; they have since been re-established by Hubert Dezamy, a French dog show judge.

+ This dog is generally healthy, but with a chance for skin or food allergies.

Catahoula Leopard Dog

Catahoula Cur / Catahoula Hog Dog / Leopard Cur

UNITED STATES

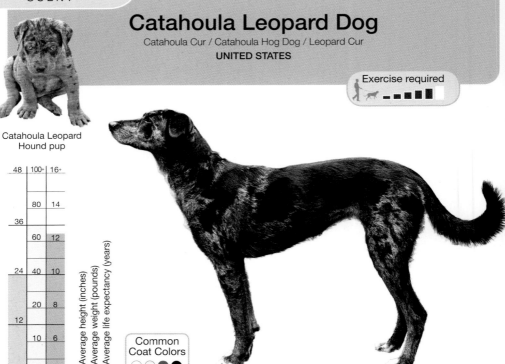

Exercise required

Catahoula Leopard
Hound pup

Average height (inches)	Average weight (pounds)	Average life expectancy (years)
48	100+	16+
	80	14
36		
	60	12
24	40	10
	20	8
12		
	10	6

Common
Coat Colors

The Catahoula Leopard Dog is a strong, independent canine who requires firm leadership. Its full name is the Louisiana Catahoula Leopard Dog, and is believed to have originated in northern Louisiana. The job of these rugged but beautiful "hog dogs" was to drive livestock to slaughter. Today, he's still more of a working dog than a pet, but he's undoubtedly versatile.

AT A GLANCE

Ease of training	▰▰ ▰▰ ▰▰ ▢▢
Affection	▰▰ ▰▰ ▢▢ ▢▢
Playfulness	▰▰ ▰▰ ▢▢ ▢▢
Good with children	▰▰ ▰▰ ▢▢ ▢▢
Good with other dogs	▰▰ ▰▰ ▢▢ ▢▢
Grooming required	▰▰ ▢▢ ▢▢ ▢▢

 The Louisiana Catahoula Leopard Dog has webbed feet—so he can negotiate swamps.

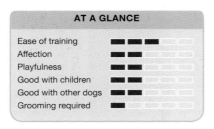 Susceptible to hip dysplasia and deafness.

HISTORY

When the first settlers arrived in Louisiana, they discovered that the state's woods were overrun with wild hogs, so they bred their own herding dogs with canines belonging to local Native Americans. The result was a tough and savvy dog capable of taking on ferocious wild hogs, as well as other fierce livestock. Additional dogs who may have figured in its ancestry are mastiffs, sighthounds, Beaucerons—even red wolves. For many years, the dogs were known as Catahoula Leopard Dog Curs. In 1979, they were formally named Louisiana Catahoula Leopard Dogs, when they were chosen to be the state canine of Louisiana.

Chien Français Blanc et Noir

FRANCE

Exercise required

Chien Français puppies

Average height (inches)	Average weight (pounds)	Average life expectancy (years)
48	100+	16+
	80	14
36		
	60	12
24	40	10
	20	8
12		
	10	6

Common Coat Colors

These lean, muscular dogs exhibit all the classic hound features. They hunt in packs and retain strong pack instincts; they give good voice when hunting; and are noted for their superb sense of smell and great staying power. Although originally developed for use on small game, they are highly regarded for hunting larger game, such as deer. The breed is friendly and easy for humans to manage.

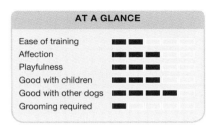

AT A GLANCE

Ease of training	
Affection	
Playfulness	
Good with children	
Good with other dogs	
Grooming required	

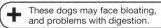
These dogs may face bloating, and problems with digestion.

! Chien Français Blanc et Noir are pack hunters, which means groups of dogs hunt together, always directed by a human, not running loose.

HISTORY

This breed is believed to have been developed during the early 1900s by Henri de Falandre, a keen huntsman. He used a foundation stock of Gascon Saintongeois and Bleu de Gascogne with some English Foxhound mixed in to provide scenting ability, stamina, and temperament. The breed was first recognized in 1957.

Chien Français Tricolore

FRANCE

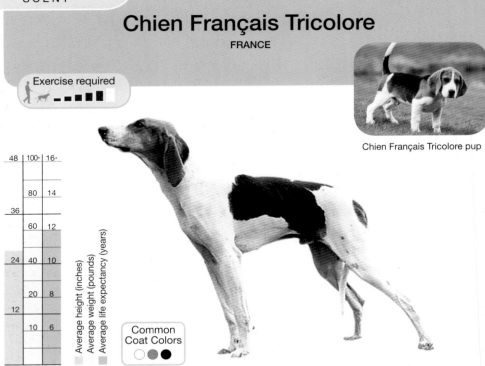

Chien Français Tricolore pup

Exercise required

48	100+	16+
	80	14
36		
	60	12
24	40	10
	20	8
12		
	10	6

Average height (inches)
Average weight (pounds)
Average life expectancy (years)

Common Coat Colors

This breed of medium to large French hound was, like the related Chien Français Blanc et Orange and the Chien Français Blanc et Noir, bred specifically to hunt large game. The hounds are always worked in packs and have a strong pack mentality, so they are not suited to living alone. They have a loud, deep bay, which is useful for the huntsman, and they can alter the tone and pitch of their bay depending on the stage of the hunt. They generally have kind natures but do not make good companion animals unless they are kept with other dogs in a rural location—they are happiest when doing what they were bred to do.

AT A GLANCE

Ease of training	■ ■ ■ ■ ■
Affection	■ ■ ■ □ □
Playfulness	■ ■ ■ ■ □
Good with children	■ ■ ■ ■ □
Good with other dogs	■ ■ □ □ □
Grooming required	■ ■ □ □ □

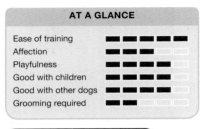

✚ Bloating, digestion issues.

HISTORY

This ancient French breed originated from the now extinct Siantonge and Gauscones hounds. It was developed by Count Joseph de Carayon-Latour in the mid nineteenth century for the purpose of tracking large game. It has a very strong pack drive but is too social to be a good guard dog and will greet strangers with a wag of its tail. It was recognized by the Fédération Cynologique Internationale in 1957 and by 2009 there were almost 2,000 dogs registered.

Cretan Hound

Kressa Kyon / Kritikos Ichnilatis

GREECE

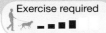
Exercise required

Cretan Hound puppies

Common Coat Colors

Average height (inches)	Average weight (pounds)	Average life expectancy (years)
48	100+	16+
	80	14
36		
	60	12
	40	10
24		
	20	8
12		
	10	6

Considered to be one of the oldest hunting dogs in Europe, this breed likely developed on the island of Crete, in Greece. Its excellent sense of scent and sight, and its speed, agility, and durability led it to become an exceptional hare hunter. These dogs are known for their guarding instincts as well as pastoral herding instincts. The Cretan Hound is nationally recognized both in Greece and in Germany.

AT A GLANCE

Ease of training	▆▆ ▆▆ ▆▆ ▆▆
Affection	▆▆ ▆▆
Playfulness	▆▆ ▆▆
Good with children	▆▆ ▆▆ ▆▆ ▆▆
Good with other dogs	▆▆ ▆▆
Grooming required	▆▆

! These dogs rarely leave Crete, except for some international dog shows in Athens.

HISTORY

A primitive hunting breed, the dog's existence on the Greek island of Crete has been documented in writing and artifacts for 3,500 years or more. This hound was extensively cultivated and used by the Minoan civilization, which, at its peak, dominated most part of the Aegean, the Cyclades islands and eastern Peloponesus.

➕ This breed tends to be very healthy.

Dachshund

Teckel / Dackel / Doxie

GERMANY / ENGLAND

Exercise required

Common Coat Colors

48	100+	16+
36	80	14
	60	12
24	40	10
	20	8
12	10	6

Average height (inches)
Average weight (pounds)
Average life expectancy (years)

Standard Dachshund

In Germany the Dachshund, which translates as "badger hound," is more commonly referred to as a Teckel. These low-slung, tenacious hunters are valued for their use on small game such as rabbit, hare, badger, and fox. They are unusual in that they can locate and track prey above ground and also dig down, kill, and retrieve prey that has gone underground. There are two recognized sizes of the Dachshund now—miniature and standard—but in Germany they are measured according to the circumferences of their chests, which determines into what size hole they can follow their prey. Dachshunds are perhaps more commonly known as companion animals today, but they are also still widely used for hunting, particularly in Germany. As companions, they are full of personality, loyal to their families, and love to have fun. They can, however, be wary of strangers and have a tendency to bark.

! A 2008 study in the journal Applied Animal Behaviour Science named the Dachshund the most aggressive of all dog breeds.

 Generally healthy, but hereditary problems can include intervertebraldisc disease and eye problems.

HISTORY

Long-bodied dogs low to the ground have been recorded since the Middle Ages. Accounts from the 1500s indicate that short-legged, powerful dogs were used in Germany for hunting badgers, and in 1685, author Christian Paullini refers to Dachshunds in his book on dogs. There are no records about how these dogs developed, but historians speculate that German Pinschers, bassetts, French hounds, and terriers might all have had some influence. Certainly the breed is designed for digging and hunting underground; they are extremely powerful but slender, and the structure of their front legs, which may incline outward slightly, allows for a free digging movement. Dachshunds became popular in England during the nineteenth century when Queen Victoria developed a fondness for them, and they made their way to the United States at around the same time. The American Kennel Club registered its first Dachshund in 1885, and the Dachshund Club of America was established in 1895.

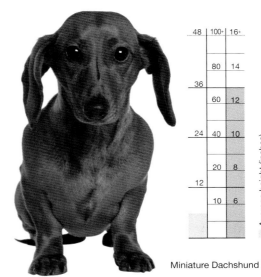

Miniature Dachshund

	Average height (inches)	Average weight (pounds)	Average life expectancy (years)
	48	100+	16+
		80	14
	36		
		60	12
	24	40	10
		20	8
	12		
		10	6

AT A GLANCE	
Ease of training	▆ ▆ ▆
Affection	▆ ▆ ▆
Playfulness	▆ ▆ ▆
Good with children	▆ ▆
Good with other dogs	▆ ▆
Grooming required	▆

Dachshund pup

83

Deutsche Bracke

GERMANY

Exercise required

Deutsche
Bracke pup

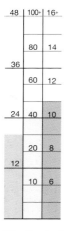

Average height (inches)
Average weight (pounds)
Average life expectancy (years)

Common
Coat Colors

The Deutsche Bracke originated in the Westphalia region of Germany, where it was used for hunting both large and small game. It has a rectangular body, somewhat narrow head, and tricolor, often bristly, short coat with white "bracken" marks. This amiable breed benefits from living with its master or family.

AT A GLANCE	
Ease of training	■ ■ ■ □ □
Affection	■ ■ ■ ■ □
Playfulness	■ ■ ■ ■ □
Good with children	■ ■ ■ ■ ■
Good with other dogs	■ ■ ■ ■ □
Grooming required	■ ■ □ □ □

! This breed is known to get along well with children and other animals.

+ This breed has no known health issues.

HISTORY

This elegant hound can be traced to eighteenth-century Germany, through various writings and artwork of the time. Enthusiasts believe these dogs descended from the Beagle, English Pointer, and various Foxhound breeds, and possibly got their voice from the Bloodhound. The turn of the twentieth century saw several breeds of German pack hounds, except for the Deutsche Bracke, go virtually extinct. The Deutschen Bracken club in Germany has fostered the breed since 1896, and in 1955 released the first official standard.

Drever

SWEDEN

Exercise required

Drever pup

48	100+	16+
	80	14
36		
	60	12
24	40	10
	20	8
12		
	10	6

Average height (inches)
Average weight (pounds)
Average life expectancy (years)

The Drever is a low-slung, versatile hound primarily used for hunting deer at slow speeds, yet it can also hunt smaller game, such as hare. Although a good-natured dog, the Drever is not suited to a non-working lifestyle.

! This dog requires firm, consistent training from an experienced owner.

✚ The dog is generally healthy.

Common Coat Colors

AT A GLANCE

Ease of training	▬▬ ▬▬ ▬▬
Affection	▬▬ ▬▬ ▬▬
Playfulness	▬▬ ▬▬
Good with children	▬▬ ▬▬
Good with other dogs	▬▬ ▬▬ ▬▬
Grooming required	▬▬

HISTORY

The breed developed in the 1850s in Germany, Austria, and Switzerland from the Westphalian Dachsbracke, and imported to Sweden in the early 1900s. In 1947 its name was changed to Drever from the Swedish "drev," meaning "drive," reflecting the breed's ability to drive game to the hunter.

Dunker

NORWAY

Exercise required

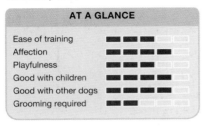

Young Dunker Hound

48	100+	16+
	80	14
36		
	60	12
24	40	10
	20	8
12		
	10	6

Average height (inches)
Average weight (pounds)
Average life expectancy (years)

Common Coat Colors

The medium-sized Dunker is a determined hunter that was developed to go after rabbits. Its coat is characteristically blue-marbled although other colors are allowed. These dogs have a relaxed nature, providing they have a proper outlet for their energy. Sadly, breed numbers are extremely low.

AT A GLANCE

Ease of training	▰▰ ▰▰ ▰
Affection	▰▰ ▰▰ ▰▰
Playfulness	▰▰ ▰▰ ▰
Good with children	▰▰ ▰▰ ▰
Good with other dogs	▰▰ ▰▰ ▰
Grooming required	▰▰ ▰

+ This breed is at risk for deafness.

! The Dunker is more popular in other countries than in its Norwegian homeland.

HISTORY

The Dunker is a specialized hare-hunting hound developed in the nineteenth century by Captain Wilhelm Dunker by crossbreeding a Russian Harlequin Hound with a number of other scent hounds. In 1902 Norwegian hare hounds were divided into two groups, the Dunker and the Hygen Hound. Deafness has become an issue—75% of all Dunkers are deaf in one or both ears.

English Foxhound

ENGLAND

Exercise required

Common Coat Colors

Average height (inches)	Average weight (pounds)	Average life expectancy (years)
48	100+	16+
	80	14
36		
	60	12
24	40	10
	20	8
12		
	10	6

English Foxhound puppy

English Foxhounds are fast, agile, and extremely enduring hounds that were bred to hunt in packs and accompany horsemen. They tend to hunt at a quick pace and are "hot-nosed" hunters, meaning they pick up and follow very fresh trails. The English Foxhound is happiest when living and working in the pack environment—they are extremely sociable and get along well with other dogs. Foxhounds are not typically kept as purely pets, despite having lovely temperaments. They are kind-natured animals and generally good with children, but their greatest joy in life is to be in the field.

AT A GLANCE

Ease of training	▬ ▬ ▬ ▬ ▬
Affection	▬ ▬ ▬
Playfulness	▬ ▬ ▬
Good with children	▬ ▬ ▬ ▬
Good with other dogs	▬ ▬ ▬ ▬
Grooming required	▬ ▬

! Foxhounds love their people, especially children, and will pine without human companionship. They should certainly have access to a securely fenced yard, but when the family is home, the Foxhound should be with them.

+ While generally healthy, they can be prone to occasional deafness or kidney disease.

HISTORY

English Foxhounds were probably created in Britain through judicious crosses of bloodhound, greyhound, and staghound types. In addition to foxes, they were also used to track stags. These dogs were brought to America by British colonists, and among the records of their history is an account of one Robert Brooke bringing them into Maryland in 1650. Notable foxhound fanciers included George Washington. Some of the English Foxhound packs that exist today in the UK can trace their lineage back to dogs in the eighteenth and nineteenth centuries.

Estonian Hound

ESTONIA

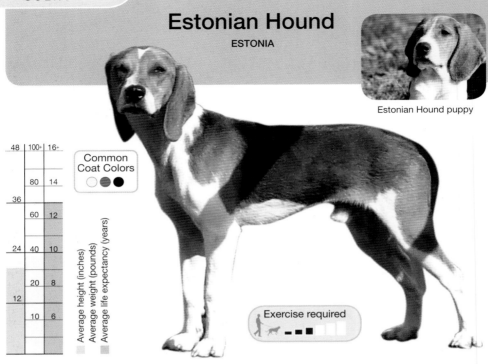

Estonian Hound puppy

48	100+	16+
	80	14
36		
	60	12
24	40	10
	20	8
12		
	10	6

Average height (inches)
Average weight (pounds)
Average life expectancy (years)

Common Coat Colors

Exercise required

Rarely seen outside their native country in Eastern Europe, these scent hounds were developed in the mid-twentieth century from Dachshunds, Foxhounds, Beagles, Swiss Bernese Hounds, Swiss Lucerne Hounds, and Russian-Polish Hounds. The Estonian Hound is a highly efficient hunter of rabbits and foxes but is forbidden to hunt hoofed animals. They are personable, intelligent dogs that can make good companions for an active home, and they excel at events like agility. However, like many pack hounds, they do not like to be left on their own, even for short periods of time.

AT A GLANCE

Ease of training	■ ■ ■ □ □
Affection	■ ■ ■ ■ □
Playfulness	■ ■ ■ □ □
Good with children	■ ■ ■ ■ □
Good with other dogs	■ ■ ■ ■ □
Grooming required	■ □ □ □ □

! The Estonian was specially developed as a hunting dog and can withstand the extreme cold of its native home.

HISTORY

The Estonian Hound is a relatively new breed and the only one to originate in Estonia. These scent hounds were developed in 1947 when the Ministry of Economy in the former USSR decided each Soviet Republic must have its own dog breed. It is now the national dog of Estonia.

+ This is a very healthy and robust breed that suffers from few hereditary conditions.

Finnish Hound

FINLAND

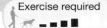

Exercise required

Finnish Hound puppy

Average height (inches)	Average weight (pounds)	Average life expectancy (years)
48	100+	16+
	80	14
36		
	60	12
24	40	10
	20	8
12		
	10	6

The breed is very popular in Finland for hunting hare and fox and is noted for its excellent voice, but it is not commonly found outside its home country.

! While energetic during a hunt, the Finnish Hound is otherwise calm and non-aggressive.

Common Coat Colors

+ This breed suffers from very few conditions, but is at risk from cerebellar ataxia.

AT A GLANCE

Ease of training	■■
Affection	■■ ■■ ■■ ■■ ■■
Playfulness	■■ ■■ ■■ ■■
Good with children	■■ ■■ ■■
Good with other dogs	■■ ■■ ■■
Grooming required	■■ ■■

HISTORY

The Finnish Hound was developed in the eighteenth century by breeders who wanted a hunting dog suited to Finland's rough, snowy, mountainous terrain and harsh climate. Foxhounds, Harriers, German, Swiss, and Polish hounds were used in the breed foundation, along with Russian hounds and local Finnish dogs. The first breed standard was written in 1893, but the modern standard was adopted in 1932.

Français Blanc et Orange

FRANCE

Exercise required

Common Coat Colors

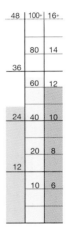

	48	100+	16+
		80	14
	36		
		60	12
	24	40	10
		20	8
	12		
		10	6

Average height (inches)
Average weight (pounds)
Average life expectancy (years)

The Chien Français Blanc et Orange originated in France. This lean, muscular breed is used for hunting in packs and descends from the old Hound of Saintonge, a type of large hunting dog. The Chien is noted for its perseverance on the hunt as well as its good nose and clear voice. Unlike many pack hounds, this dog enjoys human interaction and is relatively easy to manage.

AT A GLANCE

Ease of training	■■ ■
Affection	■■ ■■
Playfulness	■■ ■■
Good with children	■■ ■■ ■
Good with other dogs	■■ ■ ■ ■
Grooming required	■■ ■

! The Chien Francais Blanc et Orange is one of the rarest sighthounds, and is not often seen outside of France.

+ This breed is generally healthy.

HISTORY

The breed is believed to have been developed during the early 1900s by a huntsman named Henri de Falandre, using Gascon Saintongeois and Bleu de Gascogne along with some English Foxhound—and possibly French bracque breeds—to create the desired scenting ability, stamina, and temperament. This white/orange breed specifically is thought to have Billy in its background.

Grand Gascon Saintongeois

FRANCE

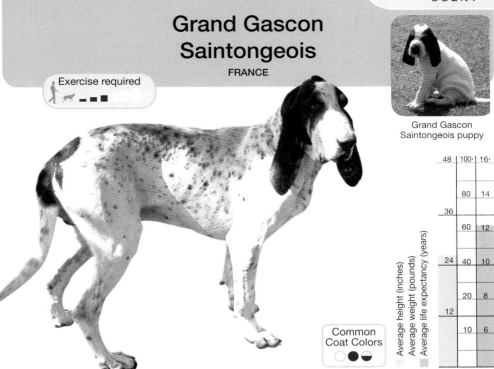

Exercise required

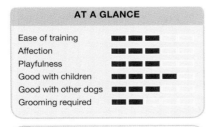

Grand Gascon Saintongeois puppy

	Average height (inches)	Average weight (pounds)	Average life expectancy (years)
	48	100+	16+
		80	14
	36		
		60	12
	24	40	10
		20	8
	12		
		10	6

Common Coat Colors

The Grand Gascon Saintongeois is a well-constructed dog, combining strength and elegance. The breed originated and was developed in France for pack hunting deer and boar; it is noted for its good nose, resounding voice, and beautiful, ground-eating gallop. It is also very affectionate off the field.

AT A GLANCE

Ease of training	■■ ■■ ■■
Affection	■■ ■■ ■■
Playfulness	■■ ■■ ■■
Good with children	■■ ■■ ■■ ■■
Good with other dogs	■■ ■■ ■■
Grooming required	■■ ■■

! This breed is found almost exclusively in southern France, and is in danger of extinction.

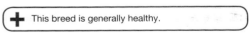 This breed is generally healthy.

HISTORY

This stately breed was created by Baron Joseph de Carayon-LaTour of Chateau Virelade, who came into possession of the only specimens of the Saintongeois Hound to survive the French Revolution—one female and two males. (The Saintongeois is now considered an extinct breed.) These he mated with Grand Bleu de Gascognes from the kennel of the Baron de Ruble. The first-generation offspring were of such magnificent quality that the two men continued to breed in such a manner, and the resulting descendants were given the name Grand Gascon-Saintongeois. The breed was first recognized by the United Kennel Club on January 1, 1993.

91

Grand Anglo-Français Blanc et Noir

FRANCE

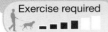
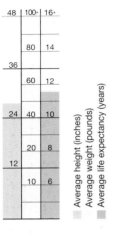

48	100+	16+
	80	14
36		
	60	12
24	40	10
	20	8
12		
	10	6

Average height (inches)
Average weight (pounds)
Average life expectancy (years)

Common Coat Colors

The Grand Anglo-Français Blanc et Noir is one of three historic Grand Anglo-Français breeds that were all derived from crossing English Foxhounds with French scent hounds. In many cases this resulted in hounds with both "hot-nose" and "cold-nose" qualities: they were able to follow a fresh, or "hot," trail at great speed, but could also follow an old, or "cold," trail with great deliberation. The Grand Anglo-Français Blanc et Noir is hunted in large packs and used for tracking large game such as deer and wild boar, though it may also be used on smaller animals, such as fox. These dogs don't make ideal companion animals—they are happiest living in a pack environment and hunting for a living.

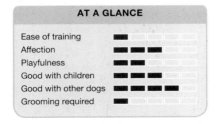

AT A GLANCE

Ease of training	■
Affection	■ ■ ■
Playfulness	■ ■
Good with children	■ ■ ■
Good with other dogs	■ ■ ■ ■
Grooming required	■

 This breed is generally very healthy.

! This dog is known to be especially stubborn, and needs an experienced and equally strong-willed owner for proper training.

HISTORY

Grand Anglo-Français Blanc et Noir is descended from crosses between the old Saintongeois Hound and Foxhounds, a type called the Bâtard Anglo-Saintongeois. The names of all the various Anglo-French hound breeds and their varieties were all officially described with the term "Anglo-Français" as of 1957.

Grand Anglo-Français Blanc et Orange

FRANCE

Exercise required

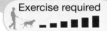

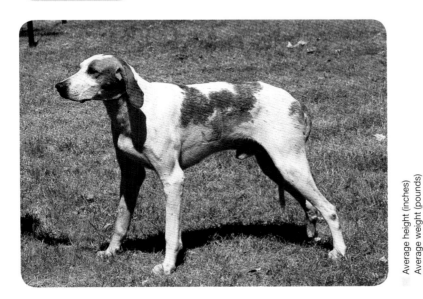

Common Coat Colors

Average height (inches)	Average weight (pounds)	Average life expectancy (years)
48	100+	16+
	80	14
36		
	60	12
24	40	10
	20	8
12		
	10	6

This is a large, rugged pack hunting hound that trails game on any terrain with vigor. Not typically seen as pets, they are nevertheless loyal to their families; most require extensive daily outings.

AT A GLANCE

Ease of training	▦ ▦
Affection	▦ ▦ ▦
Playfulness	▦ ▦
Good with children	▦ ▦ ▦
Good with other dogs	▦ ▦ ▦ ▦
Grooming required	▦

! This dog will almost never express aggression to a human, unless it thinks its family is in immediate danger.

✚ This breed is generally very healthy.

HISTORY

This breed was developed in the 1800s by crossing French scent hounds with English Foxhounds. The three Grand Anglo-Francais hounds were not divided into separate breeds until the twentieth century, when they were categorized primarily by coat color. The Grand Anglo-Français Blanc et Orange largely derived through crosses of Billy hounds and English Foxhound. Coat color is typically white/lemon or white/orange.

Grand Anglo-Francais Tricolore

FRANCE

Exercise required

Common Coat Colors

48	100+	16+
	80	14
36		
	60	12
24	40	10
	20	8
12		
	10	6

Average height (inches)
Average weight (pounds)
Average life expectancy (years)

They are a tough and rugged breed that hunts on any terrain with vigor, and are best suited for pack hunting. They are loyal to their owner and family, and are relatively easy to train.

AT A GLANCE

Ease of training	■ ■ ■ □ □ □ □
Affection	■ ■ ■ ■ □ □ □
Playfulness	■ ■ ■ □ □ □ □
Good with children	■ ■ ■ ■ □ □ □
Good with other dogs	■ ■ ■ ■ ■ □ □
Grooming required	■ □ □ □ □ □ □

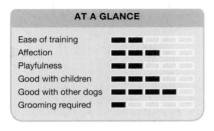

✚ This dog is generally healthy.

! This dog almost never expresses aggression toward a human unless it thinks its family is in danger.

HISTORY

This breed was developed in the 1800s by crossing French scent hounds with English Foxhounds. The three Grand Anglo-Francais hounds were not divided into separate breeds until the twentieth century, at which point they were categorized primarily by coat color. The Grand Anglo-Français Tricolore largely derived through Poitevin (tricolored) and English Foxhound crosses and exhibits the characteristic robustness of the Poitevin with the keen scenting skills of the Foxhound.

Grand Basset Griffon Vendéen

FRANCE

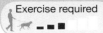
Exercise required

Common Coat Colors

The Grand Basset Griffon Vendéen is the fastest of all the basset scent hounds and is skilled in hunting hare and other small game. They also have enormous personalities, and are affectionate, kind, loyal, and charming dogs that can make wonderful companions for the right home. They are hunters foremost, however, and they will give chase if the opportunity arises and they get off-leash. They also have a reputation for being escape artists and so must have a securely fenced-in yard.

Average height (inches)	Average weight (pounds)	Average life expectancy (years)
48	100+	16+
	80	14
36		
	60	12
24	40	10
	20	8
12		
	10	6

AT A GLANCE

Ease of training	▰▰ ▰▰ ▰▰
Affection	▰▰ ▰▰ ▰▰ ▰▰
Playfulness	▰▰ ▰▰ ▰▰
Good with children	▰▰ ▰▰ ▰▰ ▰▰ ▰▰
Good with other dogs	▰▰ ▰▰ ▰▰
Grooming required	▰▰ ▰▰ ▰▰

! GBGVs are known flight risks, and might run away if left unattended.

+ This dog is prone to GBGV pain syndrome, epilepsy, and glaucoma.

HISTORY

The Grand Basset Griffon Vendéen is one of many varieties of French scent hounds that were developed centuries ago—the GBGV can be traced back to the 1500s. The name is descriptive, with "grand" meaning large, "basset" meaning low to the ground, "griffon" meaning wire-haired, and "Vendéen" referring to the part of France where the breed originated. This area of France's western coast is known for being a rugged environment with a lot of rocky terrain, thick underbrush, and brambles. Although the GBGV had been in existence for centuries, breeders didn't standardize the breed type until the late1800s. The official breed standard was adopted in 1898. At that time, they were called the Basset Griffon Francais. In 1907, when the Club du Basset Griffon Vendéen was formed, the same breed standard was used for both the Petit and Grand Basset Griffon, with the only difference being size. Often, both types—large and small Griffons—were born in the same litter. In 1909, the club rewrote the standard to recognize two types of Basset—the Petit was to be 13 to 15 inches tall and the Grand was to be 15 to 17 inches tall.

95

Grand Bleu de Gascogne

FRANCE

Exercise required

Common Coat Colors

Average height (inches)
Average weight (pounds)
Average life expectancy (years)

48	100+	16+
	80	14
36		
	60	12
24	40	10
	20	8
12		
	10	6

One of the oldest and finest hound breeds, the Grand Bleu is thought to have developed from hounds brought into France by the seafaring Phoenicians, and the now extinct Chien de Courant. These are one of the largest hound breeds and are extremely powerful. They hunt at a slow but persistent pace and have an exceptional voice. They are used on large game, such as deer and boar, and are hunted in packs. Their pack instinct is very strong, and although they have lovely temperaments they are happiest in a hunting environment.

AT A GLANCE

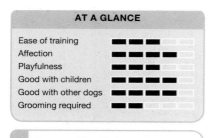

Ease of training	▪▪▪
Affection	▪▪▪▪
Playfulness	▪▪▪
Good with children	▪▪▪▪
Good with other dogs	▪▪▪▪
Grooming required	▪▪

! The name "Grand" does not necessarily refer to the dog's size; rather, the size of the game the Grand Bleu de Gascogne is suited for hunting.

HISTORY

The Grand Bleu de Gascogne may descend from dogs left by Phoenician traders, its ancestors were contemporaries with the St Hubert Hound and English Southern Hound, Comte de Foix kept a pack in the 14th century and Henry IV of France kept a pack in the late 16th & early 17th centuries. The Grand Bleu de Gascogne has a long history in the US, the first dogs were bred there in the 18th century, there are now more Grand Bleu's in the US than France. General Lafayette presented a pack of seven Grand Bleus to George Washington in 1785, who compared their melodious voices to the bells of Moscow.

 No known health risks.

Griffon Bleu de Gascogne

FRANCE

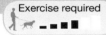

Exercise required

Griffin Bleu de Gascogne puppy

Common Coat Colors

Average height (inches)	Average weight (pounds)	Average life expectancy (years)
48	100+	16+
	80	14
36		
	60	12
24	40	10
	20	8
12		
	10	6

One of the four Bleu de Gascogne breeds, the Griffon is distinct from the other three because of its wiry coat. All three share similar roots and developed in the Pyrenean region of Gascony in southwestern France, whereas the Griffon possibly descended from the ancestors of Roman hunting dogs. They excel in tracking a variety of game and will hunt in a pack or singly. These dogs are noted for their calm, affable temperaments and easygoing natures; although not historically companion dogs, they make fine family pets once they have been properly trained and socialized.

AT A GLANCE

Ease of training	▬ ▬ ▬
Affection	▬ ▬ ▬ ▬
Playfulness	▬ ▬ ▬
Good with children	▬ ▬ ▬ ▬
Good with other dogs	▬ ▬ ▬
Grooming required	▬ ▬ ▬

! Due to its strong prey drive, this dog may not be suitable for a home with other, smaller pets.

HISTORY

The Griffon Bleu de Gascogne is descended from crosses between the Bleu de Gascogne and the Griffon Nervais, and possibly the Grand Griffon Vendéen—breeds used for hunting since before the Roman Empire. The Griffon was known in the field for its good nose and good voice. Sadly, the breed declined for many years in its home country, but it has recently begun experiencing a revival.

 This breed has no known health issues.

SCENT

Griffon Fauve de Bretagne

FRANCE

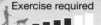
Exercise required

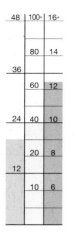

Griffon Fauve de
Bretagne pup

| 48 | 100+ | 16+ |
| 80 | 14 |
| 36 |
60	12
24	40	10
20	8
12
10	6

Average height (inches)
Average weight (pounds)
Average life expectancy (years)

Common
Coat Colors

While working, this dog is bold, dynamic, obstinate and very intelligent. With family, it is affectionate and docile. Initially, it was specialized for wolf hunting, but was later used to hunt hare and fox. It will be happiest on a farm, or in a home with lots of space and work to do.

AT A GLANCE

Ease of training	
Affection	
Playfulness	
Good with children	
Good with other dogs	
Grooming required	

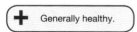
Generally healthy.

HISTORY

The Griffon Fauve de Bretagne is widely considered to be one of the oldest of the French hound breeds and dates back to the early Middle Ages. They were widespread in northern France and were typically used for hunting wolves in packs—a testament to their great bravery and tenacity. As the wolf population began to decline, breed numbers dropped, although they were still used to hunt deer, fox, hare, and wild boar. Following World War II, breeding initiatives have led to an increase in the numbers of this exceptionally gentle and charismatic hound.

Griffon Nivernais

FRANCE

Griffon Nivernais pup

Exercise required

Average height (inches) | Average weight (pounds) | Average life expectancy (years)

	48	100+	16+
		80	14
	36		
		60	12
	24	40	10
		20	8
	12		
		10	6

Common Coat Colors

The Griffon Nivernais is most associated with the mountains of Central France where they were bred to hunt wolves and wild boar. This is an exceptionally brave breed that will hunt all day in any weather, and never backs down from its prey. Like many hound breeds, these dogs also have wonderful temperaments, and although they are generally pack dogs, they can adapt to being companions as long as they have lots of activity and are not left on their own.

AT A GLANCE

Ease of training
Affection
Playfulness
Good with children
Good with other dogs
Grooming required

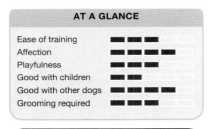

Generally healthy, chance of progressive retinal atrophy and hip dysplasia.

HISTORY

The Griffon Nivernais was a breed kept by French noblemen which disappeared after the French Revolution. The breed was reconstructed beginning in 1925, by some hunters in Morvan, modeling on the ancient types that came to Europe with the Crusaders and the type called "Canes Segusii" or the Celtic Hound by early dog writers. The original dogs were used to hunt wolves and wild boar in the fourteenth century, and were much larger than the modern-day breed. The reconstruction of the breed was done based on the Grand Griffon Vendéen. Other breeds used were the Otterhound and Foxhounds. The breed was small in number for many years, but is now experiencing a revival.

99

Hamiltonstövare

SWEDEN

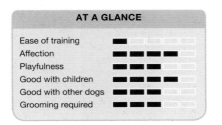

Young Hamiltonstovare
hound

Exercise required

48	100+	16+
	80	14
36		
	60	12
24	40	10
	20	8
12		
	10	6

Average height (inches)
Average weight (pounds)
Average life expectancy (years)

Common Coat Colors

The Hamiltonstövare traces to the 1800s, when it was developed by Count Adolf Patrick Hamilton, the founder of the Swedish Kennel Club. He wanted to establish a hound that could hunt hare and fox across difficult terrain in harsh weather. He used English Foxhounds, Harriers, and three German hounds that are now extinct; the foundation dogs were named Pang and Stella. The Hamiltonstövare has always hunted on its own or in pairs, never a pack. They are versatile, friendly, outgoing dogs that can make companions for an active home.

HISTORY

The Hamiltonstövare breed was developed in Sweden during the late 1800s, and so is a relatively modern breed in canine terms. The first dogs bred to create the Hamiltonstövare were an English Foxhound and a German hound, and the Hamiltonstövare has been selectively bred and improved since then to achieve the modern appearance of the dog, and its superior hunting instinct.

AT A GLANCE

Ease of training	■
Affection	■ ■ ■ ■
Playfulness	■ ■ ■
Good with children	■ ■ ■ ■
Good with other dogs	■ ■ ■
Grooming required	■ ■ ■

 Robust and healthy, though can be prone to obesity if not given proper diet/exercise.

Hanover Hound

Hanoverian Hound
FRANCE

Hanover Hound pup

Average height (inches)	Average weight (pounds)	Average life expectancy (years)
48	100+	16+
	80	14
36		
	60	12
24	40	10
	20	8
12		
	10	6

Common Coat Colors

➕ This breed has no known health issues.

The Hanover Hound is a rare hunting dog. As such, it does best where it has room to run. They are strong, intelligent and determined but obedient and will respond to firm training. They do well with children and other pets when they are raised together.

Exercise required

HISTORY

The sturdy Hanover Hound traces to the Middle Ages. They were "leash hounds" that worked on a leash as they searched for wounded game. Valuable dogs, their breeding was carefully monitored and a breed club opened in 1894. Today they are used only for large game, especially cloven-hoofed-animals.

AT A GLANCE

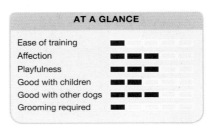

Ease of training
Affection
Playfulness
Good with children
Good with other dogs
Grooming required

Harrier

ENGLAND

**Common
Coat Colors**

Average height (inches)	Average weight (pounds)	Average life expectancy (years)
48	100+	16+
	80	14
36		
	60	12
24	40	10
	20	8
12		
	10	6

The Harrier is frequently mistaken for an oversized Beagle or a small English Foxhound, but it is a distinct breed of scenthound used to hunt hare and fox. Its history in the U.S. dates to colonial times and its lineage goes farther back still, to the early French hounds that were the ancestors of the Bloodhound and the Basset. This rare breed is primarily a pack hound, but that is no barrier to its ability to be a companion dog. Like most hounds, the Harrier is outgoing and amiable towards people. They should also be friendly towards other dogs—any aggression would make it impossible for them to be the great pack hounds they are. And because of their pack dog heritage, they dislike being alone. Harriers do best when they have human or canine company all the time. They can be very vocal and will tell you all about their day in great detail.

AT A GLANCE

Ease of training	■ ■ ■ ■
Affection	■ ■ ■
Playfulness	■ ■ ■
Good with children	■ ■ ■
Good with other dogs	■ ■ ■
Grooming required	■ ■

! Harriers love children, but they may be too rumbustious for toddlers.

+ These dogs tend to be healthy.

HISTORY

Dogs of the Harrier type, which were used to hunt hares, may have been brought to England after the Normans invaded in 1066. The first known pack of Harriers in Britain, the Penistone Pack, dated to 1260, and the line continued for at least half a millennium. Harriers are followed on foot, unlike the Foxhounds, which are ridden to on horseback, but in most other respects they are simply a smaller version of the Foxhound. The American Kennel Club recognized the Harrier as a member of the Hound Group in 1885, making it one of the oldest AKC-recognized breeds. The current Harrier Club of America was founded in 1992. Today, because of his highly specialized job, the Harrier is uncommon and ranks 188th among the breeds registered by the AKC.

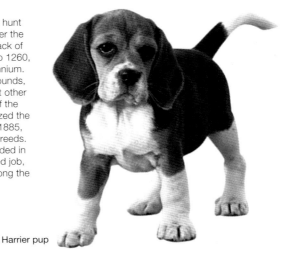

Harrier pup

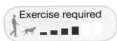

Exercise required

Hungarian Hound
Transylvanian Hound
HUNGARY

Exercise required

Hungarian Hound pup

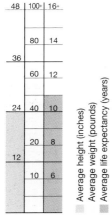

Average height (inches)
Average weight (pounds)
Average life expectancy (years)

Common Coat Colors

This rare breed of Hungarian Hound traces back to the Middle Ages when it was widespread and bred across the Carpathian Basin by aristocrats and royalty. The brave hounds were used for hunting big game such as boar, wolf, bear, and lynx in the mountains and on the plains. Due to the different terrains they hunted on, two types of hounds developed: a long-legged variety and a shorter-legged type. As large predators began to disappear, the breed began to diminish. Efforts by breeders have re-established the Transylvanian Hound, but only the long-legged variety exists today.

+ Generally healthy, chance of hip and elbow dysplasia.

AT A GLANCE

Ease of training	■ ■
Affection	■ ■ ■
Playfulness	■ ■
Good with children	■ ■
Good with other dogs	■ ■ ■
Grooming required	■

HISTORY

It is believed that the Transylvanian Hound originated in Hungary over 1,000 years ago when the Magyars came to the area. This dog breed is most likely a crossbreed between the hounds brought by the Magyars and native dogs of Hungary. The Transylvanian Hound was used as a hunting dog, especially favored by Hungarian royalty while hunting for bears and wolves in the mountains of Transylvania.

Hygenhund

NORWAY

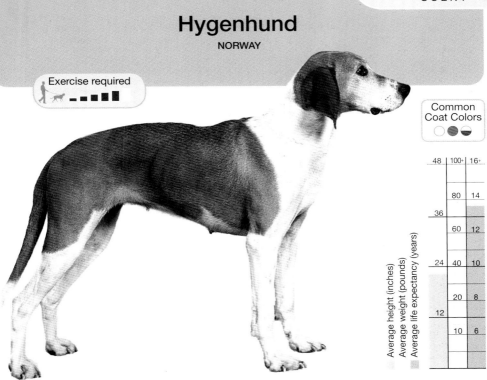

Exercise required

Common Coat Colors

Average height (inches)	Average weight (pounds)	Average life expectancy (years)
48	100+	16+
	80	14
36	60	12
24	40	10
	20	8
12	10	6

Best known for its energetic and lively nature, the Hygenhund loves to keep busy at work or play. These dogs thrive on strong and dependable relationships with humans, and often look to their owner for leadership and guidance. This breed is highly intelligent and generally easy to train. As a pet, the Hygenhund is obedient, loyal, loving, and very affectionate. It is not well-suited for full-time indoor or apartment living, however, as it enjoys spending time outdoors, taking long walks, and having plenty of room to roam, run, and play.

AT A GLANCE

Ease of training	■■ ■■ ■■
Affection	■■ ■■ ■■ ■■
Playfulness	■■ ■■ ■■
Good with children	■■ ■■ ■■ ■■
Good with other dogs	■■ ■■ ■■ ■■
Grooming required	■■ ■■

+ Exceptionally healthy.

HISTORY

This rare breed was developed by Hans Fredrik Hygen in the 1830s. Hygen's son continued his breeding program and was a founding member of the Special Club for Norwegian Hare Hounds, founded in 1902. It was also Hygen Junior who wrote the first breed standard for the Hygenhund in the same year.

! The Hygenhund is specialized for endurance hunting, and can traverse arctic terrain for miles without growing fatigued.

105

Istrian Coarse-haired Hound

CROATIA

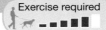

Exercise required

Common
Coat Colors

Young Istrian Coarse-
Haired Hound

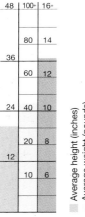

48	100+	16+
	80	14
36		
	60	12
24	40	10
	20	8
12		
	10	6

Average height (inches)
Average weight (pounds)
Average life expectancy (years)

The Istrian Coarse-haired Hound is a strong, hardy dog bred primarily for hunting—its pale wire-haired coat is dense and weather resistant. The breed is willful and can be challenging to train; as such is not especially suited to life as a companion animal.

AT A GLANCE

Ease of training	■■ ■■ ■■ □□ □□
Affection	■■ ■■ ■■ □□ □□
Playfulness	■■ ■■ □□ □□ □□
Good with children	■■ □□ □□ □□ □□
Good with other dogs	■■ ■■ ■■ □□ □□
Grooming required	■■ □□ □□ □□ □□

! This dog needs regular exercise and lots of space, and so is not especially well-suited for apartment life.

+ This breed is very healthy.

HISTORY

The Istrian Coarse-haired Hound (Croatian: istarski o'trodlaki goni', Slovene: istrski ostrodlaki goni') was developed in the mid-nineteenth century for hunting fox and rabbit. Croatian and Slovenian breeders created the rough-coated breed by crossing the French Griffon Vendeén with the Istrian Shorthaired Hound, a smooth-coated dog developed from both sight hounds and scent hounds. The new breed first took part in a conformation show in Vienna in 1866. Although its origins have been disputed by Croatians and Slovenians since the 1960s, in 2003 the the Fédération Cynologique Internationale recognized it as originating in Croatia. This dog is still used today for hunting fox, rabbits, hare, and wild boar.

Istrian Short-haired Hound

CROATIA

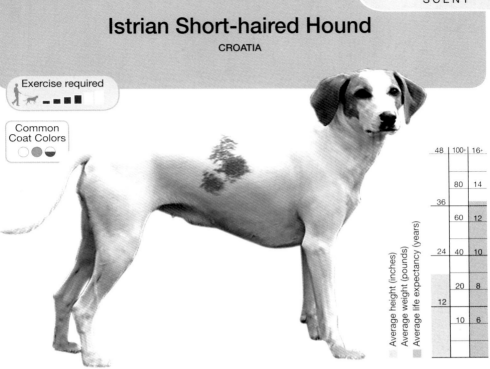

Exercise required

Common Coat Colors

Average height (inches)	Average weight (pounds)	Average life expectancy (years)
	100+	16+
48		
	80	14
36		
	60	12
24	40	10
	20	8
12		
	10	6

Dogs of similar appearance to the Istrian Shorthaired Hound appear in frescoes dating from the fifteenth century, so historians believe that this might be an ancient breed, although no actual records exist. The Istrian Shorthaired is considered to be the oldest hound breeds in the Balkan region, and gave rise to the slightly larger, wire-coated Istrian Coarse-haired Hound. Both types were prized for their hunting skills on hare, fox, and rabbit, and both are still used for hunting today. They have a docile, calm temperament when not in the field, but they can be prone to barking.

HISTORY

There is no actual proof of great antiquity for today's Istrian Shorthaired (such as written lineages going back to an earlier time), although there is much conjecture. The type is very old, and writers mentioning similar dogs include Bishop of Đakovo Petar Bakić in 1719 and the veterinarian Franjo Berti, also of Đakovo, in 1859. This general type can be seen in the Posavaz Hound and the Istrian Coarse-haired Hound as well. A stud book was established in 1924 to document the hounds that were considered part of this breed. The FCI accepted the Istrian Shorthaired Hound in 1955, but the breed standard was not published until 1973.

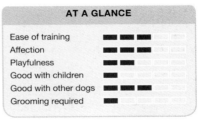

AT A GLANCE	
Ease of training	■■ ■■ ■■
Affection	■■ ■■ ■■
Playfulness	■■ ■■
Good with children	■■
Good with other dogs	■■ ■■ ■■
Grooming required	■■

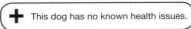
This dog has no known health issues.

107

Kerry Beagle

IRELAND

Exercise required

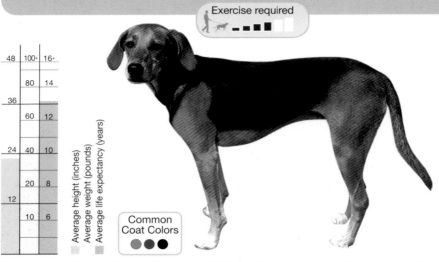

Average height (inches)
Average weight (pounds)
Average life expectancy (years)

48	100+	16+
	80	14
36		
	60	12
24	40	10
	20	8
12		
	10	6

Common
Coat Colors

Possibly one of Ireland's oldest hounds, this breed is not recognized by any major kennel clubs and is rarely seen beyond its homeland. Originally bred for tracking large game, it is now mostly used for small game such as hare, which they hunt in packs with hunters following on foot. This is a fast, enduring, broadchested hound, most often seen in black and tan. Although they are gentle, sociable dogs, as home companions they require a lot of exercise and are not suited to urban living. They are generally good with children and other dogs, but are prone to barking when left unattended.

AT A GLANCE

Ease of training	▮▮▮
Affection	▮▮▮
Playfulness	▮▮▮
Good with children	▮▮▮▮
Good with other dogs	▮▮▮▮
Grooming required	▮

! The Scarteen of Counry Limerick were once the last remaining pack of Kerry Beagles before their revival.

+ There are no health problems specific to this breed.

HISTORY

The Kerry Beagle may be one of the oldest Irish hound breeds. It is said that the "gadhar," a dog written about in ancient Irish texts, is a direct ancestor of the Kerry Beagle. This dog was most likely introduced to Ireland during sixteenth century. Although its exact history is under dispute, the Kerry Beagle is believed to be a descendant of the Old Southern Hounds. (The use of the term "beagle" is puzzling, however—the dog is a medium-sized hound.) Whatever its heritage, the Kerry Beagle was developed over time, mixed with other hound types, to create an ideal pack dog for hunting stag, and later for hare and fox. In the 1800s their numbers declined, nearly leading to the breed's extinction. Happily, the Kerry Beagle's popularity eventually increased, and even spread to other countries like the United States. The breed was formally recognized by the Irish Kennel Club in 1991.

Otterhound

ENGLAND

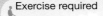

Exercise required

Otterhound pup

Average height (inches)	Average weight (pounds)	Average life expectancy (years)
48	100+	16+
	80	14
36		
	60	12
24	40	10
	20	8
12		
	10	6

Otterhounds are a delightful breed that, as the name suggests, were originally bred to hunt otters, but when otter hunting was banned the dogs declined into rarity. They have wonderful personalities, are very affectionate and can make excellent companion animals.

AT A GLANCE	
Ease of training	■■
Affection	■■ ■■ ■■
Playfulness	■■ ■■
Good with children	■■ ■■ ■■
Good with other dogs	■■ ■■ ■■ ■■
Grooming required	■■ ■■ ■■

HISTORY

These dogs are of ancient origin—the earliest mention of an Otterhound pack dates to 1653. It is believed they were smooth coated before the seventeenth century. Their dense, shaggy, protective coat is possibly the result of rough-coated French hounds introduced to the breed in the 1800s.

! A fenced yard is mandatory. Otterhounds have been known to jump fences as high as five feet, so be sure the fencing is at least six feet tall.

+ This breed is generally healthy, but there is a chance of bloating or hip dysplasia.

Perro Fino Colombiano

Colombian Fino Hound
COLOMBIA

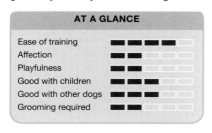

Perro Fino
Colombiano pup

Exercise required

Average height (inches)
Average weight (pounds)
Average life expectancy (years)

48	100+	16+
	80	14
36		
	60	12
24	40	10
	20	8
12		
	10	6

Common
Coat Colors

Once the hunting dog of both Colombian peasants and the artistocracy, this hound has a history that is traceable for over 200 years. The breed type was arrived at through breeding for functionality and adaptability to the Colombian landscape. Stubborn and obstinate while hunting, at home this breed is affectionate with children and makes a wonderful companion. Due to its pack-hunting nature, it is capable of working or living with other dogs and is generally friendly toward strangers.

AT A GLANCE	
Ease of training	■ ■ ■ ■ ■ □
Affection	■ ■ ■ □ □ □
Playfulness	■ ■ □ □ □ □
Good with children	■ ■ ■ ■ □ □
Good with other dogs	■ ■ ■ ■ □ □
Grooming required	■ ■ □ □ □ □

! This breed is recognized by the Colombian Kennel Club—Asociación Club Canino Colombiano.

HISTORY

The Colombian Fino Hound is a hunting dog developed in Colombia from pack hounds along with some pointing dogs imported from Continental Europe, Great Britain and North America in Colonial days.

+ This breed tends to be healthy.

Petit Basset Griffon Vendéen

PBGV

FRANCE

Exercise required

Petit Basset Griffon
Vendéen puppy

	Average height (inches)	Average weight (pounds)	Average life expectancy (years)
	48	100+	16+
		80	14
	36		
		60	12
	24	40	10
		20	8
	12		
		10	6

Common
Coat Colors

PBGVs are extroverted, friendly, and independent hounds originally bred to track hare through brambly countryside. Often called the "happy breed," PBGVs have tirelessly wagging tails, expressive, intelligent eyes, and are typically active and lively. Although they are good with children, other dogs, and pets, they may be unsuitable for very young children because of their high energy and tendency to play bite. The PBGV standard states that the dog should "give voice freely"—and as is typical of hounds, Petits are outspoken dogs. If their pack begins howling or singing, the dog will join in, with amusing results.

AT A GLANCE

Ease of training	■■ ■■ ■■
Affection	■■ ■■ ■■ ■■
Playfulness	■■ ■■ ■■
Good with children	■■ ■■
Good with other dogs	■■ ■■ ■■
Grooming required	■■ ■■

 If they can, they will either go over a fence, or under it by digging. A tall fence is recommended.

+ They are prone to PBGV pain syndrome, epilepsy, and glaucoma.

HISTORY

The Petit Basset Griffon Vendéen is one of the many small French hounds that were developed centuries ago—the PBGV can be traced back to the sixteenth century. The name is descriptive, with "petit" meaning small, "basset" meaning low to the ground, "griffon" meaning wire-haired, and "Vendéen" referring to the area of France where the breed originated. After they were recognized by the AKC in 1990, these dogs became the darlings of the show ring.

111

Petit Bleu de Gascogne

FRANCE

Petit Bleu de Gascogne pup

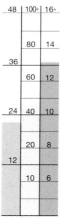

Average height (inches)
Average weight (pounds)
Average life expectancy (years)

Common Coat Colors

This ancient breed of scent hound is descended from the Grand Bleu de Gascogne and was developed in Gascony Province, on the southwest coast of France. The Petit Bleu de Gascogne was originally intended to hunt small game in packs, whereas the Grand was used on larger game. The Petit is noted for hunting methodically at a relatively moderate speed. Although these dogs are calm and easy to handle, their pack instinct is so strong they don't tend to make good pets.

AT A GLANCE

Ease of training	■■ ■■ ■■ □
Affection	■■ ■■ ■■ ■
Playfulness	■■ ■■ ■■ □
Good with children	■■ ■■ □ □
Good with other dogs	■■ ■■ ■■ □
Grooming required	■■ ■■ ■ □

HISTORY

The Grand Bleu de Gascogne's ancestors were contemporary with the St. Hubert Hounds, dogs that were hunted in packs by the fourteenth-century Comte de Foix on wolves, bears, and boars. The slightly smaller Petit Bleu de Gascogne, which was used on hares, may have existed alongside the boar-hunting dog for centuries.

+ No health problems are known to be specific to this breed.

! The name "Petit" refers to the size of game the dog hunts, not the size of the dog itself.

Phu Quoc Ridgeback

VIETNAM

The rare Phu Quoc Ridgeback is one of only three ridgeback breeds in the world. It is found on Phu Quoc Island off Vietnam's southern Kien Giang province, and it is an exceptional athlete. These dogs have keen scenting abilities on hot and cold trails, are capable of great speed, and are also excellent swimmers. They generally have good temperaments but can be inclined to bark. Because they are exceptional jumpers, they need a well-fenced, secure yard. The breed is not recognized by any major registry, and no official standard exists.

HISTORY

Native to Vietnam, the Phu Quoc Ridgeback's history has not been well documented. Enthusiasts—and a few experts—believe that all ridgeback breeds (including the Phu Quoc, Rhodesian, and Thai) originated in either Asia or Africa, due to the distinct ridge markings along the spine, though this has never been confirmed scientifically. It is also believed that, like the Thai Ridgeback, the Phu Quoc has been used as a carting, escort, hunting, and guard dog throughout its history due to its impressive appearance and muscular physique.

	48	100+	16+
		80	14
	36		
		60	12
		24	40	10
			20	8
	12		
			10	6

Average height (inches)
Average weight (pounds)
Average life expectancy (years)

Exercise required
▪ ▪ ▪ ■ ■

Common Coat Colors
● ●

Phu Quoc Ridgeback puppy

AT A GLANCE

Ease of training	■ ■ ■
Affection	■ ■ ■ ■
Playfulness	■ ■ ■
Good with children	■ ■
Good with other dogs	■ ■ ■
Grooming required	■

+ While the Phu Quoc Ridgeback is generally known as a healthy and hearty breed, they can occasionally suffer from health problems like hip dysplasia, patellar luxation—dislocation of the knee, and bloat. They are also prone to various joint problems such as arthritis.

113

Piccolo Lepraiolo Italiano

Segugio dell'Appennino

ITALY

Common Coat Colors

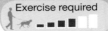

Exercise required

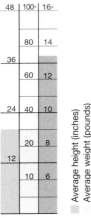

Piccolo Lepraiolo Italiano pup

Average height (inches)
Average weight (pounds)
Average life expectancy (years)

48	100+	16+
	80	14
36		
	60	12
24	40	10
	20	8
12		
	10	6

This slender hound is found both with smooth and rough coats. It is generally used for hunting hares, although it is occasionally used to hunt wild boar as well.

AT A GLANCE

Ease of training	■■ ■■ ■■ ☐ ☐
Affection	■■ ■■ ■■ ■■ ☐
Playfulness	■■ ☐ ☐ ☐
Good with children	■■ ■■ ☐ ☐ ☐
Good with other dogs	■■ ■■ ■■ ☐ ☐
Grooming required	■■ ☐ ☐ ☐ ☐

! In the Lombardy and Piedmont regions, a variant of these dogs is known as "ciaplen" amongst local hunters and has almost mythical status due to its intelligence and ability on the hunt.

HISTORY

In an attempt to secure this breed, the Società Italiana Pro Segugio (Italian Association for Scenthounds) gathered 1450 specimens in the year 2000 by scouring the Italian countryside and registered a total of 824 dogs as breed founders, thus guaranteeing ample genetic variability within the breed. Many dog breeds are derived from a very small number of founders (just nine dogs were used during the creation of the Siberian Husky) and therefore inbreeding tends to be high, resulting in an increased incidence of illness. This native breed was eventually recognized by ENCI, the Italian Kennel Club.

Plott

Plott Hound
UNITED STATES

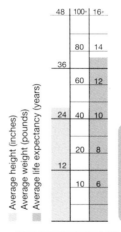

This elegant all-American hound is a spirited, fearless, and tenacious hunter that will go all day. These dogs are independent thinkers and can be headstrong and difficult to obedience train, although once they have been trained they are thoroughly rewarding dogs. They have a high activity requirement and are best suited to a hunting home. Plotts have a distinctive "chop"—a loud, ringing bark that they use when tracking. They may also be noisy if they become bored and so are not ideal for an urban environment.

HISTORY

The mountains of western North Carolina are the birthplace of one of America's few homegrown dogs: the Plott Hound. He's unique among coonhound breeds for his German heritage. The Plott's ancestors were five Hanoverian Schweisshunden—a type of Bloodhound—that accompanied German immigrant Johannes Georg Plott to western North Carolina in 1750. From those five dogs—plus a mixture of some local breeds, including curs—Plott and his descendants bred a line of dogs to hunt bears and other big predators. The early Plott dogs had multiple jobs besides hunting: they protected the home, drove livestock, and kept an eye out for the safety of the family children. These days, they continue to be employed in a variety of ways. Some are search and rescue dogs, some track cougars so they can be tagged by wildlife agencies, some continue their heritage as hunting dogs, and some have even entered the show ring. In 1960, the Emperor of Japan brought in some experts to rid the countryside of bears that were terrorizing villagers. Their "equipment" consisted of 10 Plotts. The Plott has been the official state dog of North Carolina since 1989. The breed was recognized by the United Kennel Club in 1946 and by the American Kennel Club in 2006. The Plott currently ranks 150th among the breeds registered by the AKC.

Average height (inches) / Average weight (pounds) / Average life expectancy (years)

48 | 100+ | 16+
80 | 14
36
60 | 12
24 | 40 | 10
20 | 8
12
10 | 6

Common Coat Colors

Exercise required

The Plott is the dog of choice for big-game hunters in search of bears, cougars, or hogs. They are also used to tree raccoons, and many farmers like to keep them as all-purpose dogs.

Can be prone to bloat or gastric torsion.

AT A GLANCE

Ease of training
Affection
Playfulness
Good with children
Good with other dogs
Grooming required

Polish Hound

POLAND

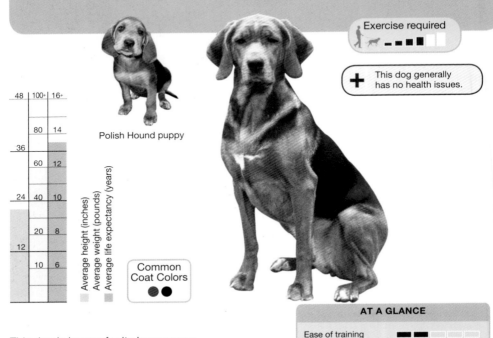

Polish Hound puppy

Average height (inches)
Average weight (pounds)
Average life expectancy (years)

48	100+	16+
	80	14
36		
	60	12
24	40	10
	20	8
12		
	10	6

Exercise required

This dog generally has no health issues.

Common Coat Colors

AT A GLANCE

Ease of training	
Affection	
Playfulness	
Good with children	
Good with other dogs	
Grooming required	

This dog is known for its keen sense of smell, and when combined with its endurance and ability to tackle harsh terrain, it's not surprising it was a prized hunter. Its stature—nearly two feet at the shoulder, made it a favorite with Polish nobility. The modern dog is sleek, with a powerful bone structure. They are mostly black and tan and have a deep, rich voice when on the hunt. These dogs are intelligent, easy to train, and make calm, affectionate pets. Although they are friendly toward other dogs, they can be protective of their homes or land. Whether this makes them good guard dogs is uncertain.

HISTORY

Polish Hounds date back to the Middle Ages, when their progenitors roamed the vast forests of Poland in search of prey. They possibly descended from the Kostroma Hound—the hound of the Tatars. Or they may have developed from local dogs crossed with the St. Hubert (Bloodhound). The early nineteenth century saw the advent of both the Polish Scent Hound and Polish Hound. Polish Hounds were primarily working dogs, however, and as a result they were not seen in the show ring until after the First World War. After the breed was threatened during World War II, two types emerged—Colonel Jozef Pawuslewicz helped standardize a lighter-boned version, while Colonel Piotr Kartawik bred a heavier-boned dog.

Polish Hunting Dog

Polish Scenthound / Gonczy Polski

POLAND

Exercise required

They may develop elbow dysplasia and gastric torsion.

Polish Hunting puppy

	Average height (inches)	Average weight (pounds)	Average life expectancy (years)
	48	100+	16+
	36	80	14
		60	12
	24	40	10
		20	8
	12		
		10	6

Common Coat Colors

The lithe, muscular Polish Hunting Dog was bred for great mobility in order to hunt or track wild boar in the rugged conditions of Poland's mountain terrain. They are trustworthy and tenacious dogs, always ready to work. This beed is also noticeably less unruly and buoyant in a home environment than the majority of other scent hounds. Although Polish Hounds have wonderful temperaments, they are inclined to be independent and noisy. They do well at agility, Frisbee, and sport tracking. Because they can be distrustful of unfamiliar people, they make effective watchdogs. This breed can also be turned into a decent guard dog, considering its territorial instinct and booming bark.

AT A GLANCE

Ease of training	■ ■
Affection	■ ■ ■ ■
Playfulness	■ ■ ■
Good with children	■ ■ ■
Good with other dogs	■ ■ ■ ■
Grooming required	■

HISTORY

Scent hounds are first mentioned in Polish literature in the fourteenth century. They were used by the aristocracy to hunt large and small game. Those early Polish Hounds are described as being mostly black and tan and having a deep, rich bark when on the hunt. In the 1600s, Poland began several centuries of political turmoil, which affected the dogs' bloodlines: many kennels were lost, and the breed was not kept pure. By the twentieth century, the original Polish Hound had almost disappeared. The breed was re-established in 1959 by hunt enthusiast Colonel Peter Kartawik, based largely on three foundation dogs: Storm, Zorka, and Chita.

117

Porcelaine
Chien de Franche Comté
FRANCE

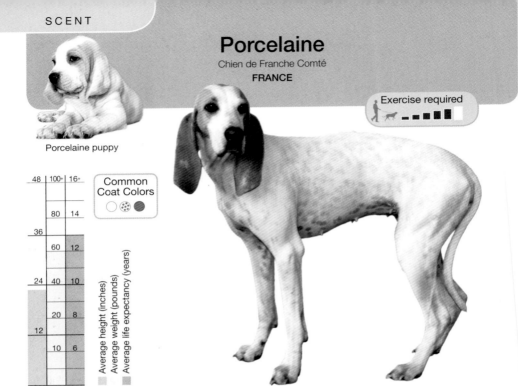

Porcelaine puppy

Exercise required

Common
Coat Colors

48	100+	16+
36	80	14
	60	12
24	40	10
	20	8
12	10	6

Average height (inches)
Average weight (pounds)
Average life expectancy (years)

This unusual-looking hound is also known as the Chien de Franché-Comté, after a region in Eastern France that borders Switzerland. Although this initially caused debate over the breed's place of origin, it has been declared a French dog. The breed takes its name from its shiny, white coat, which makes it look like a porcelain figurine. The Porcelaine is used on hare, deer, and wild boar, and in the field they are known for their excellent sense of smell and fierce independence, allowing them to hunt alone or in a pack. In the home, they are gentle and relatively easy to handle, making them fine pets, but their high energy levels demand daily, rigorous exercise.

AT A GLANCE

Ease of training	
Affection	
Playfulness	
Good with children	
Good with other dogs	
Grooming required	

➕ This breed of dog has no specific health issues.

HISTORY

Perhaps the oldest of the French scent hounds, the Porcelaine is thought to be a descendant of the English Harrier, some of the smaller Swiss Laufhounds, and the now-extinct Montaimboeuf. There have been records of the breed in France since 1845 and in Switzerland since 1880. Kept by the aristocracy on their large estates, this breed actually disappeared after the French Revolution (1789–1799). Enthusiasts reconstructed the breed in the nineteenth century, but numbers remained low. Breeders in the UK are attempting to have the dog accepted as a recognized breed.

Posavac Hound

CROATIA

Posavac puppy

Exercise required

Average height (inches)	Average weight (pounds)	Average life expectancy (years)
48	100+	16+
	80	14
36		
	60	12
24	40	10
	20	8
12		
	10	6

This breed is generally healthy.

Common Coat Colors

The sturdy, long-bodied Posavac Hound has attained regional popularity for its abilities as a hunter of small and medium game. It is also an atttactive dog, coming in several shades of reddish wheaten with white markings, and with slight feathering on its legs. While its good nose and surefootedness coupled with its speed and stamina make it an adept hunter of rabbit, fox, and deer, its obedient, docile, and affectionate nature makes it an endearing family companion. Its natural wariness of strangers and loud bark also allow the breed some effectiveness as a watchdog. The Posavac Hound gets along well with other dogs but should not be left alone with smaller pets due to its high prey drive. This dog can live in an apartment as long as its exercise needs are fulfilled—consider it the ideal jogging or hiking partner.

AT A GLANCE

Ease of training	■■■
Affection	■■■
Playfulness	■■
Good with children	■■■
Good with other dogs	■■■
Grooming required	■

HISTORY

The Posavac Hound is one of Croatia's ancient hound breeds. Its name loosely means "hound from the Sava Valley," since the densely forested Sava Valley in Central Croatia is where the breed originated. Frescoes in the Chapel of St. Mary, Beram, near the west coast city of Pazin and dating to 1474, depict hounds of similar appearance to the modern Posavac. Historians speculate that these were the modern dog's ancestors. Hounds from the Sava Valley were prized throughout Croatia and were originally called Boskini; they were not officially called Posavac until 1969.

Redbone Coonhound

UNITED STATES

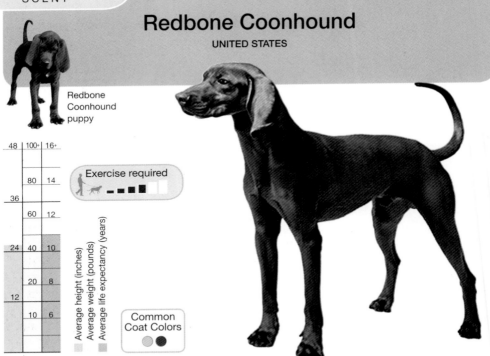

Redbone Coonhound puppy

48	100+	16+
	80	14
36		
	60	12
24	40	10
	20	8
12		
	10	6

Average height (inches)
Average weight (pounds)
Average life expectancy (years)

Exercise required

Common Coat Colors

The stylish Redbone Coonhound was developed from red foxhound types from Scotland and Ireland and was brought into the country by immigrants in the eighteenth century. The foundation of the modern Redbone is attributed to George Birdsong of Georgia—a renowned breeder and hunter. Redbones are fast and agile over a variety of terrains and are excellent swimmers. In addition to hunting raccoons, the fearless Redbones hunt larger animals, including bobcats, bears, and cougars.

AT A GLANCE

Ease of training	■ ■ ■ □ □
Affection	■ ■ ■ ■ □
Playfulness	■ ■ ■ □ □
Good with children	■ ■ □ □ □
Good with other dogs	■ ■ ■ □ □
Grooming required	■ □ □ □ □

 The man who did the most to develop the breed was named George E. L. Birdsong, a well-known fox hunter and dog breeder who lived in Georgia.

HISTORY

The Redbone is one breed that can be labeled "Made in America." Like most coonhounds, the Redbone descends from dogs of English, Scottish, Irish, French, and Swiss bloodlines. Many wealthy Europeans who settled inthe American South, brought their native hounds with them—English Foxhounds, Harriers, Grand Bleus de Gascogne, Beagles, and Bloodhounds. Over time, Southern hunters bred red dogs from this rich stock, rugged dogs that would not back down from large game and could "hound" small prey into a tree. The name came from early breeder Peter Redbone, of Tennessee. Stars of the hunting field and not the show ring, the Redbone was finally registered with the the United Kennel Club in 1902.

+ These dogs have a slight risk of progressive retinal atrophy and hip dysplasia.

Sabueso Español

Spanish Scent hound
SPAIN

Sabueso Español puppy

Exercise required
▪ ▪ ■ ■ ■

48	100+	16+
	80	14
36		
	60	12
24	40	10
	20	8
12		
	10	6

Average height (inches)
Average weight (pounds)
Average life expectancy (years)

Common Coat Colors
○ ● ◑

AT A GLANCE

Ease of training	■ ■
Affection	■ ■ ■
Playfulness	■ ■ ■
Good with children	■ ■ ■
Good with other dogs	■ ■
Grooming required	■

The Sabueso Español, or Spanish Scent Hound, originated in northern Spain many centuries ago and was used for hunting all types of large game, including bear, wolf, wild boar, and deer, and smaller animals like hare and fox. These are dedicated, driven, and tough hounds that will hunt all day long in harsh environments. By modulating their loud voices they can alert the hunters as the hunt develops. These independent dogs are bred to hunt singly or in pairs, never in packs.

HISTORY

The first description of Iberian Scenthounds appears in chapter 39 of Libro de la Montería de Alfonso XI or The Hunting Book of Alfonso XI, a medieval tome of the 14th century for a Castillian king. After that, diverse descriptions of Iberian Scenthounds appeared in various Spanish hunting books of from the fifteenth to the seventeeth centuries: two examples include *Tratado de la Montería*, or *A Treatise on Hunting* and Molina's late Renaissance book *Discurso de la Montería*, or *A Discourse on Hunting*, written in 1582. At this time, Spanish Scenthounds of the type that would become the Sabueso were used mainly in brown bear and wild boar hunting. They were also used to track wounded game by hunters called ballesteros (because they used crossbows). These hounds have been employed since very early times in "caza a trailla" — leashed hound-hunting — to scout the location of bears, wild boars, and wolves prior to the actual hunt.

✚ This breed tends to be generally healthy with no hereditary issues.

Schillerstövare

Schiller Hound
SWEDEN

Exercise required

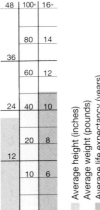

Schillerstövare puppy

48	100+	16+
	80	14
36		
	60	12
24	40	10
	20	8
12		
	10	6

Average height (inches)
Average weight (pounds)
Average life expectancy (years)

Common Coat Colors

Also known as the Schiller Hound, this large, running breed with its harsh coat is perfectly adapted to hunting in freezing weather over difficult terrain. Its chief quarry is hare and foxes. Although some believe this dog to be descended from ancient hounds, the modern breed was developed in the nineteenth century. They were named after Swedish farmer, Per Schiller (1858–1892), who developed the breed and exhibited his dogs at the first Swedish dog show in 1886. They are known to be lively and attentive companions, and make good pets, providing they get regular exercise.

AT A GLANCE

Ease of training	
Affection	
Playfulness	
Good with children	
Good with other dogs	
Grooming required	

 This breed is generally healthy and has no specific concerns.

HISTORY

The Schillerstövare originated in southern Germany, a mix of Swiss hounds and Harriers. The breed was founded on a pack of famous hounds kept at the Kaflas Estate Kennels. Swedish farmer Per Schiller acquired some of these hounds, including Tamburini and Ralla, and exhibited them at a dog show in 1886. The Swedish Kennel Club recognized the breed in 1907. It is also recognized by the Fédération Cynologique Internationale, as breed number 131. They are still used as hunting dogs, and were recognized by the United Kennel Club in the U.S. in 2006. These hounds tend to be rare and are hardly ever seen outside Sweden.

Schweizer Laufhund

Swiss Schwyz Hound
SWITZERLAND

Exercise required

Schweizer Laufhund
puppy

Average height (inches)	Average weight (pounds)	Average life expectancy (years)
48	100+	16+
	80	14
36		
	60	12
24	40	10
	20	8
12		
	10	6

Common
Coat Colors

The Swiss Schwyz Hound one of four varieties of the Schweizer Laufhund; the other hounds are the Bernese, the Jura, and the Lucernese. This breed's coat is white with orange spots or an orange-fawn saddle, sometimes very lightly speckled. The Schwyz is generally reserved for rabbit and hare, but like all Swiss Hounds, it is a hardy, vigorous, and versatile dog with great endurance. These animals are gentle, docile, and become very attached to owners who provide an active home.

AT A GLANCE

Ease of training	▪▪ ▪▪ ▪▪
Affection	▪▪ ▪▪ ▪▪
Playfulness	▪▪ ▪▪ ▪▪
Good with children	▪▪ ▪▪ ▪▪
Good with other dogs	▪▪ ▪▪ ▪▪ ▪▪
Grooming required	▪▪

These dogs are generally quite healthy.

HISTORY

A dog resembling a type of Swiss Hound was documented in Roman mosaics found in Avenches, indicating that this breed is descended from an ancient lineage. In the fifteenth century these hounds were sought by Italian dog lovers; in the 1800s it was the French who admired their way with a hare. The modern Schweizer Laufhund originated in southern Germany, a mix of Swiss hounds and the Harrier. The breed is also recognized by a number of minor registries and hunting clubs.

Segugio Italiano

ITALY

Seguigio Italiano puppy

Exercise required

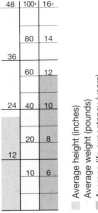

Average height (inches)
Average weight (pounds)
Average life expectancy (years)

48	100+	16+
	80	14
36		
	60	12
24	40	10
	20	8
12		
	10	6

Common
Coat Colors

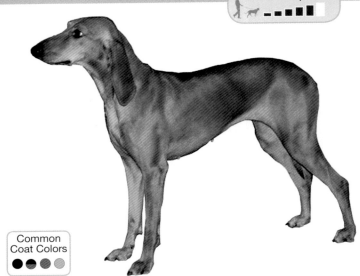

This Italian scent hound is extremely popular in its homeland, but rarely encountered beyond it. These hounds are thought to be of ancient origin, primarily used for flushing boar. They are now used for tracking hare and driving them toward the hunter. These hounds make outstanding hunters, tenacious and determined, and they can be used in packs, or singly. They are intelligent dogs that show great loyalty to their owners but can be wary of strangers. Due to their high energy demands, they are not typically kept in non-working or non-hunting homes.

AT A GLANCE

Ease of training	■■■ ▨
Affection	■■■ ▨
Playfulness	■■ ▨
Good with children	■■ ▨
Good with other dogs	■■■
Grooming required	■

+ This dog tends to be generally healthy with few issues.

HISTORY

The Segugio Italiano is an old breed whose likeness can be found in ancient sculptures and in Italian Renaissance works of art. Also known as the Italian Hound, it is believed to have developed in Italy from Phoenician sighthounds and the Celtic Hounds of southern Gaul. The addition of Mastiff blood to the lithe sighthound stock produced a dog of more substance with the ability to work quarry by scent as well as sight. Wild boar were the traditional target of the Segugio, but the end of the great forest hunts saw the numbers of purebred dogs decline. Interest in the breed was revived in the twentieth century. Careful breeding built up the numbers, and the Segugio is now extremely popular in Italy both as a hunting partner on a variety of game and as a companion. Yet it remains rare and relatively unknown outside its native land.

Segugio Maremmano
ITALY

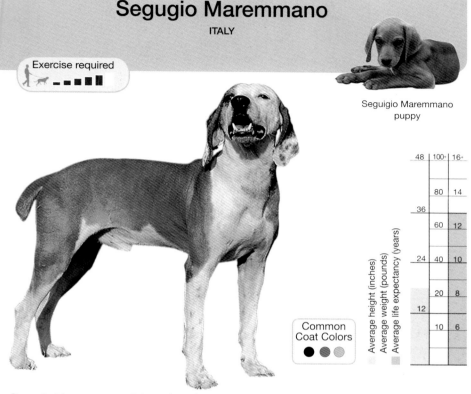

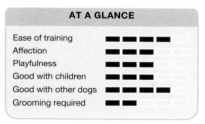

Exercise required

Seguigio Maremmano puppy

Average height (inches)	Average weight (pounds)	Average life expectancy (years)
48	100+	16+
	80	14
36		
	60	12
24	40	10
	20	8
12		
	10	6

Common Coat Colors

The Segugio Maremmano originated on the coastal plains of Maremma, in the Italian province of Tuscany. This medium-sized hound is widely used for hunting wild boar, on its own or in a pack. Because Tuscan breeders have bred their dogs chiefly for hunting ability, their appearances may vary.

AT A GLANCE

Ease of training	■ ■ ■ ■
Affection	■ ■ ■
Playfulness	■ ■ ■
Good with children	■ ■ ■
Good with other dogs	■ ■ ■ ■
Grooming required	■ ■

! Despite its small stature, this dog is strong enough—and brave enough—to hunt large game such as wild boar.

+ This breed tends to be very healthy with no known genetic disorders.

HISTORY

These dogs began to take shape as a breed around the early 1800s. Two forms eventually evolved, the short-haired and the rough-haired. The breed is recognized by ENCI (the Italian Kennel Club), which has registered 6,600 dogs as breed founders. In 2009, the breed was the third most numerous in Italy. Due to the large number of founders and the breed's genetic variability, these dogs should experience relatively few issues from genetic inbreeding.

Serbian Hound

Balkan Hound
SERBIA

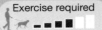

Exercise required

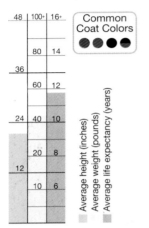

Serbian Hound puppy

48	100+	16+
	80	14
36		
	60	12
24	40	10
	20	8
12		
	10	6

Common Coat Colors

Average height (inches) · Average weight (pounds) · Average life expectancy (years)

The muscular, black and tan Serbian Hound, once known as the Balkan Hound, has been a popular hunting dog in the Balkan region of Eastern Europe for many centuries. It is possibly descended from hounds left in the area by Phoenician traders in ancient times. The breed displays a lively, robust temperament which lends itself to both hunting in the field, where these dogs are very tenacious, and to life in the home. They are kind dogs, capable of forming strong bonds with their owners. As scent hounds, they do need daily exercise with their families—playing, jogging, and even agility games.

AT A GLANCE

Ease of training	
Affection	
Playfulness	
Good with children	
Good with other dogs	
Grooming required	

HISTORY

The Serbian Hound is only one of a group of scent hounds that spread throughout the Balkans. The first record of this "Balkan Hound" comes from the eleventh century, when a man named Frank Laska described the breed in detail, along with other scent hounds of that time. The first standard written for the breed was produced in 1924, but it was not until 1940 that the Fédération Cynologique Internationale accepted the standard that had been accepted elsewhere. Because the Balkan Hound was found most widely throughout Serbia, at an FCI meeting in 1996 it was decided to officially rename it the Serbian Hound. It remains a popular hunting dog in Serbia, but is rarely seen beyond those borders.

+ This breed has no known health issues.

 This dog's name in its native language is "Srpski gonič".

Serbian Tricolor Hound

Yugoslavian Tricolor Hound / Jugoslovenski Trobojni gonic
SERBIA

Exercise required

Serbian Tricolor
Hound puppy

Average height (inches)	Average weight (pounds)	Average life expectancy (years)
48	100+	16+
	80	14
36		
	60	12
24	40	10
	20	8
12		
	10	6

Common Coat Colors

The Serbian Tricolor Hound was originally classed with the Serbian Hound, but in 1946 it got its own recognition; the two breeds are similar and share the same ancestry. The Tricolor is most commonly used for hunting large game such as wild boar, or smaller game like hare and fox. It is known for its good nose and great stamina, and will happily hunt all day long. These are loyal and devoted dogs that bond strongly with their owners.

AT A GLANCE

Ease of training	■ ■ ■
Affection	■ ■ ■ ■
Playfulness	■ ■
Good with children	■ ■ ■
Good with other dogs	■ ■ ■ ■
Grooming required	■

✚ This dog has no known health issues.

HISTORY

The Serbian Tricolor Hound is one of a group of scenthounds that has existed in the Balkans for many years, when the breed was regarded as simply a variety of other Serbian scenthounds. In 1946 this attitude was strongly refuted and the breed was granted independent status from other scenthounds and a standard was drawn up. The current dog has a deep red or fox red coat with a black mantle or saddle and white marking on the face, throat, chest, and legs. The Fédération Cynologique Internationale recognized the breed in 1961 under the name Yugoslavian Tricolor Hound. Today, the Serbian Tricolor Hound is still popular in its native country of Serbia, although it is rarely seen beyond its borders.

Styrian Coarse-haired Hound

AUSTRIA

Styrian Coarse-Haired
Hound puppy

Exercise required

48	100+	16+
36	80	14
	60	12
24	40	10
	20	8
12		
	10	6

Average height (inches)
Average weight (pounds)
Average life expectancy (years)

Common
Coat Colors

Styrian Coarse-haired Hounds are believed to have descended from the ancient Celtic Hounds of the Alps. They are sturdy dogs with medium-length drop ears, square muzzles, muscular bodies, and long tails. The coat is rough and harsh, but never shaggy, and the accepted colors are red and fawn. Among the best hunting dogs in the world, capable of taking on wild boar, these dogs should be considered as pets only by active or hunting families. They do get along well with other dogs.

AT A GLANCE

Ease of training	▪▪ ▪▪ ▪▪ ☐☐ ☐☐
Affection	▪▪ ▪▪ ▪▪ ☐☐ ☐☐
Playfulness	▪▪ ▪▪ ☐☐ ☐☐ ☐☐
Good with children	▪▪ ▪▪ ▪▪ ▪▪ ☐☐
Good with other dogs	▪▪ ▪▪ ▪▪ ☐☐ ☐☐
Grooming required	▪▪ ▪▪ ☐☐ ☐☐ ☐☐

✚ These generally healthy dogs can be prone to hip dysplasia.

HISTORY

The Styrian Coarse-haired Hound was developed in Austria by industrialist Carl Peintinger in the 1870s, and was originally known as the Peintinger Bracke. Peintinger crossed his female Hanoverian Scent Hound, Hela I, with a Coarse-haired Istrian Hound, which produced a litter of excellent hunting dogs. The best of these were selectively bred until a type began to emerge. The current hounds are tenacious and fearless hunters that give voice throughout the hunt. They are tough and enduring, often used for tracking wild boar in the Austrian mountains. Although they have pleasant temperaments, these dogs are most commonly kept as hunting companions, not as pets.

Swiss Jura Hound

Bruno Jura Hound
SWITZERLAND

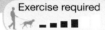
Exercise required

Swiss Jura Hound
puppy

Common Coat Colors

	48	100+	16+
		80	14
	36		
		60	12
		40	10
	24		
		20	8
	12		
		10	6

Average height (inches)
Average weight (pounds)
Average life expectancy (years)

Also known as the Bruno Jura Hound, these rare dogs have broad heads and heavy wrinkles, which differentiate them from the other Swiss hounds. They are known for hunting fox, hare, and sometimes even small deer. The Jura Hound is a skilled cold-trail follower and is capable of following the slightest trace of a scent over the rough terrain of Switzerland's Jura Mountains. The Bloodhound influence in this breed is very apparent.

AT A GLANCE

Ease of training	▬▬ ▬▬ ▬▬ ▬▬ ▬▬
Affection	▬▬ ▬▬ ▬▬
Playfulness	▬▬ ▬▬ ▬▬ ▬▬
Good with children	▬▬ ▬▬ ▬▬ ▬▬
Good with other dogs	▬▬ ▬▬ ▬▬ ▬▬
Grooming required	▬▬ ▬▬

HISTORY

The Bruno Jura Hound was developed in the Middle Ages for hunting in the Jura Mountains on the Swiss-French border. A mosaic found in Avenches places similar-looking dogs in this area at the time of the Roman Helvetia. In the fifteenth century the Swiss Hound was quite popular among Italian dog-lovers, and in the eighteenth century it was popular among the French, because of its astounding ability to hunt the speedy hare. The breed standard for the Swiss Hound was established in 1882 and revised in 1909.

✚ These dogs are generally healthy.

129

Swiss Lucerne Hound

Chien Courant Suisse / Swiss Hound
SWITZERLAND

Exercise required

Swiss Lucerne Hound puppy

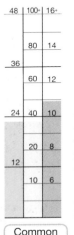

Average height (inches)
Average weight (pounds)
Average life expectancy (years)

Common Coat Colors

The influence of French hounds on their Swiss cousins is perhaps most apparent in the Swiss Lucerne Hound, which is similar in conformation and coloring to several "blue" French hound breeds. The Lucerne is steel blue, or blue mottled with patches; some have pale-yellow or tan markings on the head, chest, and legs. They were used by both Swiss nobles and commoners to track small game.

AT A GLANCE	
Ease of training	■ ■ ■ □ □
Affection	■ ■ ■ ■ □
Playfulness	■ ■ ■ □ □
Good with children	■ ■ ■ ■ □
Good with other dogs	■ ■ ■ ■ ■
Grooming required	■ □ □ □ □

HISTORY

This is one of the four Schweizer Laufhunds (Swiss "walkers") that existed for many centuries in Switzerland, all similar except for color and size. The Lucerne originated in the north-central lake region of Switzerland and probably stemmed from the French Petit Bleus Gascogne. Because Switzerland was neutral during both World Wars, their dog breeds flourished there without threat.

 This breed of hound has no known health issues.

Treeing Walker Coonhound

UNITED STATES

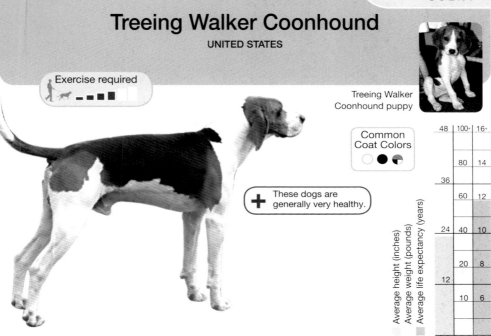

Treeing Walker
Coonhound puppy

Exercise required

Common
Coat Colors

+ These dogs are
generally very healthy.

	Average height (inches)	Average weight (pounds)	Average life expectancy (years)
		100+	16+
48			
		80	14
36			
		60	12
	24	40	10
		20	8
	12		
		10	6

The Treeing Walker Coonhound is a renowned tracker of small game. The term "walker" refers to John W. Walker and his descendants, who bred these hounds in Kentucky in the nineteenth century. These dogs have a strong desire to hunt, and if their humans don't cooperate, they might go off and see what kind of varmint they can scare up to chase. They naturally do well in coondog competitions. These dogs also crave the companionship of their owners. Non-hunters can offer them tracking competitions, search and rescue, and hiking. They generally get along well with children—although a puppy can be too rambunctious for toddlers—and other dogs. If you have cats or other small, furry pets, beware. Your Walker may view them as prey.

! The Treeing Walker is an indoor/outdoor dog. He should have a yard, but it's important for him to spend time with his people, too.

HISTORY

The Treeing Walker Coonhound is descended from the early English Foxhounds brought to America in colonial times. From those dogs evolved Virginia Hounds and Walker Foxhounds, which in turn were the progenitors of the Treeing Walker. One dog who had a huge influence on the breed in the nineteenth century was Tennessee Lead, who contributed game sense, drive, speed, and a clear, short voice. These dog were originally called English Coonhounds, but some breeders, with a different kind of dog in mind, began breeding for the qualities they valued and called their new hound the Treeing Walker. The United Kennel Club began registering the dogs as Walkers (Treeing) in 1945, a name later changed to Treeing Walker. They were recognized by the American Kennel Club in 2012.

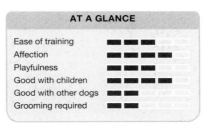

AT A GLANCE

Ease of training	■■ ■■ ■■
Affection	■■ ■■ ■■ ■■
Playfulness	■■ ■■ ■■ ■■
Good with children	■■ ■■ ■■
Good with other dogs	■■ ■■
Grooming required	■■ ■■

Tyrolean Hound

AUSTRIA

Tyrolean Hound puppy

Exercise required

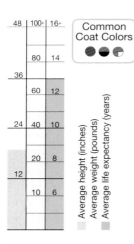

Common Coat Colors

AT A GLANCE					
Ease of training	■	■			
Affection	■	■	■		
Playfulness	■	■	■		
Good with children	■	■	■	■	■
Good with other dogs	■	■	■		
Grooming required	■				

HISTORY

The Tyrolean Hound traces to the mountainous state of Tyrol in Western Austria and to the ancient Celtic Hounds of Northern Europe. Written references to Tyroleans date back many hundreds of years, and they were a favorite of Emperior Maximillian I in the 1400s. Specific breeding for type did not begin in earnest until the 1860s, however. The breed standards were adopted in 1896, the same year the Tyrolean was first exhibited at a show in Innsbruck.

The muscular Tyrolean Hound originated in mountainous western Austria, where it was bred to hunt hare and fox and to track wounded game. It was also originally meant to hunt effectively in the snow. It is one of three Grand Brackes—or large hounds—produced in Austria to hunt on rugged terrain. The other two are the Black and Tan and the Stygian Coarse-haired. The Tyrolean is celebrated for its fine nose, its endurance, and its ability to sustain a hunt on difficult ground and during harsh weather conditions. This hound often hunts singly and excels in wooded areas and mountains. The breed is intelligent, free spirited and energetic, so needs an active, experienced owner who can handle these qualities.

 This is a healthy breed, though ticks and physical injuries are risks while hunting.

Westphalian Dachsbracke

GERMANY

Westphalian Dachsbracke
puppy

	Average height (inches)	Average weight (pounds)	Average life expectancy (years)
	48	100+	16+
		80	14
	36		
		60	12
	24	40	10
		20	8
	12		
		10	6

Common Coat Colors

This rare breed of low-slung, powerfully built hound originated in the Westphalia region of Germany and was bred to hunt small game. These dogs are dedicated and serious hunters that drive their prey toward the hunter by giving voice, and can access areas of underbrush and dense foliage that large hounds cannot. They are gentle and friendly with children and other dogs and make suitable companion animals in an active home. They also tend to be independent-minded (read: stubborn) and noisy, so would probably not do well in an apartment complex.

AT A GLANCE

Ease of training	▬ ▬
Affection	▬ ▬ ▬
Playfulness	▬ ▬ ▬
Good with children	▬ ▬ ▬
Good with other dogs	▬ ▬ ▬
Grooming required	▬

Generally healthy.

HISTORY

The Westphalian Dachsbracke is a short-legged scenthound that originated in the Westphalia region of Germany. It was also used to develop the Swedish dog, the Drever. Also known as the Westphalian Hound, it is a smaller, short-legged version of the Deutsche Bracke, which was developed by crossing the German Hound (Deutsche Bracke) with the Dachshund. This old breed got its first mention in 1886 as a variety of German Hound, though dogs of a very similar type are seen in very old European paintings.

HERDING DOGS

Aidi

Atlas Mountain dog
MOROCCO

Aidi pup

Exercise required

48	100+	16+
	80	14
36		
	60	12
24	40	10
	20	8
12		
	10	6

Average height (inches)
Average weight (pounds)
Average life expectancy (years)

Common Coat Colors

Aidis are common in their home country of Morocco, but quite rare in other countries. This breed, also known as the Atlas Mountain Dog, is an ancient dog that was originally often used for guarding livestock or hunting with sighthounds like Sloughis. Aidis are also noted for their excellent sense of smell and for their bravery. They will willingly protect their families, homes, and livestock against any predators, including wild cats. The Aidi can make a good companion animal for an active family.

AT A GLANCE

Ease of training	■ ■ ■ ■
Affection	■ ■ ■
Playfulness	■ ■ ■ ■
Good with children	■ ■ ■
Good with other dogs	■ ■
Grooming required	■ ■

+ A very healthy bredd, with very few health issues.

! The Aidi was one of the world's first professionally bred dogs.

HISTORY

The Aidi originated in North Africa, most likely in the Sahara. Though it was labeled the Atlas Sheepdog for several years—1963 to 1969—the Aidi rarely works as a sheepdog in modern life. A brave breed, the Aidi lives and works in the Atlas mountain region of Morocco, Libya, and Algeria, and serve to protect their owners and property from wildcats, large predators, and strangers. They have also been named the Berber, after being utilized by the Berber tribes, and bear slight visual similarities to the Pariah dogs that they likely descend from.

Akbash

TURKEY

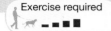

Exercise required

Common Coat Colors

Akbash pup

Average height (inches)	Average weight (pounds)	Average life expectancy (years)
48	100+	16+
	80	14
36		
	60	12
24	40	10
	20	8
12		
	10	6

These dogs are large and independent and are not suitable for first-time dog owners, although they can make companions with consistent training and socialization. It is believed that the breed has both sight hound and Mastiff in its heritage and exhibits some characteristics from each. The Akbash is an ancient breed, renowned for their bravery in warding off predators. This breed has been used for many centuries to guard livestock across the rugged interior of Turkey. The dogs live among the livestock, often unsupervised for long periods of time

AT A GLANCE

Ease of training	▰▰ ▰▰ ▰
Affection	▰▰ ▰▰
Playfulness	▰▰ ▰
Good with children	▰▰ ▰▰ ▰
Good with other dogs	▰▰ ▰
Grooming required	▰▰ ▰

 They are not suitable for first-time dog owners.

✚ The breed is known to be at a higher risk from mastocytoma (mast cell tumours) than the general population of dogs.

HISTORY

Though very little is known of the Akbash's origins, they are believed to be one of the older breeds. Two American breeders named David and Judy Nelson first began importing the Akbash into the United States in the 1970's, while the United States Department of Agriculture indoctrinated the Akbash into its predator-control program. The Akbash was recognized as a guardian breed by the United Kennel Club in 1998.

Appenzeller Sennenhund

Appenzeller Mountain Dog

SWITZERLAND

Exercise required

Appenzeller Sennenhund pup

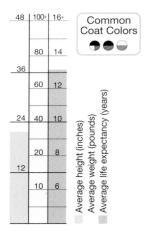

48	100+	16+
	80	14
36		
	60	12
24	40	10
	20	8
12		
	10	6

Average height (inches)
Average weight (pounds)
Average life expectancy (years)

Common Coat Colors

The ancient breed of Molossers are the ancestors of the Appenzeller Sennenhund, one of the four Swiss breeds to descend from them. For centuries, they were used to guard and shepherd livestock, watch homes, and do farm work. They are playful, energetic dogs, and are known to be intelligent, robust dogs that quickly become incredibly loyal to their families. They make suitable companion animals for active, experienced households.

AT A GLANCE

Ease of training	▣▣▣□□
Affection	▣▣▣□□
Playfulness	▣▣▣▣□
Good with children	▣▣▣□□
Good with other dogs	▣▣▣□□
Grooming required	▣▣□□□

! This dog is strong enough that its ancestors were once used to pull carts.

+ The Appenzeller Sennenhund has no significant health problems.

HISTORY

Appenzeller Sennenhunds are most likely descended from either an ancient, more general Sennenhund, or from ancient Roman cattle dogs. The first breed club for this dog, however, was founded in 1906 by Albert Heim, the same year the first stud book for the Appenzeller was written. The first breed standard was written in 1916. One possible reference to the Appenzeller's ancestors appears in an 1853 book, Tierleben der Alpenwelt, which discussed dogs in the Appenzell region. The Appenzeller Sennenhund was only recognized internationally as a distinct breed in 1989.

Australian Cattle Dog

Blue Heeler / Australian Heeler / Queensland Heeler

AUSTRALIA

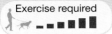

Australian Cattle
Dog pup

One of the most efficient stock dog breeds in the world, the Australian Cattle Dog was designed in the nineteenth century through careful breeding, specifically for the purpose of working cattle. Also known as the Blue Heeler, Australian Heeler, or Queensland Heeler, these dogs are also noted for their aptitude as watchdogs, as well as their cattle work. They are very protective of their families and territory, but can also make excellent family dogs if given substantial exercise and lots of diversions. With training, Australian Cattle Dogs can also make great agility show dogs.

Average height (inches)	Average weight (pounds)	Average life expectancy (years)
48	100+	16+
	80	14
36		
	60	12
24	40	10
	20	8
12		
	10	6

Generally healthy, but hereditary problems can include hip and elbow dysplasia, progressive retinol atrophy, and deafness.

AT A GLANCE

Ease of training	▰▰▰ ▰▰▰ ▰▰▰
Affection	▰▰▰ ▰▰▰ ▰▰▰
Playfulness	▰▰▰ ▰▰▰ ▰▰▰
Good with children	▰▰▰ ▰▰▰ ▰▰▰
Good with other dogs	▰▰▰ ▰▰▰ ▰▰▰
Grooming required	▰▰▰

! This dog doesn't shed year round.

HISTORY

The Australian Cattle Dog is a descendant of a type of collie called a Smithfield, which was in turn named after the Smithfield market in London, England. Smithfields were crossbred with Australian dingos and rough and smooth Scottish collies to produce a solid, non-barking working dog. The result was known as a Hall's Heeler, and became very popular among cattle workers. Later, this dog was bred with Dalmatians and black-and-tan Kelpies, which finally resulted in the modern Australian Cattle Dog; a healthy, visually unique working dog with a dingotype appearance and unusual coloring. The first breed standard was created in 1902, and the Australian Cattle Dog Club of America was officially established in the 1960's.

Australian Shepherd

UNITED STATES

Australian Shepherd pups

Exercise required

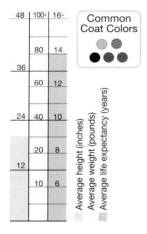

48	100+	16+
	80	14
36		
	60	12
24	40	10
	20	8
12		
	10	6

Average height (inches)
Average weight (pounds)
Average life expectancy (years)

Common Coat Colors

The Australian Shepherd, contrary to its name, originated in the United States. They are primarily used to herd sheep, but are an especially versatile breed that can adapt to most jobs. They are also often used to manage cattle, and as assistance dogs and service dogs. These dogs are very easy to train due to their exceptional intelligence, and are a lively breed that can make a good companion animal as long as they are given plenty of activity and exercise. They also need to be challenged mentally to be satisfied, aside from standard physical exercise. They are also quite good with children and animals, and excel in the fields of agility and obedience.

AT A GLANCE

Ease of training	■■■■■
Affection	■■■
Playfulness	■■■■
Good with children	■■■
Good with other dogs	■■
Grooming required	■■

 They are only suitable for a very active household.

HISTORY

The Australian Shepherd's complex history technically begins in Europe, with the Basque sheep-herders of the Pyrenees. Large numbers of the Basque people settled in Australia in the 1800s, taking their sheep and sheepdogs with them. These dogs' endurance and working skills caught the attention of American ranchers, who then began to breed and train them. With the popularization of horse riding in America's west following the Second World War, the breed came into the public eye and has just gotten stronger in the years since. They are an extremely docile and trainable breed, which has greatly contributed to their popularity.

➕ Generally healthy, but hereditary problems can include hip dysplasia, cataracts and epilepsy.

Australian Stumpy Tail Cattle Dog

AUSTRALIA

Australian Stumpy Tail
Cattle Dog pup

Common
Coat Colors

Average height (inches)	Average weight (pounds)	Average life expectancy (years)
	100+	16+
48	80	14
36	60	12
24	40	10
	20	8
12		
	10	6

Because Australian Stumpy Tail Cattle dogs were bred solely for their ability to work, without keeping their appearance in mind, they are exceptionally healthy and hardworking animals. Some of the naturally occurring stumpy-tailed dogs were excellent cattle dogs, which prompted ranchers to continue those lines. Today, these dogs are quite rare outside of Australia, but are supported by dedicated breed clubs. They can make wonderful companion animals, as long as they have lively and active homes.

AT A GLANCE

Ease of training	▬▬ ▬▬ ▬▬ ▬
Affection	▬▬ ▬▬ ▬▬ ▬▬
Playfulness	▬▬ ▬▬ ▬▬ ▬
Good with children	▬▬ ▬▬ ▬
Good with other dogs	▬▬ ▬▬ ▬
Grooming required	▬▬ ▬

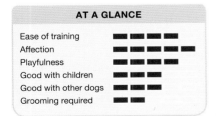

! They can make wonderful companion animals.

 A very healthy dog with no health issues.

HISTORY

The Australian Stumpy Tail Cattle Dog descended from English Smithfield Herding dogs, which were brought to Australia and bred with dingos in the early 19th century. There are few records of these dogs from the early period of their breeding, and there are differing reports of the breed's development. One account claims that drover named Timmins from Bathurst, New South Wales, crossed the Smithfield dogs with the dingo, producing a type of working dog called Timmins' Biters. In order to mute their dingo characteristics and make the dogs easier to handle.

Australian Working Kelpie

AUSTRALIA

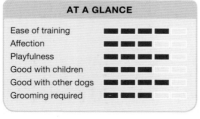

Australian Working Kelpie
pups

Exercise required

48	100+	16+
	80	14
36		
	60	12
24	40	10
	20	8
12		
	10	6

Average height (inches)
Average weight (pounds)
Average life expectancy (years)

Common Coat Colors

+ Beware of PRA (Progressive Retinal Atrophy), which is retinal degeneration causing partial to total blindness.

This breed's ancestors are three pairs of working Collies that were imported to Australia by early settlers. From these six dogs, with the addition of other Scottish working dogs, a breed was developed that was adept at working with large herds of sheep with great efficiency. The Australian Working Kelpie can work for hours at a time without growing tired, even in the harshest conditions. As they are very dexterous and intelligent dogs, Kelpies can move enormous flocks easily. They require lots of exercise and mental stimulation in order to be happy and healthy.

AT A GLANCE			
Ease of training			
Affection			
Playfulness			
Good with children			
Good with other dogs			
Grooming required			

! Problems can and will arise with meek owners.

HISTORY

The Australian Working Kelpie descends directly from simple black dogs that were known as Collies. The word "Collie" has the same root word as "coal" and "collier", or ship. Some of these Collies were imported to Australia in the early nineteenth century for stock work, and were cross-bred with other types of dogs such as the Dingo. The goal was to produce a dog that can manage sheep without direct human supervision. Today's version of the Collie was not established as a breed until about ten to fifteen years after the Kelpie was established. The first official Border Collie was not established in Australia until 1901.

Bearded Collie

Beardie
SCOTLAND

Bearded Collie pup

Exercise required

Common Coat Colors	48	100+	16+
		80	14
	36		
		60	12
		40	10
	24		
		20	8
	12		
		10	6

Average height (inches) / Average weight (pounds) / Average life expectancy (years)

The Bearded Collie, or "Beardie," primarily works with sheep but can also work with cattle or be a companion animal for an experienced and dedicated home. These versatile dogs also excel in sheepdog trials and agility training, and are intelligent and independent. These traits can make Bearded Collies destructive and stubborn, but with proper obedience training they can work in the dog's favor. They are fun loving, enthusiastic dogs with strong personalities, and thrive best when being physically and mentally challenged.

AT A GLANCE

Ease of training	▬▬▬▬
Affection	▬▬▬
Playfulness	▬▬▬▬
Good with children	▬▬▬
Good with other dogs	▬▬▬
Grooming required	▬▬▬

 Bearded Collie puppies always have a dark coat, which may lighten to another color as they mature.

Generally healthy but hereditary problems can include hip dysplasia, epilepsy, cataracts, and colonic disease.

HISTORY

Dogs of a similar appearance are found in art dating to the 1700s, but the breed was not properly documented until 1879, when they were depicted by Hugh Dalziel in his book "British Dogs." Dalziel believed that these dogs were the result of crossing English Sheepdogs and Collies. Whatever their origin, this breed is known for its long, weather-resistant, protective coats, which were perfect for the harsh Scottish weather. Bearded Collies were recognized by the American Kennel Club in 1977.

Beauceron
Berger de Beauce
FRANCE

Beauceron pup

Exercise required

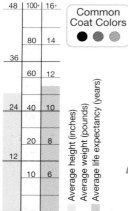

48	100+	16+
	80	14
36		
	60	12
24	40	10
	20	8
12		
	10	6

Average height (inches)
Average weight (pounds)
Average life expectancy (years)

Common Coat Colors

The Beauceron is an intelligent, bold dog, and which is thought to have originated in La Beauce, the plains region surrounding Paris. They are first mentioned in a French manuscript dating to 1578, and are the largest of the French Sheepdog breeds. They developed with no influence from other foreign breeds, and were intended to be an all-purpose farm dog. Their skillset includes, herding, guarding livestock and property, and being a companion animal. They are notably obedient, and have often been used by the French military. Though they can make good companions, they require proper socialization and a large amount of exercise in order to thrive.

AT A GLANCE

Ease of training	
Affection	
Playfulness	
Good with children	
Good with other dogs	
Grooming required	

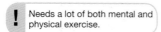

! Needs a lot of both mental and physical exercise.

+ The Beauceron is generally a healthy, hardy breed. Some lines are prone to bloat and like any breed over 40 pounds, Beaucerons are prone to hip dysplasia.

HISTORY

The Beauceron's origins are uncertain, but the earliest mention of a breed that resembles a Beauceron dates back to the 16th century. Beaucerons are notable for being the largest of all French Sheepdogs. Besides sheep, they can also herd cattle and guard homes. Their name is derived from the area surrounding Paris, known as "La Beauce."

Belgian Malinois

Chien de Berger Belge

BELGIUM

Belgian Malinois pup

Exercise required

Common Coat Colors

Average height (inches)	Average weight (lbs)	Average life expectancy
	100+	16+
	80	14
36		
	60	12
24	40	10
	20	8
12		
	10	6

The Belgian Malinois takes its name from Malines, or Mechelen, the city it originated in. The Malinois were bred to be working animals, and have become adept at livestock herding and guarding. They are exceptionally intelligent, trainable dogs, and are known to be loving with their families and owners. They also serve as good watchdogs, though they are not aggressive enough to be an actual guard dog. They need lots of exercise, and will only be suitable for the most active homes. They are popular for use in herding, sledding, tracking, and obedience competitions.

AT A GLANCE

Ease of training	▬▬▬ ▬▬▬ ▬▬▬ ▬▬
Affection	▬▬▬ ▬▬▬ ▬▬
Playfulness	▬▬▬ ▬▬▬ ▬
Good with children	▬▬▬ ▬▬▬ ▬▬
Good with other dogs	▬▬
Grooming required	▬▬▬ ▬▬▬ ▬▬

+ The breed is not known to have any specific health issues.

HISTORY

Early breeders respected the Malinois for its determined working character. Historically, it has been the preferred type of Belgian Shepherd in its homeland. It is used as a working dog for the most part, for tasks such as detecting explosives, accelerants—for arson investigations—and illegal drugs. The Malinois is also used for tracking work by the police, and makes a great search and rescue dog. The Belgian Malinois was recognized by the American Kennel Club in 1959.

 This breed's strong tracking skills make the Malinois a popular choice for the police.

Belgian Sheepdog

Groenendael

BELGIUM

Belgian Sheepdog pup

Exercise required

48	100+	16+
	80	14
36		
	60	12
24	40	10
	20	8
12		
	10	6

Average height (inches)
Average weight (pounds)
Average life expectancy (years)

Common Coat Colors
●

+ Generally healthy, but hereditary problems can include epilepsy and cancer.

! They can make wonderful, gentle, and devoted family companions for active homes.

AT A GLANCE

Ease of training	▰▰▰ ▰▰▰
Affection	▰▰▰ ▰▰▰
Playfulness	▰▰▰ ▰▰▰▰
Good with children	▰▰▰ ▰▰
Good with other dogs	▰▰ ▰▰
Grooming required	▰▰ ▰

The Belgian Sheepdog, more generally known as the Goenendael in Europe, is considered to be one of four variations of Belgian Shepherds rather than a breed of its own category. Although it was originally bred as a working sheepdog, the Belgian Sheepdog's versatile nature quickly allowed it to be used in a number of other roles due to their excellent temperaments, intelligence, trainability, and obedience. They were widely used by the military for delivering messages, as search and rescue dogs, and defense dogs during WWI and WWII. They are also frequently used by the Red Cross, and make excellent guide dogs. They can make wonderful and gentle companion animals for active homes, and are vigilant watchdogs due to their devotion to their families. However, they are happiest when working, and need an environment with lots of jobs to keep them busy.

HISTORY

The Belgian Sheepdog was first seen in the 1800s, when it was originally known as the Chien de Berger de Races Continentales, or Continental Shepherd. Because the breed is so versatile, it was used as a herder, watchdog, and companion in equal parts. It was officially named after the village of Groenendael in 1910, where there were several influential breeding kennels. The breed was recognized by the American Kennel Club as the Belgian Sheepdog in 1912.

Belgian Tervuren

Chein de berger belge

BELGIUM

Belgian Tervuren pup

Exercise required

▮ ▬ ▬ ▮ ▮ ▮

Common Coat Colors	48	100+	16+
● ● ● ●		80	14
	36		
		60	12
	24	40	10
		20	8
	12		
		10	6

Average height (inches)
Average weight (pounds)
Average life expectancy (years)

The Belgian Tervuren is another variation of the four Belgian Shepherd dogs; it is only in the United States that this dog is classified as a separate breed, rather than a variant. Tervurens are visually distinguishable from other Belgian Shepherds by their characteristic thick, double-layered coat, which usually comes in shades of mahogany. They were first used as general farm dogs, but were also well-loved for their loving nature and elegant looks. Tervurens are famously loyal and bond strongly with their owners, and are often wary of new people.

AT A GLANCE

Ease of training	▬ ▬ ▬
Affection	▬ ▬ ▬
Playfulness	▬ ▬ ▬
Good with children	▬ ▬ ▬ ▬ ▬
Good with other dogs	▬ ▬ ▬ ▬
Grooming required	▬ ▬ ▬

+ Generally healthy, but hereditary problems can include epilepsy and cancer.

! They are only suitable for a very active household.

HISTORY

The Belgian Tervuren is also known as the Chien de Berger Belge, and takes its name from the Belgian village of Tervuren. The dog breeder who founded the Belgian Tervuren—M. F. Corbeel—lived in this village, and is believed to have founded the breed through his two dogs, Tom and Poes. The dogs' daughter, Miss, was bred with a black dog named Duc de Groenendael, which in turn produced a dog named Milsart, who became the first breed standard of a Tervuren in 1907.

Bergamasco Shepherd

Cane da pastore Bergamasco
ITALY

Bergamasco Shepherd pup

Exercise required

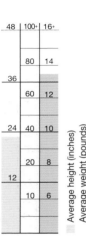

Average height (inches)
Average weight (pounds)
Average life expectancy (years)

48	100+	16+
	80	14
36		
	60	12
24	40	10
	20	8
12		
	10	6

Common Coat Colors

These extremely intelligent sheepdogs have distinctive long, thick, felt-like protective coats that insulate them from the weather and act as protective "armor." This ancient breed traditionally cared for huge flocks of sheep, solving problems independently. As a result, the Bergamasco is a quick-thinking breed that is protective and shows great devotion to its family. These dogs can make good companions for an active home but need to be properly socialized and obedience trained.

AT A GLANCE

Ease of training	
Affection	
Playfulness	
Good with children	
Good with other dogs	
Grooming required	

! The Bergamasco's coat is meant to protect him from bad weather and the predators he might have to drive off in defense of his flock.

+ Known to be healthy, slight chance of hip dysplasia.

HISTORY

The Bergamasco is an Italian Shepherd breed, named after the town in which it originated, Bergamasco. While they are common in other regions of Italy, they are most known in their hometown. They are similar in appearance to other Central European sheepdog breeds, including the heavily matted coat of the Puli. The Bergamasco nearly went extinct after World War II, as the available work—and demand—for herding dogs declined sharply. Luckily, an Italian breeder named Dr. Maria Andreoli intervened, leading a movement to save the Bergamasco.

Berger Picard
Picardy Shepherd
FRANCE

Berger Picard pup

Exercise required

Common Coat Colors

Average height (inches)	Average weight (pounds)	Average life expectancy (years)
48	100+	16+
	80	14
36		
	60	12
24	40	10
	20	8
12		
	10	6

The Berger Picard, with its wiry protective coat, hardiness, and great endurance, has changed little over the years and has always been primarily a working breed—herding, guarding livestock, watching over the home, and providing companionship. They can be wary of strangers and occasionally stubborn, but are loyal and, if properly socialized, can make good companions and watchdogs for an active home.

AT A GLANCE

Ease of training	■■■■
Affection	■■■
Playfulness	■■■
Good with children	■■■
Good with other dogs	■■■■■
Grooming required	■■

 They can be wary of strangers and occasionally stubborn.

+ The breed is known to be at a higher risk for Progressive Retinal Atrophy and hip dysplasia.

HISTORY
Before the Berger Picard was ever brought to America, it was used to herd sheep in Northern regions of France, and is most likely one of France's oldest sheepdogs. While the idea of a purebred didn't develop until the 1800s, visually similar dogs have been depicted for centuries in French works of art such as tapestries and carvings. The first known appearance of the Berger Picard was at a dog show in 1863. It participated in herding trials, though it was still a relatively uncommon dog at the time.

149

Bernese Mountain Dog

Berner Sennenhund / Bernese Cattle Dog

SWITZERLAND

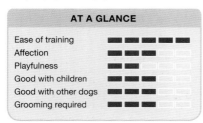

Bernese Mountain Dog pup

Exercise required

48	100+	16+
	80	14
36		
	60	12
24	40	10
	20	8
12		
	10	6

Average height (inches)
Average weight (pounds)
Average life expectancy (years)

Common Coat Colors

Generally Bernese have exceptional temperaments, calm, affectionate, and forming very strong bonds with their families. The breed has often been used for service, assistance, and mountain search and rescue. They are still also used for herding and guarding livestock and have a naturally protective instinct. Bernese make superb companions for relatively active households. They are generally good with children and other pets as long as they are introduced correctly.

AT A GLANCE

Ease of training	■■■■■
Affection	■■■■
Playfulness	■■■
Good with children	■■■■
Good with other dogs	■■■
Grooming required	■■■

! Berners are sensitive to heat and humidity.

+ Generally healthy, but hereditary problems can include hip and elbow dysplasia, cancer, cataracts, gastric torsion, and degenerative myelopathy.

HISTORY

The Bernese is generally believed to have developed from dogs introduced to the Alpine region of Switzerland by the Romans from 57 BCE. These dogs were likely to have been Molossers (mastiff types), which were then crossed with native Swiss mountain dogs. The Bernese adapted perfectly to its environment with a very thick, weatherresistant coat that also provided protection against predators.

Black Mouth Cur

Southern Cur
UNITED STATES

Black Mouth Cur pup

Exercise required

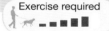

Common
Coat Colors

Average height (inches)	Average weight (pounds)	Average life expectancy (years)
48	100+	16+
	80	14
36		
	60	12
24	40	10
	20	8
12		
	10	6

The Black Mouth Cur is a notably fast, resilient dog, capable of hunting squirrel, raccoon, deer, boar, and bear. While hunting, this breed is aggressive and powerful, but is a gentle and protective companion animal when at home. They are intended to be fearless and loyal above all else, and have a strong desire to please. They are also naturally good with children, and require an owner who is experienced and comfortable enforcing authority over this dog, as it feels an instinctive need for structure.

AT A GLANCE

Ease of training	▬ ▬ ▬ ▬
Affection	▬ ▬ ▬
Playfulness	▬ ▬ ▬ ▬
Good with children	▬ ▬ ▬
Good with other dogs	▬ ▬
Grooming required	▬

! Loyalty and fearlessness are the norm.

+ The Cur are very healthy dogs with no known medical problems.

HISTORY

The origin of the Black Mouth Cur is unknown, but the most widely held belief is that it descends from several ancient European and Asian curs. The breed was developed in the Southern United States as a working farm dog, and has become relatively common in the US since the 1800s. While the name "cur" is often given to describe mixed breed dogs, the Black Mouth Cur is purebred. This dog may be related to the Southern Black Mouth Cur, originating in Alabama, the Foundation Black Mouth Cur from Texas, and the Ladner Yellow Black Mouth Cur of Mississippi.

Blue Lacy

Lacy Game Dog / Texas Blue Lacy / Lacy Hog Dog

UNITED STATES

Blue Lacy pup

Common
Coat Colors

Exercise required
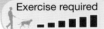

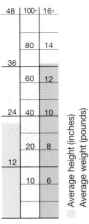

48	100+	16+
	80	14
36		
	60	12
24	40	10
	20	8
12		
	10	6

Average height (inches)
Average weight (pounds)
Average life expectancy (years)

This is an exceptionally versatile working breed that combines a strong livestock-herding instinct with excellent hunting skills. The Blue Lacy can be used as a stock dog for driving livestock, but is used more often for tracking, treeing game, running trap lines, and hunting wild hogs. Given their athleticism, they also make good agility dogs.

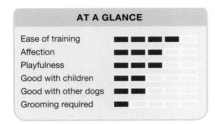

AT A GLANCE	
Ease of training	
Affection	
Playfulness	
Good with children	
Good with other dogs	
Grooming required	

Joint problems such as hip or elbow dysplasia, skin problems, and allergies are possible problems with this breed.

HISTORY

The Blue Lacy gets its name from the Lacy brothers, two Texan breeders who created the Blue Lacy in the late 1800s in order to herd wild pigs to market. The Blue Lacy is comprised of equal parts English Shepherd, Greyhound, and wolf, resulting in a strong, exceptionally healthy, medium sized working dog. The Blue Lacy is known for its speed and desire to work. In 2005, the Blue Lacy was named the state dog of Texas.

The Blue Lacy is a high energy, intense, fun, and tenacious breed.

Bohemian Shepherd

Chodský Dog

CZECH REPUBLIC

Bohemian Shepherd pup

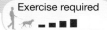

Exercise required

Common
Coat Colors

Average height (inches)	Average weight (pounds)	Average life expectancy (years)
48	100+	16+
	80	14
36		
	60	12
24	40	10
	20	8
12		
	10	6

Also known as the Chodský Dog, this is an ancient breed that has been used for centuries as a multipurpose farm dog, herding and guarding livestock and protecting homes. These dogs are widely held to have contributed to the development of the German Shepherd, and the two breeds share some similarities. The Bohemian is lively and intelligent, and it thrives when given a job to do or when mentally or physically challenged. These dogs are very people-oriented.

AT A GLANCE

Ease of training	▰ ▰ ▰ ▰
Affection	▰ ▰ ▰
Playfulness	▰ ▰
Good with children	▰ ▰
Good with other dogs	▰ ▰
Grooming required	▰ ▰ ▰

! They are excellent watchdogs.

+ An especially healthy breed when compared to similar dogs.

HISTORY

The Bohemian Shepherd originated in the 1300s in the Czech Republic, though was not professionally bred until the 1500s. Many believe this dog to be a primary ancestor of the modern German Shepherd. In 1984, a breeding program began in the Czech Republic to improve the breed's population. As of today, there are many breeders for the Bohemian Shepherd.

The Bohemian Shepherd is a Czech dog, rather than a Czechoslovakian dog; the breed was developed before the Czech and Slovak republics merged in the 1900s. While the Bohemian Shepherd was originally used to guard frontiers, they are now used primarily as herding dogs and guard dogs.

Border Collie

Scottish Sheepdog

UNITED KINGDOM

Exercise required

Generally considered the most popular sheep-herding breed in the world, there are very few other breeds that can match the Border Collie for speed, agility, working ability and drive. They are also regularly ranked within the top ten percentile of the most intelligent dog breeds, and are especially receptive to training. Border Collies are sensitive, very active dogs with great problem-solving abilities. These dogs thrive best when working or involved in intensely physical activities, and require plenty of mental and physical exercise. As their physical and intellectual needs are met, Border Collies can be active, engaging, and loving members of the family.

! The Border Collie is known to "hypnotize" sheep with its intense, focused stare.

Border Collie
puppy

AT A GLANCE

Ease of training	■ ■ ■ ■ ■
Affection	■ ■ ■ ■ ■
Playfulness	■ ■ ■ ■
Good with children	■ ■
Good with other dogs	■ ■
Grooming required	■

+ Generally healthy, but hereditary problems can include hip dysplasia, Collie Eye Anomaly, and epilepsy.

Common Coat Colors

	48	100+	16+
		80	14
36			
		60	12
	24	40	10
		20	8
12			
		10	6

Average height (inches)
Average weight (pounds)
Average life expectancy (years)

HISTORY

The Border Collie emerged from ancient British working dogs. It was first known as the Working Collie, but as it developed along the borders of Scotland and England, it was later given the name Border Collie in 1915. Queen Victoria of England heavily promoted the breed, owning several Border Collies, including one named Sharp who was often photographed with her. Old Hemp, Wilson Cap, and Wiston Cap—born in 1893, 1937, and 1963, respectively—were all extremely influential in the breeding of the modern Border Collie, with Wiston Cap's image visible on the badge of the International Sheep Dog Society.

The Border Collie dog breed was developed to gather and control sheep in the hilly border country between Scotland and England. He is known for his intense stare, or "eye," with which he controls his flock. He's a dog with unlimited energy, stamina, and working drive, all of which make him a premier herding dog; he's still used today to herd sheep on farms and ranches around the world.

Bouvier Des Ardennes

BELGIUM

Bouvier Des Ardennes pup

Exercise required

Common
Coat Colors

48	100+	16+
	80	14
36		
	60	12
24	40	10
	20	8
12		
	10	6

Average height (inches)
Average weight (pounds)
Average life expectancy (years)

The Bouvier Des Ardennes is a relatively rare breed that was first used to drive cattle and herd livestock such as sheep, pigs, and horses. They are extremely resilient, hardy dogs, as they were often required to travel long distances and work throughout the day. They have also historically been used by poachers to hunt deer and wild boar, and have the added trait of being an exemplary tracking dog, which is a characteristic not usually given to herding dogs. Given their working foundation, Bouvier Des Ardennes are obedient and receptive to training. These are tough, active, and affectionate dogs that love to play, and can make good family companions for an engaging home.

✚ This breed has no known health issues.

AT A GLANCE

Ease of training	▪▪▪ ▪▪▪ ▪▪▪
Affection	▪▪▪ ▪▪▪
Playfulness	▪▪▪ ▪▪▪
Good with children	▪▪▪
Good with other dogs	▪▪▪
Grooming required	▪▪▪ ▪▪▪

! They love to play and can make good family companions for an active home.

HISTORY

While not much is known about the origins of the Bouvier Des Ardennes, it is believed to have been well-established in France by the early 19th century, which implies that it may have been first developed in the 17th or 18th centuries. It was most likely developed before written records were kept of dog breeding, and was also most likely developed by farmers who had no interest in the dog's pedigree or history. It is almost certain, however, that the breed was developed in the Ardennes: a mountainous, heavily forested, rural area located in the South of Belgium. The first written records of this breed can all be found in the Ardennes, and no report of this breed has been found to exist in any other location prior to the 20th century. This dog is quite rare outside of its homeland, even now that it has gained more awareness.

Bouvier Des Flandres

Flanders Cattle Dog
BELGIUM

Bouvier Des Flandres pup

Exercise required
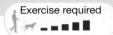

Common Coat Colors			
● ○ ● ●			

	Average height (inches)	Average weight (pounds)	Average life expectancy (years)
	48	100+	16+
		80	14
	36		
		60	12
	24	40	10
		20	8
	12		
		10	6

The Bouvier des Flandres was first developed for use by butchers, cattle traders, and farmers, and was intended to be a working dog. They moved and guarded livestock and cattle, and were required to be confident, resilient, brave, and protective of their flock. These qualities are still upheld in today's breed. The primary specification of this breed was its ability to work, rather than its appearance, and a breed standard was only drawn in 1912. Bouvier des Flandres are loving, devoted to their families, and make excellent watchdogs. They usually have calm temperaments while inside, but also require lots of exercise to keep them happy and healthy.

AT A GLANCE	
Ease of training	■ ■ ■ ■
Affection	■ ■ ■
Playfulness	■ ■ ■ ■
Good with children	■ ■ ■ ■ ■
Good with other dogs	■ ■
Grooming required	■ ■ ■

+ Bouviers are susceptible to several health problems, including hip dysplasia, glaucoma, and a heart condition called subaortic stenosis.

HISTORY

The Bouvier was bred as a farm dog originally, developed in an area of Belgium called Flanders. The Bouvier was used to drive cattle to market and pull carts, and was only recognized as an official breed in 1910, during the International Dog Show in Brussels.

 Bouviers des Flandres are rational, gentle, loyal, and protective by nature.

Boxer

German Boxer / Deutscher Boxer

GERMANY

Boxer pup

Exercise required

48	100+	16+
	80	14
36		
	60	12
24	40	10
	20	8
12		
	10	6

Average height (inches)
Average weight (pounds)
Average life expectancy (years)

Common Coat Colors

The Boxer is a versatile, high-energy dog, and is well-known for its playfulness and general state of enthusiasm. They have been used for many purposes throughout history, and were one of the first dog breeds ever employed by the German police and military, usually as couriers. Boxers are very people oriented and love to be the center of attention. Although originally bred as working dogs, they are now very popular as companion animals. They are highly intelligent as a breed and have been successfully trained as service dogs and assistance dogs; they are also very athletic and can excel at agility.

AT A GLANCE

Ease of training	▰▰▰▰▱
Affection	▰▰▰▰▱
Playfulness	▰▰▰▰▰
Good with children	▰▰▰▱▱
Good with other dogs	▰▰▰▱▱
Grooming required	▰▱▱▱▱

HISTORY

The Boxer's ancestors were bullbaiting dogs, which were bred to produce a dog that was specialized for dog-fighting contests. In the nineteenth century, however, they were more commonly used by butchers to move livestock through slaughterhouse yards, and by cattle owners to drive their herd. By 1895, a Boxer club had formed in Germany, and the first breed standard was officially made. They first arrived in the United States in the early 1900's, and were recognized by the American Kennel Club in 1904.

! Boxers are very people oriented and love to be the center of attention.

+ Generally healthy, but hereditary problems can include heart conditions, gastric torsion, cancer, and hip dysplasia.

Brazilian Mastiff

Fila Brasileiro
BRAZIL

Brazilian Mastiff pup

Exercise required

Common Coat Colors

48	100+	16+
	80	14
36		
	60	12
	24 40	10
	20	8
12		
	10	6

Average height (inches)
Average weight (pounds)
Average life expectancy (years)

The Brazilian Mastiff, or Fila Brazileiro, is an imposing, powerful breed used primarily as a guard dog and renowned for its tracking skills. The breed descends from English Mastiff, Bloodhound, and Bulldog crossed with native stock and is incredibly loyal to its family. These dogs are valued for protecting property and livestock, herding cattle, and instinctively capturing and holding game during hunts until their master arrives. As they are very mistrustful of strangers, Brazilian Mastiffs must be consistently socialized from puppyhood. This breed has been banned in some countries under dangerous-dog legislation.

AT A GLANCE

Ease of training	▪▪▪ ▪▪▪ ▪▪
Affection	▪▪▪ ▪▪▪ ▪▪
Playfulness	▪▪▪ ▪▪▪ ▪▪
Good with children	▪▪▪ ▪▪
Good with other dogs	▪▪▪ ▪▪
Grooming required	▪▪▪

 The breed is known to be at a higher risk from mastocytoma (mast cell tumours) than the general population of dogs.

HISTORY

The Brazilian Mastiff was originally designed to work on large plantations and farms in Brazil. It was primarily used to guard against thieves, drive cattle, and protect livestock from large predators such as jaguar and other large cats. The Brazilian Mastiff's usual technique is to bite onto the scruff of their target's neck, and hold it until his owner arrives. The Mastiff, the Bulldog, and the Bloodhound were likely used to develop the Brazilian Mastiff.

 ! This breed has been banned in some countries under dangerous-dog legislation.

Bucovina Shepherd Dog

Bucovina Sheepdog

SOUTH-EASTERN EUROPE

Bucovina Shepherd Dog pup

Exercise required

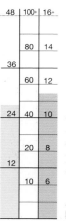

48	100+	16+
	80	14
36		
	60	12
24	40	10
	20	8
12		
	10	6

Average height (inches)
Average weight (pounds)
Average life expectancy (years)

Common
Coat Colors

This rustic breed of sheepdog developed in the Carpathian Mountains of Romania and Serbia, particularly the area of Bucovina. It is also known as the Southeastern European Shepherd, and was used by shepherds in rough mountain regions for protecting livestock, herding and moving the cattle, and guarding their farms. Bucovina Shepherd Dogs are gentle with their families and are generally known to be good with children and other animals, although they are usually quite wary of strangers. They are good watchdogs and have an intimidating bark. They do, however, need lots of exercise and consistent socialization and obedience training in order to thrive.

AT A GLANCE

Ease of training	■ ■ ■
Affection	■ ■ ■
Playfulness	■ ■ ■ ■
Good with children	■ ■ ■
Good with other dogs	■ ■ ■
Grooming required	■ ■ ■

✚ This breed has no known health issues.

HISTORY

The Bucovina Shepherd Dog is a relatively rare breed that originated in the Carpathian Mountains, in Bucovina in the North-East of Romania. In this region, this breed was used for guarding herds and property, to great success. Bucovinas are also known by the name Dulau (shepherd's dog) or Capau. The first standard was written in 1982 and updated in 2001 by the Romanian Kennel Club. The present standard, dating from March 29, 2002, was written and updated according to the model established by the 1987 FCI General Assembly from Jerusalem.

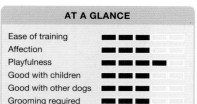

! They are good watchdogs and have an intimidating bark.

Bully

American Bulldog
UNITED STATES

Bully pup

Common Coat Colors			48	100+	16+
				80	14
			36		
				60	12
			24	40	10
				20	8
			12		
				10	6

Average height (inches)
Average weight (pounds)
Average life expectancy (years)

There are two types of American Bulldog, the Standard and the Bully. The Bully is larger, heavier, and has a shorter muzzle. This is a strong, agile breed that needs a healthy balance of both physical and mental exercise in order to thrive. This breed has a quiet, calm temperament while at home and at rest, but requires a fairly high amount of daily exercise and plenty of diversions. These are powerful dogs that can make excellent companions as long as they are properly socialized, supervised, and exercised. They have a strong pack instinct and will protect their families and property with vigor.

AT A GLANCE

Ease of training	▪▪▪ ▪▪▪ ▪▪▪
Affection	▪▪▪ ▪▪▪ ▪▪▪
Playfulness	▪▪▪ ▪▪▪ ▪▪▪
Good with children	▪▪▪ ▪▪▪
Good with other dogs	▪▪▪ ▪▪▪
Grooming required	▪▪▪

+ Generally healthy, but hereditary problems can include hip and elbow dysplasia, entropion, and cancer.

HISTORY

The breed traces back to the early bulldog types brought over to the United States during colonization. As working farm dogs, these dogs were required to be versatile, and were used for protecting homes and livestock, herding cattle, hunting large game, and serving as companions. Unfortunately, they have also been used in dog-fighting rings. One man, John D. Johnston, was particularly influential in the development of the modern breed through his breeding initiative shortly after World War II. This helped to stabilize the dwindling population of American Bulldogs, and they now have a dedicated following.

! This dog originated from the crossing of the American Pit Bull Terrier and the Staffordshire Bull Terrier.

Cão de Castro Laboreiro

Portuguese Cattle Dog

PORTUGAL

Cão de Castro Laboreiro pup

Exercise required

48	100+	16+
	80	14
36		
	60	12
24	40	10
	20	8
12		
	10	6

Average height (inches)
Average weight (pounds)
Average life expectancy (years)

Common Coat Colors

The Cão de Castro Laboreiro is a very rare breed that is named after the town of Castro Laboreiro in Northern Portugal. While there are no written records that explain this breed's origins, the Cão de Castro Laboreiro is believed to be ancient. They were most likely used by Shepherds in remote and mountainous regions for herding, guarding livestock, and guarding homes. This breed needed to be brave and aggressive enough to fight off much larger predators such as wolves, and also needed great stamina and endurance to withstand the unfriendly terrain. As farming methods changed with time, the demand for this breed began to decline.

AT A GLANCE

Ease of training	■ ■ ■
Affection	■ ■ ■ ■
Playfulness	■ ■ ■ ■
Good with children	■ ■ ■ ■
Good with other dogs	■ ■
Grooming required	■ ■

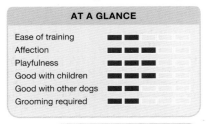

! They are now commonly used as guard dogs and companions.

+ They are generally hardy and have no known health issues.

HISTORY

The origin of the Cão de Castro Laboreiro is not known, although there are many legends regarding the breed. The Portuguese Breed Club notes that "Everything that is written about their origins is pure fiction, without any scientific or historical accuracy...data is rare, or does not exist...most guardian and herding breeds do not have records before 1900."

Cão de Fila de São Miguel

Saint Miguel Cattle Dog

SÃO MIGUEL ISLAND / PORTUGAL

Exercise required

Cão de Fila de São Miguel pup

Common Coat Colors

Average height (inches)	Average weight (pounds)	Average life expectancy (years)
48	100+	16+
	80	14
36		
	60	12
24	40	10
	20	8
12		
	10	6

This breed traces to São Miguel, an Island in the Portuguese archipelago of the Azores, where it was originally used for working cattle. Its herding technique is described in the breed standard as "biting low" when moving cattle to prevent injury to the udders. These dogs were also used for guarding livestock and property, and they exhibit the usual, traits of fearlessness and tenacity seen in other similar guardian breeds. As with any large guardian breed, they must be properly socialized and given plenty of mental and physical diversions. Today, these dogs are primarily used as companions and guard dogs and can be devoted, affectionate, and efficient in both roles.

AT A GLANCE

Ease of training	
Affection	
Playfulness	
Good with children	
Good with other dogs	
Grooming required	

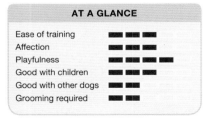

! As with any large guardian breed, they must be properly socialized.

+ They are generally hardy and have no known health issues.

HISTORY

The breed is named after its place of origin: São Miguel Island in the Azores, which was settled by the Portuguese, beginning in 1439. Another of the Azores, Terceira Island, is known for bullfights and cattle raising; large dogs used on cattle there were brought to São Miguel Island and most likely contributed to the development of the breed. According to the original breed standard, the existence of the Cão Fila de São Miguel has been documented since the early 1800s.

Carea Leonés pup

Carea Leonés

Leonese Shepherd

SPAIN

Exercise required

48	100+	16+
	80	14
36		
	60	12
24	40	10
	20	8
12		
	10	6

Average height (inches)
Average weight (pounds)
Average life expectancy (years)

Common Coat Colors

The Carea Leonés, or Leonese Sheepdog, is a breed of herding dog from León, Castile and León, Spain, and is used mainly as a sheepdog. For centuries, they tended flocks of sheep and other livestock in the mountains of the historical region of León. Because of its intelligence, the Carea Leonés, like most sheepdogs, is easy to train.

AT A GLANCE

Ease of training	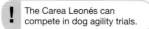
Affection	
Playfulness	
Good with children	
Good with other dogs	
Grooming required	

! The Carea Leonés can compete in dog agility trials.

+ This breed is generally hardy and have no known health issues.

HISTORY

The Carea Leonés is a dog whose physiology and temperament have been molded by its environment, including both natural and human impacts. This breed originated in regions of the province of Leónand Zamora, which was—and is— an agricultural area where crops and livestock were extremely important to the local way of life. Because of the vast amount of work necessary to keep a rural, agriculturally based population thriving and the relatively low number of available workers in such an underpopulated area, this breed was designed to work as a general, all-around farmdog to fill in where there were not enough farmhands to work. This dog was especially prized for its willpower and mental focus when working with cattle and livestock.

Carpathian Shepherd Dog

Romanian Shepherd

ROMANIA

Exercise required

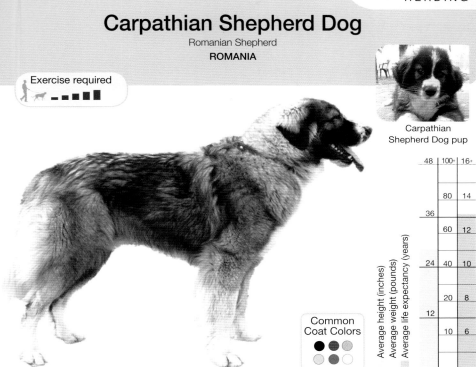

Carpathian
Shepherd Dog pup

	Average height (inches)	Average weight (pounds)	Average life expectancy (years)
	48	100+	16+
		80	14
	36		
		60	12
	24	40	10
		20	8
	12		
		10	6

Common
Coat Colors

Little is known about the Carpathian Shepherd Dog's history, except that it has perfectly adapted for its environment and role. This large, sheep-herding working breed is gentle, calm, and dignified with a natural protective instinct. It is believed to have originated in the Carpathian mountains, where it has been an invaluable part of shepherds' lives for centuries. The breed is especially well-known for its intense loyalty to its family and to the herds it protects, and will often fight off much larger predators such as wolves and lynx without hesitation.

AT A GLANCE	
Ease of training	■■ ■■ ■■
Affection	■■ ■■ ■■
Playfulness	■■ ■■ ■■
Good with children	■■ ■■ ■
Good with other dogs	■■ ■■ ■
Grooming required	■■ ■

! A very devoted, well-mannered, courageous dog.

+ The breed is known to be at a higher risk from mastocytoma (mast cell tumours) than the general population of dogs.

HISTORY

Although there is little proof one way or another, many believe that the various Carpathian Shepherd Dog breeds, as with other livestock guardian and Mountain dog breeds, are descended from dogs that were developed somewhere around 9,000 years ago in Mesopotamia, following the domestication of sheep and goats in the same area. The first breed standard was drawn up in 1934 and has been updated several times since. The National Club of Carpathian Shepherd Dog Breeders was established in Romania in 1998.

Catalan Sheepdog

Gos d'Atura Català

SPAIN

Catalan Sheepdog pup

Exercise required

48	100+	16+
	80	14
36		
	60	12
24	40	10
	20	8
12		
	10	6

Average height (inches)
Average weight (pounds)
Average life expectancy (years)

Common Coat Colors

This breed is most associated with the area around Andorra in Spain and share similarities with the Bergamasco, the Briard, the Bearded Collie, and the Portuguese Sheepdog. The Catalan Sheepdog is a versatile breed, originally bred for herding and guarding livestock. They are still used for working livestock in parts of Spain, but are now more commonly bred as companions. These intelligent and loyal dogs make good watchdogs, but need a great deal of exercise.

AT A GLANCE

Ease of training	▰▰▰ ▰▰▰ ▰▰▰
Affection	▰▰▰ ▰▰▰
Playfulness	▰▰▰ ▰▰▰ ▰▰▰
Good with children	▰▰
Good with other dogs	▰▰
Grooming required	▰▰▰ ▰▰▰

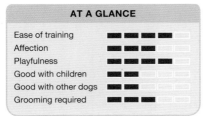

! This breed is less independent than other herders so it bonds more easily with the family.

+ Few health issues with this breed, possible chance of hip dysplasia.

HISTORY

The Catalan Sheepdog takes its name from its place of origin: Catalonia, Spain. It was most likely bred from an ancient Pyrenees breed in the Pyrenean Valley. Catalan Sheepdogs are also known as Catalonian Sheepdogs, Perros de Pastor Catalan, and the Gos d'Atura Catala. This breed has been used to guard camps and carry messages in several wars, including the Spanish Civil War. They are also often used as search-and-rescue dogs and police dogs in Spain. The breed was dwindling until the 1970s, when a group of Catalonian Sheepdog lovers started promoting it. While populations have increased, the Catalan Sheepdog remains a relatively rare breed today.

Caucasian Ovcharka

Caucasian Shepherd

GEORGIA / ARMENIA / AZERBAIJAN

Caucasian Ovcharka pup

Exercise required

	Average height (inches)	Average weight (pounds)	Average life expectancy (years)
	48	100+	16+
		80	14
	36		
		60	12
	24	40	10
		20	8
	12		
		10	6

Common Coat Colors

The Caucasian Shepherd is a large, powerful herding and guarding breed of ancient origin. While the exact location of their origin is unknown, they most likely developed within a wide area that encompasses Armenia, Azerbaijani, and Georgia, in an area with harsh terrain and physical isolation. These dogs exhibit different characteristics depending on the location of their upbringing, but all share the standard herding and guarding skills of all herding dogs. They are widely loved and respected in their homelands, and are extremely loyal and protective of their owners. This can become an issue if they are not properly socialized, and so are not appropriate for an inexperienced owner.

AT A GLANCE

Ease of training	
Affection	
Playfulness	
Good with children	
Good with other dogs	
Grooming required	

+ The breed is very hardy, but may suffer with Hip and Elbow Dysplasia.

! They can be fairly aggressive towards people they do not know.

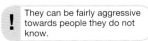

HISTORY

The Caucasian Shepherd has existed since ancient times, like many Eastern Molossers, but its first official Show-Ring appearance outside the Caucasus was not until the 1930s in Germany. They served shepherds in the Caucasus mountains as guard dogs, defending sheep from predators, mainly wolves, jackals and bears. They are still primarily used for this job, especially in Georgia, and are instrumental in the lives of many shepherds.

Collie

English Collie / Rough Collie / Scottish Collie
SCOTLAND

Collie pup

Exercise required

Common Coat Colors

48	100+	16+
	80	14
36		
	60	12
24	40	10
	20	8
12		
	10	6

Average height (inches)
Average weight (pounds)
Average life expectancy (years)

The Collie is a beautiful, well-loved dog that is known by several names: The Rough Collie, English Collie, Scottish Collie, and just "Collie." Also in play is the Smooth Collie, which is considered to be a unique breed in some countries, while others—such as the United States—consider the Smooth Collie to be little more than a coat variety of the rough-coated collie. The Collie was primarily used to herd livestock and cattle, but also has a decent level of protective and guarding instinct. Today, this lovable dog is an energetic, intelligent, and very trainable companion that is great with other animals and children.

AT A GLANCE

Ease of training	▰▰▰▰▰
Affection	▰▰▰▰
Playfulness	▰▰▰▰
Good with children	▰▰▰▰
Good with other dogs	▰▰▰
Grooming required	▰▰▰

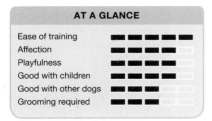

! A highly trainable companion animal that is good with children and other animals.

+ Generally healthy, but hereditary problems can include Collie eye anomaly, gastric torsion, and progressive retinal atrophy.

HISTORY

The Collie originated in the Scottish Highlands and the upland and moorland areas of the British Isles through a combination of local working stock. Borzoi was also introduced to the breed, as were Deerhounds and Greyhounds. The "Colley Club" was established in 1881 in England and set a breed standard that has not changed much since. Collies were promoted by the British Royal family; Queen Victoria became an enthusiastic owner. The breed arrived in the United States in 1879, President Calvin Coolidge and his wife had several Collies, which helped to popularize them.

Croatian Sheepdog

Hrvatski ovčar / Kroatischer Schäferhund

CROATIA

Croatian Sheepdog pup

Exercise required

Common Coat Colors

	48	100+	16+
		80	14
	36		
		60	12
		40	10
Average height (inches) Average weight (pounds) Average life expectancy (years)	24	20	8
	12		
		10	6

Croatian sheepdogs are made easily distinguishable from other breeds by their curly black coat and strong, agile form. Their history dates as far back as the fourteenth century, when very similar looking dogs were known as the Canis Pastoralis Croaticus. They were historically used for herding livestock and cattle in remote regions of Croatia, and developed into especially resilient, tough, dexterous dogs. They are an active, intelligent breed, and are adept at events like fly ball and agility. They can be loud and prone to barking, which should be discouraged during training at a young age.

AT A GLANCE

Ease of training	▬▬ ▬▬ ▬▬ ▬▬
Affection	▬▬ ▬▬ ▬▬
Playfulness	▬▬ ▬▬ ▬▬
Good with children	▬▬ ▬▬ ▬▬
Good with other dogs	▬▬ ▬▬
Grooming required	▬▬ ▬▬ ▬▬

+ They are generally hardy and have no known health issues.

 They can be prone to excessive barking, which should be discouraged.

HISTORY

A document named "Canis Pastoralis Croaticus" is the earliest written document about Croatian Sheepdogs. The document was found in the archives of the diocese of Đakovo by the "father of the breed", veterinarian Professor Dr Stjepan Romić, and is thought to have been written in the year 1374. A systematic selective-breeding program was started by the same Professor Romic in 1935 with dogs in the territory of Đakovo. After 34 years, breed was finally recognized by FCI in 1969.

Danish-Swedish Farmdog

Dansk / svensk gårdshund

DENMARK AND SOUTHERN SWEDEN

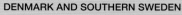

Danish-Swedish Farmdog
pup

Exercise required

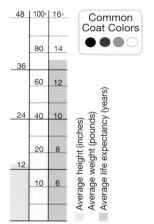

48	100+	16+
	80	14
36		
	60	12
24	40	10
	20	8
12		
	10	6

Common Coat Colors

Average height (inches) — Average weight (pounds) — Average life expectancy (years)

The Danish-Swedish Farmdog is a charismatic and versatile. This small dog took on a number of roles on the farm, including vermin control, hunting, herding, and guarding. It was often used in the circus due to its intelligence and lighthearted nature. Many believe this breed traces back to Fox Terrier and Pinscher crossbreeds. These dogs make excellent companions for an active home and are good therapy dogs.

AT A GLANCE

Ease of training	▤▤▤▤
Affection	▤▤▤▤▤
Playfulness	▤▤▤▤
Good with children	▤▤▤
Good with other dogs	▤▤
Grooming required	▤

+ They are generally hardy and have no known health issues.

HISTORY

The Danish–Swedish Farmdog first was registered as a recognized breed in Denmark and Sweden in 1987. Kennel Clubs of Denmark and Sweden convened, and agreed on the name of the breed, and also on the breed standard written by judge and breeder Lars Adeheimer of Sweden and judge Ole Staunskjaer of Denmark. The DSF was used as a farm dog for hundreds of years, and before becoming a recognized breed it was known under the local names "Skrabba", "Skåneterrier", "råttehund".

 ! These dogs make excellent companions for an active home and are good therapy dogs.

Dutch Shepherd Dog

Dutch Shepherd / Hollandse Herder

THE NETHERLANDS

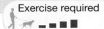

Exercise required

Dutch Shepherd
Dog pup

The Dutch Shepherd is a versatile and clever breed whose role has as farming practices have evolved over time. Originally, the breed's primary function was to herd all varieties of livestock and cattle. They had to keep the large flocks of sheep away from the crop fields, protect the vegetable patches from the hens, and gather the cows to be milked. On market day, they drove the livestock to town, and when the farmer was away, they patrolled the farm, keeping watch. As farming practices became less reliant on dogs, the breed found new roles with the police, search and rescue, and as an assistance dog. The Dutch Shepherd has a loving and calm nature and makes a good companion dog.

Average height (inches)	Average weight (pounds)	Average life expectancy (years)
48	100+	16+
	80	14
36		
	60	12
24	40	10
	20	8
12		
	10	6

+ Confirmed genetic diseases diagnosed in Dutch Shepherd Dogs include allergies (atopy), masticatory myositis, pannus, cryptorchidism, and inflammatory bowel disease.

Common
Coat Colors

AT A GLANCE

Ease of training	▪▪ ▪▪ ▪▪ ▪
Affection	▪▪ ▪▪ ▪
Playfulness	▪▪ ▪▪ ▪
Good with children	▪▪ ▪▪ ▪▪
Good with other dogs	▪▪ ▪▪
Grooming required	▪▪ ▪

! The Dutch Shepherd has a lovely nature and makes a good companion dog.

HISTORY

The Dutch Shepherd was originally intended for use as an all-purpose working dog. It was developed in 19th century Holland, and was used as a herder and farm dog. In later years, it found more work in the field of security and police work, as well as guarding property. Though they are still very popular in their homeland, they are relatively rare in other countries.

171

English Shepherd

Farm Collie

UNITED STATES

English Shepherd pup

Common
Coat Colors

Exercise required

48	100+	16+
	80	14
36		
	60	12
24	40	10
	20	8
12		
	10	6

Average height (inches)
Average weight (pounds)
Average life expectancy (years)

English Shepherds are loyal and hardworking dogs, while also being well-known for their kind and gentle temperament towards their family. If properly socialized, this dog makes a wonderful companion animal. They are also a highly intelligent, resilient breed, and has been used as a herding dog, livestock guardian, watch dog, hunting dog, vermin eradicator and a child's companion for years.

AT A GLANCE		
Ease of training	▬▬▬▬	
Affection	▬▬▬▬	
Playfulness	▬▬▬▬▬	
Good with children	▬▬▬▬▬	
Good with other dogs	▬▬▬▬▬	
Grooming required	▬▬▬	

 The English Shepherd is a highly intelligent, all-around farm dog.

✚ English Shepherds are generally healthy dogs, typically avoiding problems (like hip dysplasia) that are more common in some other breeds.

HISTORY

The English Shepherd originated between Northern England and Scotland. They first came to America with the earliest settlers, and were appreciated by American farmers for their versatility. They were frequently used to protect farms and livestock, and have been found commonly throughout farms in Europe and America for years. Despite the fact that these dogs are widely loved by farmers worldwide, they were not registered as a breed by the United Kennel Club until 1927, as they were so common and widespread that they were not seen as a single breed.

Entlebucher Mountain Dog

Entelbuch Mountain Dog / Entelbucher Cattle Dog

SWITZERLAND

Entlebucher Mountain Dog pup

Exercise required

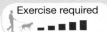

The Entlebucher is a compact, muscular dog that was traditionally used for driving herds of livestock between pastures and for gathering dairy herds to be milked. Today the breed exists in relatively small numbers, but is valued as a lively, affectionate, and intelligent companion or worker. They are steady and good-natured but also bold. Athletic and very strong, they must be kept busy playing, working, or in sports; they are not an apartment dog. They will bond with family and need lots of attention, as well as firm and experienced training, which should start early. The Entlebucher is a good watchdog and once familiar with strangers is amiable and pleasant, like all mountain dogs.

Common Coat Colors

Average height (inches) / Average weight (pounds) / Average life expectancy (years)

48	100+	16+
36	80	14
	60	12
24	40	10
	20	8
12	10	6

AT A GLANCE

Ease of training	■■ ■■ ■■ ■■
Affection	■■ ■■ ■■
Playfulness	■■ ■■ ■■ ■■
Good with children	■■ ■■ ■■
Good with other dogs	■■ ■■
Grooming required	■■

! These powerful dogs can literally pull you off your feet.

+ Entlebucher urinary syndrome is one genetic risk this breed carries.

HISTORY

This useful and versatile breed originated in the Entlebuch Valley, from where it takes its name, and is the smallest of the four Swiss Mountain Dog breeds. The breed dates back to the end of the nineteenth century, but for many years, the Entlebucher and the Appenzeller were considered the same. They were finally named two distinct breeds in 1927.

Estrela Mountain
Dog pup

Estrela Mountain Dog

Portuguese Shepherd / Cão da Serra da Estrela

PORTUGAL

Exercise required

48	100+	16+
	80	14
36		
	60	12
24	40	10
	20	8
12		
	10	6

Average height (inches)
Average weight (pounds)
Average life expectancy (years)

Common
Coat Colors

The Estrela Mountain dog is intelligent, loyal, and steadfast; affectionate to those it knows but wary of those it does not. It is known to be very protective of any children in its family. It needs early and continued socialization to be trustworthy around small pets and other dogs. As a large, athletic dog, the Estrela Mountain Dog is a formidable opponent for any predator, though as a companion animal, this is a rare occurrence. Estrelas are calm-tempered but fearless, and will not hesitate to react to danger, making it an exceptional watchdog as well as an excellent guard dog.

AT A GLANCE

Ease of training	■ ■ ■ ■
Affection	■ ■ ■
Playfulness	■ ■
Good with children	■ ■ ■
Good with other dogs	■ ■ ■
Grooming required	■ ■ ■

! It needs early and continued socialization to be trustworthy around small pets and other dogs.

+ They are a generally hardy breed and have no known health issues.

HISTORY

The Estrela Mountain dog is believed by many to be one of Portugal's oldest breeds. This breed has been protecting livestock for centuries, and have been depended by shepherds on throughout history to scare off wolves and other large predators. Over time, they began being used by the aristocracy to protect their estates. The first Estrela Mountain Dog was entered into the show ring in 1908. The first official breed standard of Estrela was established in 1933.

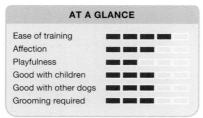

Farm Collie

Farmcollie
SCOTLAND

Farm Collie pup

Exercise required

Average height (inches)	Average weight (pounds)	Average life expectancy (years)
48	100+	16+
	80	14
36		
	60	12
24	40	10
	20	8
12		
	10	6

Common Coat Colors

Farm collies are bred for their working traits rather than their looks. The diversity of foundation stock breeds means that farm collies can vary greatly in appearance, ranging from those of a Border Collie background to those of a Rough Collie heritage. Those working traits include intelligence, loyalty, and hardiness. Farm collies are also common household pets, and sometimes trained as guide dogs for the blind. There are no current registries that include Farm Collies for show purposes.

AT A GLANCE

Ease of training	■■ ■■ ■■ ■■ ■■
Affection	■■ ■■ ■■
Playfulness	■■ ■■ ■■ ■■
Good with children	■■ ■■ ■■ ■■
Good with other dogs	■■ ■■ ■■ ■■
Grooming required	■■ ■■ ■■

 Collies are a generally healthy variety of dog, but are energetic, and need both exercise and mental stimulation.

HISTORY

In the 1860s, Queen Victoria became enamored with the breed when she visited the Scottish Highlands, and brought collies into high fashion. In the 1960s, the collie was much taller and bigger than it is today. Decades ago, collies were used for herding but they were replaced by Border Collies, which caused some generations of collies to lose their herding instinct.

! This type of dog is also friendly with other dogs and even non-canine pets.

German Shepherd

Alsatian

GERMANY

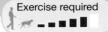

Exercise required

The German Shepherd was originally bred to be a livestock dog, to guard, herd, and drive a range of cattle and livestock. After years of selective breeding, their instincts are ingrained enough that they will still instinctively protect and herd livestock. They were widely recognized for their intelligence and receptiveness to training, and were drafted into police service soon after their popularity began to rise. They are still recognized as one of the leading police dogs in the world. With the outbreak of World War I, the German Shepherds became military dogs, delivering messages, working in search and rescue, and acting as sentries and guard dogs. They also make great guide dogs, and are adept at assisting roles in general. The first German-trained guide dog for the blind sent to the United States was named Lux, and was imported in 1925 as a gift for Minnesota senator Thomas Schall. The breed is still used for these purposes and also makes a wonderful and engaging companion animal.

German Shepherd puppies

AT A GLANCE

Ease of training	▪▪▪▪▪
Affection	▪▪▪
Playfulness	▪▪
Good with children	▪▪▪
Good with other dogs	▪▪▪
Grooming required	▪▪▪

✚ Generally healthy but hereditary problems can include hip dysplasia, degenerative myelopathy, exocrine pancreatic insufficiency, hemophilia, renal cystadenocarcinoma, pannus, panosteitis, and perianal fistula.

Common
Coat Colors

	48	100+	16+
		80	14
	36		
		60	12
Average height (inches) / Average weight (pounds) / Average life expectancy (years)	24	40	10
		20	8
	12		
		10	6

HISTORY

Captain Max von Stephanitz is generally given credit for developing the German Shepherd breed based on native working German stock. He purchased a dog named Horand von Grafrath, which had a "wolfish" appearance, from a dog show in Karlsruhe, western Germany, in 1899, and used him as the foundation of his breeding program. Stephanitz established the Society for the German Shepherd Dog, and Horand was the first dog registered. Horand's brother Kuchs was also added to the program. The motto "utility and intelligence" was adopted for the fledgling breed. In 1907 the first German Shepherd was exhibited in the United States, and the following year the American Kennel Club recognized the breed. During World War I, "German" was dropped from the breed name in the United States, and in England the breed name was changed to Alsatian, remaining as such until 1977. The full name was reinstated in the United States some years later, and by 1926 the breed accounted for 36 percent of all registered American dogs. The German Shepherd continues to be extremely popular.

! One dog named Filax of Lewanno was honored at Westminster during WWI for bringing 54 wounded soldiers to safety.

They excel as assistance dogs and have been widely used as guide dogs for the blind; the first German-trained guide dog for the blind sent to the United States was named Lux, and was imported in 1925 as a gift for Minnesota senator Thomas Schall. The breed is still used for these purposes and also makes a wonderful and engaging companion animal.

Greater Swiss Mountain Dog

Grand Bouvier Suisse

SWITZERLAND

Exercise required

The Greater Swiss Mountain Dog is the largest and oldest of the four Swiss mountain-dog breeds and has been influential in the development of other breeds, such as the St. Bernard and Rottweiler. Given their size, strength, and gentle nature, the Greater Swiss Mountain Dog was frequently used for draft purposes on small holdings and farms, as well as for herding and guarding livestock and for guarding the homestead. Today, "Swissies" compete in a number of sporting events that reflect their history, including draft and weight pulling, as well as rally, herding, tracking, and agility. These are lovely dogs that thrive in a lively home.

The Greater Swiss Mountain Dog is a draft and drover breed; it is a large, heavy-boned dog with incredible physical strength. Despite being heavy-boned and well-muscled, the dog is agile enough to perform the all-purpose farm duties of the mountainous regions of its origin.

! They are great companions if they get enough exercise, but if not, they may become destructive.

AT A GLANCE

Ease of training	■ ■ ■
Affection	■ ■ ■
Playfulness	■ ■
Good with children	■ ■ ■
Good with other dogs	■ ■
Grooming required	■ ■ ■

+ Greater Swiss Mountain Dogs have far fewer problems than more populous breeds in the similar size range.

Common Coat Colors

Average height (inches)	Average weight (pounds)	Average life expectancy (years)
	48	100+	16+
		80	14
36			
		60	12
24	40	10
	20	8
12			
	10	6

HISTORY

Two theories, equally plausible, account for the origins of this ancient breed. The first attributed to mastiff-types introduced by the Romans when they began invading the Alps from 57 BCE. Alternatively, some historians believe that the seafaring Phoenicians took large mastiff-types with them when they settled the Iberian Peninsula from roughly 1100 BCE, and that these dogs migrated eastward influencing many of the large Continental European breeds. In the harsh Alpine region, the mountain breeds developed specific traits, and were in turn bred for their working functionality. Due to their size, Swissies were often used for driving cattle and smaller livestock, and were used to do many other jobs on small farms. As farming methods changed and machinery took over, the dogs began to decrease in number. In 1908 Swiss Professor Albert Heim, a breed expert, pushed for the breed to be recognized as distinct from other mountain dogs, and they were accepted as the Greater Swiss Mountain Dog in the Swiss Stud Book. Although they are rare both in their homeland and abroad, they are supported by dedicated enthusiasts.

The Greater Swiss Mountain Dog is happy with an enthusiastic nature and strong affinity to people and children. This breed is sociable, active, calm and dignified. They do need plenty of room to exercise. They will not be happy confined to kennel life; they want to enjoy their family. They crave attention and physical contact. Greater Swiss Mountain Dogs are bold, faithful and willing workers and are eager to please. The Greater Swiss Mountain Dog is confident in nature; the breed is gentle with children.

Hovawart

Hovie

GERMANY

Exercise required

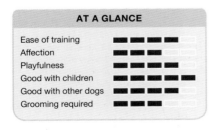

Hovawart pup

48	100+	16+
	80	14
36		
	60	12
24	40	10
	20	8
12		
	10	6

Average height (inches)
Average weight (pounds)
Average life expectancy (years)

Common Coat Colors

The Hovawart takes its name from the German words "Hova" (Hof) meaning farm, and "Wart" (wächter) meaning watchman. This name describes the primary purpose of the breed. The Hovawart is an Ancient working breed that is believed to have originated in the Harz and Black forest areas of Germany, and were bred by German Aristocrats to help guard their estates.

AT A GLANCE

Ease of training	▬▬▬ ▬▬▬ ▬▬▬ ▬▬▬
Affection	▬▬▬ ▬▬▬ ▬▬▬
Playfulness	▬▬▬ ▬▬▬ ▬▬▬
Good with children	▬▬▬ ▬▬▬ ▬▬▬ ▬▬▬ ▬▬▬
Good with other dogs	▬▬▬ ▬▬▬ ▬▬▬ ▬▬▬
Grooming required	▬▬▬ ▬▬▬ ▬▬▬

 The Hovawart is an outstanding watch dog.

+ They are generally a hardy breed and have no known health issues.

HISTORY

One of the first documented recordings of a Hovawart comes from the year 1210. In this account, a German castle—Ordensritterburg—was besieged by Slavic invaders. The castle was overrun and most of the inhabitants were killed, but the lord's infant son was saved by one of the castle's Hovawarts. Though the dog itself was injured, it dragged the child to a neighboring castle and thus saved the boy's life. This young boy, Eike von Repkow, grew up to become a legendary figure in the history of German law.

Huntaway

New Zealand Sheepdog

NEW ZEALAND

Exercise required
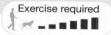

Huntaway pup

Developed in New Zealand around 100 years ago, The Huntaway was specifically bred to meet that country's demanding requirements of sheep farming. Farmers needed dogs of great endurance to work the difficult terrain, and to cope with the tough climate—they also needed dogs that barked so the farmer could find them when working at long distances. The Huntaway, was developed from the Border Collie and other herding-breed crosses, and is noted for its agility and stamina, as well as regular and sustained bark. The breed has a good temperament, but is naturally inclined to bark and is best suited to a working, rural life.

Common Coat Colors

Average height (inches)	Average weight (pounds)	Average life expectancy (years)
48	100+	16+
	80	14
36		
	60	12
24	40	10
	20	8
12		
	10	6

AT A GLANCE

Ease of training	■■■ ■■■ ■■■
Affection	■■■ ■■■
Playfulness	■■■ ■■■
Good with children	■■■ ■■ ■■■
Good with other dogs	■■■ ■■■ ■■■
Grooming required	■■■ ■■ ■■

! They are naturally inclined to bark and are best suited to a working, rural life.

HISTORY

The huntaway was developed as a breed in response to farming conditions found in the New Zealand High Country. The earliest references to huntaways are in the late 19th century. A sheepdog trial with a specific class for huntaways was advertised in the Upper Waitaki in 1870. The huntaway was further developed as a separate breed from the heading dog during the 20th Century.
As of August 2013 the Huntaway breed was recognized by the New Zealand Kennel Club. This is the first recognition of a dog breed of New Zealand origin.

+ They are generally a hardy breed and have no known health issues.

Karst Shepherd

Kraski Ovcar
SLOVENIA

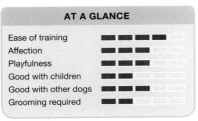

Karst Shepherd pup

Exercise required
▪ ▪ ▪ ▪ □ □

48	100+	16+
	80	14
36		
	60	12
24	40	10
	20	8
12		
	10	6

Average height (inches)
Average weight (pounds)
Average life expectancy (years)

Common
Coat Colors

The Karst Shepherd has been used for guarding and herding livestock for centuries, and was developed from ancient Molossian types. Dogs of a similar type are mentioned in Baron Vajkart Valvasor's 1689 book, The Glory of the Duchy of Carniole. The breed was originally known as the Illyrian Shepherd and was grouped with other shepherd dogs from the former Yugoslavia, but was recognized as a separate breed in 1968. The dogs are still used to guard people and livestock or as companions.

AT A GLANCE

Ease of training	▪ ▪ ▪ ▪ ▪ □
Affection	▪ ▪ ▪ ▪ □ □
Playfulness	▪ ▪ ▪ □ □ □
Good with children	▪ ▪ ▪ □ □ □
Good with other dogs	▪ ▪ ▪ ▪ □ □
Grooming required	▪ ▪ ▪ □ □ □

! The dogs are still used to guard people and livestock or as companions.

+ They are generally hardy and have no known health issues.

HISTORY

The Karst Shepherd is named after the Karst landscape that extends from Italy to Croatia and partly in Bosnia and Herzegovina, and from the Gulf of Trieste to the Dinaric Alps. The ancestral type of the modern day breed travelled with shepherds through this area. In 1689, the ethnographer Johann Weikhard von Valvasor mentioned the shepherd's dogs of the area in his work The Glory of the Duchy of Carniola. During the 20th century there were various periods when the number of Karst Shepherds was low, so to avoid inbreeding a decision was made to introduce a single male Newfoundland into the population.

King Shepherd

UNITED STATES

Exercise required
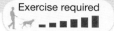

Common
Coat Colors

King Shepherd pup

	Average height (inches)	Average weight (pounds)	Average life expectancy (years)
	48	100+	16+
		80	14
	36		
		60	12
	24	40	10
		20	8
	12		
		10	6

The King Shepherd is a large, self-confident dog with a well-balanced personality. They are a naturally courageous guard and watchdog, showing courage, strength, and hardiness in their role as protector. They do not exhibit any shyness or nervousness. They are very intelligent, easy to train, faithful, and eager to please their owners. This breed makes a fine sheep-herder and working dog. They make great companions and are friendly to other animals and children.

AT A GLANCE

Ease of training	▪▪▪ ▪▪▪ ▪▪▪
Affection	▪▪▪ ▪▪▪
Playfulness	▪▪▪ ▪▪▪ ▪▪▪
Good with children	▪▪▪ ▪▪▪ ▪▪▪ ▪▪▪ ▪▪
Good with other dogs	▪▪▪ ▪▪▪ ▪▪▪ ▪▪▪
Grooming required	▪▪▪ ▪▪▪ ▪▪

+ They are generally hardy and have no known health issues.

HISTORY

This large breed was created by two American dog breeders, Shelly Watts-Cross, and David Turkheimer, who combined American and European German Shepherd Dogs, Alaskan Malamutes, American-bred German Shepherd Dogs and the Great Pyrenees. An organized dog breed club was started in 1995.

! King Shepherds are very intelligent and energetic.

Koolie

Australian Koolie / Coolie
AUSTRALIA

Koolie pup

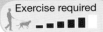

Exercise required

48	100+	16+
	80	14
36		
	60	12
24	40	10
	20	8
12		
	10	6

Average height (inches)
Average weight (pounds)
Average life expectancy (years)

Common Coat Colors

The Koolie is a working breed, bred for stamina, endurance, and responsiveness. Its natural trait is to herd anything that moves. Today we see the traditional working duties of the Koolie enlarged to include service, sports and human companionship. Koolies are generally okay with other dogs, and tolerate other species when introduced at a young age or handled by experienced owners.

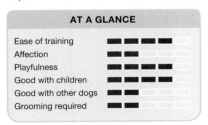

AT A GLANCE	
Ease of training	
Affection	
Playfulness	
Good with children	
Good with other dogs	
Grooming required	

 They are only suitable for a very active household.

+ Koolies have a diverse gene pool and so do not suffer from any genetic problems found in recognised breeds.

HISTORY

The Koolie is a working or herding dog that has existed in Australia since the early 19th century when it was bred from imported British working dogs—particularly the smooth coated blue merle Collie and the Black and Tan Collie from the Highlands of Scotland. Robert Kaleski, in an article on Cattle Dogs in the August 1903 issue of the Agricultural Gazette of New South Wales, describes the "Welsh heeler or merle, erroneously known as the German Collie," as a "blue-gray dog about the size and build of a smooth-haired collie, generally with wall eyes." The British background predominated in the dogs that came to be associated with the "German Collie" name.

Lancashire Heeler

Ormskirk Heeler
ENGLAND

Lancashire Heeler pup

Exercise required

Common Coat Colors

		48	100+	16+
			80	14
	36			
			60	12
		24	40	10
			20	8
	12			
			10	6

Average height (inches)
Average weight (pounds)
Average life expectancy (years)

The origins of this small, charismatic breed are not certain, but it may have developed through Welsh Corgi and Manchester Terrier crosses, possibly when Corgis were being used to drive cattle to markets from Wales into northwest England. Some historians, however, insist that the Lancashire Heeler is the older breed and that it gave rise to the Corgi! Either way, the breed was valued for driving cattle and other livestock. These are bright, cheerful dogs that enjoy family life.

AT A GLANCE

Ease of training	▬ ▬ ▬ ▬
Affection	▬ ▬ ▬ ▬
Playfulness	▬ ▬ ▬ ▬
Good with children	▬ ▬ ▬
Good with other dogs	▬ ▬ ▬
Grooming required	▬ ▬

 Despite its size, this is a strong dog capable of herding and directing much larger groups of cattle.

+ They are generally hardy and have no known health issues.

HISTORY

The Lancashire Heeler was recognized as a vulnerable native breed by The Kennel Club in 2006, which means that annual registration figures are 300 or less. Exact details of the origin of breed are unknown, however, it is accepted that a type of Welsh Corgi was used to drive livestock to the north west of England from Wales. A type of black and tan terrier called the Manchester Terrier was introduced which is thought to have resulted in what is now known as the Lancashire Heeler. The breed has been known in its home county for over a hundred and fifty years as a general purpose farm dog, capable of both ratting and herding cattle.

185

Landseer European Continental

Newfoundland

GERMANY / SWITZERLAND

Exercise required

Landseer European
Continental pup

	48	100+	16+
		80	14
36			
		60	12
24		40	10
		20	8
12			
		10	6

Average height (inches)
Average weight (pounds)
Average life expectancy (years)

Common Coat Colors

The European Continental Landseer, the other, simply known as the Landseer, is little more than a color variation of the Newfoundland. The name Landseer comes from the British painter, Sir Edwin Landseer. One of his most famous paintings, A Distinguished Member of the Humane Society, depicts a black-and-white Newfoundland. The Continental is taller than most Newfoundlands, and often has a shorter coat.

AT A GLANCE

Ease of training	
Affection	
Playfulness	
Good with children	
Good with other dogs	
Grooming required	

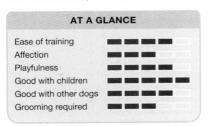

! The dog Nana in Peter Pan, although often portrayed as a St. Bernard, was intended to be a Landseer.

➕ Generally a healthy breed, but with a risk of obesity.

HISTORY

The Landseer type of dog originated in Germany and Switzerland, and is often considered by many kennel clubs to be a white and black coated variant of the black Newfoundland breed. The Landseer European Continental, however, is a distinct and separate breed that is recognized by FCI. As the Landseer is usually considered to be a variant of the Newfoundland, the breed almost became extinct when the black coated Newfoundland become fashionable. The breed's existence was also severely affected by the 2nd World War, but as a result of the efforts made by German and Swiss breeders, the Landseer was revived in the 1930s. The dog that was developed by crossing the Newfoundland with the Pyrenean Mountain dog is lighter with a less heavy coat that is relatively easy to groom.

Lapponian Herder

Lapland Reindeer dog

FINLAND

Lapponian Herder pup

Lapponian Herder

Exercise required
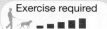

Common Coat Colors

	48	100+	16+
		80	14
	36		
		60	12
		24	40	10
			20	8
	12		
			10	6

Average height (inches)
Average weight (pounds)
Average life expectancy (years)

The Lapponian Herder is a people-oriented dog that loves being involved in any activity with its family and makes a great companion. If socialized properly, it will get along well with small children and animals. Lapponian Herders are very energetic, affectionate, and loyal working dogs, that love to please their owners and form strong bonds with their families.

AT A GLANCE

Ease of training	▬▬ ▬▬ ▬▬
Affection	▬▬ ▬▬ ▬▬
Playfulness	▬▬ ▬▬
Good with children	▬▬ ▬▬ ▬▬
Good with other dogs	▬▬ ▬▬ ▬▬
Grooming required	▬▬ ▬▬

 Lapponian Herders exhibiting basic herding instincts can be trained to compete in herding trials.

+ They are generally hardy and have no known health issues.

HISTORY

The Lapponian Herder is several centuries old, and is believed to descend from the dogs that have inhabited northern regions of Scandinavia since prehistoric periods. The origin of the breed is unknown, however, as the Lapponian Herder is dissimilar from other dogs of the same type. The earliest information on reindeer husbandry in Lapland dates back to the 16th and 17th centuries and the first mentions of reindeer-herding dogs were included in the book Lapponia, which was published in 1674.

187

McNab
McNab Border Collie
UNITED STATES

McNab pup

Exercise required

Common Coat Colors

48	100+	16+
	80	14
36		
	60	12
24	40	10
	20	8
12		
	10	6

Average height (inches)
Average weight (pounds)
Average life expectancy (years)

The McNab is a versatile livestock dog that will "head" and "heel" and is also used for hunting. They are obedient, intelligent, resilient, and affectionate. As such, McNabs are often popular with ranchers and farmers. The McNab is a breed that traces back to the late 1800s to Alexander McNab, a Scottish farmer who emigrated to Mendocino County, California. unhappy with the working ability of local dogs, he returned to Scotland and brought two Scotch Collies, Peter and Fred, back to the United States. Those were bred to Spanish dogs belonging to local Basque sheep-herders as well as to other imported Scotch Collies. While there are many characteristics of McNabs that are consistent, there is no formal breed standard.

AT A GLANCE

Ease of training	▰▰▰▰▰
Affection	▰▰▰▰
Playfulness	▰▰▰▰
Good with children	▰▰▰
Good with other dogs	▰▰▰
Grooming required	▰▰

! Though they are slowly becoming more popular, McNabs are not recognized by the American or United Kennel Clubs.

+ They are generally hardy and have no known health issues.

HISTORY
Scottish rancher, Alexander McNab, owned a 10,000-acre ranch in California, named the McNab Ranch. Because he was dissatisfied with the working ranch dogs available locally, he traveled back to Scotland in 1885 to find the type of dogs he had worked with while working with livestock. He eventually chose two male dogs which he bred with two females supposedly of Spanish origin, brought by Basque sheep herders from the Basque region of Northern Spain; these were the foundation of the modern McNab.

Miniature Australian Shepherd

Mini Aussie
UNITED STATES

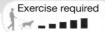

Exercise required

Miniature Australian
Shepherd pup

The Miniature Australian Shepherd was developed with the intention of creating a more compact Australian Shepherd with the same work ethic and agility. They were selectively bred for smaller size, and rapidly increased in popularity once a breed standard was defined. They are especially popular in dog agility, and do well in other dog sports including herding, obedience, disc dog, flyball and many other activities. Miniature Australian Shepherds (affectionately called "minis") function well as a family dog, but their excessive energy may need to be checked around small children. They are generally great companion dogs but do require a large amount of exercise.

Average height (inches)	Average weight (pounds)	Average life expectancy (years)
48	100+	16+
	80	14
36		
	60	12
24	40	10
	20	8
12		
	10	6

Common
Coat Colors

AT A GLANCE

Ease of training	▬ ▬ ▬ ▬
Affection	▬ ▬ ▬ ▬ ▬
Playfulness	▬ ▬ ▬ ▬
Good with children	▬ ▬ ▬
Good with other dogs	▬ ▬ ▬
Grooming required	▬ ▬ ▬

! They are easily trainable because they crave approval.

+ Eye defects of varying severity are the most common disorder in Australian Shepherds of all size varieties.

HISTORY

In 1978, a horse woman named Doris Cordova began a breeding program in Norco, California specifically to produce a very small breed based on Australian Shepherds. Her foundation stud was Cordova's Spike. Spike was placed with Bill and Sally Kennedy, also of Norco, California, to continue to develop a line of smaller dogs under the B/S kennel name. Another horseman, Chas Lasater of Valhalla Kennels, soon joined the ranks of mini breeders. In the 1980s, fanciers formed member clubs (North American Miniature Australian Shepherd Club of the USA and the Miniature Australian Shepherd Association) and registries to promote the smaller dogs in particular.

Miniature Poodle

Chien Canne
GERMANY

Miniature Poodle pup

Exercise required

48	100+	16+
	80	14
36		
	60	12
24	40	10
	20	8
12		
	10	6

Average height (inches)
Average weight (pounds)
Average life expectancy (years)

Common Coat Colors

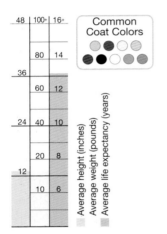

Poodles are found in three sizes—Standard, Miniature, and Toy—but all share similar traits and can make excellent family pets. The breed is noted for its loyalty and intelligence. They are delightful with their family, but can be standoffish with strangers, and are typically charismatic and full of character. With their great intelligence, Poodles make excellent gun dogs. Their origins trace back to Germany, where they were originally bred as water-retrieving dogs.

AT A GLANCE

Ease of training	▰▰▰▰▱
Affection	▰▰▰▰▱
Playfulness	▰▰▰▰▱
Good with children	▰▰▰▱▱
Good with other dogs	▰▰▰▱▱
Grooming required	▰▰▰▰▱

+ Prone to cataracts, progressive retinal atrophy (PRA) which may cause blindness, IMHA (Immune Mediated Hemolytic Anemia), heart disease, diabetes, epilepsy, runny eyes, ear infections and skin allergies.

! The Miniature Poodle is good for apartment life.

HISTORY

Poodles derive their name from the German word pudel, meaning to "splash in water," and are believed to share a similar heritage to other water-retrieving breeds, such as the Portuguese Water Dog, Irish Water Spaniel, Hungarian Water Hound, and French Barbet. The Poodle became popular in France during the eighteenth century, where it was known as the Chien Canard, meaning "duck dog." France became the breed's surrogate home, and the French Fédération Cynologique Internationale recognizes France as the breed's country of origin.

Mudi
Hungarian Mudi
HUNGARY

Mudi pup

The Mudi, also known as the "Driver Dog of Hungary," is a source of great pride amongst Hungarian Shepherds. These dogs are capable of herding and guarding livestock, hunting small game, and detecting bombs and drugs for police. While they are less popular than the Pumi and the Puli, they are nevertheless playful, intense, and friendly dogs

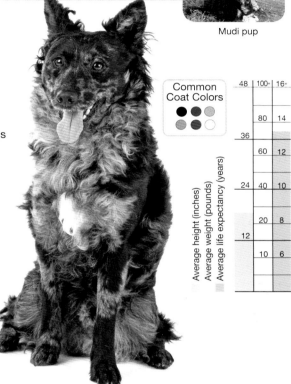

Common Coat Colors

Average height (inches)	Average weight (pounds)	Average life expectancy (years)
48	100+	16+
	80	14
36		
	60	12
24	40	10
	20	8
12		
	10	6

AT A GLANCE

Ease of training	▪▪▪ ▪▪▪ ▪▪▪
Affection	▪▪▪ ▪▪▪ ▪▪▪
Playfulness	▪▪▪ ▪▪▪ ▪▪▪
Good with children	▪▪▪ ▪▪▪ ▪▪▪
Good with other dogs	▪▪▪ ▪▪▪ ▪▪▪
Grooming required	▪▪▪ ▪▪▪

! The Mudi can live in an apartment if it is sufficiently exercised.

+ This is a fairly healthy breed, although some cases of hip dysplasia have occurred.

HISTORY

The Mudi is a herding dog breed from Hungary. It is closely related to the Puli and Pumi, from which it was separated in the 1930s. Today, the Mudi is bred for work, sport, companionship, and for showing. They continue to be used in herding, as well as participating in a variety of dog sports and competitions. In Hungarian, the plural form of Mudi is Mudik.

191

New Zealand Heading Dog

Eye Dog

NEW ZEALAND

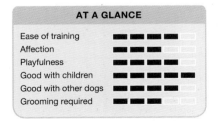

New Zealand Heading Dog pups

Exercise required

Common Coat Colors

48	100+	16+
	80	14
36		
	60	12
24	40	10
	20	8
12		
	10	6

Average height (inches)
Average weight (pounds)
Average life expectancy (years)

The New Zealand Heading Dog works in a similar manner to Border Collies, they establish intense eye contact to direct them, continually circling the flocks of sheep to move them. Also known as the Eye Dog, these dogs are extremely quick, agile, and athletic, and are highly intelligent, responding well to training. Generally, they have good temperaments but require a high-energy environment to thrive—at the very least they need plentiful exercise.

AT A GLANCE

Ease of training	
Affection	
Playfulness	
Good with children	
Good with other dogs	
Grooming required	

! If left alone for too long, they may try to escape.

+ They are generally hardy and have no known health issues.

HISTORY

Descended from the Border Collie, the New Zealand Heading Dog originated in the region around the English-Scottish border. Early pioneers brought Border Collies to New Zealand to herd sheep, and from there bred more specified dogs. Due to the Border Collie's long hair, they were bred with shorter haired dogs to create a dog better suited to the local environment. The Heading Dog has long been an important part of New Zealand sheepdog trials, which began in that country in 1867 in Wanaka. Sheepdog trials involve herding sheep around a field and into enclosures.

Newfoundland

CANADA

Newfoundland pup

Exercise required

Common Coat Colors	48	100+	16+
●●●●●		80	14
	36	60	12
		24 40	10
		20	8
	12	10	6

Average height (inches)
Average weight (pounds)
Average life expectancy (years)

This remarkable breed is known for its inherent instinct to protect and save people from danger, most notably water rescues. The "Newfie" has been remarkable servant to humankind and tales of the breed's heroism are legendary. They have a gentle, calm, and devoted temperament that makes them great companions. Newfoundlands are very large dogs but require only moderate exercise and grooming. They always welcome the opportunity to swim!

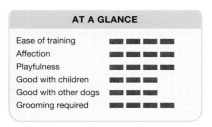

AT A GLANCE

Ease of training	▬▬ ▬▬ ▬▬ ▬▬
Affection	▬▬ ▬▬ ▬▬ ▬▬
Playfulness	▬▬ ▬▬ ▬▬ ▬▬
Good with children	▬▬ ▬▬ ▬▬
Good with other dogs	▬▬ ▬▬ ▬▬
Grooming required	▬▬ ▬▬ ▬▬ ▬▬

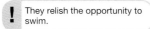

! They relish the opportunity to swim.

 Generally healthy, some hereditary problems can include hip dysplasia, elbow dysplasia, gastric torsion, subvalvular aortic stenosis, and arthritis.

HISTORY

The Newfoundland shares many traits with other Mastiffs like the St. Bernard and English Mastiff, including massive heads with very broad snouts, stout legs, a thick neck, and a very sturdy bone structure. It is descended from a breed indigenous to the island known as the lesser Newfoundland, or St. John's dog. The Newfoundland was widely used in the fishing industry in all kinds of roles, including, but not limited to, hauling nets and boats, swimming out to retrieve boats, and search and rescue. Breed numbers were decimated during the two world wars, but they have long been re-established.

193

Old English Sheepdog

Shepherd's Dog
ENGLAND

Old English
Sheepdog pup

Exercise required

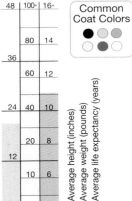

48	100+	16+
	80	14
36		
	60	12
24	40	10
	20	8
12		
	10	6

Average height (inches)
Average weight (pounds)
Average life expectancy (years)

Common Coat Colors

Distinctive for its shaggy coat and endearing appearance, this lovely breed is so beloved that the Old English Sheepdog has often been used in advertising. Despite their long coats and seeming lack of vision, however, these are agile and powerful working dogs that were favored by shepherds for their droving, herding, and protective instincts. Their remarkably thick coat serves two purposes—it insulates them against the worst of the inclement English weather and provides protection against predators.

AT A GLANCE

Ease of training	■
Affection	■ ■ ■ ■
Playfulness	■ ■ ■
Good with children	■ ■ ■
Good with other dogs	■ ■ ■ ■
Grooming required	■ ■ ■ ■

 They make wonderful family companions.

+ Generally healthy but hereditary problems can include hip dysplasia, gastric torsion, cerebellar ataxia, eye problems, and ear infections.

HISTORY

Old English Sheepdogs trace back to Russian Ovcharka and Bearded Collie ancestry, although no such early records exist. In the eighteenth century, a dog tax was introduced on pet dogs, from which working dogs were exempt—these dogs were differentiated by having "bobbed" tails. So Old English Sheepdogs had their tails docked and were often known as Bobtails. By the nineteenth century were common in the South Downs region of Sussex, in England, where they were used for driving cattle and sheep to market.

Perro de Pastor Mallorquin

Ca de Bestiar
SPAIN

Exercise required

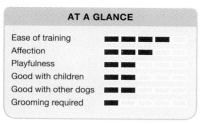

Perro de Pastor Mallorquin
pup

Common
Coat Colors

Average height (inches)	Average weight (pounds)	Average life expectancy (years)
	100+	16+
48		
	80	14
36		
	60	12
24	40	10
	20	8
12		
	10	6

Although it is unusual for a dark-coated breed to have adapted so well to a hot climate, these black livestock dogs are used across the Balearic Islands for their guarding skills as well as for general farm work. The dogs have been bred for their working skills rather than appearance and have a determinedly rugged look. The breed is best suited to a working environment or an experienced dog-owning home, as they can be aggressive to intruders as they are instinctively protective.

AT A GLANCE	
Ease of training	▬ ▬ ▬ ▬
Affection	▬ ▬ ▬
Playfulness	▬ ▬
Good with children	▬ ▬
Good with other dogs	▬ ▬
Grooming required	▬

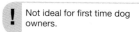

! Not ideal for first time dog owners.

+ The breed is known to be at a higher risk from mastocytoma (mast cell tumours) than the general population of dogs.

HISTORY

The Majorca Shepherd Dog has been used for herding sheep, and as a household guard dog since ancient times. Its specific origins are unknown, but it is assumed that it arrived with the conquestadors of King James I of Aragon. It began to emerge as a recognized breed in the 1970s, and the breed standard was first drafted in the 1980s.

Polish Lowland Sheepdog

Polish Owczarek Nizinny / PON

POLAND

Polish Lowland Sheepdog
pup

Exercise required

Average height (inches)
Average weight (pounds)
Average life expectancy (years)

48	100+	16+
36	80	14
	60	12
24	40	10
	20	8
12		
	10	6

Common
Coat Colors

Related to the Puli, the Polish Lowland Sheepdog also known as the Polish Owczarek Nizinny, or ONO, is popular in its homeland and increasingly popular overseas It is believed to have influenced the development of the Bearded Collie, which it closely resembles. They are fabulous working dogs and will herd sheep and cattle and are also excellent cattle and home guardian dogs. They have recently become popular companion animals and are best suited to a busy, active home.

AT A GLANCE

Ease of training	▰▰▰▰▰
Affection	▰▰▰▰
Playfulness	▰▰▰▰
Good with children	▰▰▰
Good with other dogs	▰▰▰▰
Grooming required	▰▰▰

+ Slight risk of obesity and hip dysplasia.

! They will provide a good measure of home security.

HISTORY

The Polish Lowland Sheepdog is most likely descended from Central Asian dogs that may have included the Lhasa Apso and Tibetan Terrier. Tibetan dogs were favorite among traders, which led to their introduction to Europe, where they were crossed with local sheepdogs, including the Puli. The PON has been known in Poland as a herding and flock-guarding dog since the 15th century. However, it was driven almost to extinction in World War II, only to be rescued by Dr. Danuta Hryiewicz through her dog, Smok, from which all of today's PONs are descended.

Polish Tatra Sheepdog

Tatra Mountain Sheepdog / Owczarek Tatrzanski

POLAND

Exercise required

Polish Tatra Sheepdog pup

Common Coat Colors

Average height (inches)	Average weight (pounds)	Average life expectancy (years)
48	100+	16+
	80	14
36		
	60	12
24	40	10
	20	8
12		
	10	6

This very rare breed has its origins in the Podhale region of southern Poland in the Carpathian Mountains, and has been bred over the centuries as a dedicated guardian dog for livestock, and for herding. These will remain among their flock unattended for long periods. The breed is noted for deterring predators rather than attacking, although it will attack if it is left no option. Tatras are huge, but are beautiful, gentle dogs. They have a massive build and great strength; they are vigilant watchdogs.

AT A GLANCE	
Ease of training	■■ ■■
Affection	■■ ■■ ■
Playfulness	■■ ■■
Good with children	■■ ■■
Good with other dogs	■■ ■■
Grooming required	■■ ■■

+ They are generally hardy and have no known health issues.

HISTORY

This breed sometimes goes by the names Owczarek Podhalanski and the Polish Mountain Sheepdog. It originated in the Tatra Mountain peaks of the Carpathian Mountains in the south of Poland. The breed was threatened during the Second World War because of starvation, but thanks to its intelligence and work ethic, the dog's numbers rebounded after war's end. Today, they are often used in the Tatra Mountains as guardians. Many have become purely companion dogs, although the desire to work has not left them.

! They are best suited to an experienced home.

Portuguese Sheepdog

Cão da Serra de Aires

PORTUGAL

Portuguese Sheepdog pup

Exercise required

Common Coat Colors

48	100+	16+
	80	14
36		
	60	12
24	40	10
	20	8
12		
	10	6

Average height (inches)
Average weight (pounds)
Average life expectancy (years)

The Cão da Serra de Aires, also known as the Portuguese Sheepdog, is a medium-sized breed, and is one of the indigenous regional dogs of Portugal. Its Portuguese name refers to the Serra de Aires, a mountain near Monforte in the Alentejo region. The breed is nicknamed the "cão macaco" (monkey dog, referring to the macaque or monkey) for its furry face and lively attitude. Typical coat colors include yellow, chestnut, grey, fawn, grey, and black, with tan marks.

AT A GLANCE	
Ease of training	▄▄▄
Affection	▄▄▄
Playfulness	▄▄▄▄
Good with children	▄▄▄
Good with other dogs	▄▄▄
Grooming required	▄▄▄

+ They are generally hardy and have no known health issues.

! They can live happily alongside other pets provided they have been properly socialized.

HISTORY

Traditionally these dogs were used for herding cows, sheep, and Goats (and sometimes even horses and pigs) in the Serra de Aires. It is believed to be closely related to Pyrenean and Catalan Sheepdogs, and from the Briards imported into Portugal in the early 1900s. The breed was recognized in 1996 by the Fédération Cynologique Internationale, and by the UKC in 2006.

Puli

Hungarian Puli
HUNGARY

Exercise required

Puli pup

Common Coat Colors

	48	100+	16+
		80	14
	36		
		60	12
		24	40	10
			20	8
	12		
		10	6

Average height (inches)
Average weight (pounds)
Average life expectancy (years)

The origin of the Puli is unknown. There is speculation that they arrived with the Cumans in the thirteenth century or perhaps that they developed either from herding dogs of the Magyars who settled in the Danube region in the ninth century. Both peoples had herding and guarding dogs, and the Puli, Hungarian Komondor, and Mudi are believed to share a similar heritage. Pulis are very tough working dogs whose thick corded coats provide them with protection against the elements and predators.

AT A GLANCE

Ease of training	▬ ▬ ▬ ▬
Affection	▬ ▬ ▬
Playfulness	▬ ▬ ▬
Good with children	▬ ▬ ▬
Good with other dogs	▬
Grooming required	▬ ▬ ▬ ▬ ▬ ▬

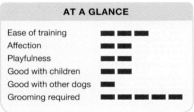

! The Puli has a unique distinctive coat.

✚ Generally healthy, skin issues if not groomed properly.

HISTORY

The Puli has been known in Hungary for at least a thousand years. Puli-type dogs were brought to Hungary by Magyar invaders. Pulis bear a resemblance to the Tibetan Terrier, and it's possible that breed is one of their ancestors. During the 17th century, the Puli almost disappeared as a breed because of interbreeding with sheepdogs from Germany and France. In 1912, a program was begun to revive the breed, and a breed standard was written in 1915 and approved by the Fédération Cynologique Internationale in 1924.

Pumi

Hungarian Herding Terrier
HUNGARY

Pumi pup

Exercise required

Average height (inches)
Average weight (pounds)
Average life expectancy (years)

48	100+	16+
	80	14
36		
	60	12
24	40	10
	20	8
12		
	10	6

Common
Coat Colors

The lovely Pumi is an engaging herding breed of similar heritage to the Puli. The Pumi is thought also to have some influence from terrier types, Briards, and possibly Keeshonds. The term Pumi was first used in 1801, but this was probably a generic term for Hungarian herding dogs. They were divided into separate breeds in 1921 by Dr. Emil Raitsis. Pumis are brave, bright, and characterful dogs that are still used for herding cattle, sheep, and pigs in addition to being used for hunting wild boar.

AT A GLANCE

Ease of training	▬▬ ▬▬ ▬▬ ▭▭
Affection	▬▬ ▬▬ ▭▭ ▭▭
Playfulness	▬▬ ▬▬ ▬▬ ▭▭
Good with children	▬▬ ▬▬ ▭▭ ▭▭
Good with other dogs	▬▬ ▬▭ ▭▭ ▭▭
Grooming required	▬▬ ▬▬ ▭▭ ▭▭

! They can have a tendency to bark but make great family companions for an active home.

+ They are generally hardy and have no known health issues.

HISTORY

The Pumi has been an established breed for more than 300 years, but wasn't officially recognized as a distinct breed around the 1920s. The Pumi is still popular in its native Hungary and was recognized by the United Kennel Club in 1996. Although the Pumi belongs to the American Kennel Club's Foundation Stock Service and is represented by the Hungarian Pumi Club of America (HPCA), it is still relatively new to the United States.

Pyrenean Mastiff

SPAIN

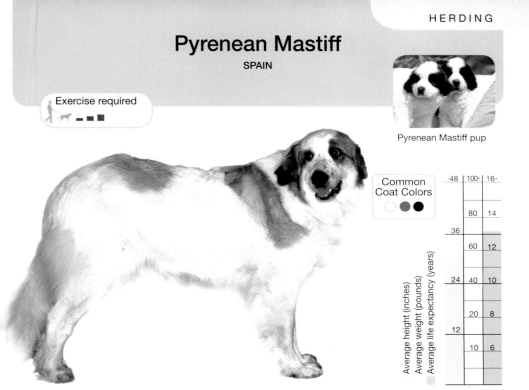

Pyrenean Mastiff pup

Exercise required

Common Coat Colors

			48	100+	16+
				80	14
			36		
				60	12
Average height (inches)	Average weight (pounds)	Average life expectancy (years)	24	40	10
				20	8
			12		
				10	6

This ancient breed descended from prehistoric Molosser dogs that lived in the Pyrenean region between Navarra Aragon. The Pyrenean Mastiff is an imposing dog that was used for herding and guarding flocks from bears and wolves, often wearing spiked metal collars to protect their necks. Predator populations diminished by the 1930s, and Pyrenean Mastiff almost disappeared with them. They were revived in the 1970s.

AT A GLANCE

Ease of training	▰▰▰ ▰▰▰ ▰▰▰
Affection	▰▰▰ ▰▰▰ ▰▰▰
Playfulness	▰▰▰ ▰▰▰
Good with children	▰▰▰ ▰▰▰ ▰▰▰
Good with other dogs	▰▰▰ ▰▰▰
Grooming required	▰▰▰ ▰▰▰ ▰▰▰

 This is not a dog that's suitable for apartment living.

+ Because of its drooping eyes, it may suffer bouts of conjunctivitis if a strict routine of eye hygiene is not initiated and adhered to.

HISTORY

The Mastiff's primary function was to heard sheep and to protect them from predatory wolves and bears. As the predator populations decreased so did the popularity and numbers of the Pyrenean Mastiff—they are expensive dogs to keep. In the 1970s a group of enthusiasts started working on recovering the breed through the few local specimens that retained typical features of the ancient mastiff. It has been on record since 1977 as a modern purebred breed by the Club del Mastin del Pirineo de España in Spain.

Pyrenean Shepherd

Berger des Pyrénées / Pastor de los Pirineos / Petit Berger / Pyrenees Sheepdog

FRANCE / SPAIN

Exercise required

Pyrenean Shepherd pup

Average height (inches)	Average weight (pounds)	Average life expectancy (years)
48	100+	16+
	80	14
36		
	60	12
24	40	10
	20	8
12		
	10	6

Common
Coat Colors

Known locally as Le Berger des Pyrenees, the lively and charismatic Pyrenean Shepherd dogs have been used for hundreds of years in the Pyrenees Mountains of southern France as the shepherd's helper, chiefly herding livestock but also providing good guardianship. The breed was virtually unknown outside its home until World War I, when thousands of them were drafted into active service and used as communications dogs— ferrying messages at high speed.

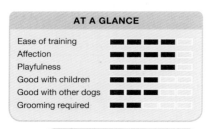

AT A GLANCE	
Ease of training	■■■■
Affection	■■■
Playfulness	■■■■
Good with children	■■
Good with other dogs	■■
Grooming required	■

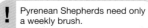

! Pyrenean Shepherds need only a weekly brush.

+ This breed remains moderately healthy. Though all adult dogs should be evaluated for hip dysplasia and eye problems.

HISTORY

Some argue that the Pyrenean Shepherd was present long before the arrival of the Roman armies that dominated Gaul and Hispania, and that they mixed with large molossers that the Romans had in their army. Other theories suggest that its origin is linked to the passage of the Vandals and Suebi through the Pyrenees to the south. After the first World War, the Pyrenean Shepherd, or "Pyr Shep", gained national recognition in France for their work as couriers, search and rescue dogs, watch dogs, and company mascots. The smooth-faced Pyrenean Shepherd may have been one of the foundation breeds for the Australian Shepherd.

Rough-haired Iletsua

Basque Shepherd dog

SPAIN

Exercise required

Common Coat Colors

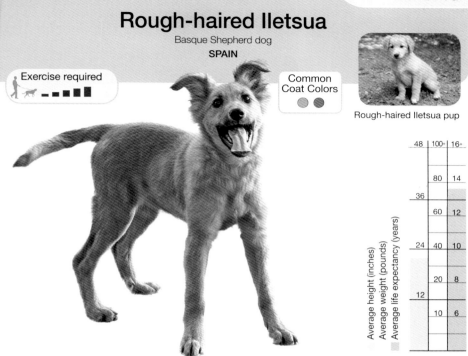

Rough-haired Iletsua pup

Average height (inches)	Average weight (pounds)	Average life expectancy (years)
48	100+	16+
	80	14
36		
	60	12
24	40	10
	20	8
12		
	10	6

The Basque Shepherd Dog originated in the Basque Country and was traditionally used by the local shepherds to help them take care of their cattle and sheep. Perro de pastor vasco (pastor vasco for short) is the Spanish name, and it is known as euskal artzain txakurra in the Basque, which is how they are known in their homeland. They are believed to have originated from Central European herding dogs.

AT A GLANCE

Ease of training	▬▬ ▬▬
Affection	▬▬ ▬▬
Playfulness	▬▬ ▬▬ ▬▬
Good with children	▬▬ ▬▬
Good with other dogs	▬▬ ▬▬
Grooming required	▬▬ ▬▬

 Iletsua means "hairy" or "shaggy" in Basque.

+ They are generally hardy and have no known health issues.

HISTORY

This is one of the oldest of all dog breeds. Remains were found in Neolithic caves that date back 12,000 years. They are thought to show that the people living in the area of what is now known as the Basque Country were once shepherds. There are representations of the Basque Shepherd Dog in sixteenth-century frescoes and paintings. Only after demonstrating their differences from other breeds such as the Pyrenean Shepherd and the Catalan Sheepdog, did the Royal Canine Society of Spain recognize the Basque Shepherd Dog as a breed with two varieties: Iletsua and Gorbeiakoa, in January 1996.

Schipperke

Spitzke

BELGIUM

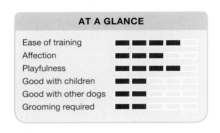

Schipperke pup

Exercise required

Average height (inches)
Average weight (pounds)
Average life expectancy (years)

48	100+	16+
36	80	14
	60	12
24	40	10
	20	8
12	10	6

Common Coat Colors

These small, black dogs were widely used for guarding and ratting by farmers, and were popular with boatmen on the waterways of Belgium and the Netherlands. It is believed that the Schipperke were related to the now-extinct Leauvenaar, which was related to the Belgian Shepherd. Their small size and protective personalities makes Schipperke's a lively breed that are well suited for a family in any living situation.

AT A GLANCE

Ease of training	
Affection	
Playfulness	
Good with children	
Good with other dogs	
Grooming required	

+ Legg-Calve-Perthes disease, autoimmune thyroiditis, epilepsy, patellar luxation.

! Schipperkes are known to live 15 years or more.

HISTORY

Originally from Belgium, this breed shares an ancestor with Leauvenaar's, which is a breed of black sheepdog. The Schipperke were bred to be small watchdogs. This differs from the Groenendael, which shares a common ancestor, but was developed to be herding dogs. The Schipperke were working dogs until 1885 when Queen Marie-Henriette owned one, instantly elevating the breed into high society and making it a fashionable dog to own. The Schipperke was recognized by the American Kennel Club in 1904.

Shetland Sheepdog

Sheltie

SCOTLAND

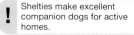
Exercise required

Shetland Sheepdog pup

Common Coat Colors	Average height (inches)	Average weight (pounds)	Average life expectancy (years)
	48	100+	16+
		80	14
	36		
		60	12
	24	40	10
		20	8
	12		
		10	6

The Shetland Sheepdog, also known as the "Sheltie", is a small working breed whose size is more than made up for by character. These dogs are very similar to working Collies, but at a much smaller scale. They share many characteristics with Collies and are exceptionally obedient dogs, making them easy to train and highly adaptable to a range of home situations. The Sheltie is both agile and highly intelligent, and is known to excel at agility and obedience classes.

AT A GLANCE

Ease of training	▰▰▰▰
Affection	▰▰▰▰
Playfulness	▰▰▰▰
Good with children	▰▰▰▰▰
Good with other dogs	▰▰▰▰
Grooming required	▰▰▰▰

! Shelties make excellent companion dogs for active homes.

+ Generally healthy, but hereditary problems can include hemophilia, cancer, Collie eye anomaly, cataracts, hip and elbow dysplasia.

HISTORY

The Shetland Sheepdog was developed on the Shetland Islands located off the northeast coast of Scotland in the 19th century. It is speculated that spitz-type dogs from Scandinavia may be an ancestor of the Sheltie, as well as smaller breeds such as the King Charles Spaniel and the Collie. Many who visited the Shetland Islands enjoyed the small dogs, and locals began to sell them to the visitors. James Loggie of Lerwick Kennels purchased many of these dogs and was one of the main early breeders. The Shetland Sheepdog was recognized by the American Kennel Club in 1911.

Shiloh Shepherd

Shiloh

UNITED STATES

Shiloh Shepherd pup

Common Coat Colors

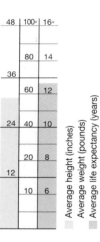

Average height (inches)
Average weight (pounds)
Average life expectancy (years)

48	100+	16+
	80	14
36		
	60	12
24	40	10
	20	8
12		
	10	6

Bred for their intelligence, size, and placid temperaments, the Shiloh Shepherd is a larger breed than the modern German Shepherd, and typically has a straighter back. They are predominantly bred as companion dogs, as Shilohs are very loyal and outgoing, and these gentle giants are excellent for working with children or other animals while still being very trainable for more practical applications such as assistive service, obedience, or herding.

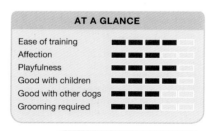

AT A GLANCE	
Ease of training	■ ■ ■ ■ ☐
Affection	■ ■ ■ ■ ■
Playfulness	■ ■ ■ ■ ■
Good with children	■ ■ ■ ■ ■
Good with other dogs	■ ■ ■ ☐ ☐
Grooming required	■ ■ ■ ☐ ☐

+ Possible issues with bloat and gastric torsion.

! Because of their gentle nature, Shiloh Shepherds are often used as therapy dogs.

HISTORY

A more modern breed, the Shiloh Shepherd was developed by Tina M. Barber of Shiloh Shepherds Kennel in New York. In an attempt to preserve the type of dog she had encountered during her childhood in Germany, she created this breed of dog which is able to be excellent family companions, intelligent, large in size, and physically and mentally strong. The International Shiloh Shepherd Dog Club was opened in 1997 and opened its own registry in 1998.

Smooth Collie

Collie

SCOTLAND

Exercise required

Smooth Collie pup

Common Coat Colors

		Average height (inches)	Average weight (pounds)	Average life expectancy (years)
		48	100+	16+
			80	14
		36		
			60	12
		24	40	10
			20	8
		12		
			10	6

Originally bred for herding livestock and protecting property, the Smooth Collie is an agile breed that make wonderful companion animals and make excellent additions to active homes. An especially athletic and energetic dog, Smooth Collies are known to excel in agility classes, herding classes, and any other manner of pursuits. They are an affection breed that will be heavily involved with family activities. They are also known to be very effective as guard dogs.

AT A GLANCE

Ease of training	▬ ▬ ▬ ▬ ▬
Affection	▬ ▬ ▬
Playfulness	▬ ▬ ▬ ▬
Good with children	▬ ▬ ▬
Good with other dogs	▬ ▬ ▬
Grooming required	▬ ▬

+ Collie eye anomaly, progressive retinal atrophy and epilepsy can be problems with this breed.

 They will vigorously bark if strangers approach their property.

HISTORY

While the modern version of this breed can be traced to the Victorian era, it is believed that the breed descended by ancient dogs bred by the Romans in approximately 400 AD. A batch of dogs were brought to Queen Victoria, and the Queen's interest in the breed made it a fashionable companion, and greatly sped along the transition from working dog to family pet.

Spanish Water Dog

Perro de Agua

SPAIN

Spanish Water Dog pup

Exercise required

Common
Coat Colors

48	100+	16+
36	80	14
	60	12
24	40	10
	20	8
12	10	6

Average height (inches)
Average weight (pounds)
Average life expectancy (years)

Bred on the Iberian Peninsula, this breed can be traced back at least 800 years. Primarily used for herding livestock in Spain, Spanish Water dogs were valued by fishermen as they guarded boats and helped to retrieve nets from the water. A vibrant and loyal breed, these dogs require a large amount of exercise, both mental and physical.

AT A GLANCE

Ease of training	
Affection	
Playfulness	
Good with children	
Good with other dogs	
Grooming required	

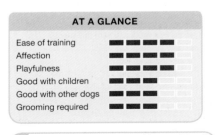

! These dogs have been used for a variety of tasks, including search and rescue, bomb detection, and therapy work.

+ Hip dysplasia, progressive retinal atrophy, addison's disease, cataracts.

HISTORY

This breed of dog originates in the wetlands of the Iberian Peninsula. The Spanish Water Dog is believed to have a common ancestor with the Portuguese Water Dog. Originally used for sheep herding, these dogs gained their notoriety by becoming a working dog for fishermen. This breed was recognized by the United Kennel Club in 2004.

St. Bernard

St. Bernhardshund / Bernhardiner

ITALY & SWITZERLAND

Exercise required

St. Bernard pup

Common Coat Colors

	48	100+	16+
		80	14
	36		
		60	12
		24	40	10
		20	8
	12		
		10	6

Average height (inches)
Average weight (pounds)
Average life expectancy (years)

Saint Bernards have functioned in the past as search-and-rescue dogs, for which the breed is famous. While they are excellent at finding people who have become lost in the mountains, they also make great companion dogs. These dogs are intelligent, kind, and protective, and make an amazing addition to a family home, provided they have the adequate space for their size. Saint Bernards are known to excel in obedience competitions, as well as draft and weight pulling.

AT A GLANCE	
Ease of training	■■ ■■ ■■
Affection	■■ ■■ ■■
Playfulness	■■ ■■
Good with children	■■ ■■ ■■ ■■ ■■
Good with other dogs	■■ ■■ ■■
Grooming required	■■ ■■ ■■

 Generally healthy, but hereditary problems can include hip and elbow dysplasia, gastric torsion, bone cancer and heart problems.

HISTORY

St. Bernards are named for the Great St. Bernard Hospice, established around 1050 by Saint Bernard de Menthon, located on a pass through the Western Alps. This hospice bred mastiff-type dogs with local farm dogs, and used them to protect livestock and property. There are early accounts of this breed rescuing lost travelers in the eighteenth century as a few of these dogs accompanied monks as they searched for survivors after storms. The American Kennel Club recognized the breed in 1885.

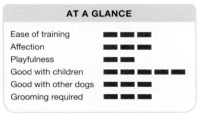 ! They make a superb addition to a family home.

Swedish Vallhund

Viking Dog / Swedish Shepherd Vallhund

SWEDEN

Swedish Vallhund pup

Exercise required

48	100+	16+
	80	14
36		
	60	12
24	40	10
	20	8
12		
	10	6

Average height (inches)
Average weight (pounds)
Average life expectancy (years)

Common Coat Colors

The Swedish Vallhund, also known as Viking Dog, is small in size but large in personality. It is hypothesized that the breed was taken to Wales around the eighth century, which lead to the creation of the Corgi breed, which are closely related to the Swedish Vallhund. The Swedish Vallhund is a multipurpose farm dog and is used to herd, hunt, track, and protecting livestock and property. Noted for its loyalty and energetic personality, this breed is a perfect fit for any active family or home.

AT A GLANCE

Ease of training	■■■■■
Affection	■■■■
Playfulness	■■■■
Good with children	■■■■■
Good with other dogs	■■■
Grooming required	■■■

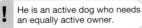

! He is an active dog who needs an equally active owner.

+ Hip dysplasia, patellar luxation, eye disease are common problems.

HISTORY

The breed is believed to have originated in Sweden, and can be traced back more than 1,000 years. It is thought that the Swedish Vallhund breed descended from the dogs of Vikings, due to their traced origins. They were used as predominantly herding dogs on farms in Sweden. The Swedish Vallhund was recognized by the Swedish Kennel Club in 1943.

Tamaskan Dog

Tam / Tamaskan Husky

FINLAND

Tamaskan Dog pup

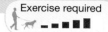

Exercise required

Common Coat Colors

	Average height (inches)	Average weight (pounds)	Average life expectancy (years)
	48	100+	16+
		80	14
	36		
		60	12
	24	40	10
		20	8
	12		
		10	6

The Tamaskan is a good family dog, being gentle with children and accepting of other dogs. Their high intelligence makes them an excellent working dog and has been known to exceed in agility and obedience as well as sled racing. This pack dog prefers not to be left alone for long periods of time. It is better suited to other human or canine company. Be sure you are this dog's pack leader, providing plenty of daily mental and physical exercise.

AT A GLANCE

Ease of training	■■ ■■ ■■ ■■
Affection	■■ ■■ ■■
Playfulness	■■ ■■ ■■ ■■
Good with children	■■ ■■ ■■
Good with other dogs	■■ ■■ ■■
Grooming required	■■ ■■ ■■

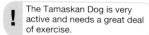

! The Tamaskan Dog is very active and needs a great deal of exercise.

+ Overall the Tamaskan breed is healthy with very few notable health issues.

HISTORY

Originating from Finland, Husky type dogs were imported from the USA in the early 1980s. These were mixed with other dogs including Siberian Husky, Alaskan Malamute and a small amount of German Shepherd. The aim was to create a breed of dog that looked like a wolf and had high intelligence and a good working ability.

Tosa
Tosa Inu / Tosa Ken
JAPAN

Tosa pup

Exercise required

48	100+	16+
36	80	14
	60	12
24	40	10
	20	8
12	10	6

Average height (inches)
Average weight (pounds)
Average life expectancy (years)

This natural guard dog is protective, courageous and fearless. It needs an owner who knows how to display leadership at all times. Socialized this dog well starting at puppyhood. Aggression and attacks on people are due to poor handling and training. Problems arise when an owner allows the dog to believe he is pack leader over humans and/or does not give the dog the mental and physical daily exercise it needs to be stable.

Common Coat Colors

AT A GLANCE

Ease of training	
Affection	
Playfulness	
Good with children	
Good with other dogs	
Grooming required	

! It is definitely unsuitable for beginner owners.

+ Bloat can be a major problem in these large dogs.

HISTORY
The Tosa has been bred for hundreds of years in Japan. The country has a long history of dog fighting, beginning in the 14th century. The Tosa is a rare breed, even in its native land and has only recently been introduced to the USA. Unfortunately, this breed is banned in some countries as a dangerous breed.

Welsh Sheepdog
Welsh Collie
WALES

Welsh Sheepdog pup

Exercise required

Average height (inches)	Average weight (pounds)	Average life expectancy (years)
48	100+	16+
	80	14
36		
	60	12
24	40	10
	20	8
12		
	10	6

Common Coat Colors

Welsh Sheepdogs are normally bred for their herding abilities rather than appearance, and so they are generally somewhat variable in build, color and size. Welsh Sheepdogs that exhibit basic herding instincts can be trained to compete in stock dog trials.

AT A GLANCE

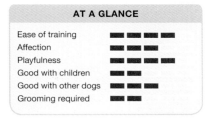

Ease of training	
Affection	
Playfulness	
Good with children	
Good with other dogs	
Grooming required	

+ They are very hardy animals but can suffer from Hip Dysplasia.

HISTORY

During the 18th century Welsh drovers taking sheep for sale took with them five or six Welsh Sheepdogs as herders on the narrow roads, guards against highwaymen, and providers of game on the route.

! Welsh Sheepdogs can compete in dog agility trials.

GUARDIAN DOGS

Abruzzese Mastiff

Pastore Abruzzese / Pastore Abruzzese / Abruzzese Sheepdog / Cane da Pecora

ITALY

Exercise required

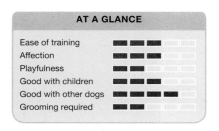

Abruzzese puppy

48+	100+	16+
	80	14
36		
	60	12
24	40	10
	20	8
12		
	10	6

Average height (inches)
Average weight (lbs)
Average life expectancy

Common Coat Colors

The enormous white Abruzzese Mastiff has long played the roles of guardian to property and protector of livestock. With its distrust of strangers—whether human or canine—this dog is not suited for the role of suburban pet. Still, its intelligence, courage, and loyalty make it a suitable companion and guard dog for experienced owners.

AT A GLANCE

Ease of training	▮▮▮▮▯▯▯
Affection	▮▮▮▮▯▯▯
Playfulness	▮▮▮▯▯▯▯
Good with children	▮▮▮▮▯▯▯
Good with other dogs	▮▮▮▮▮▯▯
Grooming required	▮▮▯▯▯▯▯

! Some Abruzzese Mastiff males reportedly exceed 220 pounds in size.

+ The Abruzzese Mastiff breed is known to be affected by hip dysplasia, bloat, sensitivity to anesthesia, and rapid weight gain.

HISTORY

The Abruzzese Mastiff is an ancient breed of sheepdog, long prized in its Italian homeland for its skill at protecting livestock. With a history that dates back at least 2,000 years, this breed is a descendant of the even more ancient Alabai and the great white dogs of the Balkans, and it is an ancestor to the Great Pyrenees and the St. Bernard. Even with its venerable history, it is no longer well-known and, like many other rare molossers (a line of large, solidly built dogs), has an uncertain future.

Alapaha Blue Blood Bulldog

Otto Bulldog

UNITED STATES

Alapaha Blue Blood Bulldog puppy

Exercise required

Common Coat Colors

	48+	100+	16+
		80	14
	36		
		60	12
		24	40	10
		20	8
	12		
		10	6

Average height (inches)
Average weight (lbs)
Average life expectancy

The sturdy, muscular Alapaha Blue Blood Bulldog is considered Southern "royalty," with a long tradition as a livestock dog. Alert and quickly trainable and with a high guarding instinct, this protective dog makes an excellent watchdog for children. It is a real lover with a lot of heart, and, for an inexperienced owner, it can be an affectionate and loyal family pet.

AT A GLANCE

Ease of training	▄▄ ▄▄ ▄▄
Affection	▄▄ ▄▄ ▄▄
Playfulness	▄▄ ▄▄ ▄▄
Good with children	▄▄ ▄▄ ▄▄
Good with other dogs	▄▄ ▄▄
Grooming required	▄▄

 This breed developed in the southern United States and may take his name from the Alapaha River in Georgia.

✚ Health issues include hip dysplasia, deafness, skin problems, and eye problems such as entropion (inversion of the eyelids).

HISTORY

The early history of this American breed is unclear, but it is most associated with the South. It is believed that its roots trace back to old bulldog types that were introduced to the United States in the 1800s. The Alapaha Blue Blood Bulldog results from three generations of a breeding program intended to rescue the "plantation dog" of southern Georgia, which was nearly extinct. They were bred for working ability, stamina, and bravery until a distinct type began to emerge.

217

Alentejo Mastiff

Rafeiro do Alentejo / Portuguese Mastiff

PORTUGAL

Alentejo Mastiff puppy

Exercise required

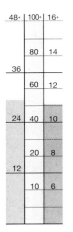

48+	100+	16+
	80	14
36		
	60	12
24	40	10
	20	8
12		
	10	6

Average height (inches)
Average weight (lbs)
Average life expectancy

Common Coat Colors

The powerful Alentejo Mastiff, with its bearlike head, is a very large molosser type of dog that originated in Portugal. Although it is not an aggressive breed, it is best raised by an experienced handler that can patiently work to properly socialize it. The well-trained adult tends to be sweet and affectionate with its family and docile with children. Brave, vigilant, and very territorial, it will protect any flock or family that it considers under its protection.

AT A GLANCE

Ease of training	■■ ■■
Affection	■■ ■■ ■■
Playfulness	■■ ■■ ■■
Good with children	■■ ■■
Good with other dogs	■■ ■■ ■■ ■■ ■■
Grooming required	■■ ■■ ■■

! The standard describes this breed as "sober"—an adjective befitting a dog with such a calm expression.

+ Little health data exists for the Alentejo Mastiff, but as with other large dogs, hip dysplasia may occur, although it is not common in this breed.

HISTORY

It is uncertain when this breed of the very ancient molosser type arrived in what is now Portugal, but it eventually became a proficient herder, known for moving flocks of sheep from Northern Portugal to the plateaus of the South, and then back again. As the practice of livestock raising began to decline, so too did the Alentejo Mastiff. Fanciers, however, have kept this dog from extinction, and although it is still listed as vulnerable, the Rafeiro is recognized internationally as a registered breed, and is still found as a companion and guard dog.

American Bulldog

Old Country Bulldog
UNITED STATES

American Bulldog puppy

Exercise required

	Average height (inches)	Average weight (lbs)	Average life expectancy
	48+	100+	16+
		80	14
	36		
		60	12
	24	40	10
		20	8
	12		
		10	6

Common Coat Colors

+ Generally healthy, but hereditary problems can include hip and elbow dysplasia, entropion, and cancer.

! Bulldogs can't swim. Their massive head, solid torso, and short legs limit their ability to stay above water.

The American Bulldog is a gentle giant—brawny and athletic in build but sweet and affectionate in temperament. This kid-loving dog needs regular physical exercise to keep fit and plenty of mental challenges to stave off boredom. Effective training is key—an owner who asserts the role of pack leader will be rewarded with a happy, loyal companion that will protect its people and property. There are two types of American Bulldog: the Standard and the Bully. The Bully is larger, stockier, and has a shorter muzzle.

AT A GLANCE

Ease of training	
Affection	
Playfulness	
Good with children	
Good with other dogs	
Grooming required	

HISTORY

Much controversy surrounds the origins of this breed, but it likely traces back to the selective breeding of bulldogs and bull terriers that British, northern European, and Spanish colonists brought to America in the 1600s and 1700s. They were versatile working farm dogs, protecting homes and livestock, herding cattle, hunting large game, and serving as companions. Sadly, they were also used for fighting. Eventually numbers dwindled, but the breeding initiative of John D. Johnston developed and revitalized the modern American Bulldog, which is now a popular breed with a dedicated following.

219

American Mastiff

UNITED STATES

American Mastiff puppy

Exercise required

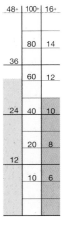

Average height (inches)
Average weight (lbs)
Average life expectancy

Common Coat Colors

The heaviest of all breeds, the American Mastiff is at heart a gentle and dignified dog. A well-trained and well-socialized mastiff will be calm and affectionate and will courageously protect its family. It loves children, but because of its vast size (often weighing more than 200 pounds), it should be supervised with them. These dogs make good companions for people who will make them part of the home and can provide them with enough space and strong leadership.

AT A GLANCE

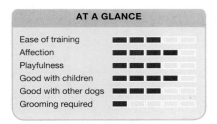

Ease of training	
Affection	
Playfulness	
Good with children	
Good with other dogs	
Grooming required	

+ Little reliable data exists on this new breed, but it is probably prone to the same problems as the English Mastiff, such as joint dysplasia and entropion.

HISTORY

The Mastiff is an ancient type that was traditionally used in war and as guard dogs, but the American Mastiff is a recent addition to the type, only gaining official purebred status in 2000. It owes its origins to Fredericka Wagner of Flying W Farms in Piketon, Ohio, who selectively bred English Mastiffs and Anatolian Shepherd Dogs to establish a breed of companion dog that would have sound health and a good-natured temperament—and would also produce less slobber than other mastiff breeds.

! All puppies are born dark and then lighten, becoming a shade of fawn by the time they reach a year old.

Anatolian Shepherd Dog

Anatolian Karabash Dog

TURKEY

Anatolian Shepherd puppy

Exercise required

	Average height (inches)	Average weight (lbs)	Average life expectancy
	48+	100+	16+
		80	14
	36		
		60	12
	24	40	10
		20	8
	12		
		10	6

Common Coat Colors

This is an ancient breed that originated in Turkey and is perfectly adapted to the harsh climate and difficult terrain of its home. The Anatolian Shepherd has been bred to guard livestock, living unsupervised among the herd, and is incredibly tough with great endurance. They can make good companion animals but thrive when given a job to do. They are loyal and protective toward their families, but are also intelligent, independent thinkers and do not always respond to commands!

AT A GLANCE

Ease of training	■■ ■■
Affection	■■ ■■
Playfulness	■■ ■■
Good with children	■■ ■■
Good with other dogs	■■ ■■
Grooming required	■■ ■■

+ Anatolian Shepherds can be prone to hip dysplasia, elbow dysplasia, hypothyroidism, and von Willebrand's disease, and thrombopathia.

HISTORY

This rugged breed originated in Asia Minor, where it was perfectly adapted to the harsh climate and difficult terrain of its home in the Anatolian plateaus. There, the nomadic population depended on sheep and goats for survival—and on the dog that protected them. For centuries, it ancestors were also combat and hunting dogs; today, it is still bred as a shepherd or guard, and as also a companion dog.

! Eager for affection, it is patient and protective of kids, but they should be supervised and properly introduced.

Armenian Gampr Dog

ARMENIA

Armenian Gampr puppy

Exercise required

Common Coat Colors

48+	100+	16+
	80	14
36		
	60	12
24	40	10
	20	8
12		
	10	6

Average height (inches)
Average weight (lbs)
Average life expectancy

Highly variable in appearance and personality, the Armenian Gampr is a very large, heavy-boned dog with a muscular physique. Known for its double coat and feathered flanks, it ranges in color from snowy white to brindled black. Bred as a livestock guardian, it can also be a lovely companion dog. It usually forms bonds with children and women first and recognizes who is the family's leader. Once this lovable dog sees that it is a valued member, it will be loyal and protective. It will, however, retain its shepherd's urge to patrol and thrives on large acreages.

AT A GLANCE

Ease of training	■■ ■■ ■■ □□
Affection	■■ ■■ ■■ □□
Playfulness	■■ ■■ ■■ □□
Good with children	■■ ■■ ■■ □□
Good with other dogs	■■ ■■ □□ □□
Grooming required	■■ ■■ □□ □□

+ Armenian Gamprs are considered to be a healthy breed with no genetic health concerns.

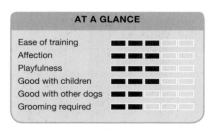

! The modern Gampr is nearly identical to it ancestors, looking and behaving much the same over 3,000 years.

HISTORY

This breed originated thousands of years ago in the Armenian Highland, now known as Anatolia, and the Southern Caucasus region. Valued as a shepherd and guard, this dog traveled with its nomadic owners and spread through Europe and Central Asia. In modern times, the USSR used Gamprs in a breeding program that produced the Caucasian Ovcharka. After its dissolution, Armenian breeders made a concerted effort to preserve the original Gampr, and this venerable breed is now officially recognized.

Bakharwal Dog

Kashmir Sheepdog / Bakarwal Mastiff

INDIA

Bakharwal Dog puppy

Exercise required

		Average height (inches)	Average weight (lbs)	Average life expectancy
		48+	100+	16+
			80	14
		36		
			60	12
		24	40	10
			20	8
		12		
			10	6

Common Coat Colors

The Bakharwal is a large, rugged sheepdog breed famous for its ferocious defense of its flock against predators. It is well-muscled and agile, with a deep chest, straight back, and broad shoulders, along with long legs that make it a superb runner and chaser. For a patient and consistent handler, this dog will express its natural gentle and obedient nature and steadfastly guard a loving family. With its high energy, it is best suited to a home that affords it a fenced place to roam, and it will treat any other pets as part of its flock.

AT A GLANCE

Ease of training	▬▬▬▬▬
Affection	▬▬▬
Playfulness	▬▬▬▬
Good with children	▬▬▬▬
Good with other dogs	▬▬▬▬
Grooming required	▬▬

+ The Bakharwal is a robust breed, and it rarely suffers from common canine health problems.

HISTORY

Its precise origins are unknown, but the Bakharwal is a slimmer variant of an ancient molosser type that traces its roots to the Himalayas. For hundreds of years, pastoral tribes of India and Pakistan, including the Gujjar, bred it to protect their livestock and settlements. From this comes its alternate breed names, Gujjar Watchdog and Gujjar Dog. Today, the Indian state of Jammu and Kashmir is the main stronghold of this breed. Its minimal recognition outside of India has put it in danger of extinction.

 The Bakharwal Dog is highly unusual in that it doesn't eat flesh and requires a milk and vegetarian diet.

Belgian Laekenois

Chien de Berger Belge
BELGUIM

Belgian Laekenois puppy

Exercise required

Common Coat Colors

48+	100+	16+	
	80	14	
36			
	60	12	
24	40	10	
	20	8	
12			
	10	6	

Average height (inches)
Average weight (lbs)
Average life expectancy

The elegant Belgian Laekenois is a strong, agile, well-muscled dog, lively and alert. It is a highly social breed and is best suited for an active family that takes it along on its adventures. Its sheepdog pedigree means it is highly intelligent and very protective, and it thrives when it has a job to perform. It excels as at police work and search and rescue, or tracking, herding, or sled pulling. It is also an excellent guide dog for the blind and assistant to the disabled.

AT A GLANCE

Ease of training	▰▰▰▰▱
Affection	▰▰▰▰▱
Playfulness	▰▰▰▱▱
Good with children	▰▰▰▱▱
Good with other dogs	▰▰▰▱▱
Grooming required	▰▰▱▱▱

 During World War I and World War II, the Belgian Laekenois was employed as a messenger dog.

➕ Generally healthy, but hereditary problems can include epilepsy and cancer.

HISTORY

Considered both the oldest and rarest of the four native Belgian breeds, the Laekenois takes its name from the Royal Castle of Laeken, home to the royal family of Belgium. In fact, it is said to have been the favorite breed of nineteenth-century Queen Marie Henriette, who used the Laekenois to guard sheep on her estate. Throughout Belgium, this ever-vigilant dog was put to work protecting livestock and property, and it was also often made the guardian of linen drying in the fields.

Berger Blanc Suisse

White Swiss Shepherd Dog / Snowy Shepherd
SWITZERLAND

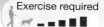

Exercise required

Berger Blanc Suisse puppy

Average height (inches)	Average weight (lbs)	Average life expectancy
48+	100+	16+
	80	14
36		
	60	12
24	40	10
	20	8
12		
	10	6

Common Coat Colors

Its snowy white coat defines the Berger Blanc Suisse—hence its alternate name, the White Swiss Shepherd Dog. It is highly intelligent and was once valued as a guardian of livestock, but it is now also often recruited for military and police work or search and rescue. This is an energetic breed that is playful with children and fits in well with an active family. It is good-natured around its family, but is wary of strangers—a trait that makes it an excellent watchdog.

AT A GLANCE

Ease of training	■■ ■■ ■■
Affection	■■ ■■ ■■
Playfulness	■■ ■■ ■■
Good with children	■■ ■■ ■■ ■■
Good with other dogs	■■ ■■
Grooming required	■■ ■■

+ This is a generally healthy breed, but hereditary problems can include hip dysplasia.

! This breed loves having tasks to perform and often excels at dog sports.

HISTORY

Sharing the same ancestry as the German Shepherd, this breed was once valued for the white coloring that made it easily distinguishable from predator wolves. As the darker colors rose in popularity, however, it was blamed for diluting the stock, resulting in a German ban on its registration. Yet, North Americans still loved the white dog. From an American-bred stud named Lobo, born in 1966, the breed was re-established in Europe, and in 2003, the FCI recognized it as the Berger Blanc Suisse.

225

Black Russian Terrier

Tchiorny Terrier / Sobaka Stalina
RUSSIA

Exercise required

Black Russian Terrier puppy

48+	100+	16+
	80	14
36		
	60	12
24	40	10
	20	8
12		
	10	6

Average height (inches) · Average weight (lbs) · Average life expectancy

Common Coat Colors

The extremely intelligent Black Russian Terrier is a fairly large dog with well-developed musculature and a distinctive wiry double coat. It is a hard-working breed, that was bred mainly as a guard dog, but it also excels as a working or sporting dog. With an experienced owner, it can be socialized as an protective and loyal companion dog that will love to play with kids.

AT A GLANCE

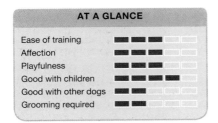

Ease of training
Affection
Playfulness
Good with children
Good with other dogs
Grooming required

! To maintain the distinctive look of its coat, this dog usually needs two to three haircuts per year.

+ This breed is prone to some hereditary diseases: hip dysplasia; elbow dysplasia; hyperurisosuria; juvenile laryngeal paralysis; progressive retinal atrophy.

HISTORY

The Black Russian Terrier is not a true terrier: its pedigree includes crossings of more than 20 breeds such as the Giant Schnauzer, Rottweiler, Newfoundland, and Airedale. In the 1930s, the state-owned Red Star Kennels in Moscow developed it to serve as a low-maintenance and robust military/working dog that was adaptable to various tasks and climates, and it originally worked with military police in prisons and at border crossings and as guard dogs in military areas.

Boerboel

South African Mastiff

SOUTH AFRICA

Boerboel puppy

Exercise required

Average height (inches)	Average weight (lbs)	Average life expectancy
48+	100+	16+
	80	14
36		
	60	12
24	40	10
	20	8
12		
	10	6

Common Coat Colors

The Boerboel is an imposing animal, with a strong bone structure and well-developed muscles so that it carries itself with confidence and powerful movement. Obedient and smart, it has strong watchdog instincts and tends to be protective of its family and territory. This breed is also very playful and affectionate and will be gentle and patient with children.

AT A GLANCE

Ease of training	■■ ■■ ■■
Affection	■■ ■■ ■■
Playfulness	■■ ■■ ■■
Good with children	■■ ■■ ■■
Good with other dogs	■■ ■■
Grooming required	■■

+ Generally healthy, but they can be prone to hip or elbow dysplasia, and juvenile epilepsy (with attacks brought on by metabolic changes or stress).

! Because it always wants to be with its owner, the Boerboel has earned the nickname Velcro dog.

HISTORY

In 1652, Dutch colonist Jan van Riebeeck arrived at the Cape of Good Hope, South Africa, with his dog, a Bullenbijter. This large, heavy mastiff bred with native South African stock, and then, over time, other sturdy European dogs introduced to the area contributed their genes to the development of the breed, resulting in a dog with mastiff appearance and great endurance and hardiness. Boerboels were required to be fearless guard dogs as well as utilitarian farmworkers.

Briard
Berger de Brie
FRANCE

Briard puppy

Exercise required

48+	100+	16+
	80	14
36		
	60	12
24	40	10
	20	8
12		
	10	6

Average height (inches)
Average weight (lbs)
Average life expectancy

Common
Coat Colors

The shaggy Briard has a long history of working with humans, which has made it very trainable and eager to please. It is a gentle, sweet-natured pet, as well as loyal and protective of its family—but it is an independent thinker and wary of strangers. This breed is intelligent and needs plenty of outdoor activity to be really happy; originally bred as a working dog, the Briard will become restless and can develop behavioral problems if not exercised enough.

AT A GLANCE	
Ease of training	▪▪▪▫▫
Affection	▪▪▪▪▪
Playfulness	▪▪▪▪▫
Good with children	▪▪▪▪▫
Good with other dogs	▪▫▫▫▫
Grooming required	▪▪▪▪▫

 Generally very healthy, but they can be prone to panosteitis, cutaneous lymphoma, progressive retinol atrophy, and hypothyroidism.

! A born worker, the Briard shines in obedience, agility, herding, carting, and tracking competitions.

HISTORY
This ancient working breed has a long history in Gaul: the eight-century Frankish King Charlemagne is depicted with Briards by his side, and, centuries later, Napoléon Bonaparte kept two Briards, possibly as guard dogs. With its fearless nature, it was long employed as a guardian of livestock herds and property. During World War I, the French army deployed it—almost to the point of extinction—as a sentry dog, ammunition carrier, messenger, and medic dog.

Broholmer

Danish Mastiff

DENMARK

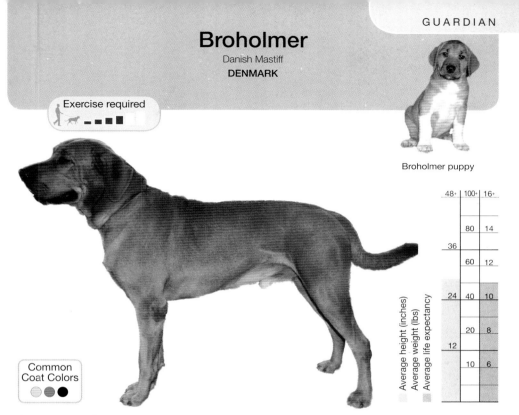

Broholmer puppy

Exercise required

▪▫▪■■

Common Coat Colors
⬤◐⬤●

	Average height (inches)	Average weight (lbs)	Average life expectancy
	48+	100+	16+
		80	14
	36		
		60	12
	24	40	10
		20	8
	12		
		10	6

A large, powerful dog with a resounding bark and dominant strut, the Broholmer strongly resembles a mastiff. Despite its imposing appearance and voice, it possesses a calm, good-tempered character. It is a natural watchdog and on the alert with strangers. A well-trained Broholmer is a friendly and loyal companion, always ready to look out for its family.

AT A GLANCE

Ease of training	▬ ▬ ▬
Affection	▬ ▬
Playfulness	▬ ▬
Good with children	▬ ▬ ▬ ▬
Good with other dogs	▬ ▬ ▬
Grooming required	▬ ▬

 The nineteenth-century Danish king, Frederick VII and his consort, Countess Danner, owned Broholmers.

✚ The Danish Broholmer is a healthy breed, though, as with larger breeds, it may be prone to canine hip dysplasia and canine bloat.

HISTORY

This rare breed developed in the 1500s from English and other mastiff types. This noble-looking dog has a long association with the Danish aristocracy, who often gave it as a gift. Named after royal gamekeeper Sehested of Broholm, by the late 1700s it had increased in number, and it was used for hunting and guarding property and livestock. The strife of World War II almost took this breed to extinction: by the 1970s, it had almost disappeared but was saved through the efforts of the Danish Kennel Club.

Bulldog

British Bulldog
ENGLAND

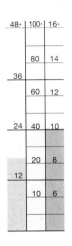

Bulldog puppy

Exercise required

48+	100+	16+
	80	14
36		
	60	12
24	40	10
	20	8
12		
	10	6

Average height (inches)
Average weight (lbs)
Average life expectancy

Common Coat Colors

The charming Bulldog of today descends from a line of bull-baiting dogs—but it looks little like its fierce ancestor and has a far different temperament. Selective breeding has produced a shorter, heavier appearance and an amiable and placid demeanor that makes it a perfect companion and family dog. It still possesses the determination and independence of its ancestors, but is also has a personable character and a distinct look that is both comical and endearing.

AT A GLANCE

Ease of training	■ ■ ■
Affection	■ ■ ■ ■ ■
Playfulness	■ ■ ■ ■
Good with children	■ ■ ■ ■ ■
Good with other dogs	■ ■ ■ ■
Grooming required	■ ■

 Generally healthy, but hereditary problems can include brachycephalic syndrome, hip dysplasia, heart conditions, cancer, and eye problems.

! Due to their oversized heads, female bulldogs have trouble giving birth and often need a caesarian.

HISTORY

The Bulldog was bred to partake in the violent sport of bull baiting. Its projecting lower jaw meant it could clamp onto a bull's nose with an unshakable grip. Brave and ferocious, it would never give up the fight. Lighter and leggier than today's Bulldog, the original had a more athletic body, but still had a low center of gravity, a plus when baiting bulls. The 1835 bull baiting ban in England saw its numbers dwindle until fanciers started breeding dogs with placid temperaments and exaggerated physical appearance.

Bullmastiff

ENGLAND

Exercise required

Bullmastiff puppy

	Average height (inches)	Average weight (lbs)	Average life expectancy
	48+	100+	16+
		80	14
	36		
		60	12
	24	40	10
		20	8
	12		
		10	6

Common Coat Colors

Beloved of the English gentry, who once relied on this large breed to guard their estates from poachers, the Bullmastiff is an athletic, quiet, and gentle dog that fits in well with an experienced dog-owning family. It must have rigorous training, but the result will be an even-tempered dog with an affectionate disposition that is tolerant of children and even the family cat. Devoted and loyal, it will be both companion and protector, craving time with its people.

AT A GLANCE

Ease of training	▬
Affection	▬ ▬ ▬
Playfulness	▬
Good with children	▬ ▬ ▬ ▬
Good with other dogs	▬ ▬ ▬
Grooming required	▬

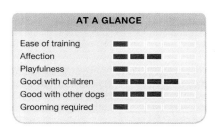

! The Bullmastiffs is known for snorting, snuffling, wheezing, grunting, and snoring. It also slobbers and drools.

+ Generally healthy, but hereditary problems include heart, skeletal and joint problems, bloat, kidney failure, hypothyroidism, entropion, cancer, and allergies.

HISTORY

The Bullmastiff breed was founded in England as early as 1795 by mating Mastiffs with Bulldogs. The 60-40 cross resulted in a calm but fearless dog, well-suited to guard large estates. Gamekeepers found it an ideal helper: powerful, intelligent, and brave. It used its stealthy tracking ability to locate poachers even in the dark. Although ferocious, it was trained to tackle the intruder, but never bite, holding him until the gamekeeper caught up. It was later used as a hunting guard, army and police dog, and as a watchdog.

Bully Kutta

Pakistani Mastiff / Sindh Mastiff / Bohli Kutta

PAKISTAN

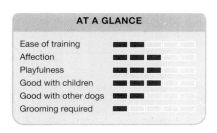

Bully Kutta puppy

Exercise required

48+	100+	16+
	80	14
36		
	60	12
24	40	10
	20	8
12		
	10	6

Average height (inches)
Average weight (lbs)
Average life expectancy

Common Coat Colors

Nicknamed the Beast from the East, the Bully Kutta is a large, powerful dog. Suited only for an experienced owner who can rigorously train and socialize it (and maintain its alpha status over it), it is a protective dog that makes an excellent guard for home and family. For a responsible owner, it can be an intensely loyal pet, and well-raised members of the breed are even good with kids, loving, and playful. It must have a lot of space and regular walks to be happy.

AT A GLANCE

Ease of training	
Affection	
Playfulness	
Good with children	
Good with other dogs	
Grooming required	

! In Punjabi (the language of the historical Province of Punjab of Pakistan), its name means "heavily wrinkled dog."

+ Generally very healthy, but they can be prone to developing arthritis, blindness, and bloating.

HISTORY

Theories abound about this breed's origin. It may be the result of the interbreeding of a mastiff-type dog already present in Pakistan or India with the Mastiffs, Bull Terriers, and other breeds that British soldiers brought with them when Britain conquered the subcontinent. Another theory suggests that the breed originated in the desert areas of Sindh—hence the alternate name Sindh Mastiff. It was bred as a guard dog, although it was also used for the now-illegal sport of dog fighting.

Cane Corso

Italian Mastiff
ITALY

Cane Corso puppy

Exercise required

		Average height (inches)	Average weight (lbs)	Average life expectancy
		48+	100+	16+
			80	14
		36		
			60	12
		24	40	10
			20	8
		12		
			10	6

Common Coat Colors

This energetic, muscular dog takes its name from the Latin word *cohors,* meaning "guardian and protector," and that is what the Cane Corso was bred to do—watch over livestock and homesteads, as well as act as a hunting dog for large or ferocious game. For a very experienced dog-owner, who will be both firm and loving, it will make a fiercely loyal and protective companion that works hard to please its family while remaining wary of strangers. Its sad eyes and wobbly muzzle belie the fact that this is an athletic breed that needs physical challenges: it is at home on a ranch or farm and will flourish as a competitor in dog sports.

AT A GLANCE

Ease of training	▬▬▬ ▬▬▬ ▬▬
Affection	▬▬▬ ▬▬▬ ▬▬▬
Playfulness	▬▬▬ ▬▬
Good with children	▬▬▬ ▬▬▬ ▬▬
Good with other dogs	▬▬
Grooming required	▬▬

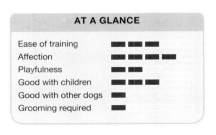

! Cane Corso are droolers and noisemakers, with a loud snore and a throaty *woo-wooooo* bark.

✚ Cane Corso health problems can include bloat, entropion, ectropion, cherry eye, hip dysplasia, epilepsy, and panosteitis.

HISTORY

This Italian dog is an ancient breed. Its genealogy probably traces back to the Canis Pugnax, a Roman war dog of the first century that would accompany its handler onto the battlefield. It also appeared in arenas, forced to fight wild animals for the spectators' amusement, and was a big-game hunting dog. Italian farmers eventually adopted this breed as a working dog, but with the decline of agriculture, it faced extinction. Happily, in the 1970s, fanciers help restore the noble Cane Corso.

Cardigan Welsh Corgi

Cardi

WALES

Cardigan Welsh Corgi puppy

Exercise required

Common Coat Colors

The Cardigan Welsh Corgi, or Cardi, is a tough and sturdy breed that earned its place as a highly prized all-weather working farm dog. Agile and bold, it could take advantage of its low-slung body to nip at the heels of the cattle in its care, urging them to move along while deftly avoiding their kicks. It also earned a reputation as an efficient vermin exterminator. Now bred mainly as a family dog, it is frisky and intelligent, with an outsize personality and an abundance of charm. Like many of its category, it craves mental and physical challenges and will make an engaging companion dog for an active family.

	Average height (inches)	Average weight (lbs)	Average life expectancy
	48+	100+	16+
		80	14
	36	60	12
	24	40	10
		20	8
	12		
		10	6

AT A GLANCE

Ease of training	■ ■ ■
Affection	■ ■ ■ ■
Playfulness	■ ■ ■ ■
Good with children	■ ■ ■ ■ ■
Good with other dogs	■ ■ ■ ■
Grooming required	■ ■ ■

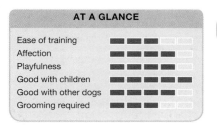

! A Cardi adores children, but it must learn to fight its instinct to "herd" them by nipping at their ankles!

+ This is a healthy breed, but hereditary problems can include intervertebral disc disease, progressive retinal atrophy, and urolithiasis.

HISTORY

The origins of the Cardigan Welsh Corgi are uncertain. Sharing ancestors with the Dachshund and the Basset Hound, it probably arrived in Wales more than 3,000 years ago, brought there by Celtic tribes who migrated from central Europe. Once ensconced in its Welsh home, it made itself indispensable to agriculture—so highly valued that an ancient law rendered severe penalties on those who harmed or stole one. Until 1934, the Cardi was considered a single breed with the Pembroke Welsh Corgi.

Central Asian Shepherd Dog

Central Asian Ovtcharka / Central Asian Sheepdog / CAS

RUSSIA

Central Asian Shepherd
Dog puppy

Exercise required

Common
Coat Colors

	Average height (inches)	Average weight (lbs)	Average life expectancy
	48+	100+	16+
		80	14
	36		
		60	12
	24	40	10
		20	8
	12		
		10	6

Large and muscular, the Central Asian Shepherd is known for its calm demeanor and fearless defense of its flock. Bred as a guard dog, it still excels at this duty. It will form a deep attachment to its master, who must be an experienced owner who can properly train and socialize this independent animal, understanding its instinctive pack mentality and establishing a leadership role over it. This dog needs ample (and fenced-in) outdoor space, and given work to accomplish, it will reward its family with steadfast loyalty and vigilant protection.

AT A GLANCE

Ease of training	▬▬ ▬▬ ▬▬
Affection	▬▬ ▬▬ ▬▬
Playfulness	▬▬ ▬▬ ▬▬
Good with children	▬▬ ▬▬ ▬▬
Good with other dogs	▬▬
Grooming required	▬▬ ▬▬

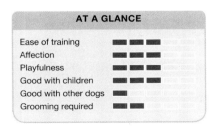

! Renown for destroying predators, it has earned the Russian name *Volkodav,* or "The Wolf Crusher."

 Bred to be healthy, it can still suffer from hip dysplasia, patellar luxation, elbow dysplasia, various joint problems, obesity, and bloat.

HISTORY

With a history dating back at least 4,000 years, the exact origins of the Central Asian Shepherd are unknown. For thousands of years, it was called into duty to protect livestock and nomadic herdsmen on the vast plains of Central Asia, where it still remains a popular working dog. Now being bred in the United States, the majority of this breed is found in areas of Iran and Afghanistan to Siberia. In Russia, where the CAS was once a stalwart, it has lost favor to the larger Caucasian Sheepdog.

Chinese Chongqing Dog

East Sichuan Hunting Dog / Linshui Dog / Pak Tin Par Dog

CHINA

Chinese Chongqing Dog puppy

Exercise required

48+	100+	16+
	80	14
36		
	60	12
24	40	10
	20	8
12		
	10	6

Average height (inches)
Average weight (lbs)
Average life expectancy

Common Coat Colors

Nearly unknown beyond the borders of its Chinese homeland, the rare Chinese Chongqing is an intelligent, dignified dog. With a fearless and alert nature, it is a natural guardian. This dog must have proper training and socialization to successfully integrate into a family, however, and demands a strong, experienced leader who communicates well with it. It does best in a quiet household, which it will guard with the utmost care and bravery. Even a well-trained Chongqing will never be friendly with newcomers and will always be on the lookout in their presence.

AT A GLANCE

Ease of training	▰▰▰
Affection	▰▰▰▰
Playfulness	▰▰▰
Good with children	▰▰▰▰
Good with other dogs	▰▰
Grooming required	▰

+ No inbreeding of this breed means that it avoids most major canine health issues, although some can develop skin problems.

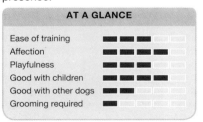

! Chongqings love exercise and make good jogging and hiking companions.

HISTORY

Pottery statuettes from the Han Dynasty (206 BC–AD 220), unearthed near the city that gives this dog its name, give researchers a clue to the breed's heritage—many of the statuettes bear a striking resemblance to the Chongqing dog of today. It was long valued as a guardian and hunter, but the establishment of the People's Republic of China in 1949 resulted in a precipitous decline in its numbers, and it was relegated to rural areas. Still an extremely rare dog, even in China, it now most often serves as a protector of family and property.

Chinese Shar-Pei

Chinese Fighting Dog
CHINA

Chinese Shar-Pei puppy

Exercise required

Average height (inches)	Average weight (lbs)	Average life expectancy
48+	100+	16+
	80	14
36		
	60	12
24	40	10
	20	8
12		
	10	6

Common Coat Colors

There is no mistaking the Shar-Pei, with its slightly oversized head, hippopotamus muzzle, blue-black tongue, and signature wrinkles. Originally bred as a fighting dog, the wrinkles enabled it to twist away from a grabbing opponent. This is a self-assured and independent breed, with a distinct stubborn streak. A well-trained Shar-Pei will integrate well with an experienced family, but, though devoted and protective, it is not a demonstrative pet and will always be reserved—or downright suspicious—with strangers. It needs lots of stimulation and loves a lively game or brisk exercise.

AT A GLANCE

Ease of training	■
Affection	■ ■ ■
Playfulness	■
Good with children	■ ■ ■ ■ ■
Good with other dogs	■ ■ ■
Grooming required	■ ■

+ Generally healthy, the Shar-Pei can suffer from hereditary problems like hip dysplasia, patellar luxation, eyelid problems, ear problems, and allergies.

! The same gene mutation that results in the Shar-Pei's trademark wrinkles has also caused wrinkling in humans.

HISTORY

This ancient breed traces it history back to the Han Dynasty (206 BC–AD 220) and may be related to the Chow Chow and the Tibetan Mastiff. It was likely developed for farming and fighting in the southern China village of Tai Leh, famous for dog fights. The Communist Revolution of 1911—and 1949 political edicts deeming pet dogs a luxury—almost eliminated the breed. In the 1960s, some were smuggled to Hong Kong and the United States, so that this rare breed now has many enthusiastic supporters worldwide.

Cimarrón Uruguayo

Uruguayan Molosser / Gaucho Dog / Cerro Largo Dog / Cimarron Creole
URUGUAY

Cimarron Uruguayo puppy

Exercise required

Common Coat Colors

48+	100+	16+
	80	14
36		
	60	12
24	40	10
	20	8
12		
	10	6

Average height (inches)
Average weight (lbs)
Average life expectancy

The only recognized native breed of Uruguay, the Cimarrón Uruguayo is a versatile dog. For much of its history, it existed as a much-reviled feral breed. When the farmers and ranchers that once hunted it discovered that the breed made an outstanding guard dog that would steadfastly defend its family and territory from all threats, they embraced it as a working dog. Still used primarily for protection, it is also a companion dog, suitable for an experienced owner.

AT A GLANCE

Ease of training	■
Affection	■ ■ ■ ■
Playfulness	■ ■ ■
Good with children	■ ■ ■
Good with other dogs	■
Grooming required	■ ■ ■

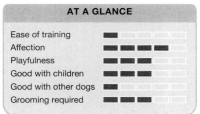

! Bounty hunters would present the dog's ears as proof of a kill, so it is said that the habit of cropping the dog's ears when young pays homage to the days when it was hunted.

 The Cimarrón Uruguayo should be tested for hip and elbow dysplasia before breeding.

HISTORY

This breed has a turbulent history, descending from dogs that were released by early European colonizers. As a feral, it adapted to its hard life, and population grew. By the eighteenth century, its numerous attacks on livestock and even humans resulted in an effort to eliminate it. The government even offered bounties for each dog killed. Yet many managed to survive, especially in the highlands of Cerro Largo, where ranchers tamed it for use as a guard dog. Its tale of survival against odds and its fierce character inspired the National Army to name it as mascot, and it was also adopted as the unofficial national symbol of Uruguay.

Czechoslovakian Vlcak

Czechoslovakian Wolfdog / Slovak Wolfdog / Czech Wolfdog

CZECHOSLOVAKIA

Exercise required

Czechoslovakian Vlcak puppy

	Average height (inches)	Average weight (lbs)	Average life expectancy
	48+	100+	16+
		80	14
	36		
		60	12
	24	40	10
		20	8
	12		
		10	6

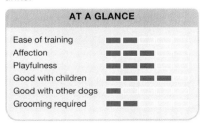

Common Coat Colors

With the sleek looks of a wolf and all the favorable qualities of a dog, the Czechoslovakian Vlcak is a remarkable breed. Rugged and lively, it is also fearless and courageous and possesses incredible endurance. It can find a place in an active, experienced household that will keep it mentally and physically challenged. It also thrives on work, making a keen guard or hunting dog or loyal service animal and successfully serves in police and search-and-rescue units.

AT A GLANCE

Ease of training
Affection
Playfulness
Good with children
Good with other dogs
Grooming required

! Barking is unnatural for this breed; they communicate in other ways (such as body language, grunts and whining).

+ It is usually very healthy, but can be prone to epilepsy, some types of cancer, degenerative myelopathy, and exocrine pancreatic insufficiency.

HISTORY

The Czechoslovakian Wolfdog can trace its history only to 1955, when breeders began crossing German Shepherds with Carpathian wolves. By 1965, a breed was born that had the trainability and temperament of dog and the courage and toughness of wolf. This new breed also retained the excellent navigational skills, night vision, and keen senses of its wolf forebear, while displaying the good nature and loyalty of a companion dog. In 1982, it was recognized as a national breed.

Doberman Pinscher

GERMANY

Exercise required

One of the most popular in the United States, the sleek Doberman Pinscher is a classic guard dog, intelligent, loyal, protective, and agile. These traits also make it suitable as a formidable police or military dog. It may be stereotyped as aggressive and vicious, but a well-trained and socialized Dobie is a gentle and affectionate dog that enjoys being a member of an active family. This natural protector loves to be close to its family, and will welcome children, friends, and guests, as long as it is treated with kindness. It is not for the laid-back, however— this dog needs plenty of stimulation and activity to truly thrive.

! Credited with saving the breed in the post-World War II era, Werner Jung risked his life to smuggle a bitch from East Germany to mate with the few Pinschers remaining.

Doberman Pinscher puppies

AT A GLANCE

Ease of training	■■■■■
Affection	■■■■
Playfulness	■■■
Good with children	■■■■
Good with other dogs	■■■
Grooming required	■

+ Generally healthy, it can suffer from hereditary problems such as cardiomyopathy, intervertebral disk disease, wobbler syndrome, and von Willebrand's disease.

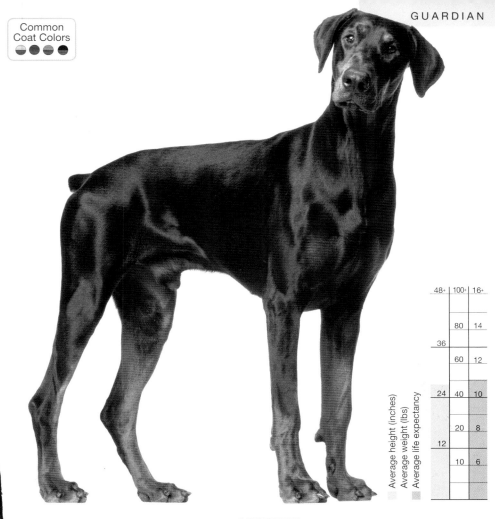

Common
Coat Colors

Average height (inches)	Average weight (lbs)	Average life expectancy
48+	100+	16+
	80	14
36		
	60	12
24	40	10
	20	8
12		
	10	6

HISTORY

The history of the Doberman begins in late-nineteenth-century Germany with Karl Friedrich Louis Dobermann, a tax collector who wanted a guard dog that would both protect him and "encourage" people to part with their money. The exact breed mix is unknown, but into the gene pool went the Rottweiler, German Shepherd, Great Dame, Black and Tan Terrier, and German Pinscher. The eventual result was a muscular dog in the characteristic black-and-tan coloring that possessed great endurance and speed and was highly trainable and intelligent.

After Dobermann's death in 1894, the Germans named the breed Dobermann-pinscher in his honor. The first Doberman was registered with the American Kennel Club in 1908, and a Doberman Club was founded in England in 1948. Its success on the battlefield and behind the lines inspired the U.S. Marine Corps to adopt it as its official war dog during World War II.

Dogo Argentino
Argentinian Mastiff / Argentine Dogo
ARGENTINA

Dogo Argentino puppy

Exercise required

Common Coat Colors

Self-confident and bold, the Dogo Argentino was developed to be a powerful hunting breed, capable of chasing down predators across the vast Argentine pampas. At that it excelled, which makes it an admirable guard dog. This is a breed for experienced owners only—it must be meticulously trained and socialized so that its stable disposition can come through. In the home, it can be a sociable pet, gentle with its human family. It bonds well with children, but their interactions must always be supervised because it is capable of unintentionally harming a child. It is dominant by nature, so an owner who knows how to assume a leadership role is best for both dog and human. If it accepts it place in the hierarchy, it will be a staunch friend and courageous protector. It needs plenty of activity and also plenty of chew toys—this dog is an inveterate chewer and needs to be distracted from making a meal of shoes or furniture.

	Average height (inches)	Average weight (lbs)	Average life expectancy
	48+	100+	16+
		80	14
	36		
		60	12
	24	40	10
		20	8
	12		
		10	6

AT A GLANCE

Ease of training	
Affection	
Playfulness	
Good with children	
Good with other dogs	
Grooming required	

 This breed is banned in some countries under various dangerous dog acts.

+ Breed health concerns may include congenital deafness (unilateral or bilateral), hip dysplasia, bloat/torsion and demodectic mange (demodex).

HISTORY
The Dogo Argentino, the sole Argentine breed recognized by the FCI, has a pedigree that dates only to the early twentieth century, when Antonio Nores Martinez began a program to breed a hunting dog that would be able to chase down and restrain big game like wild boar and puma, but still have an amiable personality that would make it a suitable family companion. Based on the now-extinct Cordoba fighting dog, it has multiple forebears, including the Great Dane, Boxer, Bull Terrier, and Dogue de Bordeaux.

Dogue de Bordeaux

French Mastiff

FRANCE

Dogue de Bordeaux puppy

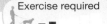

Exercise required

The extremely powerful Dogue de Bordeaux, also known as the French Mastiff, is a brave animal that was once used as a war dog valued for its ferocity in fighting conditions. Despite it violent history, this handsome, wrinkly bruiser of dog now makes a calm and gentle companion, one that will adore and protect its family. As with most guardian dogs, strict training is essential. An experienced owner with a natural air of authority is best, and to avoid aggression against other animals, it must be socialized early. A well-trained and socialized Dogue de Bordeaux will be a valued family member, but it does tend to snore loudly and drool a lot, and, unless it is alarmed, it will laze away the day, content to nap until playtime.

Common Coat Colors

Average height (inches)	Average weight (lbs)	Average life expectancy
48+	100+	16+
	80	14
36		
	60	12
24	40	10
	20	8
12		
	10	6

AT A GLANCE

Ease of training	▪
Affection	▪ ▪ ▪
Playfulness	▪ ▪ ▪
Good with children	▪ ▪ ▪
Good with other dogs	▪ ▪ ▪ ▪
Grooming required	▪ ▪

 The French Resistance used these dogs for protection—they were so good that Hitler ordered hundreds destroyed.

✚ Generally healthy, but hereditary problems can include bloat, heart problems, skin disease, eye problems, eosinophilic panosteitis, and hypothyroidism.

HISTORY

A possible descendant of the Bulldog and Tibetan Mastiff (among other breeds), by the Middle Ages, this dog was in use as a cattle driver and personal bodyguard. The French Revolution nearly spelled its doom, when many of the aristocracy's dogs were slaughtered. Both World Wars saw it drafted into active service, hauling carts and stretchers. After the war, numbers rose again through the efforts of the French Dogue de Bordeaux Club. Well established in France, it is gaining popularity worldwide.

Fila Brasileiro

Brazilian Mastiff / Cao de Fila

BRAZIL

Fila Brasileiro puppy

Exercise required

48+	100+	16+
	80	14
36		
	60	12
24	40	10
	20	8
12		
	10	6

Average height (inches)
Average weight (lbs)
Average life expectancy

Common Coat Colors

The Fila Brasileiro, or Brazilian Mastiff, shows its bloodhound ancestry in its long muzzle, drooping skin, and magnificent tracking ability. As well as working as a tracker, this strapping dog makes a vigilant guardian. It forms extremely strong bonds, and for a very experienced owner, it will prove a dedicated companion with an inbred urge to protect those it cares about. It will be gentle and patient with the children of its family, but socialization is essential, otherwise its naturally wary temperament will express itself as aggression to strangers and other animals.

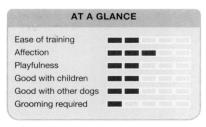

AT A GLANCE	
Ease of training	■■ ■■
Affection	■■ ■■ ■■
Playfulness	■■ ■■
Good with children	■■ ■■
Good with other dogs	■■ ■■
Grooming required	■■

 The most common problems for the breed include joint dysplasia, patellar luxation, skeletal growth abnormalities, osteochondrosis, gastric torsion, and eye problems.

HISTORY

Bred from a mix of European breeds like the English Mastiff and Bloodhound crossed with native stock, the Fila Brasileiro is valued for protecting property and livestock, herding cattle, and instinctively capturing and holding game. Slaveholders once prized this skill, using the breed to capture runaways unharmed. Banned in some countries, it is still a useful dog. Its loyalty even inspired the Brazilian saying "as faithful as a Fila."

 Its gait is similar to a camels, moving both legs on one side at a time, giving it a rolling, lateral motion.

Gaddi Kutta

Indian Panther Hound / Mahidant Mastiff

NORTHERN INDIA

Exercise required

Gaddi Kutta puppy

Common Coat Colors

Average height (inches)	Average weight (lbs)	Average life expectancy
	48+	100+	16+
		80	14
36			
		60	12
24	40	10
		20	8
12			
		10	6

As a denizen of the Himalayan ranges, the resilient Gaddi Kutta has superbly adapted itself to survive outdoors in even the harshest conditions. Himalayan shepherds employ this ferociously protective dog to guard their flocks of sheep from attacks by dangerous animals like snow leopards or bears. Surprisingly, this dog is a granivore, living on wheat flour, maize, rice-husk, and barley. Like most herding and guardian breeds, it has a keen intelligence and learns quickly. As part of a family, it is loving with children, intensely loyal, but distrustful of strangers.

AT A GLANCE

Ease of training	
Affection	
Playfulness	
Good with children	
Good with other dogs	
Grooming required	

➕ This dog is relatively robust and not inclined to illness.

! Himalayan shepherds tell of the Gaddi Dog's origin as a cross between a tiger and a dog—probably because it is as ferocious as a tiger and as loyal as a dog.

HISTORY

The Gaddi Kutta has been an important component of Himalayan life from time immemorial, but little reliable evidence exists to confirm its origins. Stories tell of the Asur King Mahidant of Meerut crossing the wild dingo-like hounds found in the Jamuna Khader region of India with the Sha-Khyi variety of Tibetan Mastiffs to produce a fierce hunting dog. This mastiff-type mountain dog is generally found only in Northern India, especially states in the Western Himalayan region.

Georgian Shepherd Dog

Georgian Mountain Dog / Tushetian Nagazi

GEORGIA

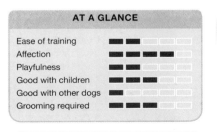

Georgian Shepherd
Dog puppy

Exercise required

Common Coat Colors

48+	100+	16+
	80	14
36		
	60	12
24	40	10
	20	8
12		
	10	6

Average height (inches)
Average weight (lbs)
Average life expectancy

The Georgian Shepherd is an ancient working breed of the molosser type found in the Caucasus. This dog is large, robust, strong boned, muscular, and athletic, with a large head and powerful legs. Used as shepherd and guard dog, it is alert, brave, and protective. With an experienced owner, a well-trained Georgian Shepherd tends to be calm, friendly, and patient with children. It has a reputation as a "one-man dog," showing unprecedented devotion to its owner.

AT A GLANCE

Ease of training	■ ■ □ □ □
Affection	■ ■ ■ □ □
Playfulness	■ ■ □ □ □
Good with children	■ ■ ■ □ □
Good with other dogs	■ □ □ □ □
Grooming required	■ ■ ■ □ □

 This rugged dog tends to be healthy and has no specific canine diseases associated with it.

! The Georgian Shepherd came to East Germany in the late 1960s to serve as a watchdog on the Berlin Wall. In 1989, when the Wall fell, about 7,000 watchdogs scattered.

HISTORY

The Georgian Shepherd is believed to be a completely natural breed that originated from the ancient molosser-type dogs of the Caucasus. In the rough terrain and climate of the region, this dog thrived as a courageous shepherd that often worked in pairs or groups. It served as the foundation for the Russian Kavlaskaya Ovtcharka after World War II and is related to many breeds native to the Caucasus. It has remained unchanged in its home region, but is largely unknown outside of Georgia.

Giant Schnauzer

GERMANY

Exercise required

Giant Schnauzer puppy

With its trademark beard and shaggy eyebrows, the Giant Schnauzer is a distinctive-looking dog. Its name is misleading—it is not a giant breed, but instead a larger relative of the Standard Schnauzer from which it was bred. It does tend to have a giant personality—this is an intelligent breed, known for its stubborn nature and problem-solving ability. A well-trained Giant is alert and driven, and it thrives on work and activities that mentally and physically challenge it, such as agility training.

It is also an energetic, charmingly curious dog that likes to be in the middle of everything and fits in well with an active family. The Giant is naturally protective of its family and makes a good watchdog.

Common Coat Colors

Average height (inches)	Average weight (lbs)	Average life expectancy
48+	100+	16+
	80	14
36		
	60	12
24	40	10
	20	8
12		
	10	6

AT A GLANCE

Ease of training	■■ ■■ ■■
Affection	■■ ■■ ■■
Playfulness	■■ ■■ ■■
Good with children	■■ ■■ ■■
Good with other dogs	■■ ■■
Grooming required	■■ ■■ ■■

! Its German name is Riesenschnauzer, which means "giant, herculean monster with a walrus mustache."

+ Giants are generally healthy, but hereditary problems can include joint dysplasia, progressive retinal atrophy, skin complaints, cancer, and heart conditions.

HISTORY

The Giant was created in Württemberg and Bavaria, probably by crossing the Standard Schnauzer with larger smooth-coated dogs, rough-haired sheepdogs, and the black Great Dane. Its original purpose was to drive cattle, but it soon became popular as a guard dog at butchers and breweries. In the early 1900s, it was trained for police work in Berlin and other German cities—a job it still holds. The first Giants came to the United States in the 1930s and have become popular working and competition dogs.

Great Dane

Deutsche Dogge / German Mastiff

GERMANY

Exercise required

The colossal Great Dane is both majestic and elegant. One of the largest breeds in the world, it is known for its size, strength and proud carriage. This is a well-muscled and leggy dog, combining the best parts of its mastiff and hound ancestors. Bred to guard aristocrats and hunt large game with them, the Great Dane has developed an appropriately noble bearing. Although noted for its ferocity on the hunt, this is not an aggressive breed and can be a marvelous companion dog if properly socialized and trained from a young age. It tends to be reserved with strangers but will be playful and affectionate with its family, including children and other family pets. It is a born watchdog—and its size alone can deter the most determined intruder.

Great Dane puppies

AT A GLANCE

Ease of training	▢▢▢
Affection	▢▢▢▢▢
Playfulness	▢▢
Good with children	▢▢▢▢
Good with other dogs	▢▢▢
Grooming required	▢

	48+	100+	16+
		80	14
	36		
		60	12
	24	40	10
		20	8
	12		
		10	6

Average height (inches)
Average weight (lbs)
Average life expectancy

Common Coat Colors

> ! Great Danes have been called the "Heartbreak Breed" because of its propensity for heart-related problems.

> + Generally very healthy, but they can be prone to teeth and gum problems, idiopathic epilepsy, hypothyroidism, and progressive retinol atrophy.

HISTORY

Great Danes got their misleading name (they are not Danish) in the 1700s when French naturalist Comte de Buffon saw them in Denmark and assumed they originated there. It is something of a mystery why the name stuck! The breed probably descended from the original Mastiff types of prehistory that migrated from Central Asia westward into Europe, developing different characteristics over time. Greyhounds, Irish Wolfhounds, and Scottish Deer-hounds are thought to have contributed to this giant breed. Historically, Great Danes were the preserve of the aristocracy and were greatly valued for their bravery when hunting. Although they often have their ears cropped in the United States, this practice was banned in England in 1894 by Edward, Prince of Wales. The breed became very popular in England, and two important kennels—the Send and Ouborough—were established in the 1920s and 1930s. Great Danes were recognized by the American Kennel Club in 1887, and since that time, the breed has consistently risen in popularity.

249

Great Pyrenees
Pyrenean Mountain Dog
FRANCE / SPAIN

Great Pyrenees puppy

Exercise required

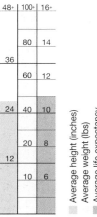

48+	100+	16+
	80	14
36		
	60	12
24	40	10
	20	8
12		
	10	6

Average height (inches)
Average weight (lbs)
Average life expectancy

Common Coat Colors

This gorgeous breed is known as the Pyrenean Mountain Dog in some countries and is instantly recognizable due to its thick, white coat and impressive size. These dogs are valued as livestock guardians and watchdogs, and will live among huge flocks of sheep unsupervised, patrolling for predators. They are formidable against intruders, but gentle and sweet-natured toward their families. These dogs are independent thinkers, which means they can be hard to train.

AT A GLANCE

Ease of training	▰▰
Affection	▰▰▰
Playfulness	▰▰▰
Good with children	▰▰▰▰
Good with other dogs	▰▰▰
Grooming required	▰▰▰

+ Generally healthy but hereditary problems can include hip dysplasia, bone cancer, and patellar luxation.

! One singular characteristic of the Great Pyrenees is the unique double dew claws on each hind leg.

HISTORY
The ancestors of this prized livestock guardian probably arrived in the Pyrenees Mountains from Central Asia by 3000 BCE. There, they began to develop in isolation, adapting to the harsh climate and treacherous terrain. A French historian from Lourdes mentioned them in 1407 as "great dogs of the mountains." In the seventeenth century, Louis XIV declared them the royal dogs of France. Some historians believe they journeyed with Basque fishermen to Newfoundland and were influential in the creation of that breed.

Greek Shepherd

Hellenikos Poimenikos

GREECE

Exercise required

Greek Shepherd puppy

Common Coat Colors

	48+	100+	16+
		80	14
36			
		60	12
	24	40	10
		20	8
12			
		10	6

Average height (inches)
Average weight (lbs)
Average life expectancy

The Greek Shepherd is a strong-willed and hardy dog with a work-oriented temperament. This breed is known to be extremely loyal toward its owner, but is otherwise not very friendly. Additionally, this breed is not known for its trainability. It is recommended that a potential owner understand the drawbacks of living with a Greek Shepherd and not simply adopt this breed as a family pet. These stubborn dogs require a strong owner with a large yard or a farm with several acres of land.

AT A GLANCE

Ease of training
Affection
Playfulness
Good with children
Good with other dogs
Grooming required

 This herding dog considers its owner as part of its pack, so it is important to establish oneself as the leader early on.

+ No diseases specific to this breed.

HISTORY

This breed has been herding sheep in Greece for hundreds of years. One dog was brought to Greece by Turkish travelers and after breeding with several native dogs, the Hellenikos Poimenikos was created. Owners realized the sheep-herding potential of this dog, and it was quickly adapted into an independently thinking working dog. Livestock farming has declined in Greece, so there are now less than 3,000 purebred Greek Shepherd dogs remaining. Since 1998, the Greek Shepherd Dog Breeding Program was implemented to help restore the dog's numbers.

Himalayan Sheepdog
Himalayan Shepherd
NEPAL / INDIA

Himalayan Sheepdog puppy

Exercise required

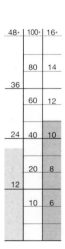

48+	100+	16+
	80	14
36		
	60	12
24	40	10
	20	8
12		
	10	6

Average height (inches)
Average weight (lbs)
Average life expectancy

This herding dog is generally kept outside, although it is loyal and playful enough to also be thought of as a companion dog. Himalayan Sheepdogs should not be kept indoors for a prolonged period of time. This breed is difficult to train and will remain obstinate unless an owner is persistent and establishes dominance. It is not recommended for homes with other pets, as this breed is known to show aggression and jealousy towards other animals.

Common Coat Colors

AT A GLANCE

Ease of training	■ ■ □ □ □
Affection	■ ■ ■ □ □
Playfulness	■ ■ ■ □ □
Good with children	■ ■ ■ □ □
Good with other dogs	■ □ □ □ □
Grooming required	■ □ □ □ □

+ Generally very healthy, but they can be prone to elbow and hip dysplasia, glaucoma, patellar luxation.

HISTORY
The exact history of this dog is unknown, but it originated as an ancient herding dog in Northern India and Nepal. This breed was also used for hunting throughout the harsh terrain of the Nepal region, although nowadays it is protective of cattle rather than a predatory dog. In modern history, the breed has rarely been found outside of India and Nepal.

! This breed's origins are similar to the Indian Mastiff and Tibetan Mastiff.

Kangal Dog

Sivas Kangal / Turkish Kangal

TURKEY

Exercise required

Kangal Dog puppy

Common Coat Colors

	48+	100+	16+
		80	14
	36		
		60	12
		24	40	10
			20	8
	12		
			10	6

Average height (inches)
Average weight (lbs)
Average life expectancy

Although the unique Kangal is often referred to as a shepherd and is usually found on farms, in reality it is a flock guardian, bred to keep away predators. This extremely protective and loyal dog is suitable as a watchdog or guard dog for a family without livestock. The breed is typically gentle with both children and small animals, despite its intimidating size. This dog is not suitable for apartments or urban living, as it requires a yard to roam in.

AT A GLANCE

Ease of training	■ ■ ■ ■ ■
Affection	■ ■ ■
Playfulness	■ ■ ■ ■
Good with children	■ ■ ■ ■
Good with other dogs	■ ■ ■ ■
Grooming required	■ ■

 Puppies need lots of attention, diversions, and moderate exercise, to prevent destructive behavior.

➕ Generally very healthy, but they can be prone to teeth and gum problems, idiopathic epilepsy, hypothyroidism, and progressive retinol atrophy.

HISTORY

It is likely this ancient livestock dog originated in the Kangal District in the Sivas Province of Turkey. Or, possibly, it was brought over from India. The Kangal was surely an early mastiff type—it is said to resemble the powerful dogs depicted in Assyrian artwork. In Turkey, this "national dog" appears on postage stamps and coins. The first Kangal was imported to the UK in 1965 and to the U.S. in 1985.

Karakachan Dog

BULGARIA

Karakachan Dog puppy

Exercise required

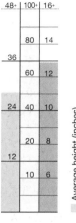

48+	100+	16+
	80	14
36		
	60	12
24	40	10
	20	8
12		
	10	6

Average height (inches)
Average weight (lbs)
Average life expectancy

Common Coat Colors

These dogs are strongly territorial and will guard homes, vehicles, livestock, and their families with great loyalty. Small numbers of the breed are used in the United States on ranches and farms in guardian-type roles. These are working dogs bred for many years to do a specific job, and they are best suited to that lifestyle. The Karakachan Dog's bravery and dignity, together with its incredible loyalty, make this dog an invaluable friend and helper.

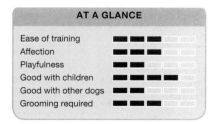

AT A GLANCE	
Ease of training	▪▪▪ ▪▪▪ ▪▪
Affection	▪▪▪ ▪▪ ▪▪
Playfulness	▪▪▪ ▪▪
Good with children	▪▪▪ ▪▪▪ ▪▪▪
Good with other dogs	▪▪▪ ▪▪
Grooming required	▪▪▪ ▪▪ ▪▪▪

! In the past, this mountain dog was widely used by the Bulgarian army as a border watchdog.

+ No diseases specific to this breed.

HISTORY

This ancient breed is named after the Karakachan people—nomadic shepherds descended from Central Europe's Thracian livestock-breeding communities. The Karakachan are noted for preserving historic breeds of sheep and horses in addition to the Karakachan Dog. The dogs are renowned for their bravery and have long been used for protecting livestock herds from wolves and other large predators.

Komondor

Hungarian Sheepdog
HUNGARY

Exercise required

Komondor puppy

	Average height (inches)	Average weight (lbs)	Average life expectancy
	48+	100+	16+
		80	14
	36		
		60	12
	24	40	10
		20	8
	12		
		10	6

Common Coat Colors

Known as the king of livestock-guardian breeds in Hungary, this distinctive breed is especially prized for its guarding instincts and has been attributed with clearing Hungary of its wolf population, with its skill and bravery. Komondors are extremely independent, which in combination with their protectiveness makes it essential that they live with an experienced dog-owning household. They are happiest when working outside and need regular obedience training and continual socialization.

AT A GLANCE

Ease of training	▪▪ ▪▪
Affection	▪▪ ▪▪ ▪▪ ▪▪
Playfulness	▪▪ ▪▪ ▪▪
Good with children	▪▪ ▪▪ ▪▪ ▪▪
Good with other dogs	▪▪ ▪▪ ▪▪
Grooming required	▪▪ ▪▪

+ Breed health concerns may include bloat (gastric dilatation and volvulus), cataracts, entropion and hip dyslpasia.

HISTORY

Komondors descend from Tibetan dogs and were brought to Hungary by Cumans, Turkic speaking, nomadic people. In the late tenth century, Mongols began to expand their territories forcing the Cumans westward. They reached the borders of Hungary in the twelfth century, where they were granted asylum under Köten Khan. The name Komondor derives from Koman-dor, meaning "Cuman dog." Today the Komondor is a fairly common breed in Hungary.

! The coat of the Komondor takes about two and a half days to dry after a bath.

255

Kuvasz

HUNGARY

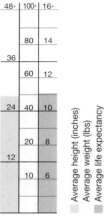

Kuvasz puppy

48+	100+	16+
	80	14
36		
	60	12
24	40	10
	20	8
12		
	10	6

Average height (inches)
Average weight (lbs)
Average life expectancy

Common Coat Colors

This large, white livestock guardian is native to Hungary. They have long been favored by the Magyar nobility who valued them for their companionship and protective instincts. Kuvasz are spirited, devoted, and protective dogs that can make good companions. However, this is a dominant breed with a huge physical presence, and they like to be in charge, so they require lots of space and consistent obedience training and socialization.

AT A GLANCE

Ease of training	■■ ■■
Affection	■■ ■■ ■■
Playfulness	■■ ■■
Good with children	■■ ■■ ■■
Good with other dogs	■■ ■■ ■■
Grooming required	■■ ■■ ■■

+ Allergic reactions, canine hip dysplasia, hypertrophic osteodystrophy, osteochondritis dissecans and skin problems.

! This breed was a popular gift to royalty, who often trusted the Kuvasz more than other people around them.

HISTORY

Throughout history these noble-looking dogs were associated with the aristocracy in Hungary; the fifteenth-century king Mathias I reputedly had a Kuvasz as a companion at all times. Their name originates in Turkey, and translates as "the armed guard of the nobility." The Kuvasz has legendary guarding skills, and they over time they were used by farmers for protecting their farms.

Leonberger

GERMANY

Leonberger puppy

Exercise required

Common Coat Colors

Average height (inches)	Average weight (lbs)	Average life expectancy
48+	100+	16+
	80	14
36		
	60	12
24	40	10
	20	8
12		
	10	6

The Leonberger's temperament is one of its most distinguishing characteristics. This breed make wonderful family companions provided they are obedience trained and socialized. They have a naturally gentle and sweet temperament and are generally good with children and other dogs. Leonbergers also have the stamina to keep up with active kids, but they can be messy to live with and have a heartbreakingly short lifespan.

AT A GLANCE

Ease of training	▰▰▰
Affection	▰▰▰▰▰
Playfulness	▰▰▰
Good with children	▰▰▰▰
Good with other dogs	▰▰▰▰
Grooming required	▰▰▰

+ Common health issues include orthopedic problems such as hip and elbow dysplasia, and eye diseases, including cataracts, entropion, and ectropion.

HISTORY

Tracing back to the nineteenth century, the Leonberger was established through the efforts of Heinrich Essig, from Leonberg in Germany. He used St. Bernards, Newfoundlands, and Great Pyrenees to establish the breed, which he exported in large numbers. These powerful dogs were used as farm dogs and for light draft. During the two World Wars, Leonbergers were used to pull the ammunition carts, among other things. The first breed standard was written in 1895.

 According to legend, the Leonberger was apparently bred as a "symbolic dog" to mimic the lion in the town crest.

Majorca Mastiff

Ca de Bou / Perro Dogo / Bull Mastiff

MAJORCA (BALEARIC ISLANDS, SPAIN)

Majorca Mastiff puppy

Exercise required

Common Coat Colors

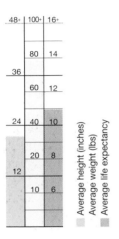

Average height (inches)
Average weight (lbs)
Average life expectancy

48+	100+	16+
	80	14
36		
	60	12
24	40	10
	20	8
12		
	10	6

The Majorca Mastiff, commonly known as the Ca de Bou, is a strong, medium-sized dog originating on the Balearic Islands of Spain. The breed is considered a particularly good herder and guardian, although it may be difficult to train with an inconsistent or undedicated owner. With enough exercise, this breed is capable of living in any environment. The protective Majorca Mastiff is well suited for families with children. These loving dogs are intelligent and loyal, but not recommended for a first-time owner.

AT A GLANCE

Ease of training	▰▰▰▰▱▱
Affection	▰▰▰▰▰▱
Playfulness	▰▰▱▱▱▱
Good with children	▰▰▰▰▱▱
Good with other dogs	▰▰▰▰▱▱
Grooming required	▰▱▱▱▱▱

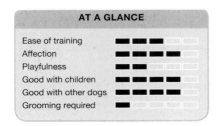

! This breed's gender can be guessed by the size of its head, as the males have a noticeably larger skull circumference.

+ Generally very healthy, but they can be prone to Hip dysplasia and other skeletal issues.

HISTORY

This breed likely originated many centuries ago in the Mediterranean and may be descended from Iberian Mastiffs that King James I of Spain brought to the Balearic Islands around 1232, which crossbred with other large herding dogs. Majorca Mastiffs were sometimes used for bull baiting—Ca de Bou means "bull-dog" in Catalan. The first dog show entry of the breed was in 1928 in Barcelona. After World War II, the breed was nearly extinct, making it necessary to crossbreed with "typey" dogs.

Maremma Sheepdog

Cane da Pastore Maremmano-Abruzzese

ITALY

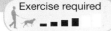

Exercise required

Maremma Sheepdog puppy

	Average height (inches)	Average weight (lbs)	Average life expectancy
	48+	100+	16+
		80	14
	36		
		60	12
	24	40	10
		20	8
	12		
		10	6

Common Coat Colors

Fearless and loyal, the Maremma can make good companions for an experienced home, but is wary of strangers because of its strong innate protectiveness. It's also inclined to be possessive so it needs to have consistent obedience training and socialization to become a good companion dog. This breed is virtually deprived of a hunting drive and therefore it's friendly with familiar non-canine animals. It will perceive a household cat as a part of its family if they have been introduced when young. This vigilant and observant breed is also a highly effective watchdog.

AT A GLANCE

Ease of training	■ ■ ■
Affection	■ ■ ■
Playfulness	■ ■ ■
Good with children	■ ■ ■
Good with other dogs	■ ■ ■
Grooming required	■ ■ ■

HISTORY

Developed in Italy's Abruzzi region in ancient times, the imposing Maremma Sheepdog has been the mainstay of shepherds' lives and work for centuries. Natural livestock guardians, Maremmas are instinctively territorial and are independent thinkers: they would be left to protect large flocks completely unattended.

! The literal English translation of the Italian name is "The dog of the shepherds of the Maremma and Abruzzese region."

+ Generally very healthy, but they can be prone to hip and joint disorders and bloat.

Mastiff

English Mastiff / Old English Mastiff
ENGLAND

Mastiff puppy

Exercise required

Average height (inches)	Average weight (lbs)	Average life expectancy
48+	100+	16+
	80	14
36		
	60	12
24	40	10
	20	8
12		
	10	6

Common Coat Colors

The classic gentle giant, the Mastiff is loving but occasionally stubborn. Mastiffs are peaceful dogs, but are fiercely protective of their family. They can make affectionate companions that are good with other dogs. Mastiffs are very good with children and treat them with great care, but caution is required around small children, simply because of the dog's great size. They are intelligent dogs, and respond well to obedience training.

AT A GLANCE

Ease of training	■■■■■
Affection	■■■■□
Playfulness	■■■■□
Good with children	■■■■□
Good with other dogs	■■■■■
Grooming required	■■□□□

+ This breed can be prone to: bloat, elbow dysplasia; hip dysplasia, cystine urolithiasis; eye problems, pulmonic stenosis, osteosarcoma and seizures.

HISTORY

Mastiff-type dogs have a long storied history but, given their size and strength, have been frequently used for bloody pursuits. The modern Mastiff is a gentle giant and couldn't be more different from its aggressive ancestors. The Mastiff was one of the predominant guard-dogs used to protect livestock and property. In this respect, they are still excellent deterrents.

 The name Mastiff probably comes from the Latin, "massivus," meaning huge, or "mastinus," meaning house dog.

Mioritic

Romanian Mioritic / Mioritic Shepherd Dog

ROMANIA

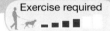
Exercise required

Mioritic puppy

	Average height (inches)	Average weight (lbs)	Average life expectancy
	48+	100+	16+
		80	14
	36		
		60	12
	24	40	10
		20	8
	12		
		10	6

Common Coat Colors

This breed has extremely strong protective instincts and is wary of strangers, but balances this with a gentle and affectionate nature. They are also notably good with children. They are generally calm and levelheaded with a degree of independent thinking, and can make excellent family companions as long as they are properly obedience trained and socialized.

AT A GLANCE

Ease of training	▰▰ ▰▰ ▰▰
Affection	▰▰ ▰▰ ▰▰ ▰▰
Playfulness	▰▰ ▰▰ ▰▰
Good with children	▰▰ ▰▰ ▰▰ ▰▰
Good with other dogs	▰▰ ▰▰ ▰▰
Grooming required	▰▰ ▰▰ ▰▰

✚ No diseases specific to this breed.

HISTORY

This large working breed originated in the relative isolation of the Carpathian Mountains in Romania. The Mioritic was bred to protect livestock from wolves and other large predators. They make fearless guardians.

! The fluffy coat can be white, cream and gray, or show patches of color.

Moscow Watchdog

Moskovskaya Storodzevay Sobaka
RUSSIA

Moscow Watchdog puppy

Exercise required

48+	100+	16+
	80	14
36		
	60	12
24	40	10
	20	8
12		
	10	6

Average height (inches)
Average weight (lbs)
Average life expectancy

Common
Coat Colors

These dogs are instinctively protective and need to be consistently obedience trained. They also require quite a lot of exercise and regular grooming. However, they also have a sweet, calm nature and can be good family companions. Other dogs may be accepted by the Moscow Watchdog, but only if they have been raised together.

AT A GLANCE		
Ease of training	■ ■ ■	
Affection	■ ■ ■	
Playfulness	■ ■ ■	
Good with children	■ ■ ■ ■	
Good with other dogs	■ ■	
Grooming required	■ ■ ■	

 They do not drool like many of the other Molossers.

+ Generally very healthy, but they can be prone to canine hip dysplasia and gastric torsion.

HISTORY
After World War II the Moscow Watchdog was developed by the General Medvedev of the Soviet army at the Central School of Military Kynology. It was created with the intention of producing a guard dog that could live in sub-zero temperatures. The breeding program involved the use of three main breeds: St. Bernards, Caucasian Ovcharkas, and Russian Spotted Hounds.

Neapolitan Mastiff

ITALY

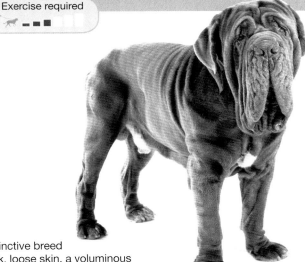

Neapolitan Mastiff puppy

Exercise required

Common Coat Colors

48+	100+	16+
	80	14
36		
	60	12
24	40	10
	20	8
12		
	10	6

Average height (inches) · Average weight (lbs) · Average life expectancy

The distinctive breed has thick, loose skin, a voluminous dewlap, lots of wrinkles, a huge frame, and a slow, almost lumbering gait. Fearless and very protective of its home and family, the Neapolitan Mastiff needs extensive socialization to learn to be around strangers, especially within the home. Without early socialization and training, Neopolitans are likely to become aggressive towards strangers and unfamiliar dogs. They are not suitable for inexperienced dog owners.

AT A GLANCE

Ease of training	■
Affection	■ ■ ■
Playfulness	■
Good with children	■ ■
Good with other dogs	■
Grooming required	■ ■

 The Neapolitan is very tolerant of pain due to the breed's fighting background and the loose skin on its body.

✚ Cherry eye, hip dysplasia, ectropion, entropion, elbow dysplasia, sebaceous adenitis, hypothyroidism, cardiomyopathy, skin infections and bloat.

HISTORY

The Neapolitan Mastiff traces its history back to the war dogs used by the Roman army, as evidenced by Roman artwork depicting massive wrinkly dogs with a similar appearance. These war dogs led to several modern Mastiff breeds, including the Neapolitan, which, over time, was bred for protecting large estates. The breed was first promoted after World War I. A breed standard was first drawn up in 1949, and was rewritten in 1971.

263

Olde English Bulldogge

UNITED STATES

Olde English Bulldogge puppy

Exercise required

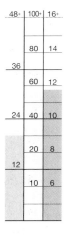

Average height (inches)	Average weight (lbs)	Average life expectancy
48+	100+	16+
	80	14
36		
	60	12
24	40	10
	20	8
12		
	10	6

Common Coat Colors

These are friendly, confident, and alert dogs that can make suitable companions and are good watchdogs. It's exceptionally patient and gentle with familiar children and will make an excellent four-legged friend for them. The well-socialised Olde English Bulldogge is usually accepting of strange people although it's rather slow to make friends with them.

AT A GLANCE

Ease of training	■ ■ ■ ■ □
Affection	■ ■ ■ □ □
Playfulness	■ ■ ■ ■ □
Good with children	■ ■ ■ ■ □
Good with other dogs	■ ■ □ □ □
Grooming required	■ □ □ □ □

+ Generally very healthy, but they can be prone to bloat and canine hip dysplasia.

! This breed likes to chew and should be supplied with plenty of toys and bones.

HISTORY

The Olde English Bulldogge was developed in Pennsylvania in the 1970s by David Leavitt. This recent breed was created using English and American Bulldogs, Bullmastiffs, and American Pit Bull Terriers. Leavitt's intention was to re-create "the Regency period bull baiter," returning to the famed athleticism of the original English Bulldog type, at the same time retaining the temperament of the modern breed. The United Kennel Club recognized the breed in 2014.

Pembroke Welsh Corgi

"Pem"
WALES

Exercise required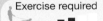

Pembroke Welsh Corgi puppy

Common Coat Colors

The Pembroke Welsh Corgi, or "Pem," as it is affectionately known, was used for droving cattle and general duties on farms. These dogs were invaluable for ridding farms of vermin, guarding against intruders, and for watching over the livestock. These endearing, intelligent dogs are still worked in some areas, but are now primarily kept as companions. They are excellent watchdogs and will protect property aggressively. They are easy to train and are good with children.

Average height (inches)	Average weight (lbs)	Average life expectancy
48+	100+	16+
	80	14
36		
	60	12
24	40	10
	20	8
12		
	10	6

AT A GLANCE

Ease of training	▪▪▪ ▪▪▪ ▪▪▪
Affection	▪▪▪ ▪▪▪ ▪▪▪ ▪▪▪
Playfulness	▪▪▪ ▪▪▪ ▪▪▪ ▪▪▪
Good with children	▪▪▪ ▪▪▪ ▪▪▪ ▪▪▪
Good with other dogs	▪▪▪ ▪▪▪ ▪▪▪ ▪▪▪
Grooming required	▪▪▪ ▪▪▪

➕ Generally healthy, but hereditary problems can include degenerative myelopathy, hip dysplasia, and progressive retinal atrophy.

! Queen Elizabeth II has owned more than 30 Pembroke Welsh Corgis during her reign.

HISTORY

The Pembroke Welsh Corgi's history is believed to date back to the ninth century when the Vikings invaded Wales, bringing with them their spitz-type dogs, which subsequently bred with native dogs. It is thought that the Swedish Vallhund, Norwegian Buhund, and Schipperke could all have influenced the development of the Pembrokeshire. Pems became hugely popular in the twentieth century when the British Royal Family began to keep them.

Perro de Presa Canario

Canary Mastiff
SPAIN

Exercise required
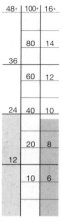

Perro de Presa Canario puppy

Common Coat Colors

	48+	100+	16+
		80	14
	36		
		60	12
	24	40	10
		20	8
	12		
		10	6

Average height (inches)
Average weight (lbs)
Average life expectancy

This is a strong-willed breed with dominant tendencies, that, combined with the dog's massive size, can make it a bit challenging to control. When properly socialized and trained, however, this dog can be calm and docile but it will always be a little bit independent. The Perro de Presa Canario is naturally protective and suspicious of strangers, so it makes a good guard dog. It is important to be careful with this breed around cats and other pets because it has a high prey drive and strong territorial instincts. They are not suitable for first-time dog owners.

AT A GLANCE

Ease of training	
Affection	
Playfulness	
Good with children	
Good with other dogs	
Grooming required	

 The Presa loves water and can be an excellent swimmer.

+ The Presa Canario can be susceptible to hip dysplasia, heart problems and mast-cell tumors and patellar evulsions, skin cysts and epilepsy.

HISTORY

Documentation on these imposing dogs goes back to the fifteenth century. They are likely descended from Mastiff-type war dogs brought to the Canary Islands by the Spanish. There, the dogs developed skills, such as guarding and driving and holding cattle. They were also popular fighting dogs, before the practice was banned. Endangered in the 1940s, the breed has rebounded and was recognized by the Real Canine Society Central of Spain in 1983.

Persian Mastiff

Sarabi Mastiff / Sarabi Shepherd Dog / Iranian Mastiff

IRAN

Persian Mastiff puppies

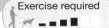

Exercise required

	Average height (inches)	Average weight (lbs)	Average life expectancy
	48+	100+	16+
		80	14
	36		
		60	12
	24	40	10
		20	8
	12		
		10	6

Common Coat Colors

The Persian Mastiff is a breed of livestock guardian dog indigenous to Sarab, a city in northwest of Iran. It has been used for centuries by Iranian shepherds to guard sheep from wolves, bears, jackals and other animals. The Sarabi Dogs are some of the most powerful dogs in the world. They are known to be loyal, extremely strong, and intelligent. They are designed specifically for guardian and shepherding work, and so are little suited for most other lifestyles.

+ Extremely healthy.

! This dog has the potential to be very aggressive to anything it sees as a threat, if it is unable to intimidate the other party into fleeing.

AT A GLANCE

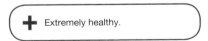

Ease of training
Affection
Playfulness
Good with children
Good with other dogs
Grooming required

HISTORY

Little is known about this dog's origin, but for the fact that the Sarabi Mastiff has been a loyal companion and guardian to shepherds in Iran for centuries. It is an extremely obscure breed outside of its native country.

Rhodesian Ridgeback

African Lion Hound / African Lion Dog

ZIMBABWE

Exercise required

The Rhodesian Ridgeback can make a wonderful family pet as long as it is properly socialized. They are a protective, territorial breed, making them very effective guard dogs. Despite their history of hunting big game they are affectionate and loyal to their families. When properly socialized, they are good with other dogs and also with children. The breed's characteristic feature is the ridge of hair running along its back in the opposite direction of the rest of its coat. They are very popular in the United States and Europe.

Rhodesian Ridgeback puppy

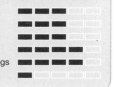

AT A GLANCE

Ease of training	■ ■ ■ ☐ ☐
Affection	■ ■ ■ ☐ ☐
Playfulness	■ ■ ■ ☐ ☐
Good with children	■ ■ ■ ■ ☐
Good with other dogs	■ ■ ■ ☐ ☐
Grooming required	■ ☐ ☐ ☐ ☐

+ Generally a very healthy breed, these dogs can sometimes develop hip or elbow dysplasia, dermoid sinus, and gastric torsion.

! The Rhodesian Ridgeback has also previously been known as African Lion Dog because of its ability to keep a lion at bay while awaiting its master's arrival.

Common Coat Colors

Average height (inches)	Average weight (lbs)	Average life expectancy
48+	100+	16+
	80	14
36		
	60	12
24	40	10
	20	8
12		
	10	6

HISTORY

The ridge along the Rhodesian's spine suggests a shared ancestry with the Thai Ridgeback and the Phu Quoc Ridgeback. These two ancient breeds may have influenced the Rhodesian Ridgeback's development when prehistoric people moved from central Asia to Africa, bringing their dogs along for hunting and protection. During the seventeenth century, European settlers moved to South Africa and also brought their dogs—Great Danes, Mastiffs, and Bloodhounds—which interbred with the African dogs, giving rise to multiple and varied types, including what is now the Rhodesian Ridgeback. These dogs were bred, most notably by early breeder Cornelius von Rooyen, to hunt big game such as lions. They became known for their unmatched bravery and were colloquially called "lion dogs."

Rottweiler

GERMANY

Exercise required

Rottweiler puppy

The Rottweiler is best-suited to an experienced dog-owning home, as it is such a big and powerful breed, and due to their size and strength, they must be properly socialized from a young age and must undergo obedience training. That said, it can make a superb companion animal when raised properly, as they are affectionate, loyal, biddable dogs that provide great home protection; and like so many of the herding and guarding breeds, the Rottweiler is a multi-skilled and exceptionally versatile breed.

AT A GLANCE

Ease of training	■■■□□
Affection	■■□□□
Playfulness	■■□□□
Good with children	■■■□□
Good with other dogs	■■□□□
Grooming required	■□□□□

+ Generally very healthy, but they can be prone to teeth and gum problems, idiopathic epilepsy, hypothyroidism, and progressive retinol atrophy.

 The dogs were known in German as Rottweiler Metzgerhund, meaning Rottweil butchers' dogs—one of their uses was to pull carts of butchered meat to market.

	48+	100+	16+
		80	14
	36		
		60	12
	24	40	10
		20	8
	12		
		10	6

Average height (inches)
Average weight (lbs)
Average life expectancy

Common Coat Colors

HISTORY

The modern Rottweiler most likely descends from the ancient Mastiffs that were bred and used by the Romans. In the first century AD, when the Romans settled in the region around the German Black Forest they took their dogs with them for hunting boar and for protection. Those animals interbred with the ancestors of breeds such as the Bernese Mountain Dog, Appenzeller, and Entlebucher. By the Middle Ages, this area had become known as "das rote wil" meaning "red roof tiles," and "rot wil" dogs became known as Rottweilers. These versatile dogs were used in many ways: in draft work, as butcher's dogs, for driving cattle, and for guarding properties. More recently they have used by the military and the police. The breed was first recognized by the American Kennel Club in 1931.

Saarlooswolfhound

NETHERLANDS / GERMANY

Saarlooswolfhound
puppy

Exercise required

Common
Coat Colors

This is an established
breed of dog
originating from wolf/
dog hybrid crosses.
It retains some of
the wolf-like and
ancient canine ways,
including an intense
pack instinct, tendency
toward shyness, and
a need to roam. These
dogs are exceptionally
strong-willed but
usually display
unwavering loyalty to the alpha human in the household. They are
still pack-oriented and need a strong leader and a social atmosphere.
Not recommended as a child companion. They are only suitable for
experienced dog-owning homes that can provide extensive space
and exercise.

	Average height (inches)	Average weight (lbs)	Average life expectancy
	48+	100+	16+
		80	14
	36		
		60	12
	24	40	10
		20	8
	12		
		10	6

AT A GLANCE

Ease of training	■
Affection	■ ■ ■
Playfulness	■ ■
Good with children	■ ■ ■
Good with other dogs	■ ■
Grooming required	■ ■

 This breed isn't naturally willing to
oblige, so only reward-based training
methods will be successful.

+ Generally healthy but this breed can be prone to
canine hip dysplasia and spondulosis of the
spine.

HISTORY

This relatively new breed was developed by Leendert
Saarloos in the twentieth century based on a male
German Shepherd named Gerard van der Fransenum
and a female wolf named Fleuri. Further German
Shepherd and wolf blood was later introduced.
Saarlooswolfhounds were originally bred to be service
or guide dogs, but proved unsuitable because they
retain the independence of the wolf.

Sage Koochee

Afghan shepherd / Kuchi dog / Sage Jangi / Jangi Spai / Kochyano Spai

AFGHANISTAN

Sage Koochee puppy

Exercise required

	Average height (inches)	Average weight (lbs)	Average life expectancy
	48+	100+	16+
		80	14
	36		
		60	12
	24	40	10
		20	8
	12		
		10	6

Common Coat Colors

The Koochee Dog is perfect for guarding, herding, or working in general; it was designed to protect and work alongside nomadic tribes, and so is hardy enough to weather harsh environments and difficult conditions for long stretches of time. It is naturally loyal, while remaining suspicious of strangers, and has a strong, solid build.

AT A GLANCE

Ease of training	▬ ▬ ▬ ▬ ▬
Affection	▬ ▬ ▬
Playfulness	▬ ▬ ▬ ▬
Good with children	▬ ▬ ▬ ▬
Good with other dogs	▬ ▬ ▬ ▬
Grooming required	▬ ▬

+ Exceptionally healthy.

! This dog has been bred entirely for its physical capabilities and temperament, and so there is no standard appearance for the Kuchi dog.

HISTORY

The Kuchi is an Afghan herding dog that gets its name from the Kuchi people of Afghanistan. Also know as the Afghan Shepherd dog, it is used as a guard dog and general working dog, protecting caravans and flocks of sheep, goats and livestock from predators and thieves. It is sometimes known as just a local variant of the Central Asian Shepherd Dog, and its status as a distinct breed has been disputed by some.

Šarplaninac

Illyrian Sheepdog / Yugoslavian Shepherd dog

SERBIA / REPUBLIC OF MACEDONIA

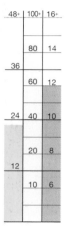

Šarplaninac puppy

Common Coat Colors

Exercise required

This is a dog breed originally from the border area between Kosovo, Macedonia, and Albania (the Sar mountains). They are preeminent livestock guardians–calm, dignified dogs that are defensive rather than aggressive–but if provoked they protect their herds with vigor. Their protectiveness transfers to their families and they are intensely loyal. They are ideal for a working, experienced home.

Average height (inches)
Average weight (lbs)
Average life expectancy

48+	100+	16+
	80	14
36		
	60	12
24	40	10
	20	8
12		
	10	6

AT A GLANCE

Ease of training	
Affection	
Playfulness	
Good with children	
Good with other dogs	
Grooming required	

 Generally very healthy, but they can be prone to canine hip dysplasia, elbow dysplasia, patellar luxation, ear infection, skin allergies, obesity and eye problems.

HISTORY

This ancient breed developed during the Roman era in the southeast mountains of the former Yugoslavia, in a region called Illyria. Initially, the breed was acknowledged by the FCI in 1939 as the Illyrian Shepherd and only in 1957 was it renamed Šarplaninac in honor of the Shar Planina mountain range where it was most often detected. The breed is a preeminent livestock guardian and has had little influence from outside breeds.

 Robust, reliable and independent, this dog is also widely used in its homeland by the police and the military.

Schapendoes
Dutch Sheepdog
NETHERLANDS

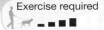
Exercise required

Schapendoes puppy

Common
Coat Colors

Until recently the Schapendoes successfully combined its herding duties with the role of a family dog. Nowadays it exists almost exclusively as a sweet-natured, devoted household pet. This dog establishes tight bonds with every family member and feels separation from them very strongly. It usually becomes especially attached to children if it has known them from an early age. Schapendoes are engaging and intelligent, and excel at events such as agility.

	48+	100+	16+
		80	14
	36		
		60	12
	24	40	10
		20	8
	12		
		10	6

Average height (inches)
Average weight (lbs)
Average life expectancy

AT A GLANCE

Ease of training	■ ■ ■
Affection	■ ■ ■ ■
Playfulness	■ ■ ■ ■
Good with children	■ ■ ■ ■
Good with other dogs	■ ■ ■
Grooming required	■ ■ ■ ■

! The breed became nearly extinct during World War II; the modern-day breed descends from just a few survivors.

+ Generally very healthy, but they can be prone to eye problems, chronic ear infections, canine hip dysplasia and elbow dysplasia.

HISTORY

The Schapendoes, or Dutch Sheepdog, developed in the Drenthe province of the Netherlands, where farmers used them for centuries to work livestock and herd; they are still used for herding today. Once widespread in the Netherlands, the breed faced extinction after World War II." It was re-established by enthusiasts, notably the Dutch author and martial-arts pioneer Pieter Toepoel. They are related to the Bearded Collie, Puli, Briard, and Owczarek Nizinny.

Shorty Bull

UNITED STATES

Shorty Bull puppy

Exercise required

Common Coat Colors

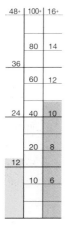

Average height (inches)
Average weight (lbs)
Average life expectancy

The shorty bull is a small, muscular dog with an even temper and a bright personality. This relatively new breed needs a dominant and experienced owner in order to function well, as it can become stubborn or disobedient with a less-assertive owner. The Shorty Bull is equally suited to life as a companion animal and a working dog.

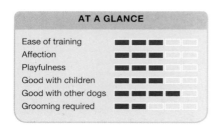

AT A GLANCE

Ease of training	
Affection	
Playfulness	
Good with children	
Good with other dogs	
Grooming required	

! These dogs tend to develop dominance issues as they age.

➕ Generally healthy, but little is known.

HISTORY

The Shorty Bull—a fairly recent breed—is currently being developed as a miniature version of the Bulldog by Jamie Sweet and Amy Krogan, two members of the U.S.-based Shorty Bull Society. This dog is more agile and athletic than the English Bull and, unlike other small bullies, it has no Boston Terrier or Pug in its lines.

Slovak Cuvac

Slovak Chuvach / Tatransky Cuvac / Slovak Tschuvatsch

SLOVAK REPUBLIC

Slovak Cuvac puppies

Exercise required

Common Coat Colors

	48+	100+	16+
		80	14
	36		
		60	12
	24	40	10
		20	8
	12		
		10	6

Average height (inches)
Average weight (lbs)
Average life expectancy

➕ Very healthy.

The Slovak Cuvac is a strong, even-tempered dog that is adept at guarding flocks of sheep and is unendingly loyal to its owner. They are known to be especially affectionate towards their family and good with children, while being aloof to strangers. This breed requires an owner who is experienced in handling herding dogs.

AT A GLANCE

Ease of training	▰▰▰
Affection	▰▰▰▰▰
Playfulness	▰▰▰
Good with children	▰▰▰▰
Good with other dogs	▰▰▰
Grooming required	▰▰▰▰

❗ This breed is known for its especially strong memory.

HISTORY

The Slovak Cuvac can be traced as far back as the 17th century, where it was used in the Slovakian region to protect livestock from wolves and other predators. As wolves began to disappear from the European mountains and more modern herding methods were practiced, the Cuvac almost became extinct. After World War II Dr. Antonin Hruza saved the dog with his successful breeding program. A standard was established and approved in 1964, and the breed was recognized internationally in 1969. This dog is similar to the slightly larger Kuvasz, and is a popular companion in Central Europe; it is also used to guard flocks, hunt big game, and perform border patrol and search and rescue.

South Russian Ovcharka

Ukrainian Ovcharka / South Russian Sheepdog
UKRAINE / RUSSIA

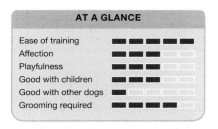

South Russian
Ovcharka puppy

Exercise required

48+	100+	16+
	80	14
36		
	60	12
24	40	10
	20	8
12		
	10	6

Average height (inches)
Average weight (lbs)
Average life expectancy

Common
Coat Colors

This large guardian breed, has a highly developed instinct to protect. South Russian Ovcharkas will defend their families rigorously, and will protect against any perceived threat. They need firm obedience training and consistent socialization, as they are extremely independent thinkers. With proper training the South Russian Ovcharka makes a great family companion and a wonderful guard dog but is not suitable for first-time dog owners.

AT A GLANCE

Ease of training	■ ■ ■ ■ ■
Affection	■ ■ ■ □ □
Playfulness	■ ■ ■ □ □
Good with children	■ ■ □ □ □
Good with other dogs	■ □ □ □ □
Grooming required	■ ■ ■ ■ □

+ Generally healthy, but hereditary problems can include hip dysplasia, entropion, heart failure, and epilepsy.

HISTORY

Ovcharka means "sheepdog", and these dogs accompanied enormous flocks of sheep on drives across Europe, from Spain to the Ukraine. The sheep were driven on foot over land—a journey that could take as long as two years. These shaggy sheepdogs crossed with local stock like the Komondor, and Caucasian Ovcharka, eventually resulting in the modern South Russian Ovcharka.

! During conflict in Russia in the 1920s breeding kennels in Ukraine and Crimea were plundered and destroyed.

Spanish Mastiff

Mastín Español

SPAIN

Spanish Mastiff puppy

Exercise required

Average height (inches)	Average weight (lbs)	Average life expectancy
48+	100+	16+
	80	14
36		
	60	12
24	40	10
	20	8
12		
	10	6

Common Coat Colors

The Spanish Mastiff is brave, protective, independent, and dignified. Its even disposition means that if fully socialized he can be reliable around strangers but it will still remain aloof. Its intimidating appearance and natural alertness make it an excellent watchdog. This breed usually accepts other canines and can be tolerant towards other animals if it has been socialized from an early age. However, these dogs are only suitable for an experienced rural home.

AT A GLANCE

Ease of training	▪▪▪▪
Affection	▪▪▪▪▪
Playfulness	▪▪
Good with children	▪▪▪▪▪
Good with other dogs	▪
Grooming required	▪▪

+ Generally very healthy, but they can be prone to canine hip dysplasia, hearts problems, eyes problems and gastric torsion.

! Puppies need lots of attention, diversions, and moderate exercise, to prevent destructive behavior.

HISTORY

This ancient breed's ancestor were possibly taken to Iberia by the Phoenicians, prior to the Roman invasions of the first century. Roman historian noted Iberian Mastiffs of great size that tended herds and fought off wolves. They were employed as war dogs and taken to the New World by conquistadors to use against the native people. Most often, however, they were used to watch over large herds of sheep and cattle.

Standard Schnauzer

GERMANY

Standard Schnauzer
puppy

Common
Coat Colors

For obvious reasons the Schnauzer takes its name from the German word "schnurrbart", which means "moustache." Their distinctive facial hair combined with their prominent eyebrows gives them a uniquely expressive look. Schnauzers are intelligent dogs and now largely a companion breed. They are good with children and other pets—as long as they are introduced correctly—and make great family pets. Socialization is important, as they can be wary of strangers.

	48+	100+	16+
		80	14
	36		
		60	12
	24	40	10
Average height (inches) / Average weight (lbs) / Average life expectancy		20	8
	12		
		10	6

! This breed has been used as hearing and therapy dogs, search and rescue dogs, and cancer and explosives detection dogs.

AT A GLANCE

Ease of training	▬▬▬▬▬
Affection	▬▬▬□□
Playfulness	▬▬▬▬□
Good with children	▬▬▬▬□
Good with other dogs	▬▬▬□□
Grooming required	▬▬□□□

 Generally very healthy, but hereditary problems can include hip dysplasia, and cancer.

HISTORY

The Standard Schnauzer traces back to at least the fourteenth century in Germany. They are believed to have originated in Württemberg and Bavaria in Southern Germany, most-likely bred from terriers and farm-dogs. The oldest of the three Schnauzer breeds, early Schnauzers were versatile farm dogs that were used for guarding property and livestock, for driving livestock, and for vermin control. In the mid-nineteenth century breeders introduced black German Poodles and gray Wolfspitz in an attempt to make Schnauzers more uniform in appearance. Schnauzers were originally called Wire Haired Pinschers; the name Schnauzer was adopted in 1879. Standard Schnauzers were recognized by the American Kennel Club in 1904.

Tibetan Mastiff

Do-Khyi

TIBET

Tibetan Mastiff puppy

Exercise required

	Average height (inches)	Average weight (lbs)	Average life expectancy
	48+	100+	16+
		80	14
	36		
		60	12
	24	40	10
		20	8
	12		
		10	6

Common Coat Colors

The Tibetan is a calm, independent, and intelligent dog that is inherently protective, making it one of the best personal and property guardians. It is a loyal family companion, it forms an unusually close relationship with its owner, and is always ready to spend time with its family— making it an excellent guardian. It's fiercely territorial though, so unknown children and adults should be careful because this breed can be aggressive; it is not suitable for first-time owners.

AT A GLANCE

Ease of training	▬
Affection	▬ ▬ ▬
Playfulness	▬ ▬
Good with children	▬ ▬ ▬
Good with other dogs	▬
Grooming required	▬ ▬ ▬

+ Generally very healthy, but this breed can be prone to canine hip dysplasia, elbow dysplasia, hypothyroidism, skin problems and heart problems.

! The name Tibetan Mastiff is a misnomer; the Tibetan Mastiff itself is not a true Mastiff.

HISTORY

The Tibetan Mastiff is one of the most ancient breeds and it is believed to have given rise to the modern Mastiff breeds, mountain dogs, and many other large working breeds. Isolated in the remote Himalayas of Tibet, Nepal, and Bhutan, the Tibetan developed uninfluenced by other breeds. Here it was a preeminent guard dog during the day; it was kept tied up in entrances and gateways and let loose at night to fend off predators and intruders. This breed is still renowned for its deep bark and protectiveness.

Tornjak

BOSNIA AND HERZEGOVINA / CROATIA

Tornjak puppy

Exercise required

Common
Coat Colors

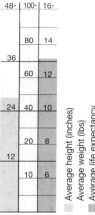

Average height (inches)
Average weight (lbs)
Average life expectancy

Native to Eastern Europe, the Tornjak is primarily a worker, bred as a livestock protection dog. A typical adult is very calm and peaceful, but when the situation demands it, it is a vigilant and alert watchdog. As a companion dog, it is best suited to an experienced home in a rural location. It requires a spacious territory to run and play and a considerable amount of exercise, including at least a daily walk of an hour or more. Without a proper amount of exercise there is a high chance of some unwelcome behavior such as chewing, aggressiveness, and constant barking.

AT A GLANCE

Ease of training	▰▰▰▰▱
Affection	▰▰▰▰▱
Playfulness	▰▰▰▰▱
Good with children	▰▰▰▰▱
Good with other dogs	▰▰▱▱▱
Grooming required	▰▰▰▱▱

+ Generally very healthy, but they can be prone to canine hip dysplasia, elbow dysplasia, von Willebrand's disease, digestive disorder, anemia and gastric torsion.

HISTORY

The large and powerful Tornjak is believed to be related to the Tibetan Mastiff. This ancient breed is mentioned in handwritten papers dated from the ninth century. The Romans used Tornjaks as dogs of war, and as guardians, and for centuries they were used primarily as livestock guardians and herding dogs in Bosnia, Herzegovina, and Croatia.

 The term "Tornjak" evolved from the Bosnian/Croatian word "tor," meaning an enclosed area for sheep.

Victorian Bulldog

UNITED KINGDOM

Exercise required

Victorian Bulldog puppy

Its intimidating appearance belies the fact that the Victorian Bulldog is really a calm, trustworthy, and extraordinarily affectionate dog. It is also known for its daunting courage and vigilant guarding capabilities. It is very much a people-oriented dog and thrives on attention. This charmer will live happily alongside other household pets that it has known since puppy-hood, but can be argumentative with strange dogs. This breed closely resembles the English Bulldog; the only distinction between the two is that the Victorian is larger.

Common Coat Colors

Average height (inches)	Average weight (lbs)	Average life expectancy
48+	100+	16+
36	80	14
24	60	12
	40	10
12	20	8
	10	6

AT A GLANCE

Ease of training	■ ■
Affection	■ ■ ■ ■ ■
Playfulness	■ ■ ■ ■
Good with children	■ ■ ■ ■ ■
Good with other dogs	■ ■ ■ ■
Grooming required	■ ■

 This breed is prone to loud snoring and excessive drooling.

✚ Because this breed has been developed to avoid health issues inherent in other Bulldogs, the Victorian Bulldog is free of genetic issues and is very hardy.

HISTORY

In the 1980s, Ken Mollett decided to create a new line of Bulldogs without the existing health issues—bulldogs that looked like the old photos of the original breed. He crossed the healthiest Bulldogs, Staffords, Bullmastiffs, and Dogue de Bordeaux he could find. By 1985, he had a dog that resembled the Victorian breed but was subject to far fewer health problems. Very few dogs from this bloodline exist.

SPORTING DOGS

American Water Spaniel

UNITED STATES

American Water Spaniel puppy

Exercise required

Common Coat Colors

48	100+	16+
	80	14
36		
	60	12
24	40	10
	20	8
12		
	10	6

Average height (inches)
Average weight (pounds)
Average life expectancy (years)

Always brown in color, these active, personable animals make excellent gundogs and are particularly suited to water retrievals and upland flushing. They also double as wonderful companions. This very vigorous breed is fond of children and makes a wonderful pet if well socialized and provided with sufficient exercise. They enjoy human company, and strive to make new friends, and while they can be protective, they are tolerant of strangers and rarely display outright aggression. Still, they make great watchdogs because they usually bark loudly when someone approaches. An innate hunter, this dog views all moving objects as potential prey, but gets on with cats and other pets if introduced at an early age.

AT A GLANCE

Ease of training		
Affection		
Playfulness		
Good with children		
Good with other dogs		
Grooming required		

 The coat of the AWS is naturally very oily to repel water and dirt, so they may leave oil spots on walls and rugs.

+ May be prone to progressive retinal atrophy, cataracts, hypothyroidism, epilepsy, allergies, baldness, hip dysplasia and diabetes.

HISTORY

This rare breed of gundog, the result of crossing the Irish Water Spaniel, Curly-Coated Retriever, Field Spaniel, and apparently the now-extinct Old English Water Spaniel, was developed in the United States in the early 1900s, and was recognized by the American Kennel Club in 1940. Over the years the numbers of the breed dwindled as hunting became more recreational than a necessity, and new breeds of dogs became popular. Thanks to Doctor F.J. Pfeifer who set up Wolf River Kennels this breed was saved.

Ariege Pointer

Braque de l'Ariège / Ariege Pointing Dog
FRANCE

Ariege Pointer puppies

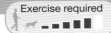
Exercise required

The Ariege Pointers are active, powerful dogs rarely seen outside their homeland, and are typically used for hunting partridge and hare. They are almost exclusively kept for their original purpose and thrive when working. They are relatively sociable but are not generally used solely as companion dogs or family pets. The Ariege Pointer tolerates strangers but interacts with them with natural wariness, although although the breed is too amiable to make a good guard dog. Being bred to work as a gundog in large packs of hunting dogs, the Ariege Pointer has an innate friendliness toward other canines, but it may not be wise to keep this hunter with small animals.

Common Coat Colors

Average height (inches)	Average weight (pounds)	Average life expectancy (years)
48	100+	16+
	80	14
36		
	60	12
24	40	10
	20	8
12		
	10	6

AT A GLANCE

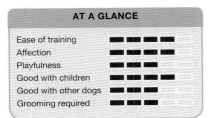

Ease of training	
Affection	
Playfulness	
Good with children	
Good with other dogs	
Grooming required	

May be prone to hip dysplasia, elbow dysplasia, cleft lip, demodex mange, ear infections, deafness, epilepsy, progressive retinal atrophy and aortic stenosis.

HISTORY

This French breed with its excellent sense of smell was developed in the nineteenth century in the Ariege area of the Pyrenees Mountains primarily as a pointing dog, by crossing Braque Saint-Germain and Braque Francais with indigenous pointing dogs. They are also useful as retrievers and for hunting. In 1990 a team of breeders began work to ensure the Braque de l'Ariège's survival. In particular Mr. Alain Deteix, who headed the team that devoted itself to the revival of part of France's National heritage.

 This breed has a baying bark and potential owners should listen to his cries before making a decision!

Barbet
FRANCE

Barbet puppy

Exercise required

Common
Coat Colors

48	100+	16+
	80	14
36		
	60	12
24	40	10
	20	8
12		
	10	6

Average height (inches)
Average weight (pounds)
Average life expectancy (years)

These dogs are superb hunters with a highly refined sense of smell that allows them to find game hidden in vegetation and along river banks. They are used for pointing, flushing, and retrieving and are particularly hardy dogs able to withstand cold water due to their thick, water-resistant coats. This dense wavy coat forms a beard on the dog's chin, giving rise to its breed name—the French word barbe means "beard." These dogs possess excellent temperaments and can make great companions, though they thrive when working and need plenty of exercise and diversions.

AT A GLANCE

Ease of training	
Affection	
Playfulness	
Good with children	
Good with other dogs	
Grooming required	

+ May be prone to hip dysplasia, hernia, elbow dysplasia, epilepsy, ear infection and undershot/overshot bite.

HISTORY

This rare French breed—there are possibly fewer than 600 worldwide— likely traces back to the fourteenth century, when it was developed to hunt water game. It is similar to the extinct English Water Dog and could be a forebear of the Briard, Poodle, and French Griffons. Early documentation has the Barbet serving as a companion, hunting dog, sailor's mate, farm helper, and guard dog. The first mention as a breed was in a book dated 1387. Today they are gundogs and family companions.

 This webbed-paw water dog gets down and dirty in pursuit of waterfowl, earning it the nickname "mud dog."

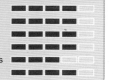

Boykin Spaniel

UNITED STATES

Boykin Spaniel puppy

Exercise required

Common Coat Colors

	Average height (inches)	Average weight (pounds)	Average life expectancy (years)
	48	100+	16+
	36	80	14
		60	12
	24	40	10
		20	8
	12		
		10	6

The Boykin Spaniel is an average-sized dog with an amicable nature and outgoing individuality. Created to hunt in the humid swamps of the southern United States in the early twentieth century, it makes a great companion for a hunter as well as for people who love hiking, boating and other activities. The Boykin Spaniel gets along with children if they have been raised together but it won't tolerate awkward toddlers or rough treatment. This breed is a wonderful playmate for older children, however, and if well socialized, it will welcome visitors to your home. They are vigilant, but too friendly to be watchdogs.

AT A GLANCE

Ease of training	▰▰▰▰▱
Affection	▰▰▰▰▰
Playfulness	▰▰▰▰▰
Good with children	▰▰▰▱▱
Good with other dogs	▰▰▰▱▱
Grooming required	▰▰▰▱▱

✚ May be prone to hip dysplasia, cataracts, ear infections, and a few localized lines have heart and skin problems.

 The forefather of the Boykin Spaniel was a homeless dog adopted in the early 1900s by Whit Boykin.

HISTORY

Described as the "dog that doesn't rock the boat," the Boykin Spaniel was developed in the 1900s as a small, robust duck-hunting dog that could fit into duck boats and blinds. They were bred by South Carolina hunters in the Wateree River Swamp area and are thought to have Springer Spaniel, Cocker Spaniel, American Water Spaniel, and Chesapeake Bay Retriever in their heritage. These are true dual-purpose dogs bred for flushing and retrieving, but they also make wonderful family companions.

Bracco Italiano

Italian Pointer

ITALY

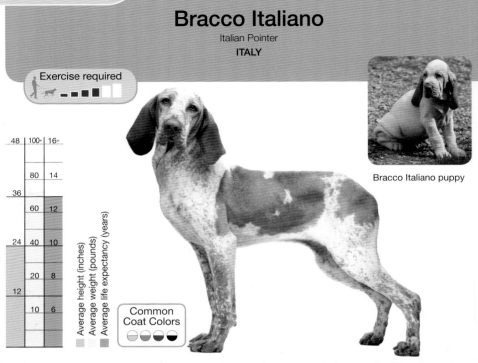

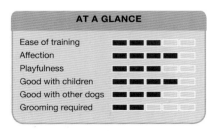
Bracco Italiano puppy

Exercise required

Average height (inches)
Average weight (pounds)
Average life expectancy (years)

48	100+	16+
	80	14
36		
	60	12
24	40	10
	20	8
12		
	10	6

Common Coat Colors

The Bracco resembles a cross between a German Shorthaired Pointer and a Bloodhound, although it is nothing like them in character. This breed is very loyal and loving, and craves being with his family, with whom it develops deep bonds. They can become upset and stressed when left alone for considerable lengths of time. Properly socialized, they are gentle with children and make good playmates. Their alertness and reserve in the presence of strangers make them decent watchdogs.

AT A GLANCE	
Ease of training	■■■ ■■■ ■■■
Affection	■■■ ■■■ ■■■
Playfulness	■■■ ■■■ ■■■
Good with children	■■■ ■■■ ■■■ ■■■
Good with other dogs	■■■ ■■■ ■■■
Grooming required	■■■ ■■■

+ This breed may be prone to hip and elbow dysplasia, entropion, ectropion, enostosis/growing pains, domitor allergies and yeast infections.

HISTORY

More hound-like in appearance than gundog, the Bracco Italiano is an ancient breed tracing back to at least the fourth and fifth centuries. They were bred by noble Italian families such as the Medicis, and were so revered they were given as gifts to visiting royalty and dignitaries. Although probably derived from ancient Egyptian hounds and Mastiff types, they developed in Italy from pointing dogs from the Piedmontese and Lombardy areas. They are highly regarded in Italy as hunt, point, and retrieve gundogs.

! They are an active breed, but require more mental exercise than physical exercise to keep them happy.

Braque d'Auvergne

FRANCE

Braque d'Auvergne puppy

Exercise required

Common
Coat Colors

The Auvergne is lively, sensitive, obedient, and affectionate. Intelligent and good natured, it makes a fine family dog and an excellent hunting partner. It gets along well with other dogs. The Braque d'Auvergne is a natural hunter who tends to work closely with its partner, checking in frequently. This trait, combined with its gentle nature and desire to please, make it a highly trainable pointer. The breed excels at hunting and trials as well as making a suitable companion for the right, active home. However, this breed would make a very ineffective guard dog as Auvergnes would warmly welcome an intruder and follow them home before they would every show aggression.

	Average height (inches)	Average weight (pounds)	Average life expectancy (years)
	48	100+	16+
		80	14
	36		
		60	12
	24	40	10
		20	8
	12		
		10	6

AT A GLANCE

Ease of training	▮▮ ▮▮
Affection	▮▮ ▮▮ ▮▮
Playfulness	▮▮ ▮▮
Good with children	▮▮ ▮▮ ▮▮
Good with other dogs	▮▮ ▮▮
Grooming required	▮▮

➕ Generally healthy but this breed may be prone to hip dysplasia, bloat and cancer.

HISTORY

This ancient breed of pointing dogs developed in the Cantal region of France and takes its name from the French word *braquer*, meaning to aim or point. As with many breeds, Braque d'Auvergne numbers were decimated during World War II, and they were threatened with extinction until breeder Andre de Tournay and his wife sought and found about twenty of the dogs. The modern Braque is descended from these. Braques arrived in the United States in the latter half of the twentieth century.

! The entire breed descends from around 20 individual dogs that survived World War II.

291

Braque du Bourbonnais

Bourbonnais Pointer

FRANCE

Braque du Bourbonnais puppy

Exercise required

Common Coat Colors

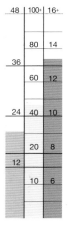

The Braque du Bourbonnais are versatile hunting dogs that work on land and in water. They are passionate, cautious, balanced, cooperative and intelligent. They adapt remarkably easily to the most varied terrains and game. This intense pointing dog can be trained easily and quickly. They are people-oriented and not happy if isolated from the family. The correctly socialised Bourbonnais will be polite, even friendly toward strangers, so they are not ideal guard dogs. The breed also typically gets along with other dogs.

AT A GLANCE	
Ease of training	
Affection	
Playfulness	
Good with children	
Good with other dogs	
Grooming required	

Eye spots should not be bigger than the palm of a hand. On the head, the two eyes must not be inside the same spot.

+ This breed may be prone to hip dysplasia, entropion or ectropion eyes and pulmonic stenosis of the heart.

HISTORY

French pointing dogs all share similar characteristics, particularly their skill at hunting, pointing, and retrieving. The Bourbonnais is thought to derive from Spanish pointers, and was first mentioned in the 1500s. The breed is usually born tail-less with a white coat coat ticked with fawn or liver. Today, these fine pointers have won favor in the U.S., Canada, and across Europe.

Braque Saint-Germain

Saint-Germain Pointng Dog
FRANCE

Exercise required

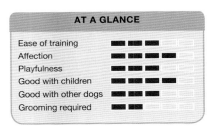

Braque Saint-Germain puppy

Common Coat Colors

		Average height (inches)	Average weight (pounds)	Average life expectancy (years)
48	100+	16+
	80	14
36		
	60	12
24	40	10
	20	8
12		
	10	6

Braque Saint-Germains are friendly animals that are incredibly loyal to their owners. In fact, some members of this cuddly breed are notorious face-lickers. However, prospective owners should be aware that as puppies these dogs can be quite boisterous and so may not be the best choice of pet for families that contain toddlers or other young children. Even so, Braque Saint-Germains do fine in households with other animals because members of this breed typically get along well with other pets.

AT A GLANCE

Ease of training	▬ ▬ ▬ ▬
Affection	▬ ▬ ▬ ▬ ▬
Playfulness	▬ ▬ ▬ ▬
Good with children	▬ ▬ ▬ ▬ ▬
Good with other dogs	▬ ▬ ▬ ▬
Grooming required	▬ ▬ ▬

 Generally very healthy but this breed may be prone to hip dysplasia.

! The breed was originally named the Braque de Compiègne after the place where the first litter was born.

HISTORY

This versatile hunting breed was developed in the 1830s at the royal kennels at Compiègne, Northern France, before being moved down to Saint Germain en Laye on the outskirts of Paris, from where it takes its name. English Pointers and different regional French pointers were used to produce the Saint-Germain, which was initially favored for the show ring rather than as a working breed. These dogs, popular in France in the 1860s, were present at the first French dog show some thirty years after their creation.

Brittany

FRANCE

Brittany puppy

Exercise required

Common
Coat Colors

48	100+	16+
	80	14
36		
	60	12
24	40	10
	20	8
12		
	10	6

Average height (inches)
Average weight (pounds)
Average life expectancy (years)

Once known as the Brittany Spaniel, but now simply the Brittany, these are busy, lively, intelligent, personable, and highly skilled hunting dogs. They have spaniel-like characteristics, particularly in their appearance, but when working, they behave more like pointers. These small, compact, leggy dogs are capable of covering a lot of ground, but they work best in a smaller range than pointers. They are excellent at pointing and holding game and retrieving on land and water, and also thrive in loving, active homes.

AT A GLANCE

Ease of training	▰▰▰▰▰
Affection	▰▰▰▰▰
Playfulness	▰▰▰▰
Good with children	▰▰▰▰
Good with other dogs	▰▰▰
Grooming required	▰

! They hold more U.S. dual titles (confirmation and field trials) than any other breed.

HISTORY

The Brittany derives from ancient stock; paintings from the seventeenth century include similar dogs, and early records date to the 1800s. Associated with Brittany, in France, they likely have English Setters and small spaniels in their heritage. Bred by the wealthy to hunt woodcock, these small dogs were useful to poachers because they were easy to hide. In the U.S. today they are popular for field trials.

+ Generally healthy but some hereditary problems can include hip dysplasia and epilepsy.

Český Fousek

Bohemian Wirehaired Pointing Griffon / Barbu Tchèque

CZECH REPUBLIC

Český Fousek
puppy

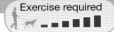

Exercise required

Common
Coat Colors

The Český Fousek is a Czech breed of versatile gundog. They are wirehaired, and have the beard and moustache ("facial furnishings") common to the wirehaired breeds. There is a dramatic difference in size between the bitches and dogs of this breed. They adapt to any sort of terrain and type of hunting—going after upland birds and waterfowl and tracking large game. They also make fantastic family dogs.

	Average height (inches)	Average weight (pounds)	Average life expectancy (years)
	48	100+	16+
		80	14
	36		
		60	12
	24	40	10
		20	8
	12		
		10	6

AT A GLANCE

Ease of training	▪▪ ▪▪ ▪▪ ▪▪
Affection	▪▪ ▪▪ ▪▪ ▪▪
Playfulness	▪▪ ▪▪ ▪▪ ▪▪
Good with children	▪▪ ▪▪ ▪▪ ▪▪
Good with other dogs	▪▪ ▪▪ ▪▪
Grooming required	▪▪ ▪

 The female Český Fousek is called "Česká Fouska."

+ Generally very healthy but this breed may be prone to alopecia and hip dysplasia.

HISTORY

The Český Fousek is thought to be an ancient breed, although written standards were first established in the nineteenth century. The breed nearly became extinct in the 1920s, and was saved by breeding with Stochelhaars. The Český Fousek was used in the creation of the foundation stock of the Slovakian Rough-Haired Pointer. Nowadays it thrives in its role as hunter and companion in its homeland and several other Europeans countries.

Chesapeake Bay Retriever

UNITED STATES

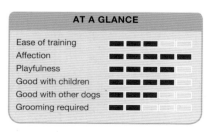

Chesapeake Bay
Retriever puppy

Exercise required

Common
Coat Colors

48	100+	16+
	80	14
36		
	60	12
24	40	10
	20	8
12		
	10	6

Average height (inches)
Average weight (pounds)
Average life expectancy (years)

The Chesapeake Bay Retriever has been bred over the last 200 years as a working gundog, and there are few breeds that surpass it in water-retrieving abilities. However, Chesapeakes also combine their brilliant working skills with a loyal, affectionate nature and can make superb family companions; they also excel at agility and working trials. They are intelligent and lively, requiring an active home, and can be independent, although with early training this can be overcome. The Chesapeake Bay Retriever was declared Maryland's official state dog in 1964.

AT A GLANCE

Ease of training	■■ ■■ ■■ □□ □□
Affection	■■ ■■ ■■ ■■ □□
Playfulness	■■ ■■ ■■ ■■ □□
Good with children	■■ ■■ ■■ ■■ □□
Good with other dogs	■■ ■■ ■■ □□ □□
Grooming required	■■ ■■ □□ □□ □□

+ Generally healthy but some hereditary problems can include hip dysplasia, cancer, and progressive retinal atrophy.

 Some of these dogs "smile" by baring their front teeth in a peculiar grin—this is a sign of joy or submissiveness.

HISTORY

In an 1845 letter, George Law described how he rescued two puppies from a floundering English ship out of Newfoundland. He called them Newfoundlands, but they were likely similar to the now-extinct St. John's Water Dog. Law landed the pups, Sailor, a male, and Canton, a female, in Maryland, where Sailor bred with Irish Water Spaniels, setters, and retrivers; Canton mixed with hunting and retrieving dogs. Their progeny all shared the same characteristics, including great skill at duck hunting.

Clumber Spaniel

ENGLAND

Clumber Spaniel puppy

Exercise required

The Clumber Spaniel is affectionate, calm, and confident, and was prized for its determination in pursuit of game. The stubborn Clumber tends to be a one-person dog that needs a strong leader, but once socialized, it will look after the whole family. These dogs can be aloof with strangers, but since they rarely bark, they don't make good watchdogs; they also lack the territorial instinct to be guard dogs. They tend to be sedate and do well in apartments. Once quite popular as companions, they are rare today.

Average height (inches)
Average weight (pounds)
Average life expectancy (years)

	48	100+	16+
		80	14
	36		
		60	12
	24	40	10
		20	8
	12		
		10	6

Common Coat Colors
○○○

AT A GLANCE

Ease of training	■■ ■■
Affection	■■ ■■
Playfulness	■■ ■■
Good with children	■■ ■■ ■■
Good with other dogs	■■ ■■ ■■
Grooming required	■■ ■■

 Prince Albert, consort of Queen Victoria, promoted this breed, as did his son, King Edward VII.

✚ Generally healthy but some hereditary problems can include entropion/ectropion eye conditions, spinal disc herniation and hip dysplasia.

HISTORY

By far the stockiest of the spaniel breeds, the Clumber traces back to at least the eighteenth century. A painting from 1788 depicts the Duke of Newcastle with several lemon-and-white dogs that appear to be Clumbers. The Duke bred them at his estate, Clumber Park, hence their name. The dogs were the preserve of the aristocracy due to their excellent noses and quiet temperament, and were not found among the "commoners." The arrived in the U.S. in the late 1800s.

Cocker Spaniel

American Cocker Spaniel

UNITED STATES

Cocker Spaniel puppies

Exercise required

Common Coat Colors

48	100+	16+
	80	14
36		
	60	12
24	40	10
	20	8
12		
	10	6

Average height (inches)
Average weight (pounds)
Average life expectancy (years)

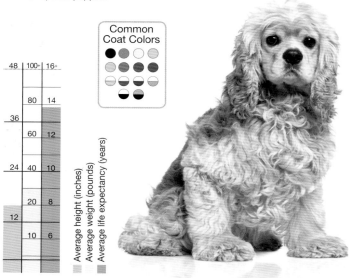

The Cocker Spaniel, or American Cocker Spaniel as they are also known, is the smallest of the sporting dogs and a truly compact athlete. These are working dogs, but they are also extremely popular as family pets and excel in this capacity. Cockers are generally friendly, cheerful, and lively companions that require vigorous daily exercise.

AT A GLANCE

Ease of training	■■
Affection	■■■■■
Playfulness	■■■■■
Good with children	■■■■
Good with other dogs	■■■■
Grooming required	■■■■

 Generally very healthy but may be prone to teeth and gum problems, idiopathic epilepsy, hypothyroidism, and progressive retinal atrophy.

! A Cocker named My Own Brucie won Best in Show at Westminster twice—in 1940 and 1941. He was known as the "most photographed dog in the world."

HISTORY

The spaniel family is large and very old—the first spaniel arrived in America on the Mayflower in 1620. These dogs were initially divided into land and water spaniels; the nineteenth century saw the advent of the breed names we know today. Cockers were first used to flush woodcock, hence the name, and later for flushing and retrieving. They are also popular field trial dogs. Although the breed originated in England, over time differences developed in the American dog, and they are now separate breeds.

Curly-Coated Retriever

ENGLAND

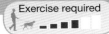

Exercise required

Curly-Coated Retriever puppy

These dogs were renowned for their stamina and ability to work all day with enthusiasm, often in severe weather or freezing water. Their tightly curled, water-resistant coat is a distinctive feature of the breed. They are loyal and highly intelligent dogs that thrive when working, but are also suited to an active family environment. The Curly-Coated Retriever is affectionate, loving and excellent with children. The more mental and physical exercise you give it, the calmer it will be. Socialize them well with people and other pets at an early age. Without proper balance in its life, it can be reserved or timid with strangers. Curly-Coated Retrievers make an ideal partner for an active family.

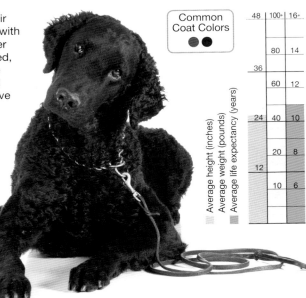

Common Coat Colors

	Average height (inches)	Average weight (pounds)	Average life expectancy (years)
	48	100+	16+
		80	14
	36		
		60	12
	24	40	10
		20	8
	12		
		10	6

AT A GLANCE

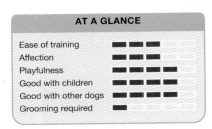

Ease of training
Affection
Playfulness
Good with children
Good with other dogs
Grooming required

! The Curly dates to the eighteenth century and is the oldest of the retrieving breeds.

+ Bloat, cancer, cardiac problems, epilepsy, exercise-induced-collapse eye problems, glycogen storage disease, and hip dysplasia.

HISTORY

The Curly-Coated Retriever was popular with gamekeepers in the early 1800s. The breed's origins are unclear, but its heritage may include the sixteenth century English Water Spaniel, the St. John's Newfoundland (also an ancestor of the Labrador), a European water retriever called the Wetterhound, and the Irish Water Spaniel. There is speculation the Poodle may also be in the mix. Curlies had made their way to the U.S. by the time of the Civil War, but they were, and still remain, a rarity.

299

Deutscher Wachtelhund
German Spaniel
GERMANY

Exercise required

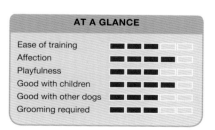

Deutscher Wachtelhund
puppy

48	100+	16+
	80	14
36		
	60	12
24	40	10
	20	8
12		
	10	6

Average height (inches)
Average weight (pounds)
Average life expectancy (years)

Common Coat Colors

This German hunting dog is often referred to as a German Spaniel, although in Germany they are not classed as spaniels. The breed was developed around 300 years ago to hunt in extreme weather over difficult terrain, and these dogs are very tough and tenacious. They are excellent trackers and flushers, and will work on land or in water hunting birds and fur game. They are renowned for going in for the kill and returning with the game to the hunter. Active and intelligent, they can make loyal family companions in a lively environment.

AT A GLANCE

Ease of training	■■ ■■ ■■ ▢▢ ▢▢
Affection	■■ ■■ ■■ ■■ ▢▢
Playfulness	■■ ■■ ■■ ▢▢ ▢▢
Good with children	■■ ■■ ■■ ■■ ▢▢
Good with other dogs	■■ ■■ ■■ ▢▢ ▢▢
Grooming required	■■ ■■ ■■ ▢▢ ▢▢

+ Generally healthy with few hereditary problems.

! Deutscher Wachtelhund actually translates as "German quail dog."

HISTORY

During the Middle Ages, only the wealthiest German families could afford kennels of hunting dogs, and they also controlled all the game. By the 1700s, though, the working classes were able to hunt, and versatile hunting dogs developed from the Stoberhund, including the Deutscher Wachtelhund, which hunted all types of game over any terrain. The breed was given official recognition in 1903 when the German Wachtelhund Club was established; the breed standard was written in 1910.

Drentsche Patrijshond

Dutch Partridge Dog
NETHERLANDS

Exercise required

Drentsche Patrijshond
puppy

Common
Coat Colors

	48	100+	16+
		80	14
	36		
		60	12
		24	40	10
			20	8
	12		
			10	6

Average height (inches)
Average weight (pounds)
Average life expectancy (years)

This versatile breed takes its name from the province of Drenthe in the Netherlands, and is also known as the Dutch Partridge Dog. This breed usually develops extremely intense attachment to all people it loves. It's prone to suffer from severe separation anxiety so owners must be willing to spend a great deal of time with them. It is considerate and gentle with children, and its fairly strong protective instinct makes it a decent watchdog. Its gentle demeanor, however, makes it unsuitable for work as a guard dog.

AT A GLANCE	
Ease of training	▬▬▬ ▬▬▬ ▬▬▬
Affection	▬▬▬ ▬▬▬ ▬▬▬
Playfulness	▬▬▬ ▬▬▬ ▬▬▬
Good with children	▬▬▬ ▬▬▬ ▬▬▬ ▬▬▬
Good with other dogs	▬▬▬ ▬▬▬ ▬▬▬
Grooming required	▬▬▬ ▬▬▬

+ Eye problems, hereditary stomatocytosis, hip dysplasia, elbow dysplasia and deafness.

! Partrijhonds appear in early Dutch paintings *The Hunter's Present* and *The Poultry Seller* by Metsu.

HISTORY

This ancient breed developed from Spanish and Flemish pointing dogs but also shares some spaniel-like attributes. In their home area of Drenthe, the dogs were used by gentry and commoners alike for hunting all types of game and vermin, for guarding the farms, and even pulling small carts. The Drentsche remains primarily a working dog, even in North America, where they are used as hunters. They are slowly gaining a reputation as loyal companion animals, however.

English Cocker Spaniel

ENGLAND

Exercise required

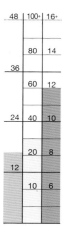

English Cocker Spaniel puppy

Average height (inches)	Average weight (pounds)	Average life expectancy (years)
48	100+	16+
36	80	14
	60	12
24	40	10
12	20	8
	10	6

The English Cocker, which is slightly larger than the American Cocker, is a lively, cheerful, busy, compact dog that makes a superb family companion and working dog. These are intelligent and inquisitive dogs, always being industrious in some manner, with their tails generally beating out a good rhythm! There is some difference between Cockers bred for showing and working, as in many breeds, but their temperament is typically universally endearing as long as they are well socialized from an early age.

Common Coat Colors

Generally healthy but some hereditary problems can include progressive retinal atrophy, familial nethropathy, and hip dysplasia.

AT A GLANCE

Ease of training	▉▉▉▉▉
Affection	▉▉▉▉▉
Playfulness	▉▉▉▉▉
Good with children	▉▉▉▉
Good with other dogs	▉▉▉
Grooming required	▉▉▉▉

 The name Cocker comes from their use to hunt woodcock in England. English Cockers also hunt other birds.

HISTORY

The earliest references to Cocker Spaniels date to the late eighteenth century. Thomas Bewick wrote in his book *A General History of Quadrupeds* about "Springers" and "Cockers" in 1790. This and other early writings reveal that Cockers were originally used in pairs and only for flushing birds. As the range on guns increased, the dogs were also trained to retrieve. The Spaniel Club was founded in England in 1885 to promote the breeding of different spaniels for different sporting events, and to create breed standards. The American Spaniel Club was formed in 1881, with one of its first objectives to differentiate between Cocker and Field Spaniels and to prevent crossbreeding. Today, English Cockers remain favorites in the show ring, as companions, and as working dogs.

English Setter

ENGLAND

English Setter puppy

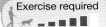

Common Coat Colors

The English Setter is one of the true "gentlemen" of the dog world. These lovely dogs combine a gentle, kind, affectionate nature with tremendous working skills and make excellent family companions. Sadly, breed numbers are now low, especially in England, but they are bred in larger numbers in the United States. Four setter breeds are recognized: the English, Irish, Irish Red and White, and the Gordon.

	48	100+	16+
		80	14
	36		
		60	12
Average height (inches)	24	40	10
Average weight (pounds)		20	8
Average life expectancy (years)	12		
		10	6

+ Generally healthy but they may be prone to teeth and gum problems, idiopathic epilepsy, hypothyroidism, and progressive retinal atrophy.

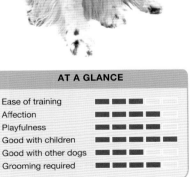

AT A GLANCE

Ease of training	■ ■ ■
Affection	■ ■ ■ ■
Playfulness	■ ■ ■ ■
Good with children	■ ■ ■ ■ ■
Good with other dogs	■ ■ ■
Grooming required	■ ■ ■ ■

! Puppies need lots of attention, diversions, and moderate exercise, to prevent destructive behavior.

HISTORY

Early English Setters are thought to have been developed by crossing Pointing and Spaniel breeds. In the 19 th century, two types of English Setters emerged—the Laverack and Llewellin strains—each taking on the name of the man who developed it. Edward Laverack carefully nurtured his own line of English Setters, creating beautiful dogs. R. Purcell Llewellin was fond of outcrosses, starting with Laverack-type dogs and then bringing in other strains to develop amazingly successful field-trial English Setters. The difference can still be seen today when comparing the somewhat smaller field setters to the show setters. The English Setter was first shown in Newcastle Upon Tyne in 1859; Laverack's beauties were especially admired in early shows. Today, the Llewellins are favored by American hunters.

English Springer Spaniel

ENGLAND

English Springer Spaniel puppy

Exercise required

Common Coat Colors

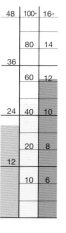

Average height (inches)
Average weight (pounds)
Average life expectancy (years)

The English Springer Spaniel is a delightful breed, full of enthusiasm for life, activity, and fun. These are extremely active dogs that have superb temperaments and make excellent companions for the right home. They are popular working gundogs, but given their intelligence and trainability are also used as drug and bomb-detection animals. They excel at agility and field trials and like nothing better than having an activity or a job to do.

AT A GLANCE

Ease of training	▰▰▰ ▰▰▰ ▰▰▰
Affection	▰▰▰ ▰▰▰ ▰▰▰
Playfulness	▰▰▰ ▰▰▰
Good with children	▰▰▰ ▰▰▰ ▰▰▰
Good with other dogs	▰▰▰ ▰▰▰ ▰▰▰
Grooming required	▰▰▰ ▰▰

 Generally healthy but some hereditary ailments can include eye disorders, hip dysplasia, and ear problems.

HISTORY

The Springer was named for its original flushing method— working patches of dense undergrowth to startle birds so they "spring" into the air. The term "spaniel" likely comes from the Roman name for Spain, where these dogs developed. The conquering Romans, keen hunters, took these dogs across Europe and into Britain. Some of the earliest Springers to arrive in America were imported by Ernest Wells in 1907. In 1910 Springer Denne Lucy was the first registered with the AKC.

 English Springer Spaniels are bred either as hunting dogs or show dogs —but never as both.

Épagneul Bleu de Picardie

Blue Picardy Spaniel

FRANCE

Exercise required

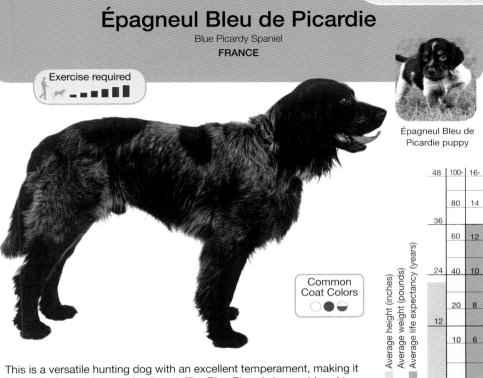

Épagneul Bleu de Picardie puppy

	48	100+	16+
		80	14
	36		
		60	12
		24	40	10
			20	8
	12		
		10	6

Average height (inches)
Average weight (pounds)
Average life expectancy (years)

Common Coat Colors

This is a versatile hunting dog with an excellent temperament, making it increasingly popular as a family pet. The Blue Picardy is considered to be a quiet breed, but needs a great deal of exercise as it has a high level of energy. It loves to play, and is a responsive and obedient breed which thrives on human companionship. It is especially good with children, and gets along well with other dogs. Similar to the Picardy Spaniel from which it is descended, it has a distinctive blue-gray coat.

AT A GLANCE

Ease of training	▬▬ ▬▬ ▬▬
Affection	▬▬ ▬▬ ▬▬ ▬▬
Playfulness	▬▬ ▬▬ ▬▬ ▬▬
Good with children	▬▬ ▬▬ ▬▬ ▬▬
Good with other dogs	▬▬ ▬▬ ▬▬
Grooming required	▬▬ ▬▬

+ The breed has no known genetic health issues, but may be prone to ear infections.

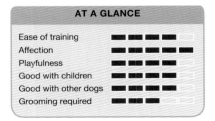

! Puppies need lots of attention, diversions, and moderate exercise, to prevent destructive behavior.

HISTORY

This unusual breed, also known as the Blue Picardy, developed in France in the early twentieth century. They were likely the offspring of English Setters and French spaniels bred in the hunting region near the mouth of the River Somme. The first blue-gray spaniel was recorded in 1875, and in 1907 the two types of Picardy Spaniels were categorized and the official club was formed. Today, they are gaining fans in the U.S. and Canada.

Field Spaniel

ENGLAND

Field Spaniel puppy

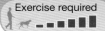
Exercise required

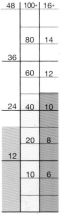

| 48 | 100+ | 16+ |
| 80 | 14 |
| 36 |
60	12
24	40	10
20	8
12
10	6

Average height (inches)
Average weight (pounds)
Average life expectancy (years)

Common Coat Colors

Field Spaniels have even temperaments and, with the right socialization, make good family companions for country life. Field Spaniels are also especially good with young children, and get on well with other dogs and cats. But they are sensitive and without attention can become nervous and anxious. They are active dogs that are still very much bred for work; they are actually described in the British Kennel Club standard as "not suitable for city living."

AT A GLANCE

Ease of training	▪▪▪▪□
Affection	▪▪▪▪▪
Playfulness	▪▪▪▪□
Good with children	▪▪▪▪□
Good with other dogs	▪▪▪□□
Grooming required	▪▪▪□□

! In 1909, a devastating fire swept through a kennel housing most of the Field Spaniels in the United States.

+ Hip and elbow dysplasia, hypothyroidism, heart problems, ear infections, eye problems, patellar luxation, Cushing's disease, cancer, and arthritis.

HISTORY

This breed developed approximately 150 years ago and went through a number of changes before arriving at the modern type. Both the English Cocker and Sussex Spaniel, along with other spaniel types, have influenced the Field Spaniel, which is noted today for its working abilities. Around the 1950s, or so, they began being bred with longer legs, making them more suitable for field work. Now rare, they are registered as a Vulnerable Native Breed by the Kennel Club of England.

Flat-Coated Retriever

ENGLAND

Exercise required

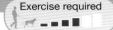

Flat-Coated Retriever
puppy

These dogs are noted for their affable, easy-going natures, making them excellent companions in the home. They are good with chldren, providing an adult remains nearby to contain their boisterous enthusiasm. These retrievers require plenty of exercise and engagement to help channel their natural sporting energy. While they will protect their owners and property with an assertive bark, they are unlikely to back up such noise with actual aggression. With their excellent sense of smell and boundless energy, they are often trained as drug-sniffer dogs. They are also used, sometimes crossed with Labs, as Guide Dogs for the Blind.

48	100+	16+
	80	14
36		
	60	12
24	40	10
	20	8
12		
	10	6

Average height (inches)
Average weight (pounds)
Average life expectancy (years)

Common Coat Colors

AT A GLANCE

Ease of training	
Affection	
Playfulness	
Good with children	
Good with other dogs	
Grooming required	

Various eye problems such as progressive retinal atrophy and glaucoma, hip dysplasia, epilepsy, diabetes, deafnes, and cancer.

! This breed has been nicknamed the Peter Pan of dogs because of its carefree attitude.

HISTORY

The Flat-Coated Retriever was developed in the early nineteenth century by crossing Newfoundland blood along with setters, spaniels, and sheepdogs, to create a retrieving dog capable of working on land and in water. They were widely used by fishermen and gamekeepers throughout England. Unique among retrievers, it was bred to be a show dog, with a breeding program begun in 1864. In 1873 Sewallis E. Shirley, founder of the English Kennel Club, helped stabilize the breed. The AKC recognized it in 1915.

French Gascony Pointer

Braque Francais / Gascogne
FRANCE

Exercise required

French Gascony
Pointer puppy

Average height (inches)
Average weight (pounds)
Average life expectancy (years)

48	100+	16+
	80	14
36		
	60	12
24	40	10
	20	8
12		
	10	6

Common
Coat Colors

This ancient French pointer is a versatile hunting dog that will flush, retrieve, and trail game. Its temperament is friendly, sociable, and submissive. It should never be subjected to harsh training methods; if well socialized with people and animals, it makes a good pet.

AT A GLANCE	
Ease of training	▬▬ ▬▬ ▬▬ □
Affection	▬▬ ▬▬ ▬▬ □
Playfulness	▬▬ ▬▬ □ □
Good with children	▬▬ ▬▬ ▬▬ □
Good with other dogs	▬▬ ▬▬ □ □
Grooming required	▬▬ □ □ □

 Hip and elbow dysplasia, patellar luxation, eye problems, pannus, demodex mange, cleft lip, acral mutilation syndrome, and aortic stenosis.

HISTORY

This breed is thought to have developed from the old Spanish Pointer in southwestern France and the central Pyrenees. At the end of the nineteenth century a search for the breeds ancestors found two separate regional varieties, the French Gascony Pointer, and the French Pyrenean Pointer. The first breed club was formed in 1850, and the standards for both breeds were written in 1880.

! Without sufficient physical activity this dog may become destructive, hyperactive, and disobedient.

French Pyrenean Pointer

Braque Français / Pyrénées / Braque Français de Petite Taille

FRANCE

Exercise required

French Pyrenean Pointer puppy

Common Coat Colors

	Average height (inches)	Average weight (pounds)	Average life expectancy (years)
	48	100+	16+
	36	80	14
		60	12
	24	40	10
		20	8
	12		
		10	6

This breed is similar to the French Gascony Pointer though slightly smaller in size and not quite as robust. Both types developed in the same area of Southwest France and the central Pyrenees and share a similar heritage. The French Pyrenean Pointer is noted as having slightly tighter skin than the Gascony, less droopy lips, and a lighter frame; their coat is also finer and shorter. The French Pyranean is a versatile and fast hunting dog with a calm temperament.

AT A GLANCE	
Ease of training	■■ ■■ ■■ ■■ □□
Affection	■■ ■■ ■■ ■■ □□
Playfulness	■■ ■■ ■■ □□ □□
Good with children	■■ ■■ ■■ ■■ □□
Good with other dogs	■■ ■■ ■■ □□ □□
Grooming required	■■ □□ □□ □□ □□

 Hip and elbow dysplasia, patellar luxation, eye problems, pannus, demodex mange, cleft lip, acral mutilation syndrome, and aortic stenosis.

! Sufficient exercise will keep these active dogs calm and relaxed indoors.

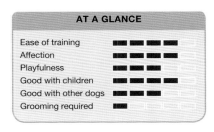

HISTORY

The original Braque Français type of pointing dog has existed since the fifteenth century. In 1975 the first French Pointing Dog-Pyranean type was brought to America, where several breeders initiated breeding programs. The dog gained further interest in the U.S. and Canada after a 1992 article in a dog magazine featured a detailed description of the breed. It was recognized by the UKC in 2006 as the Bracque Francais de Petite Taille.

French Spaniel

FRANCE

French Spaniel puppy

Exercise required

Common Coat Colors

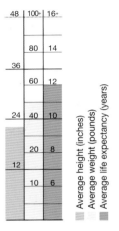

Average height (inches)
Average weight (pounds)
Average life expectancy (years)

French Spaniels are affectionate dogs suitable for an active home. Originally created in France to satisfy the need for an all-purpose hunting dog, French Spaniels gradually acquired a reputation as easy-going and affable family pets. Although they are outgoing and sweet dogs among their own people, they can be reserved or stand-offish with strangers. On the other hand, they are too sociable to make good watchdogs or guard dogs.

AT A GLANCE

Ease of training	▪▪▪▪▪
Affection	▪▪▪▪▪
Playfulness	▪▪▪▪□
Good with children	▪▪▪▪□
Good with other dogs	▪▪▪□□
Grooming required	▪▪▪□□

+ May be prone to eye problems, epilepsy and hip dysplasia.

HISTORY

The elegant and charismatic French Spaniel was first described by Gaston Phebus, Count of Foix, in his famous book on hunting, *Livre de Chasse*, although the breed undoubtedly traces back much further. During the Middle Ages, these dogs were popular among the aristocracy and were invariably found in the French royal kennels. The breed was almost unheard of outside France until the 1970s, but they are now found in England, the United States, and Canada.

 Catherine I of Russia (1684-1727) was a proud owner of a French Spaniel named Babe.

German Longhaired Pointer

Deutsch Langhaar
GERMANY

Exercise required

German Longhaired
Pointer puppy

Average height (inches)	Average weight (pounds)	Average life expectancy (years)
48	100+	16+
	80	14
36		
	60	12
24	40	10
	20	8
12		
	10	6

Common
Coat Colors

The German Longhaired Pointer is an ideal, tenacious shooting dog and works for any game on land or in water. They are hardy and enduring, with superb hunting skills and a loyal nature, but thrive in a sporting home and are not ideally suited to city life. Thanks to its docility and biddable nature this breed usually makes a terrific family pet and is also able to compete in various dog sports at the highest levels.

AT A GLANCE

Ease of training	▮▮▮
Affection	▮▮▮
Playfulness	▮▮▮
Good with children	▮▮▮▮
Good with other dogs	▮▮▮
Grooming required	▮▮▮

+ May be prone to hip dysplasia and ear infections

HISTORY

In the mid-nineteenth century, English Setter and English Pointer blood was introduced to German pointing dogs resulting in a faster, lighter animal. In 1879 the best German Longhaired Pointers were exhibited at Hanover, and a breed standard, which remains today, was drawn up. This breed is an asset to many German hunters, but it's also kept by dog enthusiasts as a loving family pet. In spite of this versatility, the breed has little recognition outside Germany.

! The "exiled" black-and-white strain of the GLP became the ancestor of the Large Munsterlander.

German Shorthaired Pointer

Deutsch Kurzhaar

GERMANY

German Shorthaired Pointer puppy

Exercise required

Average height (inches)	Average weight (pounds)	Average life expectancy (years)
48	100+	16+
	80	14
36		
	60	12
24	40	10
	20	8
12		
	10	6

Common Coat Colors

The German Shorthaired Pointer developed from ancient German hunting dogs, or bird dogs, that had been influenced by Spanish pointers and native scent hounds. The scent hound heritage gave rise to the German Shorthaired Pointer's highly tuned scenting abilities, which, with the addition of some English Foxhound and later English Pointers, led to a versatile hunting dog. Known for its intelligence and loyalty, it makes an excellent home companion.

AT A GLANCE

Ease of training	■■■■□
Affection	■■■■□
Playfulness	■■■■□
Good with children	■■■■□
Good with other dogs	■■■□□
Grooming required	■□□□□

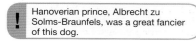

! Hanoverian prince, Albrecht zu Solms-Braunfels, was a great fancier of this dog.

+ Generally healthy but hereditary problems can include hip dysplasia, gastric torsion, von Willebrand's disease, and entropion.

HISTORY

The initial gene pool for the German Shorthaired Pointer was varied, and a number of early dogs were registered with unknown parentage. The pedigree register was established in 1872, and Hecktor I was the first dog entered into the German Kennel Club stud book. Hecktor was liver and white and described as hound-like in appearance. Nero and Treff were two other important early foundation dogs for the breed.

German Wirehaired Pointer

Deutsch Drahthaar

GERMANY

German Wirehaired Pointer puppy

Exercise required

Common Coat Colors

The modern German Wirehaired Pointer is every bit as versatile and charming as its ancestors and, although extremely energetic, can make a superb companion for an active home. The German Wirehair is smart, stubborn, energetic, hard-working, curious, and a creative thinker. All of those qualities can make him a challenge to train. So start training your puppy the day you bring him home. The German Wirehair may be devoted to its family, but with strangers, the attitude can range from aloof to downright unfriendly. This is why it's important to socialize these dogs at an early age. They may also show aggression to strange dogs and other animals.

	Average height (inches)	Average weight (pounds)	Average life expectancy (years)
	48	100+	16+
		80	14
	36		
		60	12
	24	40	10
		20	8
	12		
		10	6

AT A GLANCE

Ease of training	
Affection	
Playfulness	
Good with children	
Good with other dogs	
Grooming required	

 Prone to von Willebrand's disease, hip dysplasia and heart disease.

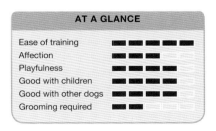 The German Wirehair's beard, whiskers, and eyebrows (known as furnishings) protect his face and eyes from injury.

HISTORY

This charismatic breed was developed in the 1800s by hunters who wanted an all-purpose hunting dog able to work in mountains, forests, and water. The German Shorthair Pointer, the Pudelpointer, Griffon, and Polish Water Dog, plus several other breeds, all contributed to the creation of the versatile Deutsch Draathar—the German Wirehair. Single hunters or small hunting parties use these dogs for tracking, locating, and pointing all manner of game.

Golden Retriever
SCOTLAND

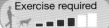
Exercise required

Goldies, as they are often called, are known for their exceptional temperaments, and although they were bred originally as working dogs, they make the transition to family companions with ease. They are still valued as gundogs, but are also used in a range of other capacities including search and rescue, drug and bomb detection, and assistance dogs for the deaf and blind. Golden Retrievers are generally easy to train, obedient, and intelligent, which combined with their gentle nature, has led to their immense popularity.

Golden Retriever puppy

AT A GLANCE

Ease of training	■■■■■
Affection	■■■■■
Playfulness	■■■■■
Good with children	■■■■
Good with other dogs	■■■■
Grooming required	■■■

! Liberty, a Golden Retriever, lived with President Gerald Ford and his family in the White House.

 Generally healthy but some hereditary problems can include cancer, hip and elbow dysplasia, heart problems, and progressive retinal atrophy.

Average height (inches)	Average weight (pounds)	Average life expectancy (years)
48	100+	16+
	80	14
36		
	60	12
24	40	10
	20	8
12		
	10	6

Common Coat Colors
○ ○ ◐ ●

HISTORY

Originally called the Yellow Retriever, the breed was developed in the nineteenth century in Scotland by Sir Dudley Coutts Marjoribanks, who kept large kennels on his estate and bred hunting dogs. One dog that helped to estabish the breed was Nous, bred to a Tweed Water Spaniel named Belle who produced four yellow puppies. These dogs were crossbred to Red Setters, Wavy Coated Retrievers, Bloodhounds, and Tweed Water Spaniels, eventually giving rise to a specific type. The first Goldie was seen at Crufts Dog Show in 1908, and in 1913, the British Kennel Club recognized the breed. The breed had arrived in the United States by the 1930s with Colonel S. Magoffin. He established the Gilnockie Kennels in Colorado, which account for many of the pedigree lines today.

Gordon Setter

SCOTLAND

Gordon Setter puppy

48	100+	16+
	80	14
36		
	60	12
24	40	10
	20	8
12		
	10	6

Average height (inches)
Average weight (pounds)
Average life expectancy (years)

Common Coat Colors

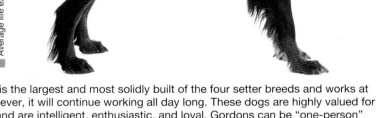

The Gordon Setter is the largest and most solidly built of the four setter breeds and works at a slower pace; however, it will continue working all day long. These dogs are highly valued for this great stamina and are intelligent, enthusiastic, and loyal. Gordons can be "one-person" dogs, and are best suited to life in a working environment.

AT A GLANCE

Ease of training	■ ■ ■
Affection	■ ■ ■ ■
Playfulness	■ ■ ■ ■ □
Good with children	■ ■ ■ ■ □
Good with other dogs	■ ■ □ □ □
Grooming required	■ ■ ■ □ □

 Developed by the Dukes of Gordon, the black-and-tan dogs were originally known as Gordon Castle Setters.

+ Generally healthy but some hereditary problems may include gastric torsion, neonatal fatalities, hip dysplasia, and cancer.

HISTORY

Gordon Setter heritage traces back to the fourteenth century to the spaniel group of hunting dogs, and there are many historic references to black-and-tan dogs of setter type. Their modern development began in the early nineteenth century on the Scottish estate of the 4th Duke of Gordon. Other kennels, including the Earl of Leicester's in northern England, also bred black-and-tan working dogs. These dogs are thought to have been crossbred with Bloodhounds to establish the Gordon Setter type.

Grand Griffon Vendéen

FRANCE

Exercise required

Common Coat Colors

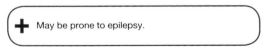

Grand Griffon Vendéen puppy

Average height (inches)	Average weight (pounds)	Average life expectancy (years)
48	100+	16+
	80	14
36		
	60	12
24	40	10
	20	8
12		
	10	6

These are friendly dogs that can be very independent and have a reputation for escaping! They have an obstinate, single-minded disposition, which is fairly typical for a scent hound. Their docile and friendly nature, however, and prepossessing appearance, make them a great choice for families with children. The Grand Griffon Vendéen was bred as a tireless hunter and therefore needs lots of intensive activity to be fully content.

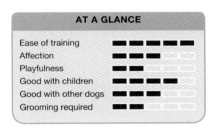

AT A GLANCE

Ease of training	■■ ■■ ■■ ■■ ■■
Affection	■■ ■■ ■■
Playfulness	■■ ■■
Good with children	■■ ■■ ■■ ■■
Good with other dogs	■■ ■■ ■■
Grooming required	■■ ■■

+ May be prone to epilepsy.

! It has a loud and beautiful voice that it uses frequently and sometimes without any reason.

HISTORY

There are several breeds of Griffon (French hunting dogs) from the Vendée region on the west coast of France, with the Grand being the largest and oldest. The breed is believed to trace back to at least the sixteenth century, when hunting was developing on a grand scale in France, becoming the sport of the royals. Accordingly, great emphasis was placed on breeding the best hunting dogs. The Grande Griffon is a brave, determined scent hound used for hunting large game, including wild boar.

Irish Red and White Setter

IRELAND

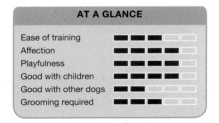

Irish Red and White
Setter puppy

Exercise required

Common
Coat Colors

48	100+	16+
	80	14
36		
	60	12
24	40	10
	20	8
12		
	10	6

Average height (inches)
Average weight (pounds)
Average life expectancy (years)

The Irish Red and White Setter is a clever, work-driven and loyal hunting dog, which adapts well to the life of a family pet. This is a joyous, sociable and spirited dog and so is recommended for active families that can provide physical and mental stimulation. They are known to be impulsive and need early and proper socialization to learn appropriate behavior.

AT A GLANCE

Ease of training	■■■■
Affection	■■■■
Playfulness	■■■■
Good with children	■■■■
Good with other dogs	■■
Grooming required	■■■

 This breed was saved through the efforts of the Rev. Noble Huston, and a Dr. Elliott following World War I.

 This breed is prone to von Willebrand's disease, eye problems, leukocyte adhesion deficiency, hip dysplasia, epilepsy and hypothyroidism.

HISTORY

The Irish Red and White Setter is not as well-known as the Irish (Red) Setter, but is thought to be the older breed. By the end of the nineteenth century, however, the Irish Setter had overtaken the Red and White, and the older breed almost became extinct. Concerted efforts from dog lovers have re-established the breed, though their numbers still remain low.

Irish Setter

IRELAND

Irish Setter puppy

Exercise required

		Average height (inches)	Average weight (pounds)	Average life expectancy (years)
48			100+	16+
			80	14
36				
			60	12
		24	40	10
			20	8
12				
			10	6

Common Coat Colors

The Irish Setter is one of the most popular of the setter breeds and is a particularly fun-loving, and lively companion, suitable for an active or working home. Popular with the aristocracy in the past, the dogs appear to have a noble air about them, which belies their outgoing and often "clownish" nature. The breed excelled in a variety of hunting activities, but especially birds. They are also popular in field trials and the show ring, with slightly different types filling each role.

AT A GLANCE

Ease of training	■ ■ ■ □ □
Affection	■ ■ ■ ■ □
Playfulness	■ ■ ■ ■ □
Good with children	■ ■ ■ □ □
Good with other dogs	■ ■ ■ ■ □
Grooming required	■ ■ ■ □ □

! Irish Setters are widely used as therapy dogs in schools and hospitals.

+ Generally healthy but some may be prone to canine leukocyte adhesion deficiency, hip dysplasia, epilepsy, bloat, hypothyroidism, and progressive retinal atrophy.

HISTORY

The Irish Setter probably developed in the eighteenth century through crosses of Irish Water Spaniels, Irish Terriers, Gordon Setters, English Setters, spaniels, and pointers. Originally bred to be red and white, the characteristic solid red color appeared in Ireland in the late 1800s and became a mark of quality. The Irish Setter was first used to "set" game, sniffing out birds hidden in undergrowth and crouching low to indicate the bird's presence. A breed club for the Irish Setter was formed in 1882.

Irish Water Spaniel

IRELAND

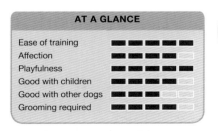

Irish Water Spaniel puppy

Exercise required

Average height (inches)
Average weight (pounds)
Average life expectancy (years)

| 48 | 100+ | 16+ |
| 80 | 14 |
| 36 |
60	12
24	40	10
20	8
12
10	6

Common
Coat Colors

The Irish Water Spaniel has a distinctive tightly curled, water-resistant coat and an unusual tail, called a "rat tail" or "whip tail." There is no mistaking this breed! They are the largest and one of the oldest spaniels. Bred as working dogs, they excel over difficult marshy or boggy terrain and are renowned for their stamina and tenacity. They are affectionate, loyal dogs with an innate sense of humor. Despite all this, they are rare.

AT A GLANCE

Ease of training	■■■■■■■
Affection	■■■■■
Playfulness	■■■■■
Good with children	■■■■
Good with other dogs	■■■
Grooming required	■■■■

+ May be prone to hip dysplasia, hypothyroidism, eye problems, ear infections, allergies, paronychia, distichiasis, and megaesophagus.

! The Irish Water Spaniel's coat is naturally oily to repel water and keep the skin underneath dry.

HISTORY

We know little about dogs that resembled the IWS throughout the ages. The breed we know today is a more recent development. Mentions of smooth-tailed spaniels from Ireland includes one that was a gift from Queen Elizabeth I's spymaster, Sir Robert Cecil, to the King of France in 1598. The dog that has the best claim to being the first modern Irish Water Spaniel was named Boatswain. He lived from 1834 to 1852, an incredibly long lifespan for the time, and sired many excellent hunting and show dogs.

Kooikerhondje

NETHERLANDS

Exercise required

Kooikerhondje puppy

	Average height (inches)	Average weight (pounds)	Average life expectancy (years)
	48	100+	16+
		80	14
	36		
		60	12
	24	40	10
		20	8
	12		
		10	6

Common Coat Colors

The Kooikerhondje is a delightful breed with spaniel-like qualities, but it is little heard of outside its homeland. This is a vivacious, vigilant, industrious, and intelligent breed that specializes in hunting ducks and exterminating vermin. Its hunting ability won it widespread acclaim by the 1600s. This breed has an independent streak so extensive socialization is necessary to ensure calm co-existence with children and other pets.

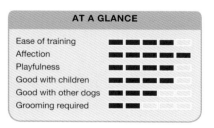

AT A GLANCE

Ease of training	▬▬▬▬
Affection	▬▬▬▬▬
Playfulness	▬▬▬▬
Good with children	▬▬▬▬
Good with other dogs	▬▬▬
Grooming required	▬▬

+ Generally very healthy but they may be prone to teeth and gum problems, idiopathic epilepsy, hypothyroidism, and progressive retinal atrophy.

HISTORY

Dating back to at least the fifteenth century, these small, orange and white dogs appear in many Dutch paintings. Developed for duck hunting, Kooikerhondje were trained to weave in and out of foliage along river banks to lure ducks into a trap. It is thought the ducks were attracted by the white feathery tail. The breed came close to extinction in the nineteenth century, but was saved largely by the work of Baroness van Hardenbroek. Kooikerhondje make superb companions and still excel in duck hunting.

! Black tips on the ears are known as earrings.

321

Labrador Retriever

CANADA / ENGLAND

Exercise required
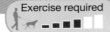

Ranked as one of the most popular dog breeds in the world, the Labrador Retriever has worked its way into the hearts of dog lovers everywhere. This breed is versatility at its best. Labs make excellent working gundogs and superb family pets, in addition to being used as service dogs, by the military, as assistance dogs, and for all manner of activities including agility and obedience. Typically Labradors are intelligent, trainable dogs that have a soft, kind nature.

Labrador Retriever pups

 Labs love food, and as growing pups will eat anything—rocks, socks, dolls—which have all been surgically removed from these dogs.

 Generally healthy but some hereditary problems can include hip dysplasia, cancer, obesity, progressive retinal atrophy, and heart problems.

AT A GLANCE

Ease of training	■ ■ ■ ■ □		
Affection	■ ■ ■ ■ ■		
Playfulness	■ ■ ■ ■ ■		
Good with children	■ ■ ■ ■ ■		
Good with other dogs	■ ■ ■ ■ ■		
Grooming required	■ ■ □ □ □		

Average height (inches)	Average weight (pounds)	Average life expectancy (years)
48	100+	16+
	80	14
36		
	60	12
24	40	10
	20	8
12		
	10	6

Common
Coat Colors

HISTORY

Labrador Retrievers trace back to the St. John's Dog found on the Canadian island of Newfoundland. Labs emerged from a mix of working stock taken to the island by Portuguese, British, and Irish fishermen who settled and traded there in the sixteenth century. The dogs were used in the fishing industry and developed into a water-loving breed with a water-resistant coat. From the early 1800s, fishermen began taking their dogs with them when traveling to Poole Harbor, England, and started to trade the dogs as well as fish. The emergence of the modern Labrador is largely attributed to the fifth Duke of Buccleuch and his brother, the Earl of Malmesbury, who bought a number of the dogs in the early nineteenth century and began developing the breed.

Lagotto Romagnolo

ITALY

Lagotto Romagnolo puppy

Exercise required

48	100+	16+
	80	14
36		
	60	12
24	40	10
	20	8
12		
	10	6

Average height (inches)
Average weight (pounds)
Average life expectancy (years)

Common Coat Colors

The Lagatto Romagnolo is an ancient breed of water-retrieving dog that comes from the Romagna sub-region of Italy. They have a distinctive curly protective coat, useful when hunting ducks in the Northern Italian marches. They began hunting truffles after the marshes were drained in the late 1800s. Today, they are the only specialized truffle-hunting breed in the world. Along with their retrieving and gun-dog skills, they are affectionate, good-natured companion dogs.

AT A GLANCE

Ease of training	■■■■ □
Affection	■■■■ □
Playfulness	■■■■ □
Good with children	■■■ □□
Good with other dogs	■■■ □□
Grooming required	■■■■■

 The name Lagotto Romagnolo is Italian for "lake dog from Romagna."

+ May be prone to epilepsy, hip dysplasia, and eye problems.

HISTORY

Initially Lagotto Romagnolo breeders concentrated on creating dogs that would be robust, with good temperaments; the resulting canines were outstanding truffle hunters, but at the cost of the breed's purity. In the 1970s, a team of Lagotto Romagnolo fanciers began efforts to re-establish the appearance and characteristics of the breed. They achieved their goal when the breed was accepted by the FCI in 2005. It still remains rare, however.

Large Münsterländer

GERMANY

Large Münsterländer puppy

Exercise required

Common Coat Colors

Average height (inches)	Average weight (pounds)	Average life expectancy (years)
48	100+	16+
	80	14
36		
	60	12
24	40	10
	20	8
12		
	10	6

This German gun-dog breed, named after the region Münster from which it originates, is a multipurpose working animal with an excellent nose and a kind, willing temperament. These active dogs are happiest when working, but they also make suitable companions for the right busy home environment. They are not difficult dogs. If one has a firm approach, even a beginner can manage this breed; however, owners must remain calm, confident, and consistent to be effective.

AT A GLANCE

Ease of training	▬ ▬ ▬ ▬
Affection	▬ ▬ ▬
Playfulness	▬ ▬ ▬ ▬
Good with children	▬ ▬ ▬ ▬
Good with other dogs	▬ ▬ ▬ ▬
Grooming required	▬ ▬ ▬

! Large Münsterländers can be recognized in artist's representations of hunting scenes as far back as the Middle Ages.

+ Generally very healthy although this breed may be prone to hip dysplasia.

HISTORY

The breed was developed from ancient long-haired hawking dogs that were found across Europe, influenced by German and, to a small degree, English pointers. They were once known as German Longhaired Pointers and have distinctive black, or black-and-white, coats. The breed first gained official recognition in the Münsterland of Northwestern Germany in the early 1900s. The Large Münsterländer was introduced to North America by Kurt von Kleist in 1966.

Montenegrin Mountain Hound

MONTENEGRO

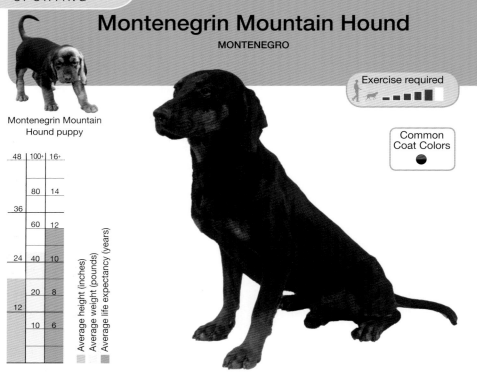

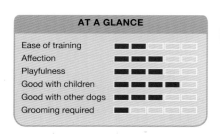

Montenegrin Mountain
Hound puppy

Exercise required

Common
Coat Colors

48	100+	16+
	80	14
36		
	60	12
24	40	10
	20	8
12		
	10	6

Average height (inches)
Average weight (pounds)
Average life expectancy (years)

This rare hound breed was formerly known as the Yugoslavian Mountain Hound and is one of several closely related Balkan hound breeds. The Montenegrin Mountain Hound is a scent hound bred specifically to work in the challenging mountain terrain of Montenegro. In its homeland it hunts a range of quarry, including foxes, hares, deer, and wild boar. They make fine additions to active homes, but are little known elsewhere in the world.

AT A GLANCE

Ease of training	■■ ■■
Affection	■■ ■■ ■■
Playfulness	■■ ■■ ■■
Good with children	■■ ■■ ■■ ■■
Good with other dogs	■■ ■■ ■■
Grooming required	■■

 This dog is called Cronogorski Planinski Gonic; "Gonic" means pinpointing prey by barking.

+ Generally very healthy but may be prone to ear infections and hip dysplasia.

HISTORY

The breed developed in the Republic of Montenegro and may be originally descended from ancient hound types introduced to the area by the Phoenicians. The first standard for the breed was drawn up in 1924 and was accepted by the United Kennel Club in the United States in 2008. These are determined, enduring, brave hunting dogs, most often used in packs and capable of hunting wild boar, deer, fox, hare, and small game. They generally have pleasant temperaments, and thrive in a working environment.

Nova Scotia Duck Tolling Retriever

CANADA

Nova Scotia Duck Tolling Retriever puppy

	48	100+	16+
		80	14
	36		
		60	12
		24	40	10
		20	8
	12		
		10	6

Average height (inches)
Average weight (pounds)
Average life expectancy (years)

Common Coat Colors

The cheerful and busy Nova Scotia Duck Tolling Retrievers are animated and versatile working gundogs. They were originally bred to work in water, but are also good upland retrievers, and are happiest when working. They have excellent temperaments and, despite their relatively small size, are tenacious and brave dogs that happily retrieve geese or wounded birds. They make good pets in active homes.

AT A GLANCE	
Ease of training	■■ ■■ ■■ ■■
Affection	■■ ■■ ■■ ■■
Playfulness	■■ ■■ ■■ ■■
Good with children	■■ ■■ ■■ ■■
Good with other dogs	■■ ■■ ■■ ■■
Grooming required	■■ ■■

✚ Generally very healthy but hereditary problems can include hip dysplasia and progressive retinal atrophy.

HISTORY

"Tolling" is a Middle English word that means "to lure or decoy game." Tolling dogs play along the shoreline attracting the attention of waterfowl, which allow their curiosity to bring them close to shore—within netting or gunshot range. It is thought that the Tolling Retriever was developed in Yarmouth County, Nova Scotia, from Red Decoy Dogs crossed with European collies. These dogs have bred true for generations now and they were accepted into the Canadian Kennel Club in 1945.

 Tollers have a unique sounding bark known as the "Toller scream," a high-pitched, howl-like, singing sound.

Old Danish Pointer
Denmark puppy

Old Danish Pointer

DENMARK

Exercise required

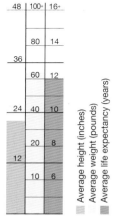

Average height (inches)
Average weight (pounds)
Average life expectancy (years)

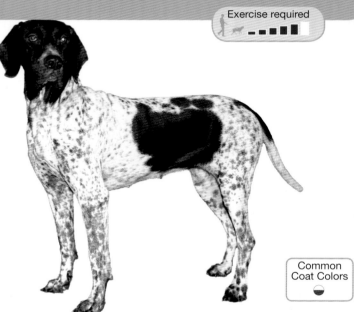

Common
Coat Colors

Bred to point grouse and quail, this dog is known for its reserved behavior in the home, where it demonstrates incredible loyalty to its master and family. It requires a certain amount of socialization to learn the basics of acceptable behavior. Thanks to its well-balanced temperament, this dog usually gets along with children and enjoys spending time with them. It makes a great companion for an active family.

AT A GLANCE

Ease of training	
Affection	
Playfulness	
Good with children	
Good with other dogs	
Grooming required	

 They are known in Denmark as Gammel Dansk Hønsehund—Old Danish Chicken Dogs.

+ No diseases specific to this breed.

HISTORY

The Old Danish Pointer is one of just a few Danish breeds and is sadly low in numbers. The breed is believed to have developed from scent hounds, including the St. Hubert's Hound, which gave rise to the Bloodhound. Breeder Morten Bak, who lived in northern Denmark during the eighteenth century, is credited with crossing local farm dogs and gypsy dogs over many generations to produce a consistent white and brown-type. Spanish pointers are also thought to have influenced this talented, low-key dog.

Picardy Spaniel

FRANCE

Exercise required

Common
Coat Colors

Picardy Spaniel puppy

	Average height (inches)	Average weight (pounds)	Average life expectancy (years)
	48	100+	16+
		80	14
	36		
		60	12
	24	40	10
		20	8
	12		
		10	6

The Picardy Spaniel is rarely seen outside France and is closely related to the French Spaniel; both breeds share several traits. Picardys are excellent hunters in both water and on land, and hunt a variety of fur and feathered game. They are gentle and playful, and a well-socialized Picardy will make a fabulous pet for families with children. This spaniel can be reserved—a result of shyness rather than suspicion. It will bark at the approach of strangers, so has potential as a watchdog, but is not an effective guard dog—it sees newcomers as potential playmates.

AT A GLANCE

Ease of training	▬ ▬ ▬ ▬
Affection	▬ ▬ ▬ ▬
Playfulness	▬ ▬ ▬ ▬
Good with children	▬ ▬ ▬ ▬
Good with other dogs	▬ ▬ ▬
Grooming required	▬ ▬

! This breed tends to experience severe separation anxiety if left alone for too long.

+ This breed is generally very healthy, but can be prone to ear infections.

HISTORY

This ancient breed developed in Picardy around the fourteenth century, when similar dogs were described by Gaston Phebus in his book, *Le Livre de Chasse*. Their popularity increased after the French Revolution, when hunting was no longer restricted to the nobility. It lost its standing as a premier hunting dog, however, in the early 1800s, when the preference changed to English hunting dogs. Its numbers declined, but it has held onto a small, loyal following. The breed was recognized in 1907.

329

Pointer

ENGLAND

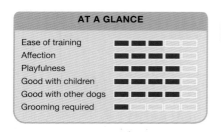

Pointer puppy

Exercise required

48	100+	16+
	80	14
36		
	60	12
24	40	10
	20	8
12		
	10	6

Average height (inches)
Average weight (pounds)
Average life expectancy (years)

Common Coat Colors

Pointers are large, elite working dogs that, like most gundog breeds, are hardwired to hunt. They were recorded in England in the 1650s, and were the first dogs known to be bred specifically to "stand" game: typically, they will locate game and then remain motionless to indicate its position to the hunter. Pointers have steady, loyal, and affectionate temperaments and can be suitable as companion dogs but only for extremely active homes.

AT A GLANCE

Ease of training	■ ■ ■ □ □
Affection	■ ■ ■ ■ □
Playfulness	■ ■ ■ ■ □
Good with children	■ ■ ■ ■ □
Good with other dogs	■ ■ ■ ■ □
Grooming required	■ □ □ □ □

 In the southern U.S., this dog is so dominant that it is often simply referred to as the "bird dog."

+ Generally healthy but some hereditary problems can include hip dysplasia and entropion.

HISTORY

Originally, Pointers in England were used by falconers and for hunting hare in conjunction with Greyhounds. Their heritage is not clear, but they probably developed from a mix of Fox Hound, Greyhound, Bloodhound, setter-types, and the Spanish Pointer. They became popular in the nineteenth century as working dogs and have changed very little in appearance since then. The breed is thought to have arrived in the United States during the Civil War. The American Kennel Club recognized the breed in 1878.

Pont-Audemer Spaniel

FRANCE

Exercise required

Pont-Audemer
Spaniel puppy

	Average height (inches)	Average weight (pounds)	Average life expectancy (years)
	48	100+	16+
		80	14
	36		
		60	12
	24	40	10
		20	8
	12		
		10	6

Common
Coat Colors

Though hardy, as well as hard-working, the breed has the typical spaniel traits of being easy to train, gentle, and affectionate. This dog, which has a fun-loving quality, is known in France as "the little clown of the marshes." The Pont-Audemer also excels at hunting in wet or swampy terrain. They are most often found in a working gundog environment and, in spite of their sweet natures, are not typically kept merely as pets.

AT A GLANCE

Ease of training	▬ ▬ ▬ ▬
Affection	▬ ▬ ▬ ▬
Playfulness	▬ ▬ ▬ ▬
Good with children	▬ ▬ ▬ ▬
Good with other dogs	▬ ▬ ▬
Grooming required	▬ ▬

 The signature topknot can take up to five years to fully develop.

✚ Generally very healthy but this breed may be prone to alopecia.

HISTORY

The rare Pont-Audemer Spaniel is thought to have developed during the nineteenth century. While the exact origins of the breed are not known, it is thought it developed from a mix of English and Irish Water Spaniels and other spaniel types, as well as setters. After World War II, breed numbers were so low that other working breeds were introduced, but numbers remain low today and the Pont-Audemer breed club has now merged with the Picardy Spaniel breed club.

Portuguese Pointer

Perdigueiro Português

PORTUGAL

Portuguese Pointer
puppy

Exercise required

Average height (inches)
Average weight (pounds)
Average life expectancy (years)

48	100+	16+
36	80	14
	60	12
24	40	10
	20	8
12		
	10	6

Common
Coat Colors

The Portuguese Pointer is considered to be one of the ultimate gundogs; its desire to please coupled with its hunting ability make this pointer a prized companion in the field. A brave and loyal watchdog, it is also reliable with children. Although not aggressive toward humans, they will bark at anything they deem suspicious. Their bark alone can deter intruders.

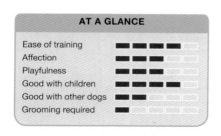

AT A GLANCE

Ease of training	▬ ▬ ▬ ▬
Affection	▬ ▬ ▬
Playfulness	▬ ▬ ▬
Good with children	▬ ▬ ▬ ▬
Good with other dogs	▬ ▬
Grooming required	▬

+ There are no diseases specific to this breed.

HISTORY

Portuguese Pointers trace back to at least the twelfth century, when they were initially bred by aristocrats. Over time, they were adopted by the working classes and became highly prized for their versatile hunting skills. The Portuguese pedigree book was established in 1932, and the standard in 1938, but the breed remains in relatively low numbers, certainly outside its homeland.

! Only this dog, and his "son," the English pointer, show this kind of skull-facial convergence.

332

Portuguese Water Dog

PORTUGAL

Exercise required

Portuguese Water Dog puppy

Average height (inches)	Average weight (pounds)	Average life expectancy (years)
48	100+	16+
	80	14
36		
	60	12
24	40	10
	20	8
12		
	10	6

Common Coat Colors

Also known as the Lion Dog, this is an intelligent, energetic breed that, with its webbed feet, muscular frame and water-resistant coat, is at home in the water. They are clipped in two ways—the lion clip with bare hindquarters and muzzle, and the retriever clip, with the coat trimmed to one inch all over. PWDs are sociable and friendly, making them ideal pets, but they also excel at hunting, obedience, service, assistance, and agility. They thrive when given a job to do.

AT A GLANCE	
Ease of training	■ ■ ■ ■
Affection	■ ■ ■ ■
Playfulness	■ ■ ■
Good with children	■ ■ ■
Good with other dogs	■ ■ ■
Grooming required	■ ■ ■

 This breed was so popular that even non-commercial fishermen would rent dogs for their fishing adventures.

✚ These dogs are generally health but some hereditary problems can include Addison's disease, progressive retinal atrophy, cancer, and hip dysplasia.

HISTORY

This ancient breed dates to pre-Christian times and likely developed on the steppes of Central Asia, spreading west into Europe with nomadic tribes. Possibly related to the German Poodle, it may be a forebear of the Irish Water Spaniel. When this once-invaluable fisherman's friend, which helped on the boats and in the water, began to disappear in the 1930s, businessman Vasco Bensaude started a breeding program in Portugal.

333

Pudelpointer

GERMANY

Exercise required

Pudelpointer
puppy

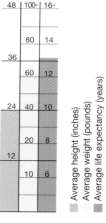

Average height (inches)
Average weight (pounds)
Average life expectancy (years)

Common
Coat Colors

The versatile Pudelpointer was developed in Germany in the late nineteenth century by crossing working German Poodles with English Pointers. This combination produced a dog with great intelligence, trainability, and a range of hunting skills. Pudelpointers work superbly both on land and in water on a variety of game. They also make wonderful companions for active homes.

AT A GLANCE

Ease of training	■■■■□
Affection	■■■■□
Playfulness	■■■□□
Good with children	■■■■□
Good with other dogs	■■■■□
Grooming required	■■□□□

! Breeders eschew club recognition: they don't want the breed split into show and working classes.

✚ There are no diseases specific to this breed.

HISTORY

In 1881, German breeder Baron von Zedlitz began engineering his ideal gundog. From seven specific poodles and nearly 100 different pointers, he developed the Pudelpointer. This new breed was easy to train, intelligent, and loved water and retrieving, like the Poodle, and was an avid hunter and natural pointer, with an excellent nose, like the English Pointer. It was also a wonderful companion in the home. Bobo Winterhelt introduced the dog to the U.S. in 1956, and in 1977 founded the Pudelpointer Club of North America in Canada.

Russian Spaniel

RUSSIA

Exercise required

Russian Spaniel puppy

Common Coat Colors

	Average height (inches)	Average weight (pounds)	Average life expectancy (years)
	48	100+	16+
	36	80	14
		60	12
	24	40	10
		20	8
	12	10	6

True to spaniel nature, these dogs are affectionate, cheerful, and lively companions who thrive leading busy, preferably working lives. Even though it is a gundog, it is also kept as a companion dog because of its easy-going nature. Russian Spaniels are trainable, make good watchdogs, and enjoy interacting with children.

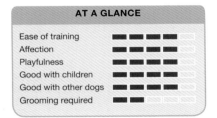

AT A GLANCE

Ease of training	▪▪▪▪
Affection	▪▪▪▪
Playfulness	▪▪▪▪
Good with children	▪▪▪▪
Good with other dogs	▪▪▪▪
Grooming required	▪▪

 A black Cocker owned by Grand Duke Nicholas Nikolaevich in the late 1800s was the first recorded spaniel in Russia.

+ These dogs are generally very healthy but can be prone to obesity, ear problems, and food allergies.

HISTORY

The Russian Spaniel was developed in the twentieth century based on crossbreeding a variety of spaniels, including the English Cocker and English Springer Spaniel. They are popular in Russia where they are used as all-around gundogs, working on marshy terrain, woodland, and uplands, and will hunt and retrieve all types of small game. Popular in its native Russia, the breed was only introduced overseas in the 1990s, and is not yet recognized by any major kennel clubs.

Saint-Usuge Spaniel

FRANCE

Saint-Usuge Spaniel puppy

Exercise required

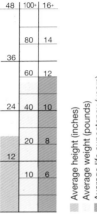

Average height (inches)
Average weight (pounds)
Average life expectancy (years)

Common Coat Colors

The Saint-Usuge Spaniel originated in the Bresse region of France. It is an intelligent, affectionate, and obedient breed that can work over a variety of terrains including forests, uplands, swamps, and in water. They are best suited to waterfowl and woodcock hunting, although they retrieve any small furred or feathered game. They also love children and make wonderful family pets. With their docile, affectionate natures, they easily enjoy apartment life.

AT A GLANCE

Ease of training	■■■■■
Affection	■■■■■
Playfulness	■■■■
Good with children	■■■■
Good with other dogs	■■■■
Grooming required	■■

+ There is no health information available on this dog at this time.

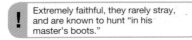

! Extremely faithful, they rarely stray, and are known to hunt "in his master's boots."

HISTORY

This relatively small French pointing spaniel, which probably dates back to the sixteenth century, had almost disappeared by the end of World War II. The breed was restored through the efforts of Father Robert Billiard. He found some of the remaining dogs in local villages and started a breeding initiative, which produced nearly 250 dogs over 33 years. The national breed club was founded in 1990; the breed was recognized by the French Kennel Club in 2003.

Slovakian Rough-Haired Pointer

SLOVAKIA

Exercise required

Slovakian Rough-Haired
Pointer puppy

Common
Coat Colors

		Average height (inches)	Average weight (pounds)	Average life expectancy (years)
		48	100+	16+
			80	14
		36		
			60	12
		24	40	10
			20	8
		12		
			10	6

The Slovakian Rough-Haired Pointer is a recently recognized gundog breed developed after WWII in Slovakia. It is known by many confusingly similar names in English, including: Slovak Wirehaired Pointer; Slovak Pointing Griffon; Slovak Wirehaired Pointing Griffon; Slovak Wirehaired Pointing Dog. Despite the nearly identical names, the SRHP is not the same as the Wirehaired Pointing Griffon, a smaller but similar breed with a slightly longer coat developed for essentially the same purposes by the Dutch. This pointer has an excellent temperament, but it is also extremely energetic and tireless. It needs an active family that can give it vigorous daily exercise.

AT A GLANCE

Ease of training	■ ■ ■ ■
Affection	■ ■ ■ ■
Playfulness	■ ■ ■ ■
Good with children	■ ■ ■ ■
Good with other dogs	■ ■ ■
Grooming required	■ ■

 This breed was given a "Meet the Breed" segment on the British broadcast of the 2007 Crufts Show.

+ They are generally healthy but can be prone to bloat, hip displasia, and idiopathic epilepsy.

HISTORY

This relatively new breed was developed during the second half of the twentieth century in Slovakia by combining Pudelpointers and more Weimaraners were recently added to increase the gene pool. These combined qualities make this pointer a tenacious gundog with great stamina, one that works on land and in water and will hunt a variety of game, including deer. They were introduced to the UK in 1997.

337

Small Münsterländer

GERMANY

Small Münsterländer puppy

Exercise required

48	100+	16+
	80	14
36		
	60	12
24	40	10
	20	8
12		
	10	6

Average height (inches)
Average weight (pounds)
Average life expectancy (years)

Common Coat Colors

These are loyal, affectionate, non-aggressive dogs that need plenty of exercise, including swimming, and particularly enjoy hunting. They are suitable as companions for an active and, preferably, hunting home. Small Munsterlanders are extremely intelligent, trainable, and attentive but require patience. When raised with other pets in the household they can coexist happily.

AT A GLANCE

Ease of training	■ ■ ■ ■ □
Affection	■ ■ ■ ■ □
Playfulness	■ ■ ■ ■ □
Good with children	■ ■ ■ ■ ■
Good with other dogs	■ ■ ■ ■ □
Grooming required	■ ■ ■ □ □

 The Small Münsterländer can retrieve a large Canada goose, which can weigh as much as 19 pounds.

+ Generally very healthy but may be prone to dry skin in colder climates and water in its ears after swimming.

HISTORY

The Small Münsterländer dates back to the Middle Ages in Europe and is a popular and versatile hunting dog. They are used to hunt a variety of different furred and feathered game and, despite their size, have historically hunted deer and wild boar. By the 1800s the breed had fallen into obscurity, kept by a few families on farms around Münster. For a half century the few dogs that were bred were primarily companions, and used when hunting to feed the family rather than for sport.

Spinone Italiano

ITALY

Spinone Italiano pup

Exercise required

This all-purpose hunting dog is highly regarded for its exceptional sense of smell. The Spinone Italiano works in a steady, methodical manner and is one of the slower, but no less effective, gun-dog breeds. They are charismatic and endearing, with excellent temperaments that match their very versatile hunting skills, which include working in water and on a variety of terrains. They also make very good family companions, usually establishing a close connection with children. They can be trained to be an excellent watchdog, although its affable character won't allow it to become a good guard dog.

Common Coat Colors

	Average height (inches)	Average weight (pounds)	Average life expectancy (years)
	48	100+	16+
		80	14
	36		
		60	12
	24	40	10
		20	8
	12		
		10	6

AT A GLANCE

Ease of training	▰▰▰▰
Affection	▰▰▰
Playfulness	▰▰▰
Good with children	▰▰▰▰
Good with other dogs	▰▰▰▰
Grooming required	▰

 Generally healthy but may be prone to ear infections, hip and elbow dysplasia, cerebellar ataxia, and gastric torision.

HISTORY

The Spinone Italiano are believed to trace back to Roman times, and clearly have pointing blood in their heritage. Several European countries claim their heritage, and any number of the claims could be true. During the Second World War, the Spinone became close to extinct. Both the war and the fact that Italian hunters had begun using other breeds (such as setters, pointers, and spaniels) caused their decline. Many breeders resorted to crossing the Spinone with other wire-haired breeds, to preserve them.

 They may have been named after an Italian thorn bush, the spino, which was a favorite hiding place for small game.

Springer Spaniel (Welsh)
WALES

Springer Spaniel (Welsh)
puppy

Exercise required

Common
Coat Colors

The Welsh Springer Spaniel are
a versatile breed that can make
a wonderful working gundog or
an affectionate family pet in an
active home. They are good-
natured and rather sociable, but
independent too. This breed
definitely shares the buoyant
nature of its English kindred and
absolutely loves vigorous games of all sorts. Severe separation anxiety can occur so they do
best in large active families where the dog won't suffer from lack of attention. However these
dogs are very loyal to their masters and treat children fondly especially if they grow up together.

	Average height (inches)	Average weight (pounds)	Average life expectancy (years)
	48	100+	16+
		80	14
	36	60	12
	24	40	10
		20	8
	12	10	6

AT A GLANCE

Ease of training	■ ■ ■
Affection	■ ■ ■ ■
Playfulness	■ ■ ■
Good with children	■ ■ ■ ■
Good with other dogs	■ ■ ■ ■
Grooming required	■ ■ ■

+ Generally healthy but this breed may be prone
to entropion, hip dysplasia, epilepsy, glaucoma,
and otitis externa.

! The Welsh Springer Spaniel was
named after its manner of springing
at game in order to flush it.

HISTORY
The ancestors to the Welsh Springer Spaniel trace far back in
history to some of the earliest hunting breeds, and developed in
the relative isolation of their homeland. Similar looking dogs can
be seen in paintings from Renaissance times. By the 1700s, the
Welsh was popular with the aristocracy, but gradually, the English
Springer began to take over. WWI caused problems for the breed
in the UK, and when the war was over there were no dogs whose
parents had registered pedigrees. The breed restarted with the
remaining unregistered dogs, and it is these dogs that formed the
modern day breed.

Stabyhoun

Stabij / Stabijhoun / Friese Stabij
NETHERLANDS

Stabyhoun puppy

Exercise required

Common Coat Colors

Average height (inches)
Average weight (pounds)
Average life expectancy (years)

The Stabyhoun, which is thought to have developed in the 1800s in Friesland, in the north western Netherlands, was highly regarded as a multipurpose dog by farmers and the working classes. Small enough to keep easily, yet large enough to be useful guard dogs, they were used for hunting on land and in water, for watching over homes, and as affectionate companions. They are highly intelligent as a breed and excel in many different types of sport and activities, such as hunting, agility, endurance, and obedience tests.

AT A GLANCE	
Ease of training	■ ■ ■
Affection	■ ■ ■ ■
Playfulness	■ ■ ■
Good with children	■ ■ ■ ■
Good with other dogs	■ ■ ■ ■
Grooming required	■ ■ ■

 The Stabyhoun is one of the top five rarest dog breeds in the world, as of 2013.

✚ May be prone to hip and elbow dysplasia, epilepsy, and congenital heart disorder.

HISTORY

The Stabyhoun is found in literature dating back to the early 1800s. It was used for hunting foxes, small game, and birds. During the hunting season, it was used as an all-round gundog. Historically, these dogs were nearly exclusively owned by farmers, whose limited financial means dictated the need for a single dog capable as an all-around working, hunting, guard and companion dog. Today the Stabyhoun enjoys a small but thoroughly devoted following among Dutch sportsmen and homeowners.

341

Standard Poodle

(Caniche / Barbone)
GERMANY

Standard Poodle puppys

Exercise required

Common Coat Colors

Poodles are found in three sizes—Standard, Miniature, and Toy—but all share similar traits and can make excellent family pets. The breed is noted for its loyalty and intelligence. They are delightful with their loved ones, but can

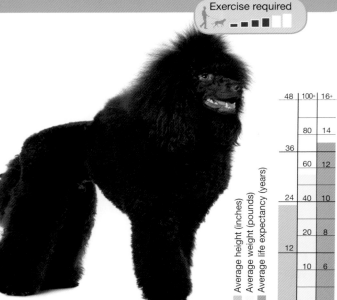

		48	100+	16+
			80	14
		36		
			60	12
Average height (inches)	Average weight (pounds) Average life expectancy (years)	24	40	10
			20	8
		12		
			10	6

be standoffish with strangers, and are typically charismatic and full of character. Although the breed requirement for the Standard Poodle is over 15 inches in height, most range from 20–26 inches and weigh up to 55 pounds. This breed is commonly thought of as French and rarely as a gundog. However, with their great intelligence, Poodles make excellent gundogs—they originated in Germany, where they were bred as water-retrieving dogs.

AT A GLANCE

Ease of training	▰▰▰▰▰
Affection	▰▰▰▰
Playfulness	▰▰▰▰
Good with children	▰▰▰
Good with other dogs	▰▰▰
Grooming required	▰▰▰▰

+ Generally healthy but hereditary problems can include hip dysplasia, cancer, Addison's disease, gastric torsion, thyroid issues, and progressive retinal atrophy.

 The trademark haircuts of this breed are derived from trims invented to make its work in the water easier.

HISTORY

Poodles derive their name from the German word pudel, meaning to "splash in water," and are believed to share a similar heritage to other water-retrieving breeds, such as the Portuguese Water Dog, Irish Water Spaniel, Hungarian Water Hound, and French Barbet.

The Poodle became popular in France during the eighteenth century, where it was known as the Chien Canard, meaning "duck dog." France became the breed's surrogate home, and the French Fédération Cynologique Internationale recognizes France as the breed's country of origin.

Sussex Spaniel

ENGLAND

Sussex Spaniel puppy

Exercise required

Common Coat Colors

	48	100+	16+
		80	14
	36		
		60	12
	24	40	10
		20	8
	12		
		10	6

Average height (inches)
Average weight (pounds)
Average life expectancy (years)

The Sussex Spaniel is a sturdily built, medium-sized, joyous and vigorous dog. The Sussex Spaniel is a slow paced, calm breed with somewhat clownish behaviour that normally keeps his energy and enthusiasm in check. He is always eager to be around people, is excellent around children, and can be quite protective of the family. They make excellent candidates for therapy dog work. Most Sussex Spaniels are primarily family pets, but they are competent enough to aid a hunter though quite stubborn to train. They tend to have a natural ability to quarter in the field, have excellent noses, and can be used to retrieve, given training.

AT A GLANCE

Ease of training	■■
Affection	■■■■
Playfulness	■■■
Good with children	■■■■
Good with other dogs	■■■
Grooming required	■■■

+ Generally healthy but may be prone to ear infections, hip dysplasia, pulmonic stenosis, patent ductus arteriosis, and intervertebral disc osteochondrosis.

! The breed is the only spaniel to howl once a game's scent is picked up.

HISTORY

The Sussex Spaniel is named after the county in England where the breed was developed and traces back to the eighteenth century. An influential figure in the breed's history was Augustus Fuller who bred them for fifty years at his kennels in Sussex, using the dogs for hunting on foot on his large estate. The Sussex was one of the original nine breeds recognized by the American Kennel Club in 1878. Nowadays, it is one of the less commonly seen Spaniel breeds.

Toy Poodle

GERMANY

Toy Poodle puppy

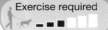

Exercise required

Common Coat Colors

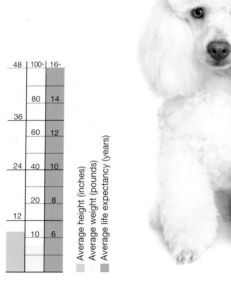

48	100+	16+
	80	14
36		
	60	12
24	40	10
	20	8
12		
	10	6

Average height (inches)
Average weight (pounds)
Average life expectancy (years)

The Toy Poodle is remarkably intelligent. Highly responsive, it is said to be one of the most trainable breeds. Sweet, cheerful, perky and lively, it likes to be with people. This breed is suited to city life but they are active little dogs that need a daily walk to behave well indoors. Socialize these dogs well and they make very good companions and even though petite, can be very good watchdogs.

AT A GLANCE		
Ease of training		
Affection		
Playfulness		
Good with children		
Good with other dogs		
Grooming required		

+ Diabetes, epilepsy, heart disorders, PRA, runny eyes, ear infections, digestive tract problems, cataracts, and progressive retinal atrophy.

HISTORY

The Poodle has been known throughout Western Europe for at least 400 years, but no one really knows the breed's true country of origin. France has taken a claim on the origin, but the AKC gives the honor to Germany, where they say it was used as a water retrieval dog. Other claims have been Denmark, or the ancient Piedmont. It is believed that the dog was a descendant of the now-extinct French Water Dog, the Barbet, and possibly the Hungarian Water Hound. The name "Poodle" most likely derives from the German word "Pudel," which means "one who plays in water."

! The "topknot" on the head is fixed in place using latex bands, because in Europe hair spray is banned.

Vizsla

HUNGARY

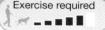

Exercise required

Vizsla puppy

Common
Coat Colors

Average height (inches)	Average weight (pounds)	Average life expectancy (years)
48	100+	16+
	80	14
36		
	60	12
24	40	10
	20	8
12		
	10	6

The Vizsla has had a history of highs and lows, facing near-extinction in the twentieth century, but has since been re-established through careful breeding and is now the national dog of Hungary. These are affectionate and lively dogs that thrive on learning and working, and are best suited to an active lifestyle. The Vizsla is a versatile gundog that works in water as well as on land and exhibits excellent pointing and retrieving skills on a range of furred and feathered game. Vizlas can make very good family dogs but do require extensive exercise.

AT A GLANCE

Ease of training	▅▅▅
Affection	▅▅▅▅▅
Playfulness	▅▅▅▅
Good with children	▅▅▅▅
Good with other dogs	▅▅▅▅
Grooming required	▅

✚ Generally healthy but hereditary problems can include hip dysplasia, epilepsy, and polymyositis.

 Vizslas served as messenger dogs during World War I.

HISTORY

Vizslas are an ancient breed that probably traces back to the Magyar people from Western and Central Asia. The breed's heritage is likely Mastiff and hound-dog crosses. By 895 CE the Magyar settled in the Carpathian Basin where they farmed and hunted, breeding their dogs to fulfill a range of roles. The earliest reference to a Vizsla dates to 1350 in a village of the same name on the Danube River. By the eighteenth century, the "golden" dogs had become the preserve of the aristocracy.

345

Weimaraner

GERMANY

Exercise required

Weimaraners developed as a result of careful and selective breeding, leading to one of the most perfect combinations of working-dog ability, companion-dog temperament, and irresistible good looks. The breed is distinctive as a result of its unusual coat coloring, which ranges from silver-gray to mouse-gray with a beautiful metallic sheen, and has led to the breed being referred to as "gray ghosts." Weimaraners can also be long haired, with that variety recognized in all countries except the United States. Weimaraners excel as working gundogs and are an intelligent and obedient breed with good stamina. Equally, they have lovely temperaments and are loyal, affectionate, and playful companions.

! The name comes from Karl August, the Grand Duke of saxe-Weimar-Eisenach, whose court, based in the city of Weimar.

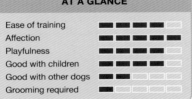

Weirmaraner pup

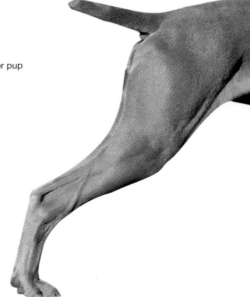

AT A GLANCE

Ease of training	▓▓▓▓▓
Affection	▓▓▓▓▓
Playfulness	▓▓▓▓▓
Good with children	▓▓▓▓
Good with other dogs	▓▓
Grooming required	▓

 Generally healthy but some hereditary problems can include hip dysplasia and gastric torsion.

Common
Coat Colors

48	100+	16+		
	80	14		
36				
	60	12		
24	40	10		
	20	8		
12				
	10	6		

Average height (inches)
Average weight (pounds)
Average life expectancy (years)

HISTORY

Little is known about the Weimaraners' early history, but they are said to have developed in the seventeenth century from early hunting dogs and bear a close resemblance to dogs in paintings from this period. The St. Hubert Hound from Belgium, which gave rise to the Bloodhound, along with old German and French hounds are often cited as the breed's ancestors. Their traceable history begins with Karl August, Grand Duke of Saxe-Weimar-Eisenach (1757–1828), who kept large kennels where he bred elite hunting dogs. These dogs were called "gray hunting dogs" and were the foundation for the modern Weimaraner. Originally, they were used for hunting big game such as bears, wolves, and wildcats. The breed was controlled and bred only by German aristocrats with the breed standard drawn up in 1896. American hunter Howard Knight was the first to import the breed to the United States, with the earliest breeding stock arriving in 1938. The Weimaraner was recognized by the American Kennel Club in 1943.

347

Wirehaired Pointing Griffon

Korthals Griffon

NETHERLANDS / FRANCE

Wirehaired Pointing Griffon puppy

Exercise required

Common Coat Colors

The Wirehaired Pointing Griffon (also called the Korthals Griffon, and the Griffon d'arrêt à poil dur Korthals in France and Quebec) is a breed of dog used in hunting as a gundog. It is sometimes considered to be Dutch in ancestry, due to the nationality of the breed founder, Eduard Karel Korthals. The Wirehaired Pointing Griffon is particularly adapted for hunting in thick undergrowth and around water, where its harsh coat is excellent protection. The Griffon is used primarily as a hunting dog for upland game birds as well as waterfowl. They are extremely people oriented and prefer to be somewhere in the vicinity of their owners, so are not suited to living outside of the home.

	Average height (inches)	Average weight (pounds)	Average life expectancy (years)
	48	100+	16+
		80	14
	36		
		60	12
	24	40	10
		20	8
	12		
		10	6

AT A GLANCE

Ease of training	■■■ ■■ □□
Affection	■■■ ■■ □□
Playfulness	■■■ ■■ □□
Good with children	■■■ ■■ ■
Good with other dogs	■■ ■■ □□
Grooming required	■■■ ■■ □□

 The AKC first erroneously registered Wirehaired Pointing Griffon as a "Russian Setter."

➕ Generally healthy but may be prone to hip dysplasia, elbow dysplasia, ear infections, panoestitis, and entropion.

HISTORY

This breed's ancestors are mentioned as early as 500 BCE, but the modern development of the breed traces only to the nineteenth century and Eduard Korthals, an avid hunter who wanted to produce a hunting dog with a protective coat and plenty of stamina that could work on all terrains. He bred griffons, spaniels, setters and German and French pointers to achieve his desired result, and then marketed the new dog across Europe. The breed is not widely known but is none-the-less a superb gundog and companion.

Wirehaired Vizsla

HUNGARY

Exercise required

Wirehaired Vizsla puppy

The Wirehaired Vizsla is a versatile, natural hunter endowed with an excellent nose and an above average trainability. Although they are lively, gentle mannered, demonstrably affectionate and sensitive, they are also fearless and possess a well-developed protective instinct. The breed has a firmness on point, is an excellent retriever, and has the determination to remain on the scent even when swimming. The overall appearance embodies the qualities of a multi-purpose pointing dog, endurance, working ability and an easily satisfied nature. This is a dog of power and drive in the field, yet is a tractable and affectionate companion in the home.

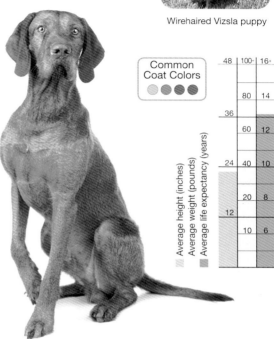

Common Coat Colors

Average height (inches)
Average weight (pounds)
Average life expectancy (years)

48	100- 16·
	80 14
36	
	60 12
	40 10
24	20 8
12	10 6

AT A GLANCE

Ease of training	
Affection	
Playfulness	
Good with children	
Good with other dogs	
Grooming required	

In Hungarian, the word Vizsla can mean either "quick" or "pointer," both of which are applicable to this breed.

+ Generally healthy but may be prone to hip dysplasia, progressive retinal atrophy, and cancer.

HISTORY

This charismatic breed traces to the 1930s when it was developed to combine the qualities of the Vizsla with a more robust frame and weather-resistant coat. As such, the Wirehaired Vizsla is better suited for water retrieving, and working in harsh terrain and frigid winter conditions. The breed's foundation traces to female Vizslas that were bred to a solid-colored wirehaired German Pointer. The Wirehaired Vizsla is not as popular as the smooth-coated breed, but is a superb working dog and a wonderful companion.

SPITZ-TYPE DOGS

Akita

Akita-Ken / Akita Inu / Japanese Akita

JAPAN / UNITED STATES

Akita puppy

Exercise required

48	100+	16+
	80	14
36		
	60	12
24	40	10
	20	8
12		
	10	6

Average height (inches)
Average weight (pounds)
Average life expectancy (years)

Common
Coat Colors

AT A GLANCE

Ease of training	■■ ■■
Affection	■■ ■■ ■■
Playfulness	■■ ■■ ■■
Good with children	■■ ■■ ■■
Good with other dogs	■■
Grooming required	■■ ■■ ■■

! Akitas have webbed toes, which help them walk on ice and snow by distributing their weight more effectively.

Bred to hunt large game, the Akita is a superbly formed, muscular dog, powerful and confident with incredible stamina. Although they are good with children and exceptionally loyal and devoted companions, they are also wary of strangers, so make excellent watch dogs. Akitas can be aggressive toward other dogs, and, given their powerful physique and complex character, the Akita is not suitable for first-time dog owners. The story of the faithful Hachiko, an Akita that waited at the train station every day for his master, even after his master's death, helped popularize this breed around the world.

Although generally healthy, hereditary problems can include auto-immune disease, hip dysplasia, progressive retinal atrophy, von Willebrands Disease, and hypothyroidism.

HISTORY

Akitas are most associated with Odate City (called Dog City) and the surrounding area of the Akita prefecture on the northern end of Honshu Island. This area was home to a number of regional types of large spitz dogs collectively called Matagi-Inu, which were used for hunting large game, as guard dogs, and for dog fighting. During the nineteenth century, European breeds like Mastiffs, German Shepherds, and Great Danes were introduced, and crossbreeding with the local stock gave rise to the Tosa Inu and increased the size of the Matagi-Inu. When original Japanese type was in danger of disappearing around 1927, a preservation society was set up and the name Akita was adopted for the Matagi-Inu. After World War II, Akitas had all but disappeared, but the breed was salvaged using two breeding lines: the Ichinoseki and the Dewa. Dogs of the Dewa line were taken to the United States and founded the American Akita, whereas those of the Ichinoseki lines gave rise to the Akita-Inu. Despite the differences between the two types, some kennel clubs have only recently acknowledged them as separate.

353

Alaskan Husky

UNITED STATES

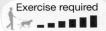

Exercise required

Alaskan Husky puppy

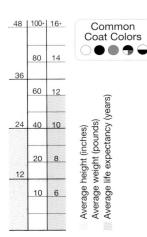

48	100+	16+
	80	14
36		
	60	12
24	40	10
	20	8
12		
	10	6

Average height (inches)
Average weight (pounds)
Average life expectancy (years)

Common Coat Colors

AT A GLANCE

Ease of training	■■ ■■ ■■
Affection	■■ ■■ ■■ ■■
Playfulness	■■ ■■ ■■ ■■ ■■
Good with children	■■ ■■ ■■
Good with other dogs	■■ ■■ ■■ ■■ ■■
Grooming required	■■ ■■ ■■

! A top-level Alaskan Husky can be worth over $10,000 due to its racing ability.

+ As hybrids, these dogs have fewer health issues, but may develop lysosomal storage disease, progressive retinal atrophy, and hypothyroidism.

The Alaskan Husky is a hybrid as opposed to a breed. Engineered with the intent of creating a highly effecient, superior sled dog, they are typically bred from various spitz types, such as the Siberian Husky and Alaskan Malamute. This dog is reputedly the best of all sled dogs, and very few purebred dogs can match its speed. Although they are viewed as working dogs rather than as companions, Alaskan Huskies are suitable for an open suburban environment; they make great companions for athletic owners who are ready for a very active pet.

HISTORY

Mushers created this dog in Alaska and Canada by breeding leggy, rangey Inuit village dogs. The breed's purpose was to perform various jobs—delivering supplies over long distances, general transportation, and sledding competitions. Alaskan Huskies vary greatly due to there being no set standard defining this type. Kennel clubs do not recognize this dog.

Alaskan Klee Kai

UNITED STATES

Exercise required

Alaskan Klee Kai puppy

Common Coat Colors

	Average height (inches)	Average weight (pounds)	Average life expectancy (years)
	48	100+	16+
		80	14
	36		
		60	12
	24	40	10
		20	8
	12		
		10	6

The Alaskan Klee Kai is an energetic and highly intelligent dog designed to resemble the Alaskan Husky. These are lively, charismatic, devoted animals that make superb family companions and trusty watchdogs. This rare breed is divided into three size categories: toy, miniature, and standard.

AT A GLANCE

Ease of training	▰▰ ▰▰ ▰▰
Affection	▰▰ ▰▰ ▰▰ ▰▰
Playfulness	▰▰ ▰▰ ▰▰ ▰▰
Good with children	▰▰ ▰▰ ▰▰ ▰▰
Good with other dogs	▰▰ ▰▰ ▰▰
Grooming required	▰▰ ▰▰ ▰▰

! This breed is not particularly aggressive, but has excellent hearing and a wariness of strangers. This makes the Klee Kai a good watchdog, but a poor guard dog.

✚ There is a possibility of juvenile cataracts, liver disease, patellar luxation, and cardiac issues.

HISTORY

The Alaskan Klee Kai is a relatively new breed that was developed in the 1970s in Wasilla, Alaska, by Linda Spurlin and her family, with the aim of producing a companion-sized husky. Siberian and Alaskan Huskies were used in the breed's foundation, along with smaller spitz-type dogs, such as the Schipperke and American Eskimo Dog to reduce the size. This breed was recognized by the United Kennel Club in 1997; it remains a rare breed, although it is growing in popularity.

Alaskan Malamute
UNITED STATES

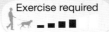
Exercise required

Alaskan Malamute
puppy

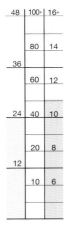

48	100+	16+
	80	14
36		
	60	12
24	40	10
	20	8
12		
	10	6

Average height (inches)
Average weight (pounds)
Average life expectancy (years)

HISTORY

The Alaskan Malamute is thought to be a descendent of ancient dogs from northwestern Alaska. These dogs were bred for utilitarian purposes, such as working and hunting. The breed became popular and highly valuable to prospectors during the Klondike Gold Rush of 1896. In 2010, this breed was named Alaska's official state dog.

Common
Coat Colors

AT A GLANCE

Ease of training	▬▬ ▬▬ ▬▬
Affection	▬▬ ▬▬ ▬▬ ▬▬
Playfulness	▬▬ ▬▬ ▬▬
Good with children	▬▬ ▬▬ ▬▬
Good with other dogs	▬▬ ▬▬
Grooming required	▬▬ ▬▬ ▬▬ ▬▬

! During World War II, these dogs were used as search and rescue dogs in Greenland.

This no-nonsense working breed has a wonderful temperament and a great spirit. Malamutes are tough, brave dogs that were instrumental in sustaining life for native cultures in Alaska. They have been used by the military, by the U.S. Postal service in remote Alaska, and by miners during the Klondike Gold Rush. As well as their main duty of sled-pulling they were also used as pack animals, carrying half their body weight in goods for up to 20 miles a day! They make fine family dogs, but only for those willing to make a substantial time commitment. Malamutes require extensive exercise, including speed work, and they are prone to digging and howling if left alone. They can also be forceful on a leash and have a strong predatory instinct for smaller animals, so a fenced-in yard is a must.

+ Hip dysplasia, elbow dysplasia, progressive retinal atrophy, and hereditary cataracts are possible ailments with this breed.

American Eskimo Dog

Eskie

UNITED STATES

American Eskimo puppy

Exercise required

48	100+	16+
	80	14
36		
	60	12
24	40	10
	20	8
12		
	10	6

Average height (inches)
Average weight (pounds)
Average life expectancy (years)

Common
Coat Colors

AT A GLANCE

Ease of training	▬▬ ▬▬ ▬▬
Affection	▬▬ ▬▬ ▬▬
Playfulness	▬▬ ▬▬ ▬▬ ▬▬
Good with children	▬▬ ▬▬ ▬▬ ▬▬
Good with other dogs	▬▬ ▬▬
Grooming required	▬▬ ▬▬ ▬▬ ▬▬ ▬▬

! Agile and eager to please, American Eskimo Dogs excel at tricks and were used as circus performers.

HISTORY

The gleaming white American Eskimo Dog, sometimes called the "Dog Beautiful," traces back to small German and other European spitz breeds brought to the United States with European immigrants. By the 1910s, these dogs had become known as the American Spitz, reflecting anti-German sentiments during and after World War I. The American Spitz grew in popularity due to its fame as a performing breed in traveling circuses and carnivals. The first dogs of the breed were registered in 1913 with the United Kennel Club under the name American Eskimo Spitz. The breed was recognized by the American Kennel Club in 1994.

Despite its name, this delightful breed has nothing to do with the Eskimo, or Inuit, culture; it is descended from European spitz breeds. These dogs are divided into toy, miniature, and standard sizes, all prized for their beautiful appearance. Not just a pretty face, "Eskies" are also charismatic, intelligent, and friendly (although independent). They make excellent companion and watchdogs, and are highly protective of their families and homes. They need plenty of exercise, though, and their spectacular coats need regular grooming. Alert and active, American Eskimo Dogs also excel in agility and love to learn new tricks. They require substantial amounts of mental stimulation as well as physical exercise, so they are happiest in an active home.

✚ Although generally healthy, some hereditary problems include hip dysplasia, cancer, Addison's disease, gastric torsion, progressive retinol atrophy, and eyelid problems.

Black Norwegian Elkhound

NORWAY

Black Norwegian Elkhound
puppy

Exercise required
■ ■ ■ ■

48	100+	16+
	80	14
36		
	60	12
24	40	10
	20	8
12		
	10	6

Average height (inches)
Average weight (pounds)
Average life expectancy (years)

Common Coat Colors
●

AT A GLANCE

Ease of training	■ ■ ■ ■
Affection	■ ■ ■ ■
Playfulness	■ ■ ■
Good with children	■ ■ ■
Good with other dogs	■ ■ ■ ■
Grooming required	■ ■ ■

! The Black Norwegian Elkhound has been a favorite of Scandinavian farmers for about two hundred years.

+ These dogs are prone to obesity, cardiac problems, elbow dysplasia, and progressive retinal atrophy.

This native Norwegian dog is a variant of the Norwegian Elkhound and is very rare outside of Scandinavia. It is classified as a hunting dog, but can be used as a watchdog, guard dog, and herder. Its dense black coat is meant to shield it from the cold weather and heavy rain that is common in Norway. Black Norwegian Elkhounds are hardy and agile dogs that can be a joy to train. They're make especially good companions for hunters because their tracking skills are well above most breeds.

HISTORY

This breed is much newer than the Grey Norwegian Elkhound and was first bred in the early 1800s. It is nearly identical to its counterpart, save for its color and heightened agility. The black variety of Norwegian Elkhounds was rejected in 1901, when the standard was set. This led to breeders focusing on scent tracking and hunting instinct, since the breed was not eligible for dog shows. The breed was close to extinction in the 1950s and remains almost unknown outside of Norway.

Canadian Eskimo Dog

Canadian Husky / Qimmiq

CANADA

Canadian Eskimo
Dog puppy

Exercise required

Common
Coat Colors

	Average height (inches)	Average weight (pounds)	Average life expectancy (years)
	48	100+	16+
		80	14
	36		
		60	12
	24	40	10
		20	8
	12		
		10	6

The Qimmiq was domesticated by the Inuit who used it as an indispensable worker. They are active, powerful animals and were used by hunters and explorers to pull heavy loads a long distance. Not usually kept as pets, they are unsuitable for children.

AT A GLANCE

Ease of training	▰ ▰ ▰
Affection	▰ ▰ ▰ ▰
Playfulness	▰ ▰ ▰
Good with children	▰ ▰ ▰
Good with other dogs	▰ ▰
Grooming required	▰ ▰ ▰

＋ This dog is prone to hip dysplasia, gastric torsion, cataracts, and arthritis.

HISTORY

The Canadian Eskimo Dog is an ancient breed, originating in the Arctic over 4,000 years ago. Once numbering in the thousands, the advent of the snowmobile made it obsolete . By the 1970s there were less than 200. A breeding kennel was started in 1972 using 19 dogs. While the breed survives today, its future is unknown.

! This dog is genetically similar to the Greenland Dog, and the two are often mistaken for one another.

Chow Chow

CHINA

Chow Chow puppy

Exercise required

The Chow Chow is a quiet, reserved, and dignified breed. These dogs are loyal to their families, but not overly demonstrative, often described as aloof. Although they are mostly companions now, historically they were used as versatile farm dogs for draft work, guarding, herding livestock, and hunting; they were even kept for their meat and were known as the "Chinese edible dog." It is one of the most unusal of all breeds, with its lion-like mane, blue-black tongue and stiff-legged gait.

Average height (inches)	Average weight (pounds)	Average life expectancy (years)
48	100+	16+
	80	14
36		
	60	12
24	40	10
	20	8
12		
	10	6

Common Coat Colors

AT A GLANCE

Ease of training	▬
Affection	▬ ▬
Playfulness	▬
Good with children	▬ ▬ ▬ ▬
Good with other dogs	▬ ▬ ▬
Grooming required	▬ ▬ ▬

+ Hip dysplasia and entropion may occur, although many breeds don't show health issues until full maturity (2-3 years old).

! The Chow is one of two AKC-registered breeds to have a blue-black tongue, the other being the Chinese Shar-Pei.

HISTORY

Recent DNA testing has revealed that the Chow Chow is directly descended from the earliest domesticated dogs and is one of the ancestors of the modern spitz-type breeds. Chow Chows are believed to have developed in the Arctic Circle before migrating south into Mongolia, Siberia, and China.

East Siberian Laika

RUSSIA

Exercise required

East Siberian Laika puppy

Common Coat Colors

	Average height (inches)	Average weight (pounds)	Average life expectancy (years)
	48	100+	16+
		80	14
	36		
		60	12
	24	40	10
		20	8
	12		
		10	6

These tough, powerful dogs are used for hunting all types of large game, such as deer and bear in deep snow, and make good guard and sled dogs. They can be suitable for urban living, and are known to be calm and good-natured, though they aren't ideal for first-time dog owners. They do best in a working environment with lots of exercise and are not recommended for a home with small animals.

AT A GLANCE

Ease of training	▬▬ ▬▬
Affection	▬▬ ▬▬ ▬▬
Playfulness	▬▬ ▬▬
Good with children	▬▬ ▬▬ ▬▬
Good with other dogs	▬▬ ▬▬
Grooming required	▬▬ ▬▬ ▬▬

 This breed is a pack dog, so once the owner establishes dominance as the pack leader, training becomes much easier.

➕ This breed may develop hip dysplasia, cancer, digestive issues, and chronic ear infections.

HISTORY

The East Siberian Laika is an ancient breed, descended from dogs taken to eastern Siberia by nomadic tribes— some migrated from the west, and others traveled north from Mongolia and China. The dogs were bred specifically to cope with the taxing climate, hostile environment, and heavy workloads, and are among the toughest of all breeds. They will take on large animals, including bears.

Eurasier

Eurasian

GERMANY

Eurasier puppy

Exercise required

■ ■■■

Average height (inches)

Average weight (pounds)

Average life expectancy (years)

48	100+	16+
	80	14
36		
	60	12
24	40	10
	20	8
12		
	10	6

Common
Coat Colors

Also known as the Eurasian, these dogs have a lovely temperament—calm, affectionate, and obedient. They are very loyal to their families, reserved but unaggressive with strangers, and generally have little—if any—hunting instinct. The Eurasier has a relatively low activity level and is happy to live in any size environment, provided it is walked twice a day.

AT A GLANCE

Ease of training	■■■ ■■■ ■■■
Affection	■■■ ■■■ ■■■ ■■■
Playfulness	■■■ ■■■ ■■■
Good with children	■■■ ■■■ ■■■ ■■■
Good with other dogs	■■■ ■■■ ■■■
Grooming required	■■■ ■■■ ■■■

! This breed was given the name Eurasier to symbolize its combined Euopean and Asian heritage.

+ Hip dyplasia, elbow dyplasia, patellar luxation, distichiasis are possible ailments with this dog.

HISTORY

This relatively new breed was developed in Germany in the 1960s strictly as a companion animal. Breeders initially crossed Chow Chows with Keeshonds, trying to reproduce the best qualities from both breeds. At first, the new breed was called the Wolf-Chow, but after Samoyed was also introduced to the mix, the name was changed to the Eurasier.

Finnish Lapphund

Lappie

FINLAND

Finnish Lapphund puppy

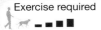

Common Coat Colors

	48	100+	16+
		80	14
	36		
		60	12
		24	40	10
			20	8
	12		
			10	6

Average height (inches)
Average weight (pounds)
Average life expectancy (years)

+ This breed is ideal for a family with small children and is known to be very responsive to kids. Lappies adapt well to the elderly, as well, and can be very gentle and sensitive.

AT A GLANCE

Ease of training	■■ ■■ ■■ ■
Affection	■■ ■■ ■■ ■
Playfulness	■■ ■■ ■■ ■
Good with children	■■ ■■ ■■ ■■ ■
Good with other dogs	■■ ■■ ■■ ■
Grooming required	■■ ■■ ■■

! This breed is ideal for a family with small children and is known to be very responsive to kids. Lappies adapt well to the elderly, as well, and can be very gentle and sensitive.

Closely related to its Swedish counterpart, this dog traces back to reindeer farmers, who relied on it to herd livestock. Although Finnish Lapphunds are now primarily pets and are among the most popular breeds in Finland, they retain strong herding instincts. They are intelligent, eager to please, and gentle, and generally get along well with children and other dogs. They can make excellent companions, and due to their courage and noisy barking, they also make good guard dogs.

HISTORY

This is a breed of ancient origin that developed across the large frozen areas of northern Finland, Sweden, Norway, and parts of Russia, and used as a reindeer herder by the Sami people. They were standardized during World War II and were in serious danger of extinction post war. The breed is believed to be the result of a cross between the Karelian Bear Dog and other reindeer-herding dogs. The breed remains popular in Europe today and is the sixth most popular companion animal in Finland.

Finnish Spitz

Finkie

FINLAND

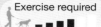

Exercise required

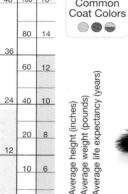

Finnish Spitz puppy

48	100+	16+
	80	14
36		
	60	12
24	40	10
	20	8
12		
	10	6

Average height (inches)
Average weight (pounds)
Average life expectancy (years)

Common Coat Colors

Also known as the Finky, this ancient Finnish breed was an essential part of early settlers' lives and was used for hunting birds and larger game. They are noted for their vigorous bark and for "giving voice" while hunting, a characteristic so highly valued that there is an annual competition in Finland to crown the dog with the greatest vocal talent as the "king of Barking." Finnish Spitzes are most adapted to hunting the capercaillie, a bird found predominately in Europe and Asia. Finkies are charismatic and make good companion animals and alert watchdogs.

AT A GLANCE

Ease of training	▬ ▬ ▬ ▬ ▬
Affection	▬ ▬ ▬
Playfulness	▬ ▬ ▬ ▬
Good with children	▬ ▬ ▬
Good with other dogs	▬ ▬ ▬ ▬
Grooming required	▬ ▬

 The Finnish Spitz became the national dog of Finland in 1979.

+ This breed is prone to hip dysplasia, patellar luxation, and epilepsy.

HISTORY

Finnish Spitz have been used for hunting game over hundreds of years. The breed almost went extinct in the late nineteenth century, but tourists Hugo Sandberg and Hugo Roos found two on a hunting trip and committed to saving the breed. The breed has weakened and re-strengthened greatly over the last century, but is now standardized and fairly popular. Almost 2,000 Finnish Spitz are registered by the Finnish Kennel Club, compared to only about 600 in the early twentieth century.

German Spitz

GERMANY

German Spitz puppy

Exercise required

Common Coat Colors

	48	100+	16+
		80	14
	36		
		60	12
		24	40	10
		20	8
	12		
		10	6

Average height (inches)
Average weight (pounds)
Average life expectancy (years)

In Germany these dogs are recognized in five different sizes: Wolfspitz (also known as the Keeshond), Giant Spitz, Mittel, Klein, and Dwarf (also known as the Pomeranian). The German Spitz is a fairly new arrival to the United States, and is registered in two sizes: the Mittel and the Klein. Both are bright, lively, bold-natured dogs that can be noisy if left alone. They thrive on company and challenges, and require only moderate amounts of exercise, but need regular grooming.

AT A GLANCE

Ease of training	▰▰ ▰▰ ▰
Affection	▰▰ ▰▰ ▰▰ ▰
Playfulness	▰▰ ▰▰ ▰
Good with children	▰▰ ▰▰ ▰▰
Good with other dogs	▰▰ ▰▰ ▰
Grooming required	▰▰ ▰▰ ▰

+ These dogs are prone to patellar luxation and eye infections.

! Following the standardization of the Pomeranian, the German Spitz became a relatively rare breed, and has even lost most of its popularity in its homeland of Germany.

HISTORY

The German Spitz traces its ancestry to ancient Nordic herding dogs used by nomadic cultures living in the frigid Arctic. These dogs, like the Samoyed, made their way to Germany and Holland, possibly with the Vikings, and were crossed with local, native sheepherding breeds. The earliest record of the German Spitz dates to 1450.

Greenland Dog

GREENLAND

Greenland Dog
puppy

Exercise required

48	100+	16+
	80	14
36		
	60	12
24	40	10
	20	8
12		
	10	6

Average height (inches)
Average weight (pounds)
Average life expectancy (years)

Common Coat Colors
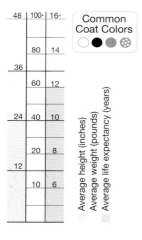

AT A GLANCE

Ease of training	▬
Affection	▬ ▬ ▬ ▬
Playfulness	▬ ▬ ▬
Good with children	▬ ▬ ▬
Good with other dogs	▬
Grooming required	▬ ▬ ▬

! This breed's thick undercoat can help it withstand temperatures as low as -75° F/-60°C.

+ The dogs are prone to lens luxation, hip and elbow dysplasia, gastric torsion, and ear infections.

The Greenland Dog is one of the powerhouse spitz breeds, and also one of the oldest. This is a remarkable sled-dog that is widely used in polar expeditions, as well as for hunting seals and polar bears. They are incredibly tough, independent, and strong, and it is essential they have consistent, patient, and firm training in addition to extensive, high-octane exercise. They are good-natured dogs, but are suitable only for an experienced home that can provide them with the exercise and supervision they need.

HISTORY

Ancient remains of spitz-type dogs found on the New Siberian Islands off of northern Russia have been dated to around 9,000 years ago, and there is evidence that the dogs reached Greenland with the Sarqaq people around 5,000 years ago.

Hokkaido-Ken

Ainu-ken / Seta / Ainu dog

JAPAN

Exercise required

Hokkaido-Ken puppy

Common Coat Colors

	48	100+	16+
		80	14
	36		
		60	12
	24	40	10
		20	8
	12		
		10	6

Average height (inches)
Average weight (pounds)
Average life expectancy (years)

This medium-size breed is one of the spitz-type dogs that are indigenous to Japan. They are ferocious and brave in field work, but if owned as a family pet, these dogs will lose much of their primal temperament and instead adapt to a calmer environment. This breed is highly motivated and intelligent and can be quick to learn with a dedicated owner. The dog has little distribution outside of Japan, although its popularity is growing.

AT A GLANCE

Ease of training	■■ ■■ ■■
Affection	■■ ■■ ■■ ■■
Playfulness	■■ ■■ ■■
Good with children	■■ ■■ ■■
Good with other dogs	■■ ■■ ■■
Grooming required	■■ ■■

 The Ainu is known for being an extremely courageous and loyal dog; some dogs have even taken on bears in order to protect their owners.

+ Roughly one third of all dogs are affected by collie eye anomaly.

HISTORY

The Hokkaido is believed to be an ancient breed; it has its roots in the Matagi-ken, a bear-hunting breed brought to Hokkaido from Tohoku by the Ainu people thousands of years ago. In 1869, English zoologist Thomas Blankiston named the breed "Hokkaido," and within 40 years it was being used by the military to search for war survivors. The breed was legally recognized as a rare protected species in 1937.

Icelandic Sheepdog

Icelandic dog
ICELAND

Icelandic Sheepdog
puppy

Exercise required

48	100+	16+
	80	14
36		
	60	12
24	40	10
	20	8
12		
	10	6

Average height (inches)
Average weight (pounds)
Average life expectancy (years)

Common
Coat Colors

AT A GLANCE

Ease of training	▬▬ ▬▬ ▬▬
Affection	▬▬ ▬▬ ▬▬ ▬▬
Playfulness	▬▬ ▬▬ ▬▬ ▬▬
Good with children	▬▬ ▬▬ ▬▬ ▬▬
Good with other dogs	▬▬ ▬▬ ▬▬
Grooming required	▬▬ ▬▬ ▬▬

! This dog neared extinction in the twentieth century due to the decline in farming, but breeders worked hard to reestablish the breed. It still remains rare today, but is no longer endangered.

+ Generally, they have few health issues, but can develop hip dysplasia and distichiasis.

The Icelandic Sheepdog is similar to the Norwegian Buhund and Welsh Corgi in temperament and appearance. They are tough and energetic as well as hardy and agile; rarely used for hunting, they excel at herding and driving sheep. They are playful, fun, and lively in nature.

HISTORY

The rugged, tough Icelandic Sheepdog traces its history to ancient times, with dog remains of a similar type uncovered in graves dating back to around 8000 BCE. Iceland was colonized in 874 by Norwegian Vikings who arrived with their dogs. These dogs adapted to the climate and terrain of Iceland, and were used for guarding property and livestock, as well as ridding farms of vermin and providing companionship. Few other dog breeds were imported over the centuries, and in 1901, the importation of any other animals onto the island was banned. This means that Icelandic Sheepdogs have been little influenced by other breeds throughout their history.

Indian Spitz

INDIA

Exercise required

Indian Spitz puppy

	48	100+	16+
		80	14
	36		
		60	12
	24	40	10
		20	8
	12		
		10	6

Average height (inches)
Average weight (pounds)
Average life expectancy (years)

Common
Coat Colors

The Indian Spitz is divided into two sizes—the Lesser Indian Spitz and the Greater Indian Spitz. Both varieties are high energy and enthusiastic, and are suitable for any living situation. They are considerded one of the most intelligent breeds and have the ability to understand human intentions.

AT A GLANCE

Ease of training	▰▰ ▰▰ ▰▰
Affection	▰▰ ▰▰ ▰▰ ▰▰
Playfulness	▰▰ ▰▰ ▰▰
Good with children	▰▰ ▰▰ ▰▰ ▰▰
Good with other dogs	▰▰ ▰▰ ▰▰
Grooming required	▰▰ ▰▰

+ This breed is prone to hip dysplasia, patellar luxation, epilepsy, and cataracts.

! This breed is known for having an adaptable diet and can survive on a diet of chicken and rice.

HISTORY

This dog was introduced into India by the British, who brought German Spitzes to the subcontinent and bred them to be suitable for a hot and humid climate. The breed resembles the German Spitz, but has a less thick coat, which helps it survive India's harsh climate, and is slightly smaller in size. This breed is currently not recognized by any kennel club.

Jämthund

Swedish Elkhound

SWEDEN

Jämthund puppy

Common Coat Colors

Exercise required

48	100+	16+
	80	14
36		
	60	12
24	40	10
	20	8
12		
	10	6

Average height (inches)
Average weight (pounds)
Average life expectancy (years)

AT A GLANCE

Ease of training	▬▬ ▬▬ ▬▬
Affection	▬▬ ▬▬ ▬▬
Playfulness	▬▬ ▬▬ ▬▬
Good with children	▬▬ ▬▬
Good with other dogs	▬▬ ▬
Grooming required	▬▬ ▬▬ ▬▬

! Swedish Elkhhounds are one of the few breeds that will face a bear.

+ The breed is prone to dysplasia, arthritis, and skin issues.

The Jämthund exhibits great versatility, with strong hunting skills, a high level of intelligence, and a stable temperament that makes this a truly exceptional dog. It is brave, courageous, and energetic—yet stoically calm. It forms a strong bond with its family and is very affectionate and friendly and is known to be good with children. This dog is willing and eager to please its owners and responds well to training. The Swedish Elkhound may display dominant behavior around other dogs, however.

HISTORY

Also known as the Swedish Elkhound, this breed was formerly grouped with the Norwegian Elkhound and was only recognized as its own breed in 1946. These dogs are most associated with the province of Jämtland in central Sweden and, despite their recent recognition, are believed to be ancient in origin. They have been used for centuries for big-game hunting, including moose and elk.

Japanese Spitz

JAPAN

Japanese Spitz puppies

Exercise required
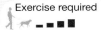

Common
Coat Colors

	Average height (inches)	Average weight (pounds)	Average life expectancy (years)
	48	100+	16+
		80	14
	36		
		60	12
	24	40	10
		20	8
	12		
		10	6

This bold and loyal breed is known to always wear a smile on its face. They are lively and will remain playful well past their puppy years. It is important to mentally engage these dogs, as they can become depressed and ill-tempered if ignored. The Japanese Spitz makes a great companion, though it is not good at being left home alone. They also need extensive grooming.

AT A GLANCE

Ease of training	■■■ ■■■ ■■■
Affection	■■■ ■■■ ■■■ ■■■
Playfulness	■■■ ■■■ ■■■ ■■■
Good with children	■■■ ■■■ ■■■ ■■■ ■■■
Good with other dogs	■■■ ■■■ ■■■
Grooming required	■■■ ■■■ ■■■ ■■■

! With a maximum life expectancy of 16 years or higher, this dog is one of the longest living small breeds.

+ These dogs are prone to patellar luxation and runny eyes due to small tear ducts.

HISTORY

This dog was initially bred in Japan in the early twentieth century by crossbreeding a number of other spitz breeds. The standard for the breed was set after World War II, and the breed became popular in the1950s, when it was exported to various countries in Europe. The breed is not recognized by the American Kennel Club, largely due to its close appearance to the American Eskimo Dog.

Kai-Ken

Kai Dog / Tora Inu / Tiger Dog
JAPAN

Exercise required

Kai-Ken pup

48	100+	16+
	80	14
36		
	60	12
24	40	10
	20	8
12		
	10	6

Average height (inches)
Average weight (pounds)
Average life expectancy (years)

Common Coat Colors

The Kai-Ken, also known as the Kai Dog or Tora Inu (Tiger Dog), is a rare Japanese breed that has started to appear outside Japan only recently. Kai-Kens are noted for their hunting abilities and are used on a range of game, including pheasants, deer, wild boar, and even bears. They tend to bond strongly with one person and are intelligent, calm, and friendly dogs that are fairly easy to train. They are very loyal and make good companions for an active, outdoor-orientated home.

AT A GLANCE

Ease of training	■ ■ ■ ■ ■
Affection	■ ■ ■
Playfulness	■ ■ ■
Good with children	■ ■ ■ ■
Good with other dogs	■ ■ ■ ■ ■
Grooming required	■ ■ ■ ■

Progressive retinal atrophy, hip dysplasia.

HISTORY

The breed is ancient in origin and traces back to the mountainous province of Kai on Honshu Island. These dogs developed in geographic isolation and have been influenced little by other breeds. The dog was designated a living natural monument of Japan in 1934.

Karelian Bear Dog

FINLAND

Exercise required

Karelian Bear Dog puppy

Average height (inches)	Average weight (pounds)	Average life expectancy (years)
48	100+	16+
	80	14
36		
	60	12
24	40	10
	20	8
12		
	10	6

Common Coat Colors

Karelian Bear Dogs are an ancient breed, traced to northwestern Europe, where spitz types were an essential part of life for farmers and peasants: guarding, hunting, and protecting. These fearless hunting dogs are used mostly on large game. Typically, they hunt silently and give voice only when the game has stopped or been treed. The Karelian Bear Dog is an active, intelligent, and independent breed that is best suited to an active, experienced home.

+ These dogs are prone to umbilical hernia, hip dysplasia, and eye problems.

! This breed has a strong hunting instinct, and is known to take on animals such as bears in order to protect their owners.

AT A GLANCE

Ease of training	▰▰▰
Affection	▰▰▰
Playfulness	▰▰▰
Good with children	▰▰▰
Good with other dogs	▰
Grooming required	▰▰

HISTORY

These dogs are associated with Karelia, a region in Russia and Finland, and likely developed from the Komi dog. They are considered a Finnish national treasure.

Keeshond

NETHERLANDS / GERMANY

Keeshond puppy

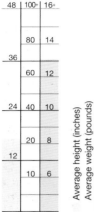

Exercise required

48	100+	16+
36	80	14
	60	12
24	40	10
	20	8
12	10	6

Average height (inches)
Average weight (pounds)
Average life expectancy (years)

Common Coat Colors

In Germany the Keeshond is considered a size variety of the German Spitz. In the United States, England, and a number of other countries, the Keeshond is recognized as a separate breed, whose history is most closely associated with the Netherlands. The Keeshond became popular there during the seventeenth century and was mostly used for guarding canal barges. This breed makes an excellent watchdog and has a fierce bark, but it is not aggressive in nature. These are highly intelligent and charismatic dogs that have been used for search and rescue, but are most commonly kept as companions.

AT A GLANCE

Ease of training
Affection
Playfulness
Good with children
Good with other dogs
Grooming required

! The Keeshond became a symbol of the Dutch Patriot political party during the eighteenth century, although the breed became rare in Holland when the Patriots were defeated.

HISTORY

This breed resembles its close cousins, specifically the German Spitz, Finnish Spitz, and Pomeranian. The breed nearly went extinct around the turn of the twentieth century, but a woman named Miss Hamilton-Fletcher convinced her parents to bring two of the dogs to England. where they revived. In 1926, a breed club was formed in England. The first American litter was bred in 1929, and the American Club was formed shortly thereafter.

+ This dog is prone to dysplasia, patellar luxation, epilepsy, and progressive retinal atrophy.

Kintamani

Kinta

INDONESIA

Kintamani puppy

Exercise required

Common Coat Colors
● ○ ○

	Average height (inches)	Average weight (pounds)	Average life expectancy (years)
	48	100+	16+
		80	14
	36		
		60	12
	24	40	10
		20	8
	12		
		10	6

This little known breed consists of friendly and intelligent dogs from Indonesia, but they remain very rare outside of the island of Bali. The Kintamani is a happy and alert dog that is ready to develop a close relationship with its owner. They have a thick double coat, with the officially accepted color being white, though it is not uncommon to see Kintamanis in other colors.

AT A GLANCE

Ease of training	▰ ▰
Affection	▰ ▰ ▰
Playfulness	▰ ▰ ▰
Good with children	▰ ▰ ▰ ▰
Good with other dogs	▰ ▰ ▰
Grooming required	▰ ▰ ▰

HISTORY

This dog originated around the famous Gunung Batur Volcano in the Northeast region of the island of Bali. It likely evolved from indigenous feral or street dogs, and is genetically also aligned with the Australian Dingo. Some time between the twelfth and sixteenth century it is believed a Chinese trader's Chow Chow bred with local Balinese dogs—and genetic studies do indicate a breed of Chinese origin in this dog's background.

 Little is known about its health issues, but the breed is generally healthy.

! One story about this dog's origin claims that it comes from a fox-wolf-dog cross.

Kishu-Ken pup

Kishu-Ken

Kishu-Inu

JAPAN

Exercise required

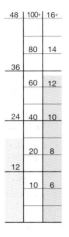

48	100+	16+
	80	14
36		
	60	12
24	40	10
	20	8
12		
	10	6

Average height (inches)
Average weight (pounds)
Average life expectancy (years)

Common
Coat Colors

The Kishu is a rare breed of Japanese spitz that is seldom seen outside its homeland. The dogs were bred white as the color of choice, but other solid colors are not uncommon. These hunting dogs are renowned for their bravery, yet in the home they are clean, quiet, and docile.

AT A GLANCE

Ease of training	■■■ ■■■ ■■■
Affection	■■■ ■■■
Playfulness	■■■ ■■
Good with children	■■■ ■■■
Good with other dogs	■■■ ■■
Grooming required	■■

 This breed is prone to hypothyroidism and entropion.

! Kishu-Ken are often used in obedience and agility competitions due to their high intelligence and athleticism.

HISTORY

These dogs have ancient roots and developed in the rugged, isolated mountains of Kishu, now the Wakayama Prefecture. They were, and are, used for hunting deer and wild boar and excel in this role. Originally Kishu-Kens exhibited a range of coat colors, but hunters came to prefer pure white dogs because they were easier to spot in the forest underbrush.

Labrador Husky

CANADA

Labrador Husky puppy

Exercise required
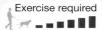

Common Coat Colors
●○◐◑◒

	Average height (inches)	Average weight (pounds)	Average life expectancy (years)
	48	100+	16+
		80	14
	36		
		60	12
	24	40	10
		20	8
	12		
		10	6

The Labrador Husky was bred as a fast, strong sled dog in the Martime provinces of Canada. Despite its name, it is not a mix of the Siberian Husky and Labrador Retriever. Unlike other northern breeds, these dogs are not aggresive to strangers. They also do well with children and are relatively easy to train. As pack animals, they enjoy the company of other dogs.

AT A GLANCE

Ease of training	▰▰ ▰▰
Affection	▰▰ ▰▰ ▰▰ ▰▰
Playfulness	▰▰ ▰▰ ▰▰ ▰▰
Good with children	▰▰ ▰▰ ▰▰
Good with other dogs	▰▰ ▰▰ ▰▰
Grooming required	▰▰ ▰▰ ▰▰

! This dog is happiest in a cold climate due to its thick double coat and should not be kept in temperate climates.

+ These dogs are prone to eye problems, notably corneal dystrophy and progressive retinal atrophy.

HISTORY

This breed originated in the Labrador portion of Newfoundland and Labrador. Its ancestors were brought to the region by the Inuit some time around 1300 AD. The dog evolved in relative isolation, although some breeders have recently crossed it with Alaskan Malamutes or German Shepherds in order to create a larger and stronger dog. They remain unrecognized by any kennel clubs and are little known outside Canada.

379

Nordic Spitz

Norrbottenspets

SWEDEN / FINLAND

Nordic Spitz pup

Exercise required

48	100+	16+
	80	14
36		
	60	12
24	40	10
	20	8
12		
	10	6

Average height (inches)
Average weight (pounds)
Average life expectancy (years)

Common Coat Colors

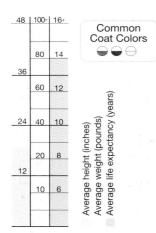

This dog was primarily bred as a hunting dog. Nordic Spitzes are unique for using three senses—sight, scent, and hearing—for tracking, unlike most dogs, which typically use either sight or scent. This light, agile breed is a powerful hunter and best suited as a companion to an active owner or family. Norrbottenspets make excellent watchdogs due to their wariness of strangers and rapid, aggressive barking.

AT A GLANCE

Ease of training	▬▬ ▬▬
Affection	▬▬ ▬▬ ▬▬
Playfulness	▬▬ ▬▬ ▬▬ ▬▬
Good with children	▬▬ ▬▬ ▬▬ ▬▬
Good with other dogs	▬▬ ▬▬ ▬▬
Grooming required	▬▬ ▬▬ ▬▬

 This breed is able to bark up to 120 times per minute, which helps it confuse its prey and muffle the sounds of the dog's hunting companions.

✚ The breed is prone to hip dysplasia, patellar luxation, and diabetes.

HISTORY

This breed gets its name from Norrbotten, Sweden, although Sweden and Finland argue about the true origin of this dog. The Norbottenspets came close to extinction toward the end of World War I, but a breeding program in the 1950s saved the breed from disappearing. The breed's official name and standard were set in 1967 by the Swedish Kennel Club, although the Finns call the dog the "Pohjanpystykorva." Breeders follow very strict breeding practices in both Finland and Sweden in order to preserve the dog's health and characteristics.

Northern Inuit Dog

NI Dog

**ORIGINAL STOCK FROM CANADA,
DEVELOPED IN THE UK**

Exercise required

Northern Inuit pup

	Average height (inches)	Average weight (pounds)	Average life expectancy (years)
	48	100+	16+
		80	14
	36		
		60	12
	24	40	10
		20	8
	12		
		10	6

Common
Coat Colors

The large, athletic Northern Inuit Dog is a recent crossbreed developed in the 1980s in the United Kingdom from Husky, Malamute and Shepherd stock with Canadian origins. While generally friendly, calm and outgoing, this breed is not for the faint of heart—it is known to be stubborn and difficult to train. Northern Inuit Dogs require a consistent and strong owner who is ready to commit to their dog's socialization. This dog may develop separation anxiety if ignored or if the owner is away; they often do better with another dog for company.

AT A GLANCE

Ease of training	▬
Affection	▬ ▬ ▬
Playfulness	▬ ▬ ▬ ▬
Good with children	▬ ▬ ▬ ▬
Good with other dogs	▬ ▬ ▬ ▬
Grooming required	▬ ▬ ▬ ▬

✚ Like all big dogs, this breed is prone to hip dysplasia and elbow dysplasia.

HISTORY

One possible origin story is that the breed's founder Eddie Harrison bred this dog in the late 1980s by combining several rescue dogs with Siberian Huskies, Alaskan Malamutes, and German Shepherds. This breed was meant to resemble a wolf, but still retain the gentler qualities and trainable nature of the dog.

! These dogs are famous for being cast as the Direwolves in the 2011 HBO series *Game of Thrones*.

Norwegian Buhund

Norsk Buhund / Norwegian Sheepdog
NORWAY

Exercise required

Norwegian Buhund pup

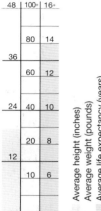

Average height (inches)
Average weight (pounds)
Average life expectancy (years)

Common
Coat Colors

The modern Buhund developed in western Norway, where they were used as general-purpose farm dogs—herding and guarding livestock, hunting small game, and guarding property.

AT A GLANCE

Ease of training	■■ ■■ ■■
Affection	■■ ■ ■■
Playfulness	■■ ■ ■■
Good with children	■■ ■ ■ ■
Good with other dogs	■■ ■ ■
Grooming required	■■ ■ ■

+ This breed may develop Inherited eye issues and hip dysplasia.

HISTORY

This ancient breed is documented as having accompanied the Vikings on their frequent journeys, both on sea and land. A Viking grave excavated in ancient Gokstad and dating from around 900 AD, revealed skeletons from six dogs of various sizes, the representatives of modern-day Buhunds.

! Despite having a long history in Europe, this breed was not brought to England or most other European countries until after World War II.

Norwegian Elkhound

Grey Norwegian Elkhound / Norsk Elghund

NORWAY

Exercise required

Norwegian Elkhound
puppy

Average height (inches)	Average weight (pounds)	Average life expectancy (years)
48	100+	16+
	80	14
36		
	60	12
24	40	10
	20	8
12		
	10	6

Common
Coat Colors

One of the more ancient of the spitz-type breeds, sturdy, compact Norwegian Elkhounds have served as hunters, guardians, herders, and defenders. They were bred to track moose (elk), but will also tackle bears or wolves. These bold, playful dogs form a close bond with their owners, and their natural vigilance and sharp, ready bark means they are good watchdogs.

AT A GLANCE

Ease of training	▮▮▮ ▮▮▮ ▮▮▮ ▮▮▮
Affection	▮▮▮ ▮▮▮ ▮▮▮ ▮▮▮ ▮
Playfulness	▮▮▮ ▮▮▮ ▮▮▮ ▮▮▮
Good with children	▮▮▮ ▮▮ ▮▮▮ ▮▮▮
Good with other dogs	▮▮▮ ▮▮▮ ▮▮▮ ▮▮▮
Grooming required	▮▮▮ ▮▮▮ ▮▮

! In Norway, this dog is known as the "Norsk Elghund," which translates to "Norwegian Moose Dog."

✚ The breed is prone to Fanconi syndrome, hypothyroidism, progressive retinal atrophy, and sebaceous cysts.

HISTORY

Although its origins are obscure, this dog originated in Norway in ancient times—skeletons resembling the breed have been dated to 5000 BCE. Almost certainly the Vikings used this dog's ancestors for hunting. Genetically, the Elkhound is the result of a female wolf-male dog hybridization that took place post domestication. The breed came to England in the late 1800s and was admitted to the Kennel Club in 1901.

Norwegian Lundehund

NORWAY

Exercise required

Common
Coat Colors

48	100+	16+
	80	14
36		
	60	12
24	40	10
	20	8
12		
	10	6

Average height (inches)
Average weight (pounds)
Average life expectancy (years)

Norwegian Lundehund pup

The Norwegian Lundehund, the "puffin dog", are canine contortionists. The dogs were used on the Norwegian coast where Atlantic puffins were used by villagers for food and feathers. Their six muscled toes and full-body flexibility helped them climb cliffs and retrieve the heavy puffins from their crevice nests. Lundehunds have a natural small-prey drive and they can be barky, but they are playful, gregarious and wonderful companions to patient, experienced owners.

AT A GLANCE

Ease of training	▬▬ ▬▬
Affection	▬▬ ▬▬ ▬▬
Playfulness	▬▬ ▬▬ ▬▬
Good with children	▬▬ ▬▬ ▬▬ ▬▬
Good with other dogs	▬▬ ▬▬ ▬▬ ▬▬ ▬▬
Grooming required	▬▬ ▬▬

! This dog loves to run and play with other dogs and will thrive as a second or third dog for a loving owner.

+ This dog may be prone to Lundehund intestinal syndrome, rapid weight gain/obesity, and progressive retinal atrophy.

HISTORY

The Norwegian Lundehund takes its name from the Norwegian word lunde, meaning "puffin". The breed can be traced to the 1500s and were used to hunt puffins on Norway's North Atlantic coast and neighboring islands. When puffins were named a protected species, the dogs were no longer essential and declined greatly in numbers. The breed barely survived two canine distemper epidemics — post-World War II and in 1963 — leaving only six dogs. No longer endangered, this rare breed made its debut at the Westminster Kennel Club Dog Show in 2012.

Pungsan

Poongsan

NORTH KOREA

Pungsan puppy

Exercise required

Common
Coat Colors

Average height (inches)	Average weight (pounds)	Average life expectancy (years)
48	100+	16+
	80	14
36		
	60	12
24	40	10
	20	8
12		
	10	6

The thick-coated Pungsan is a hunting dog from North Korea, where they were used for hunting large animals, including Amur tigers. Because they developed in mountainous regions, these dogs evolved to become strong and agile. The breed is rare, and hardly known outside its own country.

AT A GLANCE

Ease of training	■■■ ■■■ ■■■ ■■■ ■■■
Affection	■■■ ■■■ ■■■
Playfulness	■■■ ■■■ ■■■ ■■■
Good with children	■■■ ■■
Good with other dogs	■■■
Grooming required	■■■ ■■■ ■■■

! These loyal dogs may become so focused on their families that they ignore everyone else. They are reportedly good with children, but need to be socialized properly with other pets. These puppies a great chewers, so keep valuables out of their reach.

+ This dog is prone to hip and elbow dysplasia, cancer, ear infections, entropian, ectropian, and obesity.

Although its exact origins are unknown, the Pungsan is believed to have been bred as a hunting dog during the early years of the Joseon Dynasty (1392–1897). What is known is that they originated in the mountainous region in the north known as Pungsan. In old Korean tales, these dogs were celebrated for their cleverness and loyalty, as well as their hunting ability.

385

Russo-European Laika

RUSSIA

Russo-European
Laika pup

Exercise required

48	100+	16+
	80	14
36		
	60	12
24	40	10
	20	8
12		
	10	6

Average height (inches)
Average weight (pounds)
Average life expectancy (years)

Common
Coat Colors

Lively and excitable, the Russo-European Laika needs a lot of exercise and a large area to thrive. Affectionate and good with children, these dogs make fine family pets. They are also effective watchdogs—they are typically cautious with strangers and are known to be territorial.

AT A GLANCE

Ease of training	▮▮ ▮▮
Affection	▮▮ ▮▮ ▮▮
Playfulness	▮▮ ▮▮
Good with children	▮▮ ▮▮ ▮▮
Good with other dogs	▮▮
Grooming required	▮▮ ▮▮

+ One of the healthier breeds, minor problems include monorchidism and umbilical hernias.

! Without enough stimulation from its owner, this dog can become bored and destructive. It's important to keep this dog engaged and give it plenty of opportunities to run free.

HISTORY

Initially bred for hunting, the Russo-European Laika would locate prey, bark to alert its human compainions, and then hold or tree the prey until the hunters arrived. The dog is believed to have originated in the harsh northern Arctic regions of Russia. Studies have found that the Russo-European Laika is closely related to the wolf, and it is possibly one of the oldest dog breeds in existence.

Samoyed

Bjelkie/"The Smiling Dog"

RUSSIA

Exercise required

Samoyed puppy

	48	100+	16+
		80	14
	36		
		60	12
		24	40	10
		20	8
	12		
		10	6

Average height (inches)
Average weight (pounds)
Average life expectancy (years)

Common
Coat Colors

Samoyeds, with their "Sammie smiles," are known to be one of the friendliest and best-natured Nordic breeds. They have a thick, double-layer coat, triangular ears, and a distinct, bushy tail that lies over their backs. The breed can be independent, and while some may require extensive training, most Sammies are good with children, affable with strangers, and remain playful even into old age.

AT A GLANCE

Ease of training	▬ ▬ ▬
Affection	▬ ▬ ▬ ▬ ▬
Playfulness	▬ ▬ ▬ ▬ ▬
Good with children	▬ ▬ ▬ ▬ ▬
Good with other dogs	▬ ▬ ▬ ▬ ▬
Grooming required	▬ ▬ ▬

+ This breed is prone to gastric torsion, hip dysplasia.

! Samoyeds were used by the American military during World War II. One Samoyed, named Frosty of Rimini, served his country so well, he was awarded the Good Conduct Medal and a Victory Medal.

HISTORY

Native to Russia, Samoyed are descended from the Nenets Herding Laika, a spitz used in Siberia for sledding, herding, and guarding. The breed lived in nearly complete isolation until the 1600s, when the Russians began to explore and colonize Siberia. Their lack of genetic diversity has resulted in a number of geneticc disorders, such as Samoyed hereditary glomerulopathy, a renal disease.

Seppala Siberian Sleddog

Seppala Siberian Sheepdog
CANADA

Seppala Siberian
Sleddog pup

Exercise required

Common
Coat Colors

The Seppala Siberian Sleddog is a working dog developed in early twentieth century Canada for competitive sled racing—and which later became popular in New England. Seppalas are known for their high work ethic and a greater ease of training than most other sled dogs. This energetic breed requires a dedicated owner, however, because it retains some primitive canine qualities. This breed shares a similar ancestor to the Siberian Husky and is much like that breed in temperament.

AT A GLANCE

Ease of training
Affection
Playfulness
Good with children
Good with other dogs
Grooming required

This breed is prone to allergies, cancer, and eye problems such as cataracts.

! For half a century, this dog shared the same registry as the Siberian Husky, despite being a distinct breed.

HISTORY

This "master" sled dog was named after its breeder, legendary sled driver Leonhard Seppala, who bred this dog in Alaska, using dogs he exported from eastern Siberia. The focus was on performance, so they were never bred for strict conformation or the show ring. Several Seppala breeders worked to keep the breed going over the decades, although this dog remains rare nowadays.

Shiba Inu

Shiba-Ken / Little Brushwood Dog

JAPAN

Shiba Inu puppy

Exercise required

Average height (inches)	Average weight (pounds)	Average life expectancy (years)
48	100+	16+
	80	14
36		
	60	12
24	40	10
	20	8
12		
	10	6

Common Coat Colors

Once bred to hunt, the Shiba Inu is now the most common companion dog in Japan. It is a small, compact dog, with well-developed muscles and a permanently alert expression. The breed also has a double coat, much like the the Akita. In the home, these dogs do best without small children or other dogs—they still retain the prey drive of a hunter and can also be quite independent.

AT A GLANCE

Ease of training	
Affection	
Playfulness	
Good with children	
Good with other dogs	
Grooming required	

! This dog came to the U.S. relatively recently, but quickly rose to the top 50 most popular dogs in America. The Shiba Inu has especially found popularity on the internet, with famous examples such as Mari the Shiba and Doge.

HISTORY

The Shiba Inu is considered a basal breed, one that predates the emergence of modern breeds in the 1800s. Sometimes known as the "Little Brushwood Dog," it was able to hunt small prey in dense brushwood. It was one of the most popular dog breeds for many years in Japan. In the aftermath of World War II, however, the Shiba Inu went through a sharp decline due to a food shortage and a distemper epidemic. In more recent times, its popularity has spread to many countries, including the U.S.

+ The breed is prone to allergies, chylothorax, hyperthyroidism, and hip dysplasia.

389

Siberian Husky

SIBERIA

Exercise required

It is easy to see why many people are drawn to the Siberian's wolf-like looks, but be warned, this athletic, intelligent dog can be independent and challenging for first-time dog owners. Huskies are notorious escapologist and need a fenced yard that is sunk into the ground to prevent them digging out. This beautiful dog has a thick coat that comes in a wide range of colors and markings. Their piercing blue or multi-colored eye and striking facial masks only add to the appeal of this breed.

! Siberian Huskies have very loving and loyal natures, but they also require extensive exercise. They should only be considered as pets by families or individuals that have an active lifestyle.

+ This breed is prone to corneal dystrophy, canine glaucoma, and progressive retinal atrophy.

HISTORY

These huskies trace back at least three thousand years; they were bred by the Chukchi people of Siberia—a hunter-gatherer culture that bred them for pulling sleds, herding livestock, and protecting their homes. During World War II, the dogs were used primarily for search and rescue missions, and it was around that time that the breed arrived in England.

Siberian Husky
pups

Average height (inches)	Average weight (pounds)	Average life expectancy (years)
48	100+	16+
	80	14
36		
	60	12
24	40	10
	20	8
12		
	10	6

Common
Coat Colors

AT A GLANCE	
Ease of training	▪
Affection	▪ ▪ ▪ ▪ ▪
Playfulness	▪ ▪ ▪ ▪
Good with children	▪ ▪ ▪ ▪ ▪
Good with other dogs	▪ ▪ ▪
Grooming required	▪ ▪ ▪

Shikoku pup

Shikoku

Shikoku-Ken

JAPAN

Exercise required
▬ ▬ ▮ ▮ ▮

Common
Coat Colors
⬤ ⬤ ◯

48	100+	16+
	80	14
36		
	60	12
24	40	10
	20	8
12		
	10	6

Average height (inches)
Average weight (pounds)
Average life expectancy (years)

This native dog of Japan has been used to hunt deer and wild boar for centuries. Somewhere between the Akita Inu and the Shiba Inu in size, these dogs are tough, brave, agile, and loyal to their masters and familys. They reportedly love to learn and do well in obedience and agiliy. Unless well socialized, however, their high prey drive makes them a risk to smaller pets.

AT A GLANCE

Ease of training	▬ ▬
Affection	▬ ▬ ▬
Playfulness	▬ ▬ ▬
Good with children	▬ ▬ ▬
Good with other dogs	▬
Grooming required	▬ ▬ ▬

+ These dogs are prone to panosteitis, hip dysplasia, entropion, and allergies.

! The Shikoku is a rare dog, even in Japan; in 1937 the breed was established as one of that countrys national treasures.

HISTORY

Originating on the island of Shikoku, Japan, this primitive breed developed in genetic isolation, in the mountains of Kochi Prefecture, where it was split into two groups, the Eastern and the Western Shikoku. In the twentieth century, the Japanese re-evaluated the dogs and classified them as the Awa, the Hongawa, and the Hata—named for the areas in which they were bred.

Swedish Lapphund
The "Lappie"
SWEDEN

Swedish Lapphund puppy

Exercise required

Common Coat Colors

	Average height (inches)	Average weight (pounds)	Average life expectancy (years)
	48	100+	16+
		80	14
	36		
		60	12
	24	40	10
		20	8
	12		
		10	6

The Swedish Lapphund is a medium-sized working breed native to Lapland in northern Sweden. It is known for its fearsome bark, and was commonly used for hunting, guarding, and herding. It is also one of Sweden's oldest and rarest breeds, which has led to its being identified as the "the black beauty of Norrland." In the home, these dogs are friendly, playful, and rarely aggressive.

AT A GLANCE

Ease of training	▬
Affection	▬ ▬ ▬ ▬ ▬
Playfulness	▬ ▬ ▬ ▬
Good with children	▬ ▬ ▬ ▬
Good with other dogs	▬ ▬ ▬
Grooming required	▬ ▬ ▬

! The Swedish Lapphund is the national dog of Sweden. Only a few thousand of the breed exist.

+ This dog is prone to diabetes mellitus and progressive retinal atrophy.

HISTORY
The origin of the Swedish Lapphund can be traced back to the nomadic Sami People of Lapland, whose lives revolved around their reindeer. The Swedish Lapphund herded these reindeer with its bark, making the breed invaluable to the community. Due to this legacy of hard work, as well as the rugged terrain of its homeland, the Swedish Lapphund became resilient, intelligent, and independent.

Thai Bangkaew Dog

THAILAND

Thai Bangkaew pup

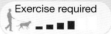

Exercise required

Common Coat Colors

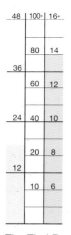

48	100+	16+
	80	14
36		
	60	12
24	40	10
	20	8
12		
	10	6

Average height (inches)
Average weight (pounds)
Average life expectancy (years)

The Thai Bangkaew Dog is a medium-sized Asian spitz breed. Compact and squarely built, the Thai Bangkaew has two coats: a short undercoat coupled with a coat of longer guard hairs. These inteligent, robust dogs are lively and loyal to their families, and make excellent watchdogs.

AT A GLANCE

Ease of training	▄▄ ▄▄
Affection	▄▄ ▄▄ ▄▄
Playfulness	▄▄ ▄▄ ▄▄
Good with children	▄▄ ▄▄
Good with other dogs	▄▄
Grooming required	▄▄ ▄▄ ▄▄

+ They may be prone to dysplasia, patellar luxation, liver disease, and chronic ear infections.

! Seasonal flooding of the Bangkaew region created isolation and a limited canine gene pool, leading to the inbreeding that created this dog.

HISTORY

Tracing back to Bangkaew, a village in the Phitsanulok Province in central Thailand, this breed is said to have originated when a black-and-white dog named Tah Nim bred with a jackal, then appeared near a local monastery to have her puppies. Genetic studies do show jackal bloodlines. Popular in Thailand today, this dog is rarely seen beyond its home borders.

Volpino Italiano

Italian Spitz / Florentine Spitz
ITALY

Volpino Italiano puppy

Exercise required

48	100+	16+		
	80	14		
36				
	60	12		
24	40	10		
	20	8		
12				
	10	6		

Average height (inches)
Average weight (pounds)
Average life expectancy (years)

Common Coat Colors

Florentine Spitzes are lively and playful dogs with an ancient heritage. They have been favorites of Italian royalty, especially noble ladies, for centuries. In Italian, the name translates to "little fox," which perfectly describes the dog's pert, alert appearance. Although they resemble Pomeranians, they are much older, with very different backgrounds. In the home, they are affectionate and active.

AT A GLANCE

Ease of training	▬ ▬ ▬ ▬
Affection	▬ ▬ ▬ ▬ ▬
Playfulness	▬ ▬ ▬ ▬
Good with children	▬ ▬ ▬ ▬
Good with other dogs	▬ ▬ ▬ ▬ ▬
Grooming required	▬ ▬ ▬

✚ This breed is enerally healthy, but can develop heart problems and cataracts. It is also threatened by primary lens luxation.

HISTORY

Based on specimens found in peat bogs, this spitz's ancestry may go back as far as 4000 BCE. The dog was initially used as a watchdog that was meant to alert larger guard dogs, such as Mastiffs, of an intruder. The breed nearly became extinct in the 1960s, but it was somewhat successfully revived in 1984. Today there are roughly 2,000 dogs registered worldwide, with 120 registered each year in Italy. They remain a rare breed.

! Legend has it that Michelangelo was accompanied by Volpinos when he painted the Sistine Chapel's ceiling.

West Siberian Laika

Zapadno-Sibirskaïa Laïka

RUSSIA

West Siberian
Laika pup

Exercise required

48	100+	16+
	80	14
36		
	60	12
24	40	10
	20	8
12		
	10	6

Average height (inches)
Average weight (pounds)
Average life expectancy (years)

Common
Coat Colors

The West Siberian Laika is a powerful, rugged hunting dog, devloped as a barking pointer—locating game, barking to alert the hunter, then holding the prey. Originating from a group of aboriginal spitz breeds assciated with different ethnic groups—and numbering in the dozens—the WSL began to take its modern shape after World War II. They are affectinate loyal dogs, that can be territoral with other males and may see cats outside the household as prey to be pursued and treed.

AT A GLANCE

Ease of training	▬ ▬ ▬
Affection	▬ ▬ ▬ ▬
Playfulness	▬ ▬ ▬ ▬
Good with children	▬ ▬ ▬
Good with other dogs	▬ ▬
Grooming required	▬ ▬ ▬ ▬

! The hardy West Siberian Laika is known to be one of the healthiest dogs in the world, and unlike other breeds, their health issues tend to be minor.

+ "One of the healthiest dogs in the world"– umbilical hernia and monorchidism are infrequent but potential occurrences.

HISTORY

This dog originated in northeasern Russia, where it was commonly used in the nineteenth century for selective hunting—meaning it could focus solely on a certain species. Many owners benefitted financially from dogs that could seek out only the rarest and most valuable game animals. In the late 1900s, deforestation lessened the number of Siberian hunting dogs, including the WSL. During the 1960s, this breed was exported to the U.S, where it became part of the pet trade.

Yakutian Laika

Yakut Laika

RUSSIA

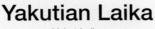

Exercise required

Yakutian Laika puppy

Common
Coat Colors

	Average height (inches)	Average weight (pounds)	Average life expectancy (years)
	48	100+	16+
		80	14
	36		
		60	12
	24	40	10
		20	8
	12		
		10	6

This striking black and white dog originated along the Arctic seashore of the Yakutia Republic. They are versatile workers that can serve their owners as reindeer-herders, hunting dogs, or sled dogs. Althought they can be aggressive toward predators, they are gentle and loving with humans. Yakutian Laikas do best in active homes; they are high-energy dogs that need daily exercise.

AT A GLANCE

Ease of training	▪▪▪
Affection	▪▪▪▪
Playfulness	▪▪▪
Good with children	▪▪▪
Good with other dogs	▪▪▪
Grooming required	▪▪▪

None.

! Although it's known as a working dog, this breed makes an excellent watchdog due to its sensitive nose and ears and its wariness of strangers.

HISTORY

This ancient dog was developed by native Yakuts to hunt mammals and birds. The breed became especially popular in the seventeenth century when demand for white polar foxes spiked. As a result, Yakutian Laikas became a favorite for those in need of sled dogs for hunting.

TERRIERS

Affenpinscher

Affen / Affie / Monkey Dog

GERMANY

Affenpinscher pup

Exercise required

48	100+	16+
	80	14
36		
	60	12
24	40	10
	20	8
12		
	10	6

Average height (inches)
Average weight (pounds)
Average life expectancy (years)

Common Coat Colors
●

The German word "affenpinscher" translates to "monkey terrier," an appropriate description for these small, cheeky dogs. Known as "diablotin moustachu", or "moustached little devil" in France, they make fun, lively, though occasionally stubborn companions. The Affenpinscher is bold, athletic, playful, and occasionally noisy, but generally good with other pets.

AT A GLANCE	
Ease of training	■ ■ ■ ■ ☐
Affection	■ ■ ■ ■ ☐
Playfulness	■ ■ ■ ■ ☐
Good with children	■ ■ ■ ☐ ☐
Good with other dogs	■ ■ ■ ☐ ☐
Grooming required	■ ■ ■ ☐ ☐

! This dog is mostly quiet, but can become very excited if attacked or threatened, and shows no fear.

+ The Affenpinscher is prone to hip dysplasia. As with many small breeds of dog, they are prone to collapsed trachea.

HISTORY

Although the breed's origins are undocumented, dogs of the Affenpinscher type have been known since about 1600. These were somewhat larger, about 12 to 13 inches tall, with coat colors of gray, fawn, black, tan and red. By the seventeenth century, white small terriers of this type were widespread in Germany; and depictions of similar dogs appeared in earlier paintings. Affenpinschers were often kept on farms as ratters but were also popular as ladies' pets.

Airedale Terrier

Waterside Terrier / Bingley Terrier

UNITED KINGDOM

Airedale Terrier pup

Exercise required

Average height (inches)	Average weight (pounds)	Average life expectancy (years)
48	100+	16+
	80	14
36		
	60	12
24	40	10
	20	8
12		
	10	6

Common Coat Colors

The tallest of the terrier breeds, the Airedale is often referred to as the "King of Terriers." They are extremely versatile dogs that have been used to perform a variety of functions since their development during the nineteenth century. Their intelligence and trainability has led to their use in the police force and military. This breed also have superb hunting, tracking, and retrieving skills, that were widely used on farms as ratters.

AT A GLANCE

Ease of training	▰ ▰ ▰
Affection	▰ ▰ ▰
Playfulness	▰ ▰ ▰ ▰
Good with children	▰ ▰ ▰ ▰
Good with other dogs	▰ ▰
Grooming required	▰ ▰ ▰ ▰

✚ Airedales can be affected by hip dysplasia. Like most terriers, they have a propensity towards dermatitis. Skin disorders may go unnoticed in Airedales because of their hard, dense, wiry coats.

 This dog's coat is hypoallergenic; that is, it tends not to generate allergic reactions in people.

HISTORY

Although their heritage is largely unknown, they are believed to have developed from the extinct Black and Tan Rough Terrier from the South Yorkshire area, crossed with Bull and Irish Terriers. Its name has alternated between Working, Bingley, or Waterside Terriers for some years before being named Airedale Terriers in 1879.

American Hairless Terrier

AHT

UNITED STATES

American Hairless Terrier pup

Exercise required

Common Coat Colors

48	100+	16+
	80	14
36		
	60	12
24	40	10
	20	8
12		
	10	6

Average height (inches)
Average weight (pounds)
Average life expectancy (years)

Although they are terriers by heritage, the American Hairless Terrier (AHT) is a lively, charismatic, and affectionate companion breed that were specifically designed for companionship. They are playful, intelligent, trainable, and thus enjoy activities like agility and obedience. They can be quite compatible and friendly with cats if they are raised alongside them and generally get along well with other dogs as well.

AT A GLANCE

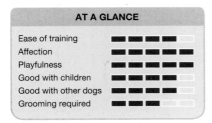

Ease of training

Affection

Playfulness

Good with children

Good with other dogs

Grooming required

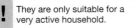
 They are only suitable for a very active household.

+ They can be affected by eye problems and hip dysplasia and are predisposed to immune-mediated rheumatic disease.

HISTORY

The AHT were initially developed from a mixed breed of terriers known as Feists which were brought to North America from Europe in the eighteenth century. Another breed, the Rat Terrier was bred by integrating the Feist breed with Beagle, Italian Greyhound and Miniature Pinscher bloodlines in the late nineteenth century. The first AHT was borne from a Rat Terrier litter almost a century later in the state of Louisiana, United States. Pleased with its appearance, the owners Edwin and Willie Scott bred her aiming to reproduce her hairless quality.

American Pit Bull Terrier

APBT / Pit Bull / Pit APBT / Pit

UNITED STATES

American Pit Bull Terrier pup

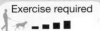
Exercise required

Average height (inches)	Average weight (pounds)	Average life expectancy (years)
48	100+	16+
	80	14
36		
	60	12
24	40	10
	20	8
12		
	10	6

Common Coat Colors

Immigrants and ranchers often took these crossbred dogs to the United States for ranch work and for their participation in activities such as hunting, guarding and fighting. Contrastingly, the American Pit Bull is banned is banned or restricted in some countries due to its potential for aggressive behavior.. However, they can make loyal, friendly companions if properly socialized, trained and cared for.

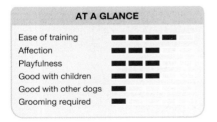

AT A GLANCE	
Ease of training	■ ■ ■
Affection	■ ■ ■
Playfulness	■ ■ ■
Good with children	■ ■ ■
Good with other dogs	■
Grooming required	■

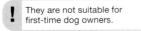
! They are not suitable for first-time dog owners.

+ The breed tends to have a higher-than-average incidence of hip dysplasia.

HISTORY

With similar ancestry to the American Staffordshire Terrier, the American Pit Bull Terrier traces back to English Bulldog and Terrier breeds. Faster, more athletic Bulldogs were bred by English dog breeders by crossing a variety of regional terriers in the nineteenth century. The resulting breed became known as the Bull and Terrier, Half and Half, Pit Dog, or Pit Bull terrier; "pit" refers to their participation in dog fights often held in pits to contain the gruesome "entertainment".

403

American Staffordshire Terrier

AmStaff / Stafford

UNITED STATES

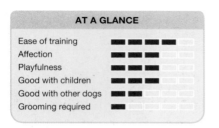

American Staffordshire
Terrier pup

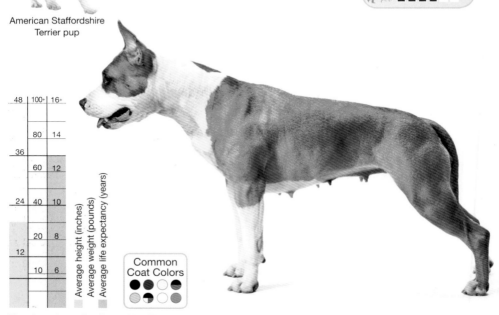

48	100+	16+
	80	14
36		
	60	12
24	40	10
	20	8
12		
	10	6

Average height (inches)
Average weight (pounds)
Average life expectancy (years)

Common Coat Colors

The American Staffordshire Terrier are easy to handle and gentle, despite being a dog fighting breed. They are characteristically affectionate, playful and loyal. Although they may be aggressive toward other dogs, with proper training and socialization that can be overcome.

AT A GLANCE

Ease of training	▬▬▬▬
Affection	▬▬▬
Playfulness	▬▬▬
Good with children	▬▬▬
Good with other dogs	▬▬
Grooming required	▬

! They are not suitable for first-time dog owners

+ Notable issues related to health and well-being include: Congenital heart disease, Elbow and hip dysplasia and Luxating patella

HISTORY

Bred from both English Bulldog and Terrier crosses like the American Pit Bull Terrier, the American Staffordshire Terrier (renamed from Bull and Terrier in 1969) were brought by immigrants to the United States. Compared to their relatives in England, the immigrated dogs became much larger and more powerful.

Australian Silky Terrier

Silky

AUSTRALIA

Australian Silky Terrier pup

Exercise required

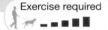

Common Coat Colors

	Average height (inches)	Average weight (pounds)	Average life expectancy (years)
	48	100+	16+
		80	14
	36		
		60	12
	24	40	10
		20	8
	12		
		10	6

An intelligent, friendly, spirited and self-assured breed, the Silky Terrier enjoys chasing small animals and is perseverant in a fight. An excellent watchdog despite their small size, as being sensitive to strangers, they are quick to sound the alarm.

AT A GLANCE

Ease of training	■■ ■■ ■■ ■
Affection	■■ ■■ ■■
Playfulness	■■ ■■ ■■
Good with children	■■ ■■
Good with other dogs	■■ ■■ ■■
Grooming required	■■ ■■ ■■ ■■

 Terriers are known to have teeth and gum problems

! It is important they are kept busy and social to discourage boredom

HISTORY

The Australian Silky Terrier is a small breed of dog developed in Australia with ancestral types and breeds from Great Britain. They are closely related and share similar characteristics to the Australian Terrier and the Yorkshire Terrier. Solely known as the Silky Terrier in North America, the breed is known as the Australian Silky Terrier in the rest of the world.

Australian Terrier

Aussie
AUSTRALIA

Australian Terrier pup

Exercise required

Common
Coat Colors

48	100+	16+	
	80	14	
36			
	60	12	
24	40	10	Average height (inches) Average weight (pounds) Average life expectancy (years)
	20	8	
12			
	10	6	

Australian Terriers were often used mainly as ratters to control rat populations around gold mines, harbor areas and farms. Small but with the confidence of a large breed, they are wonderful watchdogs and sensitive to strangers. They are energetic with a spirited, mischievous personality, and strongly attached to family.

AT A GLANCE	
Ease of training	▪▪▪▪☐
Affection	▪▪▪☐☐
Playfulness	▪▪▪▪☐
Good with children	▪▪▪▪▪
Good with other dogs	▪▪▪▪☐
Grooming required	▪▪▪☐☐

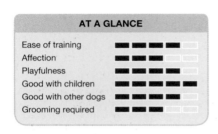

! The Aussie is a typical terrier, he loves to bark, dig, and chase

+ Australian Terriers are generally healthy but can be prone to certain conditions and diseases; Patellar luxation and Legg-perthes

HISTORY

Bred to be small, tough, suited for an Australian climate, and capable as ratters and watchdogs, the breed incorporated a mix of mostly British terrier breeds, including the Dandie Dinmont, Skye, Manchester, and Yorkshire Terriers in Tasmania. They were also used occasionally as sheep herders. The Australian Terrier was the first Australian breed be recognized and shown in its home country.

Austrian Pinscher

Austrian Shorthaired Pinscher

AUSTRIA

Exercise required

Austrian Pinscher pup

	Average height (inches)	Average weight (pounds)	Average life expectancy (years)
	48	100+	16+
		80	14
	36		
		60	12
	24	40	10
		20	8
	12		
		10	6

Common Coat Colors

Austrian Pinschers are calm, affectionate, and loyal. Their wariness around strangers and loud bark allow them to be good watchdogs. Although their wary nature carries over to other animals, they generally get along well other dogs.

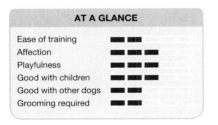

AT A GLANCE	
Ease of training	▪▪ ▪▪
Affection	▪▪ ▪▪ ▪▪
Playfulness	▪▪ ▪▪ ▪▪
Good with children	▪▪ ▪▪ ▪▪
Good with other dogs	▪▪ ▪▪ ▪▪
Grooming required	▪▪ ▪▪

✚ The Austrian Pinscher may prone to hip dysplasia and some may have a heart condition that is inherited.

! Socialization and training are important.

HISTORY

Descended from an ancient breed, the Austrian Pinscher was a valued and versatile working farm dog in the nineteenth century with a natural instinct as a ratter and for working cattle. The Austrian Pinscher was first recognized as a breed in 1928.

Bedlington Terrier

Rothbury Terrier / Rodbery Terrier / Rothbury's Lamb

ENGLAND

Exercise required

Known for its speed, the Bedlington Terrier is one of the fastest of its kind. They are an affectionate, calm and demonstrative breed, but are noted to be reserved and aggressive with other dogs at times. They are often compared to a miniature version of the Scottish Deerhound.

Bedlington Terrier pup

AT A GLANCE		
Ease of training		
Affection		
Playfulness		
Good with children		
Good with other dogs		
Grooming required		

➕ Bedlington Terriers are more prone to copper toxicosis than most other dog breeds.

Bedlington Terrier pup

! Their coats require a lot of upkeep.

Common Coat Colors

Dogs are usually born dark, and their color fades as they age, maturing into a pale bluish-gray, Blue, sandy, or liver, with or without tan markings

Average height (inches)
Average weight (pounds)
Average life expectancy (years)

48	100+	16+
	80	14
36		
	60	12
24	40	10
	20	8
12		
	10	6

HISTORY

The Bedlington Terrier was bred in Northumberland, some with pedigrees that trace back to the eighteenth century. Originally named the Rothbury or Rodbury Terrier until 1825 when renamed after a northern mining town of Bedlington, England, the breed is thought to contain bloodlines from Whippet, Rough-Coated Scottish Terrier, and Dandie Dinmont breeds. However, their precise origins are uncertain.

Border Terrier

Coquete Terrier / Redesdale Terrier

SCOTLAND / ENGLAND

Exercise required

Border Terrier pup

48	100+	16+
	80	14
36		
	60	12
24	40	10
	20	8
12		
	10	6

Average height (inches)
Average weight (pounds)
Average life expectancy (years)

Common Coat Colors

This charismatic breed developed along the border areas of Northumberland and Scotland, they were mainly used to hunt foxes and other small prey. Their reputation as exceptionally tough, rugged, and plucky little dogs makes them great hunting partners.

AT A GLANCE

Ease of training	■ ■ ■ ■ ▢
Affection	■ ■ ■ ▢ ▢
Playfulness	■ ■ ■ ▢ ▢
Good with children	■ ■ ■ ■ ■
Good with other dogs	■ ■ ■ ▢ ▢
Grooming required	■ ■ ▢ ▢ ▢

+ Borders are a generally hardy breed, though there are certain genetic health problems associated with them, including hip dysplasia.

! Borders generally get along well with other dogs, but are prone to barking if they get bored.

HISTORY

Originally referred to as the Coquetdale or Redesdale Terrier which was derived from its area of origin, the breed's name was altered to the Border Terrier by the late nineteenth century presumably due to its long history with the Border Hunt in Northumberland. They are share bloodlines from both the Bedlington and Dandie Dinmont Terrier. In 1920, the breed was recognized by the Kennel Club, and in the same year, the Border Terrier Club formed.

Brazilian Terrier

Fox Paulistinha / Terrier Brasileiro
BRAZIL

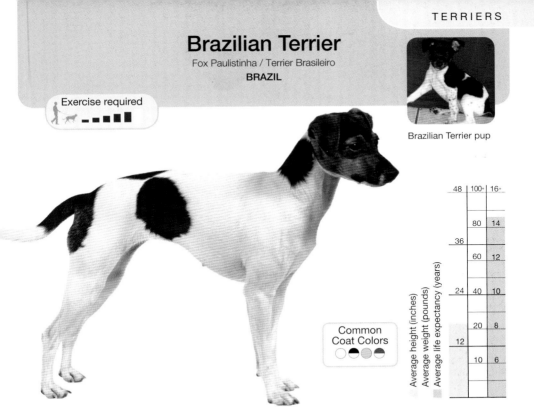

Brazilian Terrier pup

Exercise required

Common Coat Colors

Average height (inches)
Average weight (pounds)
Average life expectancy (years)

48	100+	16+
	80	14
36	60	12
24	40	10
	20	8
12		
	10	6

With similar temperament as a Jack Russell Terrier, the Brazilian Terrier is alert, perky, spirited and intelligent. Their friendliness and playfulness make them great in active homes but are needful of a firm, consistent and confident pack leader, otherwise they will become independent, willful and determined. They are effective, obedient, fearless watchdogs, and their adaptability to their environment makes them tenacious hunter partners.

AT A GLANCE

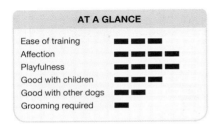

Ease of training
Affection
Playfulness
Good with children
Good with other dogs
Grooming required

! Their hunting instinct is the strongest among average terriers; they should not be trusted with small animals.

+ A very hardy breed, not known to have any health problems.

HISTORY

Various terrier breeds including Pinschers, Jack Russell and Fox Terriers, were brought by European immigrants to Brazil for the breeding of the Brazilian Terrier. Today, the Brazilian bears a close resemblance to the Jack Russell Terrier and shares many of its qualities. This breed is still used on farms and in homes as ratters, but it has also become popular as a companion as well as an efficient watchdog.

Bull Terrier

English Bull Terrier / Bully / The White Cavalier / Gladiator
ENGLAND

Exercise required

Known for their enormous personalities and sense of fun, Bull Terriers are humorous, assertive, bold, and affectionate dogs. At times they can be stubborn, and without early socialization and training, can be aggressive toward other dogs, animals, and strangers. However, Bull Terriers thrive in the company of familiar people, and should live indoors with family.

AT A GLANCE

Ease of training	
Affection	
Playfulness	
Good with children	
Good with other dogs	
Grooming required	

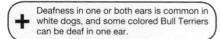
+ Deafness in one or both ears is common in white dogs, and some colored Bull Terriers can be deaf in one ear.

Bull Terrier puppy

! They don't do well when left alone for long periods and will wreak destruction when bored.

Average height (inches)	Average weight (pounds)	Average life expectancy (years)
48	100+	16+
	80	14
36		
	60	12
24	40	10
	20	8
12		
	10	6

Common Coat Colors

Bull Terriers come in two color varieties: white and colored. White Bull Terriers are solid white, with or without colored markings on the head but nowhere else on the body. Colored Bull Terriers are any color other than white or any color with white markings.

HISTORY

Breeder James Hinks aimed to create a "Gentleman's Companion", specifically a white dog, during the mid nineteenth century. He crossed Bulldogs and Terriers that were originally bred for fighting with Dalmations and now extinct English White terriers and created an earlier form of the Bull Terrier, the White Cavalier. Other breeds such as Greyhound, Spanish Pointer, Foxhound, Whippet, Borzoi, and Collie breeds were introduced to achieve the head's distinctive curved profile. Later in the twentieth century, Staffordshires were also incorporated to introduce color to the breed.

413

Cairn Terrier

SCOTLAND

Cairn Terrier pup

Exercise required

Common Coat Colors

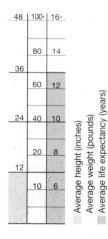

Average height (inches)
Average weight (pounds)
Average life expectancy (years)

48	100+	16+
	80	14
36		
	60	12
24	40	10
	20	8
12		
	10	6

Due to their fearlessness, these plucky, cheeky dogs love to hunt and are prized for their ability to catch otters and badgers. However, they are stubborn and do not retreat from a fight. They often stand up to other larger dogs, and can be aggressive.

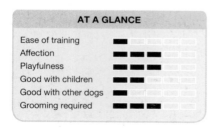

AT A GLANCE

Ease of training	■
Affection	■ ■ ■
Playfulness	■ ■ ■
Good with children	■ ■
Good with other dogs	■
Grooming required	■ ■ ■

! The Cairn is a terrier, which means his natural instincts are to bark, dig, and chase.

+ Cairns are generally healthy, but like all breeds, they're prone to certain health conditions, such as craniomandibular osteopathy, cryptorchidism and hypothyroidism.

HISTORY

The Cairn Terrier breed traces back to the indigenous working terriers of the Scottish Highlands and islands, developed from the same stock that also developed the Skye, Scottish, and West Highland White Terriers. The small, rugged working dog breed were first mentioned in the sixteenth century, and were most valued for their hunting abilities, being described as "earth dogges." During the nineteenth century, with an effort to distinguish between the different types of terrier, the Cairn was differentiated from the Short-Coated or Prick-Ear Skye breed.

Cesky Terrier

Czech Terrier

CZECH REPUBLIC

Exercise required

🚶 ▬ ▬ ■ ■

Common Coat Colors

●●○◔

Cesky Terriers have a soft bluish-gray coat that ranges from silver to dark charcoal.

Cesky Terrier pup

	Average height (inches)	Average weight (pounds)	Average life expectancy (years)
	48	100+	16+
	36	80	14
		60	12
	24	40	10
		20	8
	12	10	6

Cesky Terriers are great hunters and have a pleasant temperament. Although they are generally good with children, they can be aggressive with other dogs without careful socialization. They are bright, active, and engaging, and serve well as watchdogs. Unlike most other terriers, their coats are trimmed with clippers instead of stripped.

AT A GLANCE

Ease of training	▬ ▬ ▬ ▬
Affection	▬ ▬ ▬
Playfulness	▬ ▬ ▬ ▬
Good with children	▬ ▬ ▬ ▬ ▬
Good with other dogs	▬ ▬ ▬ ▬
Grooming required	▬ ▬ ▬

➕ A very hardy breed, not known to have any health problems.

 Puppies are all black, and the coat lightens over the first few years of life.

HISTORY

Geneticist and dog breeder Frantisek Horak developed the Cesky or Czech Terrier in the mid-twentieth century. He had bred Scottish and Sealyham Terriers separately but believed a better breed of hunting dog could be created by crossbreeding the two. After a decade of breeding, by 1959 he successfully developed a standard, the Cesky, specifically used to hunt foxes, rabbits, pheasants and ducks.

415

Chilean Fox Terrier

Ratonero

CHILE

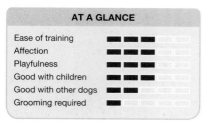

Chilean Fox Terrier pup

Exercise required

48	100+	16+
	80	14
36		
	60	12
24	40	10
	20	8
12		
	10	6

Average height (inches)
Average weight (pounds)
Average life expectancy (years)

Common
Coat Colors

A superb ratter, attaining the name "Ratonero" or "rat hunter," the Chilean Fox Terrier are one of the healthiest and cleanest dog breeds. They are smart problem solvers, with tremendous tenacity and a loyal, devoted nature. However, they are prone to barking and wary of other people and dogs. Their ease of training, affection, and energy constitute a great family dog, best suited for an inclusive, active home.

AT A GLANCE

Ease of training	▪▪▪ ▪▪▪ ▪▪▪
Affection	▪▪▪ ▪▪▪ ▪▪▪
Playfulness	▪▪▪ ▪▪▪ ▪▪▪
Good with children	▪▪▪ ▪▪▪ ▪▪▪
Good with other dogs	▪▪▪ ▪▪▪
Grooming required	▪▪▪

+ A very hardy breed, not known to have any health problems.

HISTORY

Traced to the nineteenth century, the Chilean Fox Terrier was developed through a crossbreeding of the European Fox Terrier to which they bear more of a resemblance and a native Chilean stock of unknown heritage. They adapted perfectly to the climate and terrain of Chile over time, becoming popular among farmers.

! Can be prone to barking.

Dandie Dinmont Terrier

Dandie / Hindlee Terrier
SCOTLAND

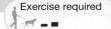
Exercise required

Dandie Dinmont Terrier pup

Average height (inches)	Average weight (pounds)	Average life expectancy (years)
48	100+	16+
	80	14
36		
	60	12
24	40	10
	20	8
12		
	10	6

Common Coat Colors

With a calm and reserved character, the Dandie Dinmont Terrier is nicknamed "the Gentleman of the Terrier Family". Although seemingly composed, the breed retains the terrier tenacity and hunting ability. Due to their small size and moderate exercise needs, the Dandie Dinmont is well suited to both city and country homes. Mostly playful, loyal, and brave dogs, they can, however, be reserved with strangers and aggressive toward other dogs.

AT A GLANCE

Ease of training	▭▭ ▭▭
Affection	▭▭ ▭▭ ▭▭
Playfulness	▭▭ ▭▭ ▭
Good with children	▭▭ ▭▭
Good with other dogs	▭▭ ▭▭ ▭
Grooming required	▭

! Be sure to keep your Dandie on leash when he's not in a secure area.

+ The breed is known to be at a higher risk from mastocytoma (mast cell tumours) than the general population of dogs.

HISTORY

Although their precise heritage is unknown, the Dandie Dinmont is known to have lived around the border of Scotland and England for centuries. They were mostly kept by farmers as hunters for a variety of prey including otters and badgers during the eighteenth century. Previously known as Pepper and Mustard terriers due to their coats, the dogs were renamed Dandie Dinmonts in the early nineteenth century due to a publication in 1815 of the novel Guy Mannering by Sir Walter Scott. A breeder of Dandie Dinmonts named his own terriers and those like his after a terrier-owning character from this novel.

417

Dutch Smoushond
Dutch Ratter / Hollandse Smoushond
NETHERLANDS

Exercise required

Dutch Smoushond pup

48	100+	16+
	80	14
36		
	60	12
24	40	10
	20	8
12		
	10	6

Average height (inches)
Average weight (pounds)
Average life expectancy (years)

Common Coat Colors

Descended from a terrier-like ratter in Germany and the Netherlands, the Dutch Smoushond is a small breed of dog related to the Schnauzer and is known to be devoted affectionate, and lively in nature. However, it is a rare breed, little known to those outside the Netherlands.

AT A GLANCE	
Ease of training	■ ■ ■
Affection	■ ■ ■ ■
Playfulness	■ ■ ■
Good with children	■ ■ ■
Good with other dogs	■ ■ ■
Grooming required	■ ■

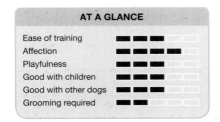

! The Dutch Smoushond will do okay in an apartment as long as it gets adequate exercise.

+ A very hardy breed, not known to have any health problems.

HISTORY
After World War II, the breed of Dutch Terrier almost disappeared, but was re-established by the efforts of a handful of breeders. The Smoushound is believed to be traced back to the Schnauzer, possibly as a color variant, although this position has been rejected by some breeders. They were popular as a gentleman's stable dog, coach dog or ratter in the nineteenth century. During the 1970's the breed was reconstructed, including a mix of terrier breeds crossed with a few remaining dogs of the original breed.

English Toy Terrier

Black and Tan
ENGLAND

Exercise required

Common
Coat Colors
●●●

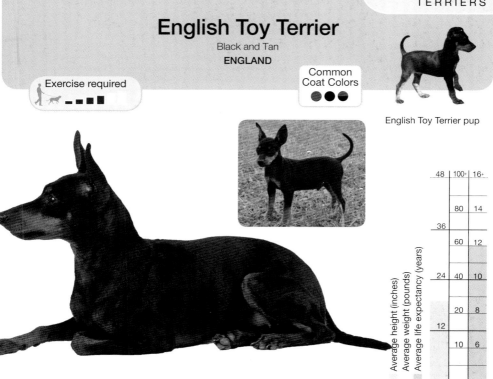

English Toy Terrier pup

Average height (inches)	Average weight (pounds)	Average life expectancy (years)
48	100+	16+
	80	14
36		
	60	12
24	40	10
	20	8
12		
	10	6

Sometimes mistaken as a miniature Doberman, the English Toy Terriers are charming, lively and gregarious dogs with a drive to chase small animals. Although they are intelligent and relatively easy to train, they may show aggression to unfamiliar dogs if not properly socialized. Otherwise, most English toy terriers are lovable, friendly, intelligent, but prone to barking.

AT A GLANCE

Ease of training	▬▬ ▬▬ ▬▬
Affection	▬▬ ▬▬ ▬▬
Playfulness	▬▬ ▬▬ ▬▬
Good with children	▬▬ ▬▬ ▬▬
Good with other dogs	▬▬ ▬▬ ▬▬
Grooming required	▬▬ ▬▬ ▬▬

+ Skin problems are documented in this breed, with demodectic mange one of the most common ailments.

HISTORY

English Toy Terriers were known to be the best ratting dogs around in the nineteenth century England. Along with the use of their abilities to control vermin on farms, towns, factories, dockyards and homes, they were also used for the popular sport of ratting. In public houses and venues across the country, dogs were placed in "rat pits" and judged on the number of rats killed and their speed. A fad of miniaturizing the breed arose and almost led to its eradication. However, the breed was salvaged by a few breeders who reinstated their qualities.

! They enjoy exercise, but they also like plenty of cuddles.

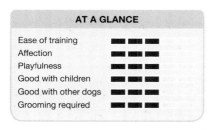

419

German Pinscher

Deutscher Pinscher
GERMANY

German Pinscher pup

Exercise required

48	100+	16+
	80	14
36		
	60	12
24	40	10
	20	8
12		
	10	6

Common Coat Colors

Average height (inches)
Average weight (pounds)
Average life expectancy (years)

German Pinschers are friendly, fiercely protective and devoted, and if well trained can be trusted with other animals and children. Due to their high intelligence and quick ability to learn, they do not require extensive, repetitive training. They can be wary of strangers and other dogs, and thus also make good watchdogs.

AT A GLANCE

Ease of training	▄▄▄▄
Affection	▄▄▄▄▄
Playfulness	▄▄▄▄▄
Good with children	▄▄▄
Good with other dogs	▄▄
Grooming required	▄

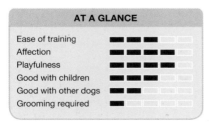

! This breed needs a firm, experienced owner who is consistent in training.

+ Due to the small gene pool of the German Pinscher, breeders should health test their dogs for hereditary cataracts, hip dysplasia and elbow dysplasia.

HISTORY

Widespread in Germany by the nineteenth century, the German Pinscher was valued as a ratter, stable dog and watchdog. In 1895, the Pinscher Club was founded by Josef Bertha and within the year, the breed was officially recognized. However, by the end of World War II, the breed almost went extinct. But Werner Jung reestablished the population by breeding his female Pinschers, Kitty V. Bodenstrand and Jutta, with some oversized Miniature Pinschers. All German Pinschers today trace back to this line.

Glen of Imaal Terrier

Irish Glen of Imaal Terrier / Wicklow Terrier

IRELAND

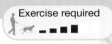

Exercise required

Glen of Imaal Terrier pup

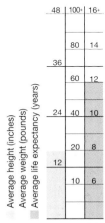

	Average height (inches)	Average weight (pounds)	Average life expectancy (years)
	48	100+	16+
		80	14
	36		
		60	12
	24	40	10
		20	8
	12		
		10	6

Common Coat Colors

Also called the Irish Glen of Imaal or Wicklow Terrier, this breed developed during the late sixteenth century at the time of Elizabeth I's reign. She hired French Mercenaries who brought their low-slung hounds along, to put down civil unrest in Ireland. The soldiers that remained in the area bred their own dogs with a local terrier stock, eventually producing the Glen of Imaal breed. These dogs are "strong dogs" unlike most terriers which are "sounders". They were trained to hunt prey down by silently entering its den rather than bark to indicate its location.

AT A GLANCE

Ease of training	▰ ▰ ▰ ▰
Affection	▰ ▰ ▰
Playfulness	▰ ▰ ▰ ▰
Good with children	▰ ▰ ▰ ▰ ▰
Good with other dogs	▰ ▰ ▰ ▰
Grooming required	▰ ▰ ▰

+ Generally very healthy, but hereditary problems may include progressive retinal atrophy.

HISTORY

This small, tough terrier breed is one of the oldest of the four native Irish dog breeds. Having developed in the remote valley of Glen of Imaal in the Western Wicklow mountains, an area of harsh terrain and difficult living, they were often used to protect rural farms from intruders and vermin, guard livestock, and hunt. This breed was also known to be fighting dogs as well as "turnspit" dogs who run on a wheel to cook meat in kitchens.

! Glens are intelligent and can have a stubborn streak, so consistency and firmness is essential in training puppies.

421

Irish Terrier

Irish Red Terrier
IRELAND

Irish Terrier pup

Exercise required

48	100+	16+	
	80	14	
36			
	60	12	
24	40	10	
	20	8	
12			
	10	6	

Average height (inches)
Average weight (pounds)
Average life expectancy (years)

Common Coat Colors

Noted for their bravery and cheerful personalities, the Irish Terrier is often described as "the poor man's sentinel", "the farmer's friend", and "the gentleman's favorite". However, this breed is also known to be aggressive with other dogs and are often reserved with strangers.

AT A GLANCE

Ease of training	▪▪ ▪▪
Affection	▪▪ ▪▪ ▪▪
Playfulness	▪▪ ▪▪ ▪▪ ▪▪
Good with children	▪▪ ▪▪ ▪▪
Good with other dogs	▪▪
Grooming required	▪▪ ▪▪ ▪▪

 Irish Terriers must have regular opportunities to burn off their energy.

+ The Irish Terrier is a vigorous breed and doesn't have any common health problems.

HISTORY

Descended from the now-extinct Black and Tan, and Wheaten-colored Terriers, the Irish Terrier is one of the oldest Terrier breeds. Recognized in 1875 in a dog show in Glasgow, Scotland, these dogs are famously versatile. For centuries they were used as farm, hunting, and guard dogs, and they were also widely in both World Wars by the military.

Jagdterrier

Deutscher Jagdterrier / German Hunt Terrier
GERMANY

Jagdterrier pup

Exercise required

! They have a high exercise requirement and are best suited to a hunting home.

Common Coat Colors
●●●

	Average height (inches)	Average weight (pounds)	Average life expectancy (years)
	48	100+	16+
		80	14
	36		
		60	12
	24	40	10
		20	8
	12		
		10	6

Bred to be fearless hunting dogs, the Jagdterrier were used to hunt wild boars, badgers, foxes, weasels, raccoons, and squirrels. They drove animals out of thickets and tracked escaped wounded animals. Due to their intelligence and adaptability, Jagdterriers can make good pets, however they are primarily a hunting dog with strong prey drive. However, they are devoted, loyal, protective and wary of strangers, thus make excellent watch or guard dogs.

AT A GLANCE

Ease of training	▪▪ ▪▪
Affection	▪▪ ▪▪ ▪▪
Playfulness	▪▪ ▪▪ ▪▪
Good with children	▪▪ ▪▪ ▪▪
Good with other dogs	▪▪ ▪▪ ▪▪
Grooming required	▪▪ ▪▪ ▪▪

➕ Jagdterriers are generally healthy dogs.

HISTORY

Developed in Germany in the twentieth century, Breeders crossed English Fox Terriers with Black and Tan Hunting Terriers to specifically create a better hunting dog. Many years were spent selectively breeding for hunting skills and eventually bred the Jagdterrier.

Jack Russell Terrier

Jack

ENGLAND

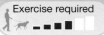
Exercise required

Although the Jack Russell Terrier is one of the best-known and most recognized breeds, they are often confused with the Parson Russell Terrier. The breed is sometimes subdivided into Jack Russells and Russells, the latter a shorter-legged, stockier variety. "Jack" in Jack Russell describes a small dog with a character of a large dog. With a tremendous personality, they are lively, intelligent, independent, energetic, nosey and needful of attention. Although they are devoted to their families, without thorough socialization, they can be aggressive with other dogs.

Jack Russell
Terrier pup

AT A GLANCE

Ease of training	■ ■ ■
Affection	■ ■ ■
Playfulness	■ ■ ■
Good with children	■ ■ ■
Good with other dogs	■ ■ ■
Grooming required	■ ■

Although generally healthy, some health problems include lens luxation and progressive retinal atrophy.

Wirehaired Jack
Russell Terrier

Average height (inches)	Average weight (pounds)	Average life expectancy (years)
48	100+	16+
	80	14
36		
	60	12
24	40	10
	20	8
12		
	10	6

Common
Coat Colors

HISTORY

With the efforts of Reverend John Russell, a fox-hunting, dog-breeding enthusiast, the Jack Russell, sharing ancestry with the Parson Russell Terrier, was developed around the nineteenth century. A pack of Fox Terriers, bred by Russell during this time and largely white in color, became known as Parson Jack Russell Terriers. These were bred for their working ability and appearance. However, from these terriers a shorter-legged, long-bodied version developed and were used instead for hunting small animals. Initially called "Puddin' Dogs" and "Shorties", these terriers became known as the Jack Russell Terrier.

! Jack Russell Terriers have a low boredom threshold and need to be entertained.

Kerry Blue Terrier

Irish Blue Terrier

IRELAND

Exercise required

Kerry Blue Terriers or "Kerries" are versatile dogs with clearly defined personalities, having many functions for many years in rural Ireland. They are intelligent hunting dogs with great instincts that are able to hunt small animals and retrieve from land and water. They are have been used as capable herders and vigilant watchdogs. Although they may be aggressive towards other dogs and pets, they are relatively easy to train, reserved with strangers and loyal to family.

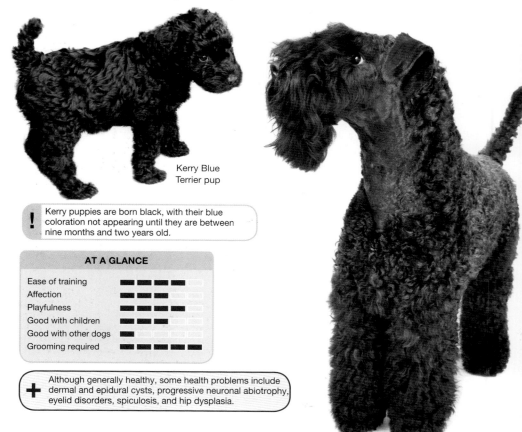

Kerry Blue Terrier pup

! Kerry puppies are born black, with their blue coloration not appearing until they are between nine months and two years old.

AT A GLANCE

Ease of training	■■■■□
Affection	■■■□□
Playfulness	■■■■□
Good with children	■■■□□
Good with other dogs	■□□□□
Grooming required	■■■■■

+ Although generally healthy, some health problems include dermal and epidural cysts, progressive neuronal abiotrophy, eyelid disorders, spiculosis, and hip dysplasia.

Average height (inches)	Average weight (pounds)	Average life expectancy (years)
48	100+	16+
	80	14
36		
	60	12
24	40	10
	20	8
12		
	10	6

Common Coat Colors

HISTORY

Most associated with the mountains of Kerry and Lake Killarney in Ireland, where they are believed to have developed, the breed's history is somewhat uncertain with many tales attempting to explain its origin. One tells of a blue dog from a shipwrecked Russian ship or Spanish Armada that swam ashore to Tralee Bay where it bred with local dogs and gave rise to the Kerry Blue. However, realistically, the breed was likely a cross of Irish Wolfhounds and local terrier-types developed by farmers to produce a robust, hardy, and versatile dog, allegedly favored by poachers. Kerry Blue Terriers were recognized as a breed in Ireland in 1916 and accounted for 25% of all registrations in the Irish Kennel Club by the 1920s. They were first seen at the Crufts, the world's largest dog show in 1922 and in the same year, made an appearance at the American Westminister Dog Show.

Kromfohrländer

Länder / Kromi

GERMANY

Kromfohrländer pup

Exercise required

48	100+	16+
	80	14
36		
	60	12
24	40	10
	20	8
12		
	10	6

Average height (inches)
Average weight (pounds)
Average life expectancy (years)

Common Coat Colors

A very lively, good-natured, intelligent breed, the Kromfohrländer is a very friendly dog and very attached to their owners and families. Unlike most terrier breeds, they have a comparatively weak hunting instinct, but are somewhat more compatible with strangers and children.

AT A GLANCE

Ease of training	
Affection	
Playfulness	
Good with children	
Good with other dogs	
Grooming required	

+ The breed has a known genetic predisposition to certain hereditary health defects, including epilepsy, cystinuria, and keratosis, or foot corns, as well as patellar luxation.

HISTORY

The Kromfohrländer traces to Peter, a stray farm dog crossed with a Grand Griffon Vendéen and Wire Fox Terrier. In the 1940s Peter was adopted by American servicemen in northern France and later ended up in Germany. There, Ilsa Shleifenbaum, a dog breeder, bred him with a Fox Terrier that produced puppies with similar traits, forming this new and rare breed.

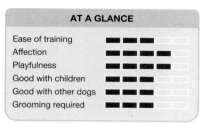

! The Kromfohrländer is one of the very newest of all dog breeds.

Lakeland Terrier

ENGLAND

Lakeland Terrier pup

Exercise required

		Average height (inches)	Average weight (pounds)	Average life expectancy (years)
	48		100+	16+
			80	14
	36			
			60	12
		24	40	10
			20	8
		12		
			10	6

Common Coat Colors

Known for their fearlessness and endurance, the Lakeland Terrier often accompanied Foxhound packs on hunts, indicating locations of small animals in burrows. They are a popular breed, bold, playful, sensitive and family-friendly, but require patient and consistent training. It is often described as 'rascally' and is known to dig holes.

AT A GLANCE	
Ease of training	■ ■
Affection	■ ■ ■
Playfulness	■ ■ ■ ■
Good with children	■ ■ ■
Good with other dogs	■ ■ ■
Grooming required	■ ■ ■

 Lakeland Terriers are excitable dogs and have a lot of energy.

+ Lakeland Terriers are a hardy breed and don't suffer from any known hereditary health problems.

HISTORY

These Terriers developed in the Lake District of northern England primarily as a ratter and was given the name "Lakeland" in 1921. Champion Stingray of Derryabah, or Skipper, is a particularly famous Lakeland is who won Best in Show at Crufts in 1961 and in the following year won Best in Show at Westminster in the United States.

Manchester Terrier
The Gentleman's Terrier
ENGLAND

Exercise required

Common Coat Colors

48	100+	16+
	80	14
36		
	60	12
24	40	10
	20	8
12		
	10	6

Average height (inches)
Average weight (pounds)
Average life expectancy (years)

Manchester Terrier pup

Although originally meant for ratting, the Manchester Terrier were also kept as pets by the middle and upper classes due to their elegant appearance. Devoted, loyal, and intelligent, they can be independent and are often reserved with strangers. A smaller sub-breed with pointed, erect ears, the Toy Manchester Terrier, was recognized by the AKC in 1958.

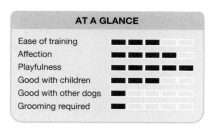

AT A GLANCE

Ease of training	
Affection	
Playfulness	
Good with children	
Good with other dogs	
Grooming required	

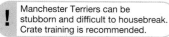

 Manchester Terriers can be stubborn and difficult to housebreak. Crate training is recommended.

+ Manchesters are generally healthy, but like all breeds, they're prone to certain health conditions such as glaucoma, von Willebrand's Disease and heat bumps.

HISTORY

The Manchester Terrier traces back to the original Black-and-Tan Terrier, widespread by the sixteenth century. Much less refined than the modern Manchester Terrier, previously these dogs were used to control huge populations of rats. As a result, they became associated with the mining areas, factories, wharves, and farms of northern England. During the nineteenth century, the Whippet breed was introduced and incorporated to the Manchester breed, developing a faster and sleeker appearance.

Minature Bull Terrier

ENGLAND

Minature Bull Terrier pup

	Average height (inches)	Average weight (pounds)	Average life expectancy (years)
	48	100+	16+
		80	14
	36		
		60	12
	24	40	10
		20	8
	12		
		10	6

Common Coat Colors

Identical to the Bull Terrier in every aspect other than size, the Miniature Bull Terrier is a devoted, loyal and fun breed. They have a sense of humor but can be single-minded, stubborn and often require much attention.

AT A GLANCE

Ease of training	▮▮ ▮▮
Affection	▮▮ ▮▮ ▮▮
Playfulness	▮▮ ▮▮ ▮▮
Good with children	▮▮ ▮▮ ▮▮ ▮▮ ▮▮
Good with other dogs	▮▮ ▮▮ ▮▮
Grooming required	▮▮

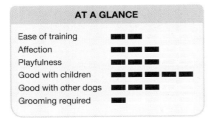

! They make great dogs for people with limited space.

+ Miniature Bull Terriers are generally quite healthy, but there are hearing, eye, skin, kidney, heart and knee problems in some dogs. Deafness occurs in both colored and white Bull Terrier (Miniature). Puppies can be born unilaterally deaf (deaf in one ear) or bilaterally deaf (deaf in both ears).

HISTORY

The Miniature Bull Terrier shares the same history and ancestry as the Bull Terrier. A toy version was attempted to be bread but was largely unsuccessful. The first dog show that held a class for Miniature Bull Terriers was held in 1863. But it was only until 1938 when the Miniature Bull Terrier Club was established.

Miniature Fox Terrier

Toy Fox Terrier / Mini Foxie

AUSTRALIA

Miniature Fox Terrier pup

Exercise required

Common Coat Colors

48	100+	16+
	80	14
36		
	60	12
24	40	10
	20	8
12		
	10	6

Average height (inches)
Average weight (pounds)
Average life expectancy (years)

Primarily bred to hunt small mammals, Miniature Fox Terriers are known for their speed and agility. Due to their smaller size and ruthlessness in their attacks, they have been incredibly useful on many farms since the nineteenth century. However, they have proved to be well-suited in urban environments as domestic pets. Their small size, short clean hair, and loyalty to their owners make them good pets, especially with households with small children.

AT A GLANCE

Ease of training	■■ ■■ ■■
Affection	■■ ■■ ■■
Playfulness	■■ ■■ ■■
Good with children	■■ ■■ ■■ ■■
Good with other dogs	■■ ■■ ■■
Grooming required	■■ ■■

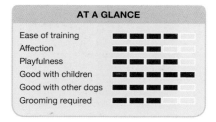

! They thrive on positive socialization and are happy to be rewarded with pats rather than treats when being trained.

 Miniature Fox Terriers are generally healthy and hardy despite their size. They need little maintenance.

HISTORY

Miniature Fox Terriers and Toy Fox Terriers were developed from the same lines of ancestry that produced the Jack Russell, Rat, and Tenterfield Terriers. Many pedigrees can be traced back to "Foiler", the first Fox Terrier to be registered with the Kennel Club in Britain, in 1876.

Miniature Schnauzer

Zwergschnauzer (Dwarf Schnauzer)

GERMANY

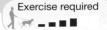

Exercise required

Miniature Schnauzer pup

48	100+	16+
	80	14
36		
	60	12
24	40	10
	20	8
12		
	10	6

Average height (inches)
Average weight (pounds)
Average life expectancy (years)

Common Coat Colors

Although mainly used as ratters on farms and houses, the size of the Miniature Schnauzer makes it ideal for an urban lifestyle. They are bold, lively, intelligent, gregarious, and a breed that is relatively easy to train, thus make great family pets. Although they are inclined to bark, as a result they make excellent watchdogs.

AT A GLANCE

Ease of training	▰▰▰
Affection	▰▰▰
Playfulness	▰▰▰▰
Good with children	▰▰▰
Good with other dogs	▰▰▰
Grooming required	▰▰▰

+ Miniature Schnauzers may suffer health problems associated with high fat levels. Such problems include hyperlipidemia, which may increase the possibility of pancreatitis. Other issues which may affect this breed are diabetes, bladder stones and eye problems.

HISTORY

The Standard Schnauzer has its earliest records of its history in Germany from the late nineteenth century. Like many terrier breeds, the Schnauzer was bred to be a medium-sized farm dog capable of ratting, herding and guarding property. However, farmers desired a smaller, more compact breed and thus incorporated the Standard with Affenpinscher and Miniature Poodle breeds. The first recorded Miniature Schnauzer appeared in 1888.

! All Schnauzers have a high prey drive, which means they may attack other small pets.

433

Mountain Feist

Treeing Feist / American Treeing Feist / American Feist

NORTH AMERICA

Mountain Feist pup

Exercise required

Common Coat Colors

48	100+	16+
	80	14
36		
	60	12
24	40	10
	20	8
12		
	10	6

Average height (inches)
Average weight (pounds)
Average life expectancy (years)

Due to their curiosity, intelligence, alertness and energy, Mountain Feist are well suited as both hunting or companion dogs. They are great at hunting small animals and larger game, but are also very protective of their families.

AT A GLANCE

Ease of training	■ ■
Affection	■ ■ ■
Playfulness	■ ■ ■
Good with children	■ ■ ■
Good with other dogs	■ ■ ■
Grooming required	■ ■ ■

+ They are generally healthy dogs.

HISTORY

Native to the Southern Appalachian and Ozark Mountains, written accounts of the Mountain Feist are centuries old, including diary entries by George Washington, a poem written by Abraham Lincoln entitled "The Bear Hunt", and William Faulker's *Go Down Moses*. Although the length of their existence is uncertain, they played a vital role in the lives of early pioneers in the United States.

! Feist Terriers are very vocal dogs, communicating with growls, bays, and barks.

Nippon Terrier

Japanese Terrier / Nihon Terrier / Nihon Teria

JAPAN

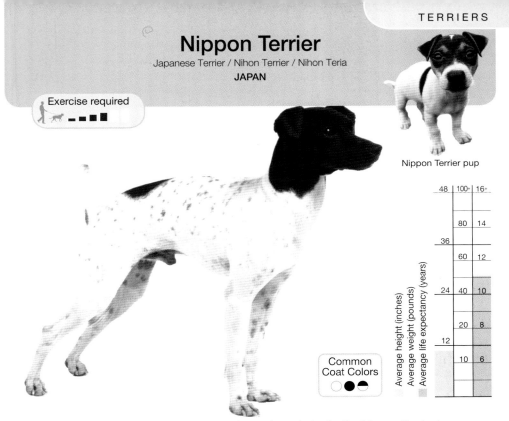

Exercise required

Nippon Terrier pup

Average height (inches)	Average weight (pounds)	Average life expectancy (years)
48	100+	16+
36	80	14
	60	12
24	40	10
	20	8
12		
	10	6

Common Coat Colors

A breed small in size with a compact, muscular and sturdy body, the Nippon Terrier has a cheerful, active temperament. Although they are spirited, lively and love to chase small mammals, they are a bit cautious and are not recommended for households with small children. Nevertheless, the breed is well-known for its vigor and loyalty.

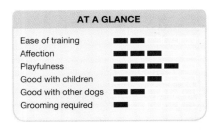

AT A GLANCE

Ease of training	
Affection	
Playfulness	
Good with children	
Good with other dogs	
Grooming required	

! It should have adequate amount of daily exercises in order to stay healthy and animated.

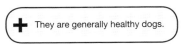

They are generally healthy dogs.

HISTORY

The Nippon Terrier developed from Fox Terriers brought to Japan by Dutch and British Ships in the seventeenth century, which were inbred with local dogs and small pointers. This breed unlike most terriers were bred and valued not as ratters but as beloved companion dogs. In 1930 the Japanese Kennel Club recognized the breed.

Norfolk Terrier

ENGLAND

Exercise required

Norfolk Terrier pup

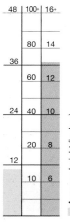

Average height (inches)
Average weight (pounds)
Average life expectancy (years)

48	100+	16+
	80	14
36		
	60	12
24	40	10
	20	8
12		
	10	6

The primary role of this breed was a fox-bolter. The Norfolk Terrier has a remarkably cheerful and fearless temperament, regardless of being one of the smallest working Terrier breeds. They have much spirit, and make tough, determined, and dedicated hunters. An ideal pet for city-dwellers, it enjoys the company of children.

Common Coat Colors

AT A GLANCE

Ease of training	■	■	■	
Affection	■	■	■	
Playfulness	■	■	■	
Good with children	■	■	■	■
Good with other dogs	■	■	■	
Grooming required	■	■		

Considered a "big dog in a small package." Alert, gregarious, and nimble, they are loyal companions with the heart of a working terrier.

+ Mitral valve disease (MVD) is a life-threatening heart abnormality that reputable Norfolk breeders are working to reduce or completely eradicate in the breed.

HISTORY

Frank "Roughrider" Jones developed a breed of terriers in Norfolk, England, which were recognized by the English Kennel Club as the Norwich Terriers in 1932. However in 1964 the club distinguished the terriers into two breeds, the Norwich and Norfolk, both with different standard and different characteristics. The most obvious differences in the ears: the Norwich has pricked ears, and the Norfolk, droopy ears.

Norwich Terrier

ENGLAND

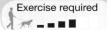
Exercise required

Norwich Terrier pup

Similarly to the Norfolk Terrier, the Norwich terrier also has a large personality and drive regardless of its small size. A wonderful companion for an active individual or family, the Norwich Terriers are spirited, bold, enduring dogs that are affectionate, loyal, entertaining, but often independent.

Common Coat Colors

	48	100+	16+
		80	14
	36		
		60	12
Average height (inches)	24	40	10
Average weight (pounds)		20	8
Average life expectancy (years)	12		
		10	6

AT A GLANCE

Ease of training	■ ■ ■
Affection	■ ■ ■ ■
Playfulness	■ ■ ■
Good with children	■ ■ ■
Good with other dogs	■ ■ ■
Grooming required	■ ■ ■

The Norwich is a rare and therefore expensive breed.

Cataracts are recognized as a disorder that has been reported sporadically. There are also instances of epilepsy, narrow tracheas, luxating patellas, hip dysplasia, mitral valve disease, portosystemic shunts, atopy and incorrect bites.

HISTORY

With the same ancestry as Norfolk Terriers, the Norwich Terrier share the same early history. However, during the nineteenth century when the keeping of terriers became fashionable to Cambridge students, the Norwich Terrier developed into its own breed. Students bought several dogs from a local dealer named Charles Lawrence, and these dogs became known as the Trumpington Terriers, named after Trumpington Street where many of the students resided. A puppy named "Rags", a cross between a long red-haired Trumpington terrier and a Scottish Terrier type, was the first known Norwich terrier with its distinctive pricked ears and great hunting instincts.

437

Parson Russell Terrier

Parson / Parson Jack Russell Terrier
ENGLAND

Exercise required

The standard has changed little over the years due to the hard work of breeders to maintain the working quality of the Parson Russell Breed. They are dedicated, fearless and tenacious, best suited as hunters and working dogs, although they are often kept as companions. These dogs are reserved with strangers, and due to their relatively low tolerance level they can be aggressive with other dogs, and easily become snappy, noisy and bad tempered. While as a result of their temperament they not suitable for households with young children, the Parson Russell are outgoing and loyal to their families.

Parson Russell Terrier puppy

AT A GLANCE	
Ease of training	
Affection	
Playfulness	
Good with children	
Good with other dogs	
Grooming required	

+ Although generally healthy, some problems can include lens luxation, progressive retinal atrophy, and late onset ataxia.

	Average height (inches)	Average weight (pounds)	Average life expectancy (years)
	48	100+	16+
		80	14
	36		
		60	12
	24	40	10
		20	8
	12		
		10	6

Common
Coat Colors

! Parson Russell Terriers have a high hunting drive and will roam if left unattended. It is essential they have a well-fenced yard!

HISTORY

Like the Jack Russell Terrier, the Parson Russell Terrier was developed by the fox hunting enthusiast, Reverend John Russell in the nineteenth century. He owned a pack of Fox Terriers that became known as Parson Russell Terriers, most of which traced back to a Terrier named Trump that he bought in 1819. He bred his dogs specifically for their working qualities, unconcerned with appearance as he shunned the show world. However, other breeders took the opportunity to develop the Parson Russells for the show ring themselves, creating a gradual change in the original breed.

Patterdale Terrier

Black Fell Terrier
ENGLAND

Exercise required

48	100+	16+
36	80	14
	60	12
24	40	10
	20	8
12		
	10	6

Average height (inches)
Average weight (pounds)
Average life expectancy (years)

Common Coat Colors

Patterdale Terrier pups

The Patterdale Terriers primarily worked with fox hunters and Foxhound packs. Because of their size, they were able to follow foxes into tight crevices and holes. Initially a working terrier breed, Patterdales also can make good companions for active homes.

AT A GLANCE

Ease of training	
Affection	
Playfulness	
Good with children	
Good with other dogs	
Grooming required	

+ A hardy breed with no known health problems

HISTORY

This enduring breed described as being "tough as nails", originated from the steep, rocky, terrain and harsh climate of the Lake District in northern England. The Patterdales were bred from Fell Terrier types by multiple breeders including an Ullswater Hunter, J. Bowman, Cyril Breay, Frank Buck, and Brian Nuttall.

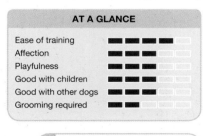

! The Patterdale Terrier is not recommended for apartment life.

Plummer Terrier

Plummer

ENGLAND

Plummer Terrier pup

Exercise required

Common Coat Colors			48	100+	16+
				80	14
			36		
				60	12
			24	40	10
				20	8
			12		
				10	6

Average height (inches) · Average weight (pounds) · Average life expectancy (years)

The Plummer Terrier is very energetic breed and needs sufficient exercise; otherwise with a lack of activity, the breed may become a nuisance. Because of its need for activity, they prefer to live in large spaces and take long, brisk walks. But if their level of exercise is met, they are pleasant and playful dogs.

AT A GLANCE

Ease of training	▰▰ ▰▰
Affection	▰▰ ▰▰ ▰▰
Playfulness	▰▰ ▰▰ ▰▰ ▰▰
Good with children	▰▰ ▰▰ ▰▰
Good with other dogs	▰▰ ▰▰ ▰▰
Grooming required	▰▰

 The Plummer Terrier will do okay in an apartment if it is sufficiently exercised, but will do best with at least an average-sized yard.

Patellar luxation and related orthopedic complaints have been identified in the breed, although not with any great recurrence.

HISTORY

Named after its breeder, Dr David Brian Plummer, the Plummer Terrier was bred as a ratter and an all-purpose working dog in the 1960's in the Midlands. This breed combines bloodlines from Beagles, Jack Russell, and Red Fell Terriers, with Bull Terriers incorporated later. The Plummer was highly valued for its acute senses and abilities as a hunter, but was often criticized for its larger size and appearance. Many described the breed as a "genetic monster", boasting ugly and undesirable traits. As a result such characteristics have been selectively bred out, potentially removing outcrosses from the breed.

Rat Terrier

American Rat Terrier / Ratting Terrier / Decker Giant

UNITED STATES

Rat Terrier pup

Exercise required

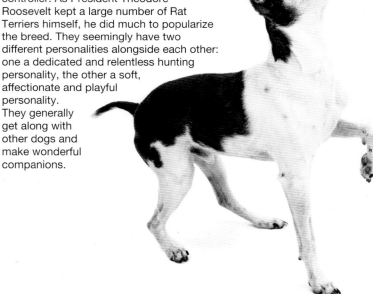

The Rat Terrier was a very successful ratter both for the sport and as a vermin controller. As President Theodore Roosevelt kept a large number of Rat Terriers himself, he did much to popularize the breed. They seemingly have two different personalities alongside each other: one a dedicated and relentless hunting personality, the other a soft, affectionate and playful personality. They generally get along with other dogs and make wonderful companions.

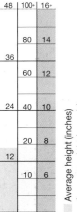

Average height (inches)
Average weight (pounds)
Average life expectancy (years)

48	100+	16+
	80	14
36		
	60	12
24	40	10
	20	8
12		
	10	6

Common Coat Colors

AT A GLANCE

Ease of training	▮▮▮▮
Affection	▮▮▮▮
Playfulness	▮▮▮▮
Good with children	▮▮▮▮
Good with other dogs	▮▮▮▮
Grooming required	▮

 The social sensitivity of Rat Terriers makes them very trainable and easy to live with.

+ The Canine Health Information Center (CHIC) recommends that Rat Terriers be tested for patellar luxation, cardiac abnormalities, hip dysplasia, and Legg-Calvé-Perthes syndrome.

HISTORY

The Rat Terrier is an American breed believed to be traced primarily to the Manchester Terrier and Smooth Fox Terrier crosses brought by English immigrants in the late nineteenth century. They were highly prized for their rat-killing abilities. However, other breeds including the Italian Greyhound and Beagle were incorporated to further increase the Rat Terrier's speed and hunting skills.

Ratonero Bodeguero Andaluz

Perro Ratonero Andaluz / Andalusian Wine-Cellar Rat-Hunting Dog

SPAIN

Exercise required

Ratonero Bodeguero
Andaluz pup

Common
Coat Colors

always tricolored
(a solid white body
with a black and
tan head)

Average height (inches)	Average weight (pounds)	Average life expectancy (years)
	48	100+	16+
		80	14
36			
		60	12
	24	40	10
		20	8
12			
		10	6

The Ratonero Bodeguero Andaluz, Spanish for "Andalusian wine-cellar rat-hunting dog" is a Spanish breed of the terrier type. As illustrated by its name, the breeds main function was to hunt rats and mice hidden in wine cellars in Andalusia, Spain. Therefore they naturally are lively and brave with strong hunting instincts, but are nonetheless friendly and good with children.

AT A GLANCE

Ease of training
Affection
Playfulness
Good with children
Good with other dogs
Grooming required

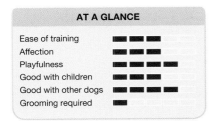

These dogs should not be
trusted with non-canine pets.

No diseases specific to this breed

HISTORY

Several hundred years ago, English wine merchants settled in the Sherry-producing region of Spain, Marco de Jerez, and brought the ancestors of Fox Terriers along with them. They were crossed with local dogs for the purpose of vermin control. Later, in the 1900's, the Toy Terrier was introduced into the breed.

Russian Black Terrier

Tchiorny Terrier

RUSSIA

Russian Black Terrier pup

Exercise required

Common Coat Colors

48	100+	16+
	80	14
36		
	60	12
24	40	10
	20	8
12		
	10	6

Average height (inches)
Average weight (pounds)
Average life expectancy (years)

The Russian Black Terrier has a very desirable character and temperament. A calm, confident, courageous and self-assured dog, this breed is very intelligent, adaptable and easy to train. They were initially bred as protective guard dogs and thus are also alert, responsive, fearless and deeply loyal to family, but are often wary of strangers.

AT A GLANCE

Ease of training	
Affection	
Playfulness	
Good with children	
Good with other dogs	
Grooming required	

 Shyness or excessive excitability is a serious fault.

+ Generally healthy, however it is prone to certain hereditary diseases: hip dysplasia, elbow dysplasia hyperuricosuria

HISTORY

The Russian Black Terrier was developed after the World War II by the Russian army to create a breed that was able to cope with the extremely cold Russian climate. The Giant Schnauzer, Airedale Terrier and Rottweiler breeds were mainly used. The FCI recognized the Russian Black Terrier as a breed in 1984.

Scottish Terrier

Scottie

SCOTLAND

Scottish Terrier pup

Exercise required

Common Coat Colors

		48	100+	16+
Average height (inches)	Average weight (pounds)	Average life expectancy (years)	80	14
		36		
			60	12
		24	40	10
			20	8
		12		
			10	6

The Scottish Terrier is a distinguished and prized member of the terrier family. Also known as a "Diehard" due to its tenacious character, these dogs were historically bred as working and hunting dogs. Recently, the breed has been developed into a more glamourous and sophisticated breed, and greatly differs in appearance from its ancestors. Nonetheless, Scottish Terriers have retained their innate hunting instinct, and are determined, fearless and ready for action. They can be aggressive towards other dogs but are loyal, devoted and affectionate with their families.

AT A GLANCE

Ease of training	▬ ▬ ▬ ▬
Affection	▬ ▬ ▬
Playfulness	▬ ▬ ▬ ▬
Good with children	▬ ▬ ▬ ▬
Good with other dogs	▬
Grooming required	▬ ▬ ▬ ▬

 Scotties are extremely independent and can be difficult to train. Start puppies young!

+ Problems can include Scottie cramp, von Willebrand's disease, Cushings syndrome, hypothyroidism, epilepsy, craniomandibular osteopathy, and cerebellar abiotrophy.

HISTORY

Historically, Scottish Terriers bred in the Scottish Highlands for the purpose of hunting small animals and killing vermin on large estates. The modern breed traces back to a nineteenth-century Aberdeen strain, specifically known as the the Aberdeen Terriers. Early breeder, Baptain Mackie, took his own Aberdeen Terrier to southern England in the 1870s and bred them to the type known today.

Sealyham Terrier
Welsh Border Terrier / Cowley Terrier
WALES

Exercise required

Sealyham Terrier pup

48	100+	16+
	80	14
36		
	60	12
24	40	10
	20	8
12		
	10	6

Average height (inches)
Average weight (pounds)
Average life expectancy (years)

Common Coat Colors

The Sealyham Terrier or "Sealy" was once one of the UK's most popular terrier breeds. However, today the breed is very uncommon and is the UK's most endangered native breed, according to the English Kennel Club. The Sealyham has a high prey drive and can be aggressive towards dogs and wary of strangers, but also can be a loyal and devoted companion dog.

AT A GLANCE

Ease of training	
Affection	
Playfulness	
Good with children	
Good with other dogs	
Grooming required	

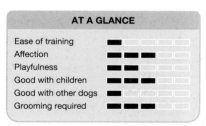

! Although happy in the company of others, they are fine if left alone.

+ This is a hardy breed with few breed specific health problems. The main hereditary problem highlighted by the American Sealyham Terrier Club is an eye condition called lens luxation, for which there are DNA tests. Lens luxation is a condition in which the lens slips out of position in the eyeball due to the weakening of the fibers that hold it in place

HISTORY

In the late nineteenth century, Captain John Edwardes developed the Sealyham Terrier breed on his Sealyham Estate in Haverfordwest, Wales. He desired a dog that was brave and agile enough to hunt badgers, otters and foxes, and as a result, crossed multiple breeds of terrier types including Dandie Dinmonts, Fox Terriers, and West Highland Whites breeds. They were capable of digging prey from holes and were used to accompany Otter hounds. The English Kennel Club recognized the breed in 1910 and the American Kennel Club in 1911.

Skye Terrier

SCOTLAND

Exercise required

Skye Terrier pup

Average height (inches)	Average weight (pounds)	Average life expectancy (years)
48	100+	16+
	80	14
36		
	60	12
24	40	10
	20	8
12		
	10	6

Common Coat Colors

Skye Terriers are highly skilled and fearless hunters, capable of hunting foxes, otters, rats and other small animals. Their long coats protect them from prey and weather. They are affectionate and loyal dogs who are aggressive with other dogs and wary of strangers, making good watchdogs.

AT A GLANCE

Ease of training	■ ■ ■
Affection	■ ■ ■ ■
Playfulness	■ ■ ■
Good with children	■ ■ ■
Good with other dogs	■
Grooming required	■ ■ ■ ■ ■

! Skye Terriers can be very destructive if they are bored or are frequently left alone for long. periods.

+ The Skye Terrier is a very healthy breed. The only issue that's a potential concern is orthopedic problems that could occur during growth.

HISTORY

One of the oldest Scottish Terrier breeds, the Skye Terrier developed in northwestern Scotland on the Isle of Skye over 400 years ago. Over the centuries the characteristics of the breed were unaffected and remain relatively unchanged today. Although they were widespread during the nineteenth century they are seen less often today.

447

Smooth Fox Terrier

Fox Terrier

ENGLAND

Smooth Fox Terrier pup

48	100+	16+
36	80	14
	60	12
24	40	10
	20	8
12		
	10	6

Average height (inches) / Average weight (pounds) / Average life expectancy (years)

Common Coat Colors

Favored by hunters during the nineteenth century, the Smooth Fox Terrier often accompanied Foxhound packs on hunts. Fox Terriers would locate a fox when hidden underground in a burrow and bark vigorously to alert the hunters of its location. As a result they have a tendency to bark and dig. And although they are wary of strangers and other dogs, they make lively companions in active homes.

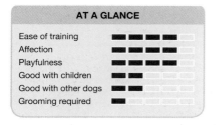

AT A GLANCE

Ease of training	▬▬▬▬▬▬
Affection	▬▬▬▬▬
Playfulness	▬▬▬▬▬▬
Good with children	▬▬▬
Good with other dogs	▬▬▬
Grooming required	▬

 This highly energetic dog is not recommended for sedentary owners

+ Genetically quite healthy. Some known health problems are deafness, luxating patellas and a variety of eye disorders such as lens luxation, distichiasis, and cataracts.

HISTORY

Once thought of as one breed, the Smooth and Wire Fox Terriers were classed and often bred together until the end of the nineteenth century when breeders began to distinguish between the two types. In 1876, the officers of the Fox Terrier Club officially established separate breed standards. The Smooth Fox Terrier is believed to have bloodlines from Beagles, Greyhounds, Old English, Black and Tan, and Bull Terriers breeds.

Soft-Coated Wheaten Terrier

Irish Soft-Coated Wheaten Terrier
IRELAND

Soft-Coated
Wheaten Terrier pup

Exercise required

	Average height (inches)	Average weight (pounds)	Average life expectancy (years)
48		100+	16+
		80	14
36			
		60	12
	24	40	10
		20	8
	12		
		10	6

Common
Coat Colors

Despite its long heritage, the Soft-Coated Wheaten Terrier was only recognized as a distinct breed in the twentieth century. Known as one of the three long-legged terrier breeds native to Ireland, they developed into versatile farm dogs which underline the breed today. They are charming, engaging and independent, and are gentle and calm unlike most terrier breeds, making them an ideal family companion. With patience these dogs are relatively easy to train and are accepting of other dogs.

AT A GLANCE	
Ease of training	▄▄ ▄▄
Affection	▄▄ ▄▄ ▄▄ ▄▄ ▄▄
Playfulness	▄▄ ▄▄ ▄▄ ▄▄
Good with children	▄▄ ▄▄ ▄▄ ▄▄
Good with other dogs	▄▄ ▄▄ ▄▄ ▄▄
Grooming required	▄▄ ▄▄ ▄▄

+ Although generally healthy, problems can include renal dysplasia and protein-losing diseases.

! It requires patience and consistent positive training.

HISTORY

The Soft-Coated Wheaten Terrier shares the same roots as the Kerry Blue and Irish Terriers which all are exhibited in the class of "Irish Terriers" in Ireland in the nineteenth century. The breed traces back to a general farm dog that was extremely willing and spirited. They were popular and widespread on rural properties for their use in hunting, herding, guarding and for companionship. The last of the Irish Terrier breeds to be accepted, the Soft-Coated Wheaten Terrier was recognized by the Irish Kennel Club in 1937, making its debut in the Irish Kennel Club Championship Show in 1938, on St. Patrick's Day.

Staffordshire Bull Terrier

Staffy / Staffy Bull / Staffy Dog / Nanny Dog

ENGLAND

Exercise required

Staffordshire Bull Terriers or "Staffies" have superb temperaments and, despite their bloody heritage, are known for their affection for children, acquiring the nickname "Nanny Dogs". They are reliable, loyal and devoted dogs, and generally get along well with other dogs and humans. The Staffy is intelligent, easy to train and dependable, but given their lovely nature they are not very good watchdogs!

Staffordshire Bull Terrier pup

AT A GLANCE					
Ease of training	■	■	■	■	
Affection	■	■	■		
Playfulness	■	■	■	■	
Good with children	■	■	■	■	■
Good with other dogs	■	■	■	■	
Grooming required	■	■	■		

+ Staffordshire Bull Terriers are known to suffer from hereditary cataracts (HC) and L-2-hydroxyglutaric aciduria (L2HGA)—a metabolic disorder resulting in behavioural changes and dementia-like symptoms.

! SBTs enjoy their comforts and will readily join you on the sofa or bed if allowed.

Common Coat Colors

Red, fawn, white; black, brindle, or blue; with or without white

	Average height (inches)	Average weight (pounds)	Average life expectancy (years)
	48	100+	16+
		80	14
	36		
		60	12
	24	40	10
		20	8
	12		
		10	6

HISTORY

The Staffordshire Bull Terrier is related to the early Bulldog and terrier breeds that were bred for dog fighting and animal fighting. During the early nineteenth century when dog fighting reached an ascendency, they were characterized by their bravery and fierceness in battle, but also by their gentleness with their handlers. The breed was named after the area to which they were most associated. They were recognized by the Kennel Club of the United Kingdom in 1935 and the American Kennel Club in 1974.

Sporting Lucas Terrier

SCOTLAND

Sporting Lucas Terrier pup

48	100+	16+
	80	14
36		
	60	12
24	40	10
	20	8
12		
	10	6

Average height (inches)
Average weight (pounds)
Average life expectancy (years)

Common Coat Colors

A small, relatively unknown terrier breed, the Sporting Lucas Terrier is named after its breeder, Sir Jocelyn Lucas. A determined, self-confident, fearless, and lively breed, they love to hunt and enjoy much exercise. They are independent, yet easily trainable.

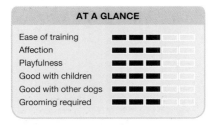

AT A GLANCE

Ease of training	
Affection	
Playfulness	
Good with children	
Good with other dogs	
Grooming required	

! They are only suitable for a very active household.

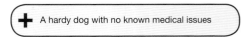
A hardy dog with no known medical issues

HISTORY

In the mid twentieth century, Sir Jocelyn Lucas, famous for his pack of Sealyhams from his renowned Ilmer kennels, developed the Sporting Lucas Terrier. He was concerned the Sealyham was becoming cloddy, and so crossed them with a Norfolk Terrier, resulting in the Lucas Terrier. However, over time the breed began to lose some of its desirable characteristics that Sir Jocelyn admired, so in the late twentieth century, the expertise of Brian Plummer was asked to step in. Plummer's intervention led to the present generation—a dog that is equally comfortable in the field and the home. But whatever this terrier is used for, there's never a dull moment with one about.

Teddy Roosevelt Terrier

UNITED STATES

Teddy Roosevelt Terrier pup

Exercise required

Less common problems may include allergies, bite problems (malocclusions), hip dysplasia, elbow dysplasia, and subluxating patella as these are problems that appear in the dog's cousin, the Rat Terrier.

Common Coat Colors

Average height (inches)	Average weight (pounds)	Average life expectancy (years)
48	100+	16+
	80	14
36		
	60	12
24	40	10
	20	8
12		
	10	6

Like the Rat Terrier, the Teddy Roosevelt Terrier is low-set, muscular, and active, and was originally meant as a hunting companion. Today, it is bred for its hunting instincts, soundness of health, great temperament and its appearance. Their prey drive is higher than average and they are capable of hunting down small to medium sized prey; but as a result they will also dig frequently, leaving many trails of holes. These dogs are protective and territorial, making excellent watchdogs, and become very attached to family with enough interaction and affection.

AT A GLANCE

Ease of training	▬▬ ▬▬ ▬▬ ▬
Affection	▬▬ ▬▬ ▬▬
Playfulness	▬▬ ▬▬ ▬▬
Good with children	▬▬ ▬▬ ▬▬
Good with other dogs	▬▬ ▬▬ ▬▬ ▬
Grooming required	▬▬ ▬▬ ▬▬

! Teddies are very smart and loyal, which makes them easy to train.

HISTORY

An American breed, the Teddy Roosevelt Terrier was developed from a variety of breeds brought over by working-class English immigrants, including the Manchester Terrier, Smooth Fox Terrier, Bull Terrier, Whippet, and Beagle to use as ratters on farms, factories, harbors and on industrial sites. A terrier with uniform characteristics , known as the Rat Terrier began to emerge from the crossing of these breeds and was named after its skilled hunting abilities. The shorter-legged variety of the Rat Terrier became known as the Teddy Roosevelt Terrier due to the President's affection for the breed.

Tenterfield Terrier pup

Tenterfield Terrier

AUSTRALIA

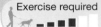

48	100+	16+
	80	14
36		
	60	12
24	40	10
	20	8
12		
	10	6

Average height (inches)
Average weight (pounds)
Average life expectancy (years)

Common
Coat Colors

With many desirable qualities, the Tenterfield Terrier is a great choice as a working dog and a magnificent companion. They are strong, agile, and energetic with great adaptability and pleasant proportions, they are also brave, smart, independent, eager, and attentive. Although much patience is needed to train terriers, they respond well to methods of training that use positive reinforcement; yelling will not get a good response from this sensitive breed. They are friendly and love to cuddle up in their owner's laps. All told, this terrier is a talented working dog and a wonderful companion.

AT A GLANCE

Ease of training	■■ ■■ ■■ □□ □□
Affection	■■ ■■ ■■ □□ □□
Playfulness	■■ ■■ ■■ ■■ □□
Good with children	■■ ■■ ■■ ■■ □□
Good with other dogs	■■ ■■ ■■ ■■ □□
Grooming required	■■ □□ □□ □□ □□

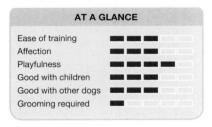

! Like all terriers, it takes loving patience to train them.

+ A hardy dog with no known medical issues

HISTORY

The ancestors of the Tenterfield Terrier arrived in Australia with the first European settlers, who sailed from Portsmouth on England's south coast. They were brought along because of their ability to kill vermin that would often spread disease around on the ships.

Tibetan Terrier

TIBET

Tibetan Terrier pup

Exercise required

Common Coat Colors

Average height (inches)	Average weight (pounds)	Average life expectancy (years)
48	100·	16·
	80	14
36		
	60	12
24	40	10
	20	8
12		
	10	6

Tibetan Terriers are medium-sized dogs that are courageous, dedicated, sweet, and gentle, but nevertheless make a great watchdog. They have great endurance and agility, however, they are a control-seeking, strong-willed and dominant breed. Be sure you are this dog's pack leader; Tibetans that believe they are alpha become willful and begin to bark in excess, telling you what to do and trying to control everything and "run the show."

AT A GLANCE

Ease of training	▬ ▬ ▬ ▬
Affection	▬ ▬ ▬
Playfulness	▬ ▬ ▬ ▬
Good with children	▬ ▬ ▬ ▬ ▬
Good with other dogs	▬ ▬ ▬ ▬
Grooming required	▬ ▬ ▬

 Although Tibetan Terriers can learn quickly, they may be stubborn when it comes to obeying commands.

 Tibetan Terriers are generally healthy but may suffer with progressive retinal atrophy and/or patellar luxation.

HISTORY

Similar to the Tibetan Spaniel, the Tibetan Terrier has a history of more than 2,000 years with their roots associated with monasteries built in the Himalayan Mountains, where they were bred. This earned them the name "Holy Dogs of Tibet." They guarded livestock and the monasteries, and provided companionship. They first arrived in the West in the mid twentieth century.

Toy Fox Terrier

American Toy Terrier / Amertoy

UNITED STATES

Toy Fox Terrier pup

Exercise required

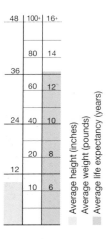

Average height (inches)
Average weight (pounds)
Average life expectancy (years)

Common
Coat Colors

Toy Fox Terriers combine typical terrier qualities such as smartness and liveliness with their admirable hunting skills, but they frequently bark, dig, and chase after small prey as well. Nevertheless, with their love of attention and activity, they make great companions for lively people.

AT A GLANCE

Ease of training	▪▪▪▪
Affection	▪▪▪▪▪
Playfulness	▪▪▪▪
Good with children	▪▪▪
Good with other dogs	▪▪▪
Grooming required	▪

! Toy Fox Terriers adapt well to apartment life but love to have room to run.

+ Toy Fox Terriers are generally healthy, but like all breeds, they're prone to certain health conditions. Demodectic Mange, Patellar Luxation, Legg-Calve-Perthes Disease, von Willebrand's Disease.

HISTORY

In the beginning of the twentieth century, Toy Fox Terriers were bred in the United States by crossing small Smooth Fox Terriers and different toy breeds, such as Manchester Terriers, Miniature Pinschers, Greyhounds, and Chihuahuas.

Toy Manchester Terrier

UNITED STATES (ORIGINS IN ENGLAND)

Toy Manchester Terrier pups

Exercise required

Common Coat Colors

Average height (inches)	Average weight (pounds)	Average life expectancy (years)
48	100	16
	80	14
36		
	60	12
24	40	10
	20	8
12		
	10	6

Toy Manchester Terriers are graceful, spirited dogs that are a miniature version of the original Manchester breed. They have a slightly curved back with a smooth and lustrous coat. They walk freely and effortlessly with an eager and alert expression. They do have hunting instincts, similar to most other terriers, and enjoy chasing small animals, but are considered to be one of the most gentle and caring breeds. They are curious and playful around familiar people, yet may become shy and reserved near strangers.

AT A GLANCE

Ease of training	■ ■ ■ ■
Affection	■ ■ ■
Playfulness	■ ■ ■ ■ ■
Good with children	■ ■ ■
Good with other dogs	■ ■ ■ ■
Grooming required	■

+ No major concerns with this breed of dog.

HISTORY

Until 1923, the Manchester Terrier was believed to the same breed as the ancestors of the Black and Tan Terrier. Throughout time, the Manchester Terrier was assumed to have been influenced by a mixing with other breeds, specifically the Italian Greyhound which contributes to their wide range of sizes. In 1881, a toy version was described and recorded because of consumer preference for small dogs. Breeders actually created even smaller dogs, but the outcome was an increase in frailty, so they altered their process and developed miniature, not tiny versions.

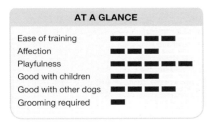

! It enjoys a romp outdoors, but it hates the cold.

457

Welsh Terrier

Welshie
WALES

Exercise required

Originating from Wales, the Welsh Terrier is likely the oldest dog breed in the United Kingdom that still exists today. They are currently classified as endangered species according to the English Kennel Club. Approximately 300 of them are registered yearly, in contrast to the most popular breeds which are registered in the tens of thousands. Their original role was to hunt otters, badgers, or any small and medium sized prey, and they are still capable as hunting dogs. They are easier to train compared to other terrier breeds with their calm, amiable, dignified and tactful personality.

AT A GLANCE

Ease of training	■■■□□□
Affection	■■■■□□
Playfulness	■■■■□□
Good with children	■■■■□□
Good with other dogs	■■□□□□
Grooming required	■■■■■□

+ Generally exceptionally healthy, but hereditary problems may include primary lens luxation.

Welsh Terrier pup

	Average height (inches)	Average weight (pounds)	Average life expectancy (years)
	48	100+	16+
		80	14
	36		
		60	12
	24	40	10
		20	8
	12		
		10	6

Common Coat Colors

HISTORY

The Welsh Terrier is a primitive breed that originated in a relatively isolated location in Wales. They are thought to be a relative of the extinct broken-coated Black and Tan Old English Terrier. A significant aspect of this breed is their exceptional sense of smell. This ability, along with their remarkable bravery, are helpful for their primary role in hunting and chasing their game into burrows.

! Maintaining obedience in a Welsh Terrier can be an ongoing challenge, and it is important to reinforce training constantly.

West Highland White Terrier

SCOTLAND

West Highland
White Terrier pup

Exercise required

48	100+	16+
	80	14
36		
	60	12
24	40	10
	20	8
12		
	10	6

Average height (inches)
Average weight (pounds)
Average life expectancy (years)

Common
Coat Colors

The West Highland White, affectionately known as a Westie, has a lively, warmhearted nature. Although the breed originated at the end of the nineteenth century, with a relatively short history it has become very popular. They are cheerful, outgoing, and lively dogs, but needful of much attention and prone to barking and digging. They are occasionally stubborn and independent and require patient training.

AT A GLANCE

Ease of training	■■ ■■ ■■
Affection	■■ ■■
Playfulness	■■ ■■ ■
Good with children	■■ ■■ ■■ ■
Good with other dogs	■■ ■■ ■
Grooming required	■■ ■■

+ Although generally healthy, problems can include Legg-Calvé-Perthes, patellar luxation, atopic dermatitis, dry eye, lymphoma, and inflammatory bowel disease.

! Westies are born with droopy ears that gradually become pricked by about three months, or in some cases, a little later.

HISTORY

By the seventeenth century, a range of terrier types developed regional differences in Scotland with evidence of white terrier types developing on the Isle of Skye and on the western Highlands. Due to their rugged and enduring characteristics, the West Highland White was bred specifically for hunting aggressive prey like badgers and foxes. Colonel Edward Donald Malcolm of the Poltalloch Estate is said have influenced the breed's development at the end of the nineteenth century.

Wire Fox Terrier

Wirehaired Terrier
ENGLAND

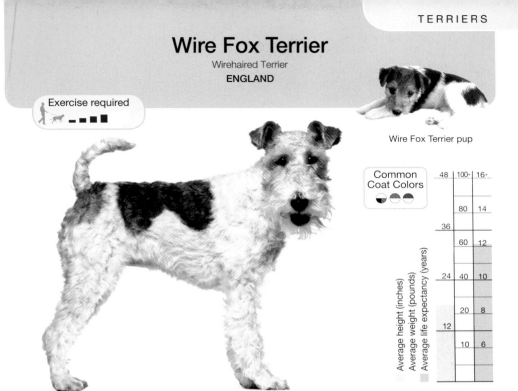

Wire Fox Terrier pup

Exercise required

Common Coat Colors

	48	100+	16+
		80	14
	36		
		60	12
		24	40	10
			20	8
	12		
		10	6

Average height (inches)
Average weight (pounds)
Average life expectancy (years)

These intelligent, engaging, energetic dogs love to hunt, play, dig, and bark. They make wonderful companions in active homes, but may need high fences to keep them from roaming. Keeping one as a pet needs firm control to redirect their prey instincts and provide the dog with sufficient exercise and diversion.

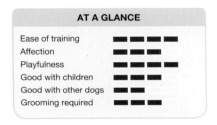

AT A GLANCE

Ease of training	▬ ▬ ▬ ▬
Affection	▬ ▬ ▬
Playfulness	▬ ▬ ▬ ▬
Good with children	▬ ▬ ▬
Good with other dogs	▬ ▬
Grooming required	▬ ▬ ▬

! A low threshold for boredom makes exercise and stimulation necessary.

+ Epilepsy may have a genetic component in this breed. Other concerns are post-nasal drip, lens luxation, distichiasis, cataracts, Legg-Calvé-Perthes syndrome, shoulder dislocation and mast cell tumors

HISTORY

The Wire Fox Terrier has a similar history to that of the Smooth Fox Terrier. Both breeds commonly accompanied fox hunters to scout and determine the location of foxes hidden in burrows. However some speculate that the Wire Fox Terriers descended from the rough-coated Black and Tan Terriers. The oldest recorded Wire Fox Terrier, Old Tip, was bred by the Master of the Sinnington Hounds in Yorkshire during 1866. Old Tip sired three champions, significantly contributing to the development of the breed's lineage.

461

COMPANION DOGS

Bichon Frisée

Bichon Tenerife
SPAIN

Bichon Frisée pup

Exercise required

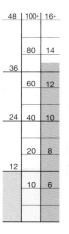

Common
Coat Colors

A hypoallergenic breed, Bichons are playful and affectionate dogs that love human company. Although this breed is prone to barking, Bichons make a great family dog and are well suited for apartment living.

AT A GLANCE	
Ease of training	
Affection	
Playfulness	
Good with children	
Good with other dogs	
Grooming required	

Urinary infections and kidney stones are common in Bichons. Also prone to orthopedic issues such as luxating patella and hip dysplasia. Ear infections are extremely common as well due to profuse hair in the ear canals.

HISTORY

These small, friendly dogs have been associated with the Spanish island, Tenerife, since the fourteenth century. It is likely they were originally brought by sailors to trade with the islanders. By the sixteenth century, Bichons have become favored pets among the nobility of the French, Spanish and Italians, becoming increasingly evident in their artwork. In the nineteenth century, they were used to perform tricks by circuses.

 This breed was once used by Spanish sailors as goodwill ambassadors when traveling abroad.

Bolognese

Bichon Bolognese
ITALY

Bolognese pup

Common
Coat Colors
○○○

48	100+	16+
	80	14
36		
	60	12
	40	10
24		
	20	8
12		
	10	6

Average height (inches)
Average weight (pounds)
Average life expectancy (years)

Exercise required

As these dogs are an intelligent, inquisitive, and playful breed, their affectionate nature allows for strong bonds between family and children, and can create healthy relationships with other dogs. They can be prone to barking.

AT A GLANCE

Ease of training	■ ■ ■ ■
Affection	■ ■ ■ ■ ■
Playfulness	■ ■ ■ ■ ■
Good with children	■ ■ ■ ■
Good with other dogs	■ ■ ■
Grooming required	■ ■ ■

+ Prone to orthopedic issues such as luxating patella and hip dysplasia. Ear infections are extremely common as well due to profuse hair in the ear canals.

! The Bolognese is very similar to the Bichon Frisée, although this dog originated in Italy.

HISTORY

The Bolognese is part of the Bichon family which descends from the Barbet breed, which is historically known as Barbichon. They are closely related to the Bichon Frise, but originate in northern Italy around the city of Bologna. Italian nobility often favored the breed and they were regularly given as valuable gifts among noble families.

Boston Terrier

Boston Bull / Boxwood / American Gentleman

UNITED STATES

Adult Boston Terrier

Boston Terrier puppy

Common Coat Colors

Exercise required

AT A GLANCE

Ease of training	
Affection	
Playfulness	
Good with children	
Good with other dogs	
Grooming required	

! The Boston Terrier is the first dog breed developed in America.

 Generally healthy, but hereditary problems can include luxating patellas, deafness, heart murmur, mast-cell tumors, and allergies.

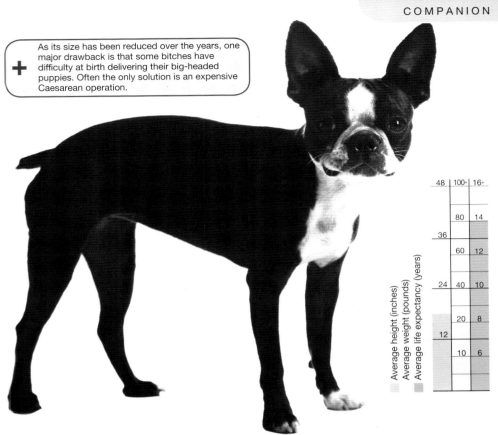

As its size has been reduced over the years, one major drawback is that some bitches have difficulty at birth delivering their big-headed puppies. Often the only solution is an expensive Caesarean operation.

Average height (inches)	Average weight (pounds)	Average life expectancy (years)
48	100+	16+
	80	14
36		
	60	12
24	40	10
	20	8
12		
	10	6

Due to its dapper appearance and gentle disposition, the Boston Terrier is sometimes referred to as the "American Gentleman", despite being bred from fighting stock that traces back to the American Civil War. These dogs are dignified, loyal, intelligent, agile and relatively easy to train. They are often used as therapy dogs. Like many terrier breeds, they have a tendency for stubbornness at times.

HISTORY

The Boston Terrier was developed at the end of the nineteenth century in Boston, Massachusetts and can be traced to British Bulldog and White English Terrier crosses. The first Boston Terrier type, known as Tom, was sired by the son of Robert Hooper's dog, Judge in 1877. In 1893 the breed was recognized by the American Kennel Club.

Brussels Griffon

Griffon Bruxellois

BELGIUM

Exercise required

Common Coat Colors

! This dog was originally bred in Belgium to hunt rats.

Average height (inches)	Average weight (pounds)	Average life expectancy (years)
48	100+	16+
	80	14
36		
	60	12
24	40	10
	20	8
12		
	10	6

A breed of ancient origin supposedly first documented in Jan Van Eyck's fifteenth century painting, "The Marriage of Giovanni Arnolfini", the Brussels Griffon is a fun, plucky companion breed. Also known as the Griffon Bruxellois, these dogs enjoy long walks, however are equally comfortable with inactivity and relaxation. Although they can be prone to barking, they exhibit many admirable terrier qualities and are spirited, bold, outgoing and friendly.

Brussels Griffon puppy

AT A GLANCE				
Ease of training	▬	▬	▬	
Affection	▬	▬	▬	▬
Playfulness	▬	▬	▬	
Good with children	▬	▬		
Good with other dogs	▬	▬	▬	
Grooming required	▬	▬	▬	

Jan Van Eyck's fifteenth century painting, *"The Marriage of Giovanni Arnolfini"*

HISTORY

The Brussels Griffon is a descendant of a rough-coated terrier type. For decades they were popular as a guard dog on horse-drawn cabs as well as a ratter on farms. During the nineteenth century, there was some Pug, Affenpinscher, and King Charles Spaniel added to the Brussels Griffon mix.

 Luxating patellas, eye diseases such as progressive retinal atrophy, syringomyelia, and hip dysplasia

469

Cavalier King Charles Spaniel

Cavalier

ENGLAND

Exercise required

48	100+	16+
	80	14
36		
	60	12
24	40	10
	20	8
12		
	10	6

Average height (inches)
Average weight (pounds)
Average life expectancy (years)

Common Coat Colors

The affectionate, calm, quiet, playful Cavalier King Charles spaniel has a lovely temperament, and is renowned for its gentle disposition and sweet nature. They generally have healthy relationships with other dogs and pets, and are friendly with strangers, making them poor as watchdogs but excellent as lap dogs. These dogs enjoy running and many other activities, and will often flush small game from undergrowth.

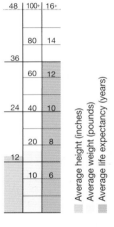

Cavalier King Charles Spaniel pup

 Cavalier King Charles Spaniels are named after King Charles II. An urban legend states that he decreed that no King Charles Spaniel could be barred from a public space, and many believe this decree is still in place today.

+ Heart conditions, patellar luxation, hip dysplasia, deafness, brachycephalic airway obstruction syndrome

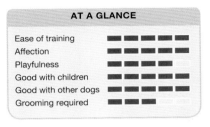

Cavalier King Charles
Spaniel pup

HISTORY

This breed's roots goes back many centuries, sharing the same early history as the smaller King Charles Spaniel—or English Toy Spaniel in the United States—despite differing considerably in appearance, especially in the shape of the head. These spaniel types have appeared in European paintings since the sixteenth century, when they were thought of as "comforters", and were primarily owned by the aristocracy. They are particularly associated with England's King Charles I whose own spaniel, Rogue, is said to have been at his side at his execution. However, the breed's name is derived from King Charles II, the Cavalier King. He adored the little dogs, and ensured that they could escort him anywhere by decreeing they were allowed entrance into any public building—even Parliament. It was not until 1928 that the breed was given its name when their standard was drawn up.

AT A GLANCE

Ease of training	▬▬▬▬▬
Affection	▬▬▬▬▬
Playfulness	▬▬▬▬
Good with children	▬▬▬▬▬
Good with other dogs	▬▬▬▬
Grooming required	▬▬▬

Chihuahua

MEXICO

Exercise required

48 | 100+ | 16+

80 | 14

36

60 | 12

24 | 40 | 10

20 | 8

12

10 | 6

Average height (inches)
Average weight (pounds)
Average life expectancy (years)

Common
Coat Colors

Although the Chihuahua is the world's smallest dog breed, it has an enormous personality. These dogs often need lots of attention, and dislike being left alone. This constant need of company creates strong bonds with their owners, but they are very inclined to bark and be wary of strangers. Although they may need extra care when interacting with larger breeds due to their tiny size, they do generally get along well with other dogs. They are frequently used in advertising and have appeared in a number of Hollywood movies.

! Chihuahuas did not become popular until the mid-twentieth century, with their popularity in the United States boosted by Xavier Cugat, the famous Rumba King, whose Chihuahuas appeared with him on his weekly television shows.

AT A GLANCE

Ease of training	▰▰
Affection	▰▰▰▰▰
Playfulness	▰▰▰
Good with children	▰▰▰▰▰
Good with other dogs	▰▰
Grooming required	▰▰

HISTORY

Tracing back to the state of
Chihuahua in northern Mexico,
remains and figurine portrayals of
Chihuahuas have been found in early
graves, some thousands of years
old. Dogs were an important part of
early Central and South American life
three thousand years ago, including
the Techichi Dogs of the Toltecs and
the Xoloitzcuintli of the Aztecs. It was
believed that dogs carried the spirits
of the deceased to the underworld,
so were frequently sacrificed or
painted on pottery to be placed in
graves. Unearthed skeletal remains
are similar to modern chihuahuas.
In the fifteenth century, when the
Spanish conquistadors arrived on the
continent and plundered the native
cultures, they had no interest in these
little dogs, which became feral. They
were rediscovered in Chihuahua
300 years later in the mid-nineteenth
century and slowly spread to the
United States and England.

Chihuahua pup

 Prone to rheumatism, slipped stifle, colds, gum
problems, corneal dryness, and secondary
glaucoma

473

Chinese Crested

"Dr. Seuss Dog"

CHINA

Chinese Crested
Hairless pup

Exercise required

	48	100+	16+
		80	14
	36		
		60	12
	24	40	10
		20	8
	12		
		10	6

Average height (inches)
Average weight (pounds)
Average life expectancy (years)

Common Coat Colors

The Chinese Crested comes in two dramatically different looking varieties: the Powderpuff variety is entirely covered with a long double, straight, silky coat. The hairless variety is hairless, with soft, smooth skin except for its soft, silky hair on its head, tail, and feet known as the crest, plume, and socks respectively. Regardless of their differences, the two types often come from the same litter. These affectionate dogs are fun and playful, and reside well with children, strangers, and other dogs. The skin of the hairless variety can be susceptible to dryness and sunburn, and needs protection from the elements.

AT A GLANCE

Ease of training	■ ■ ■ ■ □
Affection	■ ■ ■ ■ ■
Playfulness	■ ■ ■ ■ ■
Good with children	■ ■ ■ ■ □
Good with other dogs	■ ■ ■ ■ □
Grooming required	■ ■ ■ □ □

! These dogs are known as the "Dr. Seuss Dog" because of their resemblance to characters from Dr. Seuss' stories.

+ Generally healthy, but problems can include primary lens luxation, progressive retinal atrophy, and patellar luxation.

HISTORY

The Hairless variety has existed in China since at least the sixteenth century. They became popular with Chinese seafarers, and were frequently used for ratting on board ships and were often traded as curiosities when the ships reached shore. Chinese Crested dogs arrived in England as part of a zoological show in the mid-nineteenth century, and were introduced to the United States a few decades later. They were first registered in 1881. The American Chinese Crested Club, was founded in 1978.

Chinese Imperial

Lion Dogs / Foo Dogs / Sleeve Dogs

CHINA

Chinese Imperial puppy

48	100-	16+
	80	14
36		
	60	12
	40	10
24		
	20	8
12		
	10	6

Average height (inches)
Average weight (pounds)
Average life expectancy (years)

Common Coat Colors

The Chinese Imperial is a close relative of the larger Shih Tzu, and can be traced back to imperial China. Bred to resemble miniature lions, these dogs were an important and revered symbol of the Buddhist faith. Chinese Imperials have a lovely sweet temperament. They are a bold, loyal, and playful companion breed, enjoying human company and affection. These dogs are friendly with other dogs and children, and have great bonds with their families. However, given their small size, they should be given plentiful attention and not left unattended in the company of larger dogs.

Exercise required

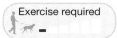

! Nobility used to keep this breed in the sleeve of their robes

AT A GLANCE

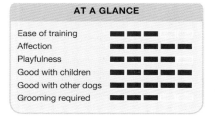

Ease of training	
Affection	
Playfulness	
Good with children	
Good with other dogs	
Grooming required	

+ Hypoglycemia, slipped stifle and spinal disc disease, plus ear infections.

HISTORY

The Chinese Imperial was first bred in China around 700 AD. However, they were not recognized as a breed in their own right in the West—separate from the Shih Tzu—until March 2005.

475

Chinook

UNITED STATES

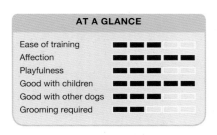

Chinook puppy

Exercise required

48	100+	16+
	80	14
36		
	60	12
24	40	10
	20	8
12		
	10	6

Average height (inches)
Average weight (pounds)
Average life expectancy (years)

Common Coat Colors

The Chinook is known for its special devotion toward children, and is an affectionate and playful family companion. The breed's founder, Polar Explorer Arthur Treadwell Walden, made it famous through his many expeditions, where his dogs proved themselves as effective as other established sled breeds such as the Husky. Although originally kept mainly as a working breed, today Chinooks are chiefly a companion breed. They are best suited to active homes and excel at sledding, agility, and other energetic activities.

AT A GLANCE

Ease of training	
Affection	
Playfulness	
Good with children	
Good with other dogs	
Grooming required	

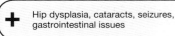

+ Hip dysplasia, cataracts, seizures, gastrointestinal issues

HISTORY

The Chinook, one of just a few all-American breeds, was developed in the early 1900s in New Hampshire by a polar explorer, Arthur Treadwell Walden It can be traced back to a single ancestor. The first of this breed, named Chinook, was one of three pups born to a Northern Husky. He was outstanding sled dog with strength of larger freight dogs but with the speed of smaller sled dogs.

! In the 1960s this breed was declared the rarest breed on Earth, as only 125 existed. At one point only 28 of the dogs remained, with only 12 capable of breeding.

Coton de Tulear

"Cotie"

MADAGASCAR

Exercise required

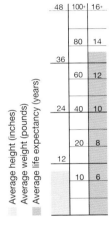

Common
Coat Colors

Average height (inches)	Average weight (pounds)	Average life expectancy (years)
48	100+	16+
	80	14
36		
	60	12
24	40	10
	20	8
12		
	10	6

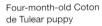

Four-month-old Coton
de Tulear puppy

A rare breed originally from Madagascar, their name is derived from the cotton-like appearance of their coat, and from the Madagascan town of Tulear. For centuries they have been bred specifically as companion dogs. They are bright, easy-to-train, cheerful, friendly dogs, but are prone to barking. Coton de Tulears make great family dogs and will take part in many activities; it is, however, a sensitive breed, and requires much early socialization and attention.

AT A GLANCE

Ease of training	▬ ▬ ▬ ▬ ▬
Affection	▬ ▬ ▬ ▬ ▬
Playfulness	▬ ▬ ▬ ▬ ▬
Good with children	▬ ▬ ▬ ▬ ▬
Good with other dogs	▬ ▬ ▬
Grooming required	▬ ▬ ▬ ▬ ▬

! Females Coties are more independent than males and often rule over them

HISTORY

Although there are many tales of its origins, Coton de Tulears were most likely developed from small Bichon-type dogs popular amongst sailors and merchants. Bichons arrived in Madagascar in the fifteenth century when Tulear was a thriving port. Many different Bichon-types interbred and over time, a distinct type developed that was unique to the island. They were given to the Malagasy Royals and nobles as gifts and were adopted by the ruling "Merina" dynasty so that others were unable to own them. Known as the Royal Dog of Madagascar, Coton de Tulears are now the island's official dog.

Dalmatian

Carriage Dog / Spotted Coach Dog / Leopard Carriage Dog / Firehouse Dog / Plum Pudding Dog/"Dal"

CROATIA

Exercise required

Common Coat Colors

A young Dalmatian

The beloved Dalmatian is a highly distinctive breed with its striking spotted coat. These elegant dogs combine a playful personality with great versatility and thus historically have been used in a range of roles: for hunting and ratting; as farm dogs and watch dogs; as circus performers, firehouse dogs, and carriage dogs; and more recently as companions. They are sometimes reserved with strangers and are occasionally aggressive toward other dogs, but are intelligent and trainable.

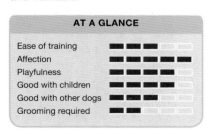

AT A GLANCE

Ease of training	
Affection	
Playfulness	
Good with children	
Good with other dogs	
Grooming required	

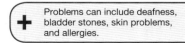

+ Problems can include deafness, bladder stones, skin problems, and allergies.

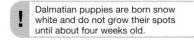

! Dalmatian puppies are born snow white and do not grow their spots until about four weeks old.

48	100+	16+
	80	14
36		
	60	12
24	40	10
	20	8
12		
	10	6

Average height (inches)
Average weight (pounds)
Average life expectancy (years)

HISTORY

Although dalmatians are mostly associated with England and the United States, records of spotted dogs have appeared in Italian Renaissance art, and even in artefacts frm Ancient Egypt. In the sixteenth century, a letter written by Serbian poet, Jurij Dalmatin, refers to two spotted Turkish dogs that he bred, perhaps creating the first Dalmatian. Since the sixteenth century in England, they were favored as coaching dogs, acting as guards for unattended coaches and horses to deter highwaymen. Dalmatians became known as English Coach Dogs or Spotted Dicks. Across the Atlantic, in the United States, they became known as Firehouse Dogs, as they were used to accompany early fire trucks, running ahead of them to clear the way. In 1951 the National Fire Protection Association designated a Dalmatian named Sparky as their official mascot. Following the release of Disney's 101 Dalmatians in 1961, the popularity of the breed increased significantly, and it has been a popular companion ever since.

Elo
GERMANY

Elo pup

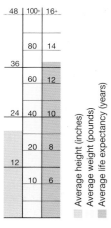

Average height (inches)
Average weight (pounds)
Average life expectancy (years)

48	100+	16+
	80	14
36		
	60	12
24	40	10
	20	8
12		
	10	6

The Elo is the direct result of a German couple's experiment to create the perfect pet with regard to temperament and behavioral characteristics, rather than appearance. The experiment began in 1987, and involved three breeds, resulting in the Elo's varied appearance, not dissimilar to modern "designer" breeds. Common traits include distinctive Spitz-type erect ears and curly, bushy tails. Clearly the experiment was a success, as the Elo is affectionate, loyal, and lively.

AT A GLANCE

Ease of training	▬ ▬ ▬ ▬
Affection	▬ ▬ ▬ ▬ ▬
Playfulness	▬ ▬ ▬ ▬
Good with children	▬ ▬ ▬ ▬ ▬
Good with other dogs	▬ ▬ ▬
Grooming required	▬ ▬ ▬

 This breed's name is trademarked and development of Elos has been closely supervised by the Elo Breeding and Research Association.

+ Susceptible to inbreeding because of small population size (and its after-effects of inbreeding depression) and distichia

HISTORY

In 1987, Marita and Heinz Szobries crossed their Bobtails and Eurasiers to create "the perfect pet." Later, the Chow Chow breed was incorporated and the resulting dog was named "Elo", derived from letters from the names of the three breeds.

Common Coat Colors

Exercise required
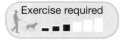

French Bulldog

"Frenchie"

FRANCE

French Bulldog pup

Average height (inches)	Average weight (pounds)	Average life expectancy (years)
48	100+	16+
36	80	14
	60	12
24	40	10
	20	8
12		
	10	6

Exercise required

! Most French bulldog puppies are born by Caesarean section because their heads are too big for the birth canal.

Common Coat Colors

Often described as the "clowns of the dog world", French Bulldogs have a keen sense of humor. They are sweet-natured dogs and have solid and muscular frames, despite their small height. They are affectionate, eager to please, exceptionally bright, and devoted to their families. At times they can be stubborn, but they are generally cheerful, friendly dogs.

AT A GLANCE

Ease of training	▬▬ ▬▬
Affection	▬▬ ▬▬ ▬▬ ▬▬
Playfulness	▬▬ ▬▬ ▬▬
Good with children	▬▬ ▬▬ ▬▬
Good with other dogs	▬▬ ▬▬ ▬▬
Grooming required	▬▬

➕ Although generally healthy, problems can include heart conditions, patellar luxation, hip dysplasia, deafness, and brachycephalic airway obstruction syndrome, brachycephalic syndrome, von Willebrand's disease, intervertebral disc disease, and entropion.

HISTORY

The breed traces back to British Bulldogs and Bullenbeissers, which were both used for dogfighting and bull baiting. However, when these activities were outlawed in England in 1835, they were bred to be smaller they became fashionable as companions. In the nineteenth century, many English craftsmen and traders moved to France bringing their small bulldog types with them. These dogs were bred with the French Bullenbeissers, resulting in a small bulldog type called, Bouledouge Francais. In 1893, some of these French Bulldogs arrived in England, and the breed was established in the United States around the same time. Some Frenchies still exhibited rose ears, and in 1897, the French Bulldog Club of America wrote a new standard specifying their now distinctive bat ears, the prominent feature of the breed. In 1902, the French Bulldog Club of England was formed.

Havanese

Bichon Havanês

CUBA

Exercise required

48	100+	16+
	80	14
36		
	60	12
24	40	10
	20	8
12		
	10	6

Average height (inches)
Average weight (pounds)
Average life expectancy (years)

Originally called the Bichon Havanais or Havana Silk Dog, the Havanese is the Cuban member of the Bichon family. These ancient long-haired Bichon-type dogs developed regional variations, eventually leading to the breed recognized today. The Havanese is ideal for a family pet: trainable, intelligent, and naturally affectionate. They are energetic and require regular light exercise. The breed's non-shedding coat makes it hypoallergenic, but it requires a lot of grooming.

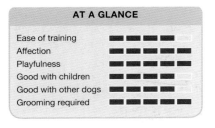

AT A GLANCE

Ease of training	
Affection	
Playfulness	
Good with children	
Good with other dogs	
Grooming required	

Hip dysplasia, elbow dysplasia, chondrodysplasia (abnormally short limbs. Disorder is commonly mislabeled as dwarfism)

HISTORY

In the late fifteenth century, the Spanish began settling in Cuba with their Bichon breeds These began to interbreed and over time developed into the Havanese. Europeans visiting the island brought them back with them, and by the mid-1800s they had become popular amongst the French, English and Spanish royalty.

Havanese pup

Havanese are the only
breed native to Cuba,
and thus, are the
national dog of Cuba.

Common
Coat Colors

COMPANION

Japanese Chin

Japanese Spaniel

JAPAN / CHINA

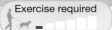

Exercise required

48	100+	16+
	80	14
36		
	60	12
24	40	10
	20	8
12		
	10	6

Average height (inches)
Average weight (pounds)
Average life expectancy (years)

Common Coat Colors

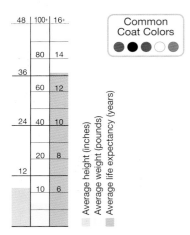

Its name is misleading, as the Japanese Chin is an ancient breed that traces to China. Closely related to the Pekingese breed, they are delightful, affectionate, devoted and playful companions. They were dispersed throughout the ancient world through the Silk Road, from which they made their way to Japan, where they became the preserve of the Imperial households. In the late nineteenth century, the breed was recognized by the American Kennel Club.

AT A GLANCE

Ease of training	▪▪▪
Affection	▪▪▪▪
Playfulness	▪▪▪
Good with children	▪▪
Good with other dogs	▪▪▪
Grooming required	▪

 The Japanese Chin was unknown to the outside world until 1853 when Commodore Matthew C. Perry helped to open Japan to international trade.

✚ Can suffer with atrioventricular endocardiosis, progressive retinal atrophy, patellar luxation, heart murmurs

HISTORY

No one knows for sure how the Chinese "Japanese" Chin arrived in Japan. One theory proposes that 1300 years ago the rulers of Korea gave the dogs to Japanese royalty as a gift. Each noble house in Japan bred to its own standards, leading to the many variations in size, coat density, and personality.

484

King Charles Spaniel

English Toy Spaniel / Charlies

ENGLAND

King Charles Spaniel puppy

Exercise required

Common Coat Colors

			48	100+	16+
				80	14
			36		
				60	12
			24	40	10
				20	8
			12		
				10	6

Average height (inches)
Average weight (pounds)
Average life expectancy (years)

! King Charles Spaniels were said to have been black and tan during the time of King Charles II. The different colors of this breed emerged much later.

+ Can suffer with cataracts, corneal dystrophy, distichia, entropion, and keratitis.

The King Charles Spaniel, also known as the English Toy Spaniel, is a close relative of the Cavalier King Charles Spaniel. The breed was a favorite of King Charles II of England, and their exceptionally long ears resembled the wigs worn by the aristocracy in the seventeenth century. They are loyal and devoted dogs, adoring of their families. They are often independent, stubborn, and wary of strangers, but are also calm, generally quiet, playful, and enjoy a good walk.

HISTORY

First seen in Europe during the sixteenth century, the breed is believed to have originated in the Far East. They were first linked with the English royal family during the reign of Queen Mary I.

AT A GLANCE

Ease of training	▬▬ ▬▬ ▬▬ ▬▬ ▬▬
Affection	▬▬ ▬▬ ▬▬
Playfulness	▬▬ ▬▬ ▬▬
Good with children	▬▬ ▬▬ ▬▬
Good with other dogs	▬▬ ▬▬ ▬▬
Grooming required	▬▬ ▬▬

Kyi-Leo

UNITED STATES

Kyi-Leo pup

Exercise required

48	100+	16+
	80	14
36		
	60	12
24	40	10
	20	8
12		
	10	6

Average height (inches)
Average weight (pounds)
Average life expectancy (years)

Common Coat Colors

Recognized only by the American Rare Breed Association, the Kyi-Leo is one of the original "designer dogs." Developed in San Francisco in the 1950s by crossing a Lhasa Apso and a Maltese, this breed is affectionate, lively, playful, and devoted to their families but they can be stubborn and may be wary of strangers. In 1972 the breed was named the Kyi-Leoi: Kyi, from the Tibetan word for "dog", and Leo, from the Latin for "lion."

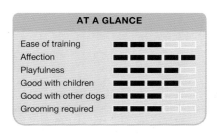

AT A GLANCE

Ease of training	■ ■ ■ ■ □ □
Affection	■ ■ ■ ■ ■ □
Playfulness	■ ■ ■ ■ ■ □
Good with children	■ ■ ■ ■ □ □
Good with other dogs	■ ■ ■ ■ □ □
Grooming required	■ ■ ■ □ □ □

! This dog's name was officially registered as a trademark by the Kyi-Leo Club in 1995.

+ Slipped patella, back pains, and can easily become overweight due to their small frame.

HISTORY

In the 1950s the Kyi-Leo was first introduced to the San Francisco Bay area via the accidental crossing of a Maltese and Lhasa Apso. The "breed" slowly spread throughout the U.S. It would be considered a "designer dog" had it not recently been recognized as a legitimate breed by the American Rare Breed Association.

Lhasa Apso

TIBET

Lhasa Apso pup

Exercise required

48	100+	16+
	80	14
36		
	60	12
24	40	10
	20	8
12		
	10	6

Average height (inches)
Average weight (pounds)
Average life expectancy (years)

Common Coat Colors

Lhasa Apso is an ancient dog breed developed in remote Tibet, relatively uninfluenced by other breeds. Closely associated with the spiritual beliefs of Buddhism and its monasteries where they were bred, they are revered, and considered to be an incarnation of the mythical Tibetan snow lion. These dogs are charismatic, affectionate, playful, and protective. They make good watchdogs as they can be wary of strangers.

AT A GLANCE

Ease of training	▰▰ ▰▰
Affection	▰▰ ▰▰ ▰▰
Playfulness	▰▰ ▰▰ ▰▰ ▰▰
Good with children	▰▰ ▰▰ ▰▰ ▰▰
Good with other dogs	▰▰ ▰▰ ▰▰
Grooming required	▰▰ ▰▰ ▰▰ ▰▰

 In Tibet this dog is known as "Apso Seng Kyi", which translates to "bearded lion dog."

✚ Sebaceous adenitis, progressive retinal atrophy, and prone to eye diseases.

HISTORY

This is one of the most ancient companion breeds, having been kept for centuries by Tibetan monks. They were jealously guarded from outside influences. Some believed that when the monks died, they were reincarnated as one as these sacred dogs. Originating from a very small breed of mountain wolf, the breed is over 4000 years old. They were brought to England from the Indian subcontinent in the early 1900s.

Löwchen

Little Lion Dog

GERMANY

Exercise required

Löwchen puppies

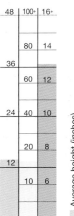

48	100+	16+
	80	14
36		
	60	12
24	40	10
	20	8
12		
	10	6

Average height (inches)
Average weight (pounds)
Average life expectancy (years)

Common Coat Colors

The Löwchen, also known as "the Little Lion Dog", can be traced as far back as the sixteenth century when they began to appear in German paintings. They are cheerful, playful, eager-to-please dogs that have great personalities, but are prone to barking.

AT A GLANCE

Ease of training	■ ■ ■ □ □
Affection	■ ■ ■ □ □
Playfulness	■ ■ ■ ■ □
Good with children	■ ■ ■ ■ ■
Good with other dogs	■ ■ ■ ■ □
Grooming required	■ ■ ■ ■ □

! This dog is referred to as the Little Lion Dog because its haircut resembles a lion.

+ Cataracts, progressive retinal atrophy, patellar luxation

HISTORY

Löwchen were always meant as a companion dog, but were sometimes used as rodent hunters and watchdogs. During World War II the breed virtually disappeared but was revived through the efforts of Belgian breeder, Madame Bennert, and German breeder, Dr. Hans Rickert.

Maltese

Maltese Lion Dog
MALTA

Exercise required

Maltese puppy

			Average height (inches)	Average weight (pounds)	Average life expectancy (years)
48	100+	16+			
	80	14			
36					
	60	12			
	40	10			
24					
	20	8			
12					
	10	6			

Common Coat Colors

The Maltese's distinctive long, silky white coat has ensured its popularity among the European aristocracy for centuries. Although gentle and affectionate, these little dogs are are also intelligent, lively, and fearless. Being wary of strangers they have a tendency to bark, and therefore make good watchdogs.

AT A GLANCE

Ease of training	▪▪▪ ▪▪▪ ▪▪▪
Affection	▪▪▪ ▪▪▪ ▪▪▪
Playfulness	▪▪▪ ▪▪▪ ▪▪▪
Good with children	▪▪▪ ▪▪▪ ▪▪▪
Good with other dogs	▪▪▪ ▪▪▪
Grooming required	▪▪▪ ▪▪▪ ▪▪▪

! This is a very popular breed for crossbreeding. By the nineteenth century, there were as many as nine different breeds of the Maltese.

+ Patellar luxation, portosystemic liver shunt, progressive retinal atrophy, hypoglycemia

HISTORY

Indigenous to the island of Malta, where its name is derived (named by the Romans) the Maltese is an ancient Bichon breed with Spaniel roots. They were first seen in the U.S. in the nineteenth century and first entered in the Westminster Kennel Club shows in the 1870s.

Miniature Pinscher

"Min-Pin"/Zwergpinscher

GERMANY

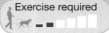

Exercise required

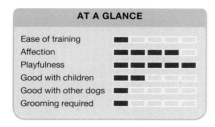

Miniature Pinscher
puppy

Common
Coat Colors

48	100+	16+
	80	14
36		
	60	12
24	40	10
	20	8
12		
	10	6

Average height (inches)
Average weight (pounds)
Average life expectancy (years)

Commonly known as the "Min-Pin", the Miniature Pinscher is believed to have developed from German Pinschers crossed with Dachshunds and Italian Greyhounds several hundred years ago—their likeness appears in historic artwork. They gained American Kennel Club recognition in 1929, ten years after they arrived in the United States. They are fearless, inquisitive, and independent but self-possessed, stubborn, and feisty.

AT A GLANCE

Ease of training	■
Affection	■■■■
Playfulness	■■■■
Good with children	■■
Good with other dogs	■
Grooming required	■

The Miniature Pinscher is often called the "King of the Toys" due to its hardiness and courage.

+ Progressive retinal atrophy, Legg-Calve-Perthes disease, epilepsy

HISTORY

Long thought to be an ancient breed, the breed traces back only several hundred years. Miniature Pinschers first appeared in Germany, used as rodent hunters in homes and stables. After the formation of the Pinscher Klub in 1895 the development of the dog increased rapidly.

Miniature Shar Pei

Mini Pei

CHINA

Exercise required

Miniature Shar Pei puppy

Common
Coat Colors

Average height (inches)	Average weight (pounds)	Average life expectancy (years)
48	100+	16+
	80	14
36		
	60	12
24	40	10
	20	8
12		
	10	6

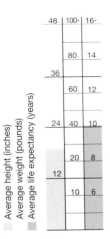

The Miniature Shar Pei, affectionately known as the Mini Pei, is an affectionate dog, known for its loyalty and ability to create exceptionally strong bonds with a devoted owner.

AT A GLANCE

Ease of training	▪▪▪ ▪
Affection	▪▪▪ ▪
Playfulness	▪▪ ▪
Good with children	▪▪▪ ▪ ▪
Good with other dogs	▪▪▪ ▪
Grooming required	▪▪ ▪

+ Prone to amolydosis and skin problems

HISTORY

The breed is a purebred Shar-Pei which has been selectively bred to express the recessive gene that gives the dog its small size. Although originally kept as a general-purpose farm dog, today it is kept as a companion dog.

! Miniature SharPeis are known for hating water and will do anything to avoid it.

Papillon

Continental Toy Spaniel

FRANCE

Exercise required

Young Papillon

Average height (inches)
Average weight (pounds)
Average life expectancy (years)

48	100+	16+
	80	14
36		
	60	12
24	40	10
	20	8
12		
	10	6

Common Coat Colors

The name, Papillon, is derived from the French word for "butterfly," after the breed's large ears which resembles a butterfly's wings. These are great companion dogs whose dainty, elegant looks and excellent character contribute to their enormous popularity. These joyful, charming, playful, affectionate dogs are devoted to their families. They are also intelligent, friendly, agile and easily trained, and therefore make perfect therapy dogs.

AT A GLANCE	
Ease of training	■ ■ ■ ■ ■
Affection	■ ■ ■ ■ ■
Playfulness	■ ■ ■ ■ ■
Good with children	■ ■ ■ ☐ ☐
Good with other dogs	■ ■ ■ ■ ☐
Grooming required	■ ■ ■ ☐ ☐

! The Papillon has a long association with royalty. One apocryphal tale says that Marie Antoinette walked to the guillotine clutching her dog under her arm.

+ Patellar luxation, dental issues, and seizures

HISTORY

These small dogs were favored by the nobility as "comforters" or lap dogs. Although France is listed as their country of origin, they developed all over Europe, including Belgium, Spain, and Italy, portrayed in many pieces of artwork since the sixteenth century. Papillons became a regular at the French Court and were kept by a succession of French royals. The breed arrived in the United States in the early twentieth century with the first Papillon named Joujou having registered with the American Kennel Club in 1915. The breed traces to a dwarf-spaniel type referred to as the Titian Spaniel or Toy Spaniel that became popular throughout Europe by the sixteenth century.

Pekingese

Peke

CHINA

Exercise required

Pekingese pup

Common Coat Colors

Pekingese are known to snore loudly due to their short noses.

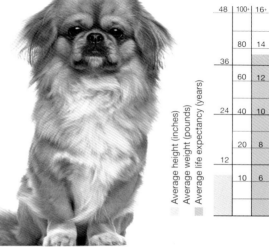

	Average height (inches)	Average weight (pounds)	Average life expectancy (years)
	48	100+	16+
		80	14
	36		
		60	12
	24	40	10
		20	8
	12		
		10	6

The proud, aloof Pekingese is a dignified breed that are devoted, affectionate and loyal to their families, but are characteristically not fond of strangers. These dogs are also independent and are difficult to train and stubborn. They have big personalities, and require a special understanding and empathy, but with patience they can be quiet, calm, and reserved companions.

AT A GLANCE

Ease of training	▬
Affection	▬ ▬
Playfulness	▬
Good with children	▬ ▬
Good with other dogs	▬ ▬ ▬ ▬
Grooming required	▬ ▬ ▬ ▬ ▬

✚ Although generally healthy, some health problems can include brachycephalic airway obstruction syndrome, back problems, eye problems, and patellar luxation.

HISTORY

An ancient breed closely associated with China's emperors and ruling elite, they were bred specifically to resemble miniature lions, a revered Buddhist symbol. The dogs were bred in great numbers at China's royal palace, and they became known as Foo Dogs, and were tended to by eunuchs. Statues of Pekingese were placed outside Buddhist temples or used as amulets. In 1860, the British ransacked the Imperial Summer Palace in Beijing, retrieving five Pekingese Dogs that were later bred in England. They arrived in the United States by the early 1900s, two dogs were gifted by the Empress Dowager Cixi — one to Alice Roosevelt, daughter of Theodore Roosevelt, and one to financier J. P. Morgan.

Phalène

Moth-eared Toy Spaniel

FRANCE

Phalène pup

Exercise required

Common Coat Colors

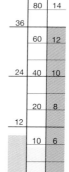

Average height (inches)	Average weight (pounds)	Average life expectancy (years)
48	100+	16+
	80	14
36		
	60	12
24	40	10
	20	8
12		
	10	6

These sweet little dogs trace back to at least the sixteenth century as is evidenced in paintings of the time. Believed to be the older of the two types of Papillon, the Phalène was once more popular than its prick-eared relative. At the end of the nineteenth century the Phalène started to disappear and thus, within the last fifty years or so there has been a concerted effort to reestablish the Phalène. The Phalène is a delightful, charming, friendly, playful, sweet, and calm, great as a family dog. Because of its similarity to the Papillion in every aspect but its "drop-ears", the Phalène is not recognized as a separate breed by all kennel clubs.

AT A GLANCE	
Ease of training	■ ■ ■ ■ ■
Affection	■ ■ ■ ■ ■
Playfulness	■ ■ ■ ■ ■
Good with children	■ ■ ■ □ □
Good with other dogs	■ ■ ■ ■ □
Grooming required	■ ■ ■ □ □

HISTORY

The earliest form of the Papillon, the Phalène gained popularity during the early nineteenth century. Although it became endangered in the mid-20th century, it was prevented from becoming extinct.

! This dog is not recognized as an individual breed by the American Kennel Club, although nations that use the World Canine Organization do recognize it as a unique breed.

Pomeranian

Deutscher Spitz / Zergspitz / Pom / Pom Pom

GERMANY

Pomeranian puppies

Common Coat Colors
● ○ ● ●

Exercise required
🚶 🐕 −

A member of the spitz family, Pomeranians are lively, inquisitive, and playful dogs. However, they are independent, stubborn, and hard to train.

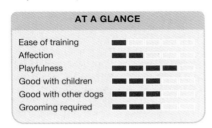

AT A GLANCE	
Ease of training	▰
Affection	▰ ▰
Playfulness	▰ ▰ ▰ ▰
Good with children	▰ ▰ ▰
Good with other dogs	▰ ▰ ▰
Grooming required	▰ ▰ ▰

! Since 1988, this breed has ranked among the top 20 most popular breeds in the U.S.A.

HISTORY

Although the breed traces its ancestry to the Arctic, the Pomeranian was developed in Germany as the smallest of the German Wolfspitzen. Queen Victoria popularized the breed in England, and her own Pomeranian, Turi, was with her when she died. The first "Pom" was registered in the United States in the late 1980s, and the breed's popularity rapidly increased thereafter.

+ Mild deafness, ametropia, microphthalmia, and colobomas

495

Pug

Chinese Pug / Dutch Bulldog / Dutch Mastiff

CHINA

Multum in parvo, or "much in a little" in Latin, as the Pug is often described as the perfect description for this delightful breed that is full of personality and charisma. They have a lively, gregarious, eager to please, playful nature making them great companion dogs. Renowned for their sense of humor and comic behavior, they can also be dignified and rather regal, depending on their mood. Negatives: Pugs are often stubborn and prone to snoring and wheezing.

 Pugs love to get on furniture. If you want a dog that doesn't sit on your sofa, a Pug probably isn't for you.

 Although generally healthy, problems can include brachycephalic airway obstruction syndrome, back problems, eye problems, patellar luxation, hip dysplasia, and Pug-dog encephalitis.

Exercise required

Pug pup

		48	100+	16+	
			80	14	
		36			
			60	12	
		24	40	10	Average height (inches)
			20	8	Average weight (pounds)
		12			Average life expectancy (years)
Common Coat Colors			10	6	

HISTORY

The Chinese philosopher Confucius wrote about "short-mouthed dogs," and is thought to have referred to the Lo-Chiang-Sze or early Pug types, this ancient breed is thought to date back to 400 BCE. Pugs were an icon of China's elite and were treated with lavish care. The breed arrived in England in 1688 and similarly became fashionable among the aristocracy, its popularity spreading to France and Russia. In the mid 1860s, the first Pugs are thought to have arrived in the United States.

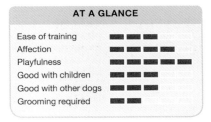

AT A GLANCE	
Ease of training	■■ ■■ ■■
Affection	■■ ■■ ■■ ■■
Playfulness	■■ ■■ ■■ ■■ ■■
Good with children	■■ ■■ ■■ ■■
Good with other dogs	■■ ■■ ■■ ■■
Grooming required	■■ ■■

Russian Toy

Russkiy Toy / Russian Toy Terrier
RUSSIA

Exercise required

Common Coat Colors

Long-haired Russian Toy

48	100+	16+
	80	14
36		
	60	12
24	40	10
	20	8
12		
	10	6

Average height (inches)
Average weight (pounds)
Average life expectancy (years)

The Russian Toy, or Russkiy Toy, a small but feisty breed, is found in both long- and smooth-coat varieties. These dogs have a keen instinct for ratting and are wary of strangers, but make good watchdogs and are lively and playful with their families.

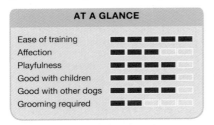

AT A GLANCE	
Ease of training	■■■■■
Affection	■■■
Playfulness	■■■
Good with children	■■■
Good with other dogs	■■■
Grooming required	■■

 This dog makes a great watchdog, as it is wary of strangers and will bark loudly when an intruder is present.

+ Requires help of a veterinarian to remove deciduous teeth. Also prone to patellar luxation and bone fractures due to their small size.

HISTORY

The Russian Toy is a new dog breed that was developed in Russia in the mid-twentieth century based on the English Toy Terrier. Breeders began to reestablish once popular English breeds which have disappeared from all but Russia. And after some years of development, a new type emerged that was later recognized as a distinct breed.

Shih Tzu

Chinese Lion Breed
CHINA

Exercise required

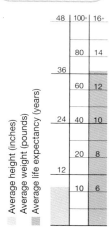

Average height (inches)	Average weight (pounds)	Average life expectancy (years)
48	100+	16+
	80	14
36		
	60	12
24	40	10
	20	8
12		
	10	6

Common Coat Colors

! Shih Tzu puppies, like all puppies, can be easily injured and should never be left unattended with small children.

A cheerful, sparky, and gregarious companion, the Shih Tzu love to play. They have sweet natures and are kind, gentle, and calm around the house. Despite their friendly character, they are very prone to barking when threatened or uncomfortable, and thus make excellent, but noisy watchdogs.

AT A GLANCE

Ease of training	■■■■
Affection	■■■■
Playfulness	■■■■■
Good with children	■■■■
Good with other dogs	■■■■
Grooming required	■■■■■

+ Although generally healthy, problems can include dry eye, progressive retinal atrophy, bladder stones, ear problems, hernias, diabetes, patellar luxation, and liver shunt.

HISTORY

The Shih Tzu is an ancient breed with traces to "Lion Dogs" bred by Buddhist monks in Tibet which were used in conjunction with the larger Tibetan Mastiff as guard dogs. The "Lion Dogs" became very popular in China, particularly with the Manchu emperors of the Qing Dynasty, and eventually developed differently from those from the Tibetan Plateau—one became the Shih Tzu, the other the Lhasa Apso breed. Shih Tzus were bred extensively in the nineteenth century by the Empress Cixi, who kept large kennels of Shih Tzus but also of Pugs and Pekingese. They arrived in England in the late 1920s and were not imported to the United States in significant numbers until the 1950s, but soon became popular within a decade.

499

Small Greek Domestic Dog

Meliteo Kinidio / Kokoni

GREECE

Exercise required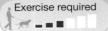

Common Coat Colors

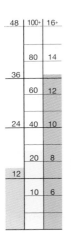

Average height (inches)
Average weight (pounds)
Average life expectancy (years)

Lively, and versatile companions, the Greek Domestic dog is suitable both as lap dog or as a very noisy watchdog. But these dogs also make a great ratter.

AT A GLANCE

Ease of training	▬ ▬ ▬
Affection	▬ ▬ ▬ ▬
Playfulness	▬ ▬ ▬ ▬
Good with children	▬ ▬ ▬
Good with other dogs	▬ ▬ ▬
Grooming required	▬ ▬

! Its name, Meliteo Kinidio, translates to "little dog from Malta."

+ No major health issues are known.

HISTORY

An ancient breed, also known for many years as the Meliteo Kinidio, was considered a variant of the Alopekis, another small Greek breed. However, the Greek Domestic Dog is now categorized as a separate breed, but are rarely seen or heard of beyond Greece.

Tibetan Spaniel

Simkhyi

TIBET

Tibetan Spaniel puppy

Exercise required

		48	100+	16+
			80	14
		36		
			60	12
		24	40	10
			20	8
		12		
			10	6

Average height (inches)
Average weight (pounds)
Average life expectancy (years)

Common Coat Colors

The Tibetan Spaniel was developed more than 2000 years ago. Similarly to many dog breeds of the Himalayan Area, it has a history associated with Buddhism. Also known as "Lion Dogs" and bred by Tibetan monks, they were used as watchdogs in the monasteries and believed to bring good luck. They would stand on the exterior walls and sound an alarm when necessary and turn prayer wheels The breed arrived in England in 1898 and about 70 years later in United States. These devoted, sensitive, intelligent dogs thrive on the companionship of their families.

AT A GLANCE

Ease of training	▰ ▰ ▰
Affection	▰ ▰ ▰ ▰
Playfulness	▰ ▰ ▰
Good with children	▰ ▰ ▰ ▰ ▰
Good with other dogs	▰ ▰ ▰ ▰
Grooming required	▰ ▰ ▰

+ Progressive retinal atrophy and patellar luxation.

! This dog is not a true spaniel, although it may have been given this name due to its resemblance to the lapdog version of hunting spaniels, such as the Cavalier King Charles Spaniel.

HISTORY

The Tibetan Spaniel is an ancient Asian breed frequently given as gifts to ambassadors visiting China, facilitating the spread of the breed worldwide. In 1960, the breed was recognized by the England Kennel Club. Presently, the breed is relatively rare nowadays, and does not rank in the top 100 breeds registered by the AKC.

Yorkshire Terrier

Yorkie

ENGLAND

Exercise required

"Yorkies," are somewhat self-important busy, active little dogs. They enjoy and bask in unadulterated admiration and affection. Self-confident and playful, they have huge personalities. Despite their diminutive size, they can be aggressive toward other dogs and are often wary of strangers, and are thus very inclined to bark. Although renowned for being pampered and coiffed, Yorkies enjoy running and still have the terrier instinct to chase (very) small rodents.

 Yorkie puppies are born black. Their tan or blue-and-tan coloring emerges gradually as they mature.

 Although generally healthy, some health problems can include portosystemic shunts, hypothyroidism, renal failure, and patellar luxation.

Yorkshire Terrier pups

48	100+	16+
	80	14
36		
	60	12
24	40	10
	20	8
12		
	10	6

Average height (inches)
Average weight (pounds)
Average life expectancy (years)

HISTORY

The Yorkie developed in the nineteenth century in northern England, from small terrier-types favored by mill owners. The terriers, were valued for keeping rodent populations at bay, were largely introduced by immigrant workers from Scotland.. Breeds such as the now-extinct Waterside, and Old English Toy Terrier are all thought to be part of the Yorkie. 'Huddersfield' was the most influential early Yorkie—he won numerous show classes and ratting events. All of today's Yorkies trace back to Huddersfield through his ten sons and one daughter. Yorkies were first recognized by the American Kennel Club in 1885.

Common Coat Colors
● ●

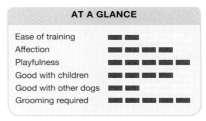

AT A GLANCE

Ease of training	▬ ▬
Affection	▬ ▬ ▬
Playfulness	▬ ▬ ▬ ▬
Good with children	▬ ▬ ▬
Good with other dogs	▬ ▬
Grooming required	▬ ▬ ▬

DESIGNER DOGS

Aussledoodle pup

Aussiedoodle

Aussiepoo

UNITED STATES

Exercise required

48	100+	16+
	80	14
36		
	60	12
24	40	10
	20	8
12		
	10	6

Average height (inches)
Average weight (pounds)
Average life expectancy (years)

Common
Coat Colors

AT A GLANCE

Ease of training	■■ ■
Affection	■■ ■ ■ ■
Playfulness	■■ ■ ■
Good with children	■■ ■ ■
Good with other dogs	■■ ■ ■
Grooming required	■■ ■ ■

! The Aussiedoodle is more popular in the United States than in Australia. That is because Australian shepherds were developed in the Western US, not Australia.

+ Susceptible to some of the same hereditary diseases as the parent breeds such as hip dysplasia, patellar luxation, and cataracts.

Also recognized as "Aussiepoo", the Aussiedoodle is a crossbreed of the Australian Shepherd and the Poodle. This breed is somewhat hypoallergenic due to its Poodle genes, and is playful, friendly, and compatible with both kids and other animals, making it an excellent family pet. The height and size of this loyal and intelligent breed varies greatly and is dependent upon the characteristics of its parents.

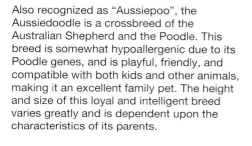

HISTORY

As a crossbreed, very little is known about its history. It is believed to have developed in the late twentieth century to create a smaller dog with hypoallergenic qualities, while retaining its Shepherd characteristics.

Beaglier puppy

Beaglier

AUSTRALIA

Exercise required

■ ▪ ▪ ■

48	100+	16+
	80	14
36		
	60	12
24	40	10
	20	8
12		
	10	6

Average height (inches)
Average weight (pounds)
Average life expectancy (years)

Common Coat Colors

A cross between the Beagle and the Cavalier King Charles Spaniel, the Beaglier is a playful, affectionate breed. They are friendly and compatible with both children and other pets, but are not recommended for small apartment living due to their need for large space to meet their need for play and activity. They are sensitive and wary towards strangers and thus make great watchdogs.

AT A GLANCE

Ease of training	■ ■ ■ ■
Affection	■ ■ ■ ■ ■
Playfulness	■ ■ ■ ■ ■
Good with children	■ ■ ■ ■
Good with other dogs	■ ■ ■ ■ ■
Grooming required	■ ■ ■

! Beagliers do not make good guard dogs, but are known to bark loudly at abnormal sounds or strangers, so they make good watchdogs.

+ Epilepsy, patellar luxation, progressive retinal atrophy. Inherited health issues are largely based on their parent breeds.

HISTORY

During the late twentieth century, the Beaglier became popular through crossbreeding programs in Australia. Breeders endeavored to develop a small but healthy and energetic dog while tempering the Beagle's hunting temperament.

DESIGNER

Bichpoo

Poochon / Bichonpoo

UNITED STATES

Exercise required

Bichpoo pup

Common
Coat Colors

	48	100+	16+
		80	14
	36		
		60	12
	24	40	10
		20	8
	12		
		10	6

Average height (inches)
Average weight (pounds)
Average life expectancy (years)

The Bichpoo is a cross between a Bichon Frise and a Poodle. Depending on the size of its parent Poodle, whether they are standard, miniature or toy, this generally small dog can vary in size and appearance. Bichpoos are sensitive, affectionate dogs with boundless energy. They are well-suited to smaller living environments like an apartment and make excellent companions.

AT A GLANCE

Ease of training	▬▬ ▬▬ ▬▬
Affection	▬▬ ▬▬ ▬▬ ▬▬
Playfulness	▬▬ ▬▬ ▬▬ ▬▬
Good with children	▬▬ ▬▬ ▬▬ ▬▬
Good with other dogs	▬▬ ▬▬ ▬▬ ▬▬
Grooming required	▬▬ ▬▬ ▬▬

+ This breed is known for being healthier than either of its parents, but may still experience problems such as progressive retinal atrophy and patellar luxation.

HISTORY

The Bichpoo originated in the United States but is known to display an irregular set of traits, diversifying in characteristics over time. This breed is eligible for registration though the American Canine Hybrid Club.

 A Bichpoo owner must be ready to play with its dog often, since this breed is known for having sudden energy spikes.

509

Borador

UNITED STATES

Borador puppy

Exercise required

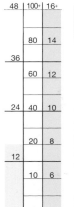

48	100+	16+
	80	14
36		
	60	12
24	40	10
	20	8
12		
	10	6

Average height (inches)
Average weight (pounds)
Average life expectancy (years)

Common Coat Colors

AT A GLANCE

Ease of training	▬ ▬ ▬
Affection	▬ ▬ ▬ ▬
Playfulness	▬ ▬ ▬
Good with children	▬ ▬ ▬
Good with other dogs	▬ ▬ ▬ ▬
Grooming required	▬ ▬ ▬

! The Borador is able to learn to fetch very quickly due to the "retriever" quality it inherits from its Lab parent.

+ Moderate tendency to get fat if not properly exercised, hip and elbow dysplasia, eye problems, ear infections.

510

The Borador is a cross between two highly intelligent and extremely popular breeds: the Border Collie and the Labrador Retriever. Although they are extremely intelligent and obedient, much commitment is required when training the Borador. This multi-talented, versatile breed have great energy and require consistent, high levels of exercise, and therefore may not be suitable for urban environments. They do, however, make an excellent companion and family dog.

HISTORY
A relatively new crossbreed that is recognized by the Designer Breed Registry, the Borador originated in the United States.

Cavachon
UNITED STATES

Cavachon puppy

Exercise required

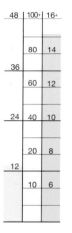

48	100+	16+
	80	14
36		
	60	12
24	40	10
	20	8
12		
	10	6

Average height (inches)
Average weight (pounds)
Average life expectancy (years)

Common
Coat Colors

The Cavachon is a crossbreed of the Cavalier King Charles Spaniel and Bichon Frise. This relatively quiet tiny breed are lovable, intelligent and ideally suited to small-space urban family environments.

AT A GLANCE

Ease of training	▬▬▬▬
Affection	▬▬▬▬▬
Playfulness	▬▬▬▬
Good with children	▬▬▬▬
Good with other dogs	▬▬▬▬▬
Grooming required	▬▬▬▬

! Well-groomed Cavachons have relatively short coats, but this small dog's coat can grow as long as 5" if not properly maintained.

+ Typically have the same potential health issues as other small dogs, such as ear infections, heart murmurs, and eye ulcerations (comes from hair rubbing the cornea).

Chion

Papihuahua / Pap-Chi / Chi-A-Pap

UNITED STATES

Chion puppy

Exercise required

	48	100+	16+
		80	14
	36		
		60	12
	24	40	10
		20	8
	12		
		10	6

Average height (inches)
Average weight (pounds)
Average life expectancy (years)

Common
Coat Colors

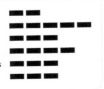

AT A GLANCE

Ease of training	▬ ▬
Affection	▬ ▬ ▬ ▬ ▬
Playfulness	▬ ▬ ▬
Good with children	▬ ▬ ▬
Good with other dogs	▬ ▬ ▬
Grooming required	▬ ▬ ▬

Known to be extremely loving and loyal, the Chion is a crossbreed of the Chihuahua and Papillon. They are relatively quiet and protective but may bark loudly when exposed to unfamiliar environments and strangers. Due to their small size, they are delicate and should not be kept around small children. Otherwise, they make an excellent companion or family dog for an affectionate family living in smaller urban areas.

! Chions are often bred back to Chihuahuas or Papillons.

 Patellar luxation, soft spot on skull (sensitive and prone to injury), prone to catching colds

513

Chizer

Schnauchi / Miniature Schnauzer Chihuahua Mix

UNITED STATES

Chizer puppy

Exercise required

48	100+	16+
	80	14
36		
	60	12
24	40	10
	20	8
12		
	10	6

Average height (inches)
Average weight (pounds)
Average life expectancy (years)

Common Coat Colors

AT A GLANCE

Ease of training	▬▬ ▬▬ ▬▬
Affection	▬▬ ▬▬ ▬▬ ▬▬
Playfulness	▬▬ ▬▬ ▬▬
Good with children	▬▬ ▬▬ ▬▬ ▬▬
Good with other dogs	▬▬ ▬▬ ▬▬ ▬▬
Grooming required	▬▬ ▬▬ ▬▬ ▬▬

! Toy dog, companion dog, lap dog, guard dog

A cross between the Chihuahua and the Miniature Schnauzer, the Chizer's appearance may vary greatly depending on the characteristics of their parents. They typically range around 10–14 inches in height and 8–15 pounds in weight, and come in a variety of colors often grey, black, brown or white. The general character of the Chizer combines the active personality of a Miniature Schnauzer and the big, bold attitude of a Chihuahua. They are fiercely loyal, but affectionate and gentle. Given their small size, the Chizer is great for apartment living and easy to train, but requires regular grooming and trimming around the eyes, ears and nose. They have a tendency to bark; due to a keen sense of hearing, they respond to the slightest noise.

Chorkie

Yorkiehuahua

UNITED STATES

Chorkie puppy

Exercise required

Common Coat Colors

	Average height (inches)	Average weight (pounds)	Average life expectancy (years)
	48	100+	16+
		80	14
	36		
		60	12
	24	40	10
		20	8
	12		
		10	6

AT A GLANCE

Ease of training

Affection

Playfulness

Good with children

Good with other dogs

Grooming required

The Chorkie is a cross between the Yorkshire Terrier and the Chihuahua. Depending on the relative proportions of its parent breeds, the Chorkies qualities and temperament may vary greatly. A protective, low-maintenance breed, they are suitable for most environments. But due to its small size, they are not suitable for families with small children as they may be more susceptible to injuries.

! Chorkies love to play outside, although their long coats bring the outdoors inside if not properly maintained.

+ Patelllar luxation, dental issues, epilepsy, portosystemic shunts (all issues are dependent upon parent)

515

Cockapoo

UNITED STATES

Cockapoo puppy

Exercise required

48	100+	16+
	80	14
36		
	60	12
24	40	10
	20	8
12		
	10	6

Average height (inches)
Average weight (pounds)
Average life expectancy (years)

Common Coat Colors

AT A GLANCE

Ease of training	■ ■ ■ ■
Affection	■ ■ ■ ■ ■
Playfulness	■ ■ ■ ■ ■
Good with children	■ ■ ■ ■
Good with other dogs	■ ■ ■ ■
Grooming required	■ ■ ■

! The Cockapoo is a non-shedding dog due to being part Poodle, which makes it a reliable option for those allergic to dog hair.

+ Cataracts, patellar luxation, hip dysplasia, liver disease

One of the older of the "new breeds", the Cockapoo is a mixture of the American Cocker Spaniel or English Cocker Spaniel and Poodle. Similar to most hybrid breeds, there is a variation in appearance and character dependent on the parents. Sizes vary on whether the Parent Poodle is standard, miniature or toy, and attributes vary depending on whether the Parent Spaniel is English or American. Nevertheless, Cockapoos make great companion dogs, often are renowned for their friendly personalities.

HISTORY

When Cockapoos were developed in the mid twentieth century, they rose in popularity very quickly. Although the crossing of the two breeds may have been initially accidental, the resulting dog was well received. It remains one of the most popular of the "designer" dogs to this day. Various clubs such as the Cockapoo Club of America (1999) and the American Cockapoo Club (2004) formed to create a breed standard within the past two decades.

Doxiepoo

UNITED STATES

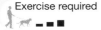

Exercise required

Doxiepoo puppy

Common Coat Colors

	48	100+	16+
		80	14
	36		
		60	12
	24	40	10
		20	8
	12		
		10	6

Average height (inches)
Average weight (pounds)
Average life expectancy (years)

The Doxiepoo is a mix of Dachshund and Poodle breeds. They frequently compete in obedience and agility competitions and are especially popular in the southern United States. Doxiepoos are adaptable to either small or large homes, urban or rural. Because they are so easy to train and maintain they make excellent companions.

AT A GLANCE

Ease of training	▰ ▰ ▰ ▰
Affection	▰ ▰ ▰ ▰ ▰ ▰
Playfulness	▰ ▰ ▰
Good with children	▰ ▰ ▰
Good with other dogs	▰ ▰ ▰
Grooming required	▰ ▰ ▰

+ Susceptible to the same health problems as the Dachshund and Poodle, although the mixing may lower chances of certain diseases. Prone to back problems, epilepsy, deafness, hip displasia, and patellar luxation.

! This breed's name spelling varies greatly. It is known as the Doxie-poo, Doxipoo, Doxi-poo, or even Doxypoo.

Goldendoodle

UNITED STATES

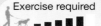
Exercise required

Goldendoodle puppy

48	100+	16+
	80	14
36		
	60	12
24	40	10
	20	8
12		
	10	6

Average height (inches)
Average weight (pounds)
Average life expectancy (years)

Common Coat Colors

AT A GLANCE

Ease of training	■■■ ■■
Affection	■■■ ■■
Playfulness	■■■ ■■
Good with children	■■■ ■■
Good with other dogs	■■■ ■■
Grooming required	■■ ■

! Goldendoodle puppies go through several coat changes before they develop their adult coats at about one year of age. Their shaggy eyebrows and beards begin forming as puppies and are noticeable, but take some time to develop fully.

+ Generally exceptionally healthy, but some issues might include elbow and patellar luxation, von Willebrand disease, progressive retinal atrophy, and hip dysplasia

Developed in the United States in the late twentieth century, the Goldendoodle is a cross between the Golden Retriever and the Poodle. They have become enormously popular in the United States, Australia, and England. Their low-shedding and low-dander coat makes them partially hypoallergenic, and thus more suitable for allergy sufferers. These dogs are intelligent, friendly, and playful, but require lots of exercise. These gregarious dogs tend to develop very strong bonds with their owners and make wonderful companions.

HISTORY

Following quickly on the heels of the development of the Australian Labradoodle, the Goldendoodle appeared as a deliberate hybrid in the late twentieth century. Breeders noticed a successful breeding of small hybrid crosses with Poodles and so determined to develop a large but similar crossbreed.

Gollie

Golden Collie

ENGLAND / UNITED STATES

Gollie puppy

Exercise required

48	100+	16+
	80	14
36		
	60	12
24	40	10
	20	8
12		
	10	6

Average height (inches)
Average weight (pounds)
Average life expectancy (years)

Common Coat Colors

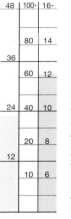

The Golden Collie or "Gollie" is a crossbreed of the Collie and Golden Retriever. They frequently retain the characteristics of both parents including the Golden Retriever's soft mouth and love of water and the Collie's herding instincts. Generally they are very intelligent, alert and active. Good with family members and easy to train, the Gollie requires considerable activity and exercise and may not be best suited to urban living. They come in a variety of colors but are most often shades of cream, red-brown or black.

AT A GLANCE

Ease of training	■■■■
Affection	■■■■
Playfulness	■■■
Good with children	■■■■
Good with other dogs	■■■
Grooming required	■■■

 Gollies have a very strong herding instinct and will chase cars or people if not kept active both mentally and physically.

+ Hip dysplasia, arthritis, eye issues, cancer

Jack-a-Bee

ENGLAND / UNITED STATES

Jack-a-Bee puppy

Exercise required

+ Generally healthy due to hybrid genetics, but prone to glaucoma and patellar luxation

48	100+	16+
	80	14
36		
	60	12
	40	10
24		
	20	8
12		
	10	6

Average height (inches)
Average weight (pounds)
Average life expectancy (years)

Common Coat Colors

AT A GLANCE

Ease of training	■
Affection	■ ■ ■ ■
Playfulness	■ ■ ■ ■ ■
Good with children	■ ■ ■ ■
Good with other dogs	■ ■ ■ ■
Grooming required	■

! The Jack-A-Bee is a high-energy dog that can suffer from separation anxiety. Owners should properly train and crate their dogs to decrease the likelihood of chewing household furnishings.

A crossbreed between Jack Russell Terriers and Beagles, these small to medium sized dogs are loyal, energetic and playful. From their Beagle parents, the Jack-a-Bee retains their hunting instincts and highly sensitive nose. However, due to their independence and tenacity, they are not always responsive and are prone to wandering, and thus require consistent obedience training. Be especially careful when walking off-lead in woods or wilderness, as they are easily distracted by smells and movement, and may not respond to recall commands.

Jack-a-Poo

Jackadoodle / Poojack

ENGLAND / UNITED STATES

Jack-a-poo puppy

Exercise required

48	100+	16+
	80	14
36		
	60	12
24	40	10
	20	8
12		
	10	6

Average height (inches)
Average weight (pounds)
Average life expectancy (years)

Common
Coat Colors

AT A GLANCE

Ease of training	■■■ ■■
Affection	■■ ■■
Playfulness	■■ ■■ ■■ ■
Good with children	■■ ■■ ■
Good with other dogs	■■ ■ ■
Grooming required	■■ ■ ■

! The Jack-a-Poo is a good option for someone who wants Jack Russell characteristics in their dog, but is allergic, since the Jack-a-Poo inherits hypoallergenic qualities.

A fairly new hybrid, the Jack-a-Poo is a crossbreed between the Jack Russell Terrier and Miniature Poodle. As the breed was developed recently, its appearance will not have standardized for several more generations. Nevertheless, they are loving, cheery, family-oriented dogs that make excellent companions. They are intelligent, active and highly trainable, but require regular physical and mental exercise.

+ Addison's disease, bloat, epilepsy, eye problems, patellar luxation

Labradoodle

Australian Labradoodle
AUSTRALIA

Exercise required

Labradoodle puppy

Labradoodles are a cross between the Labrador Retriever and the Poodle. Established four decades ago, this breed encompasses the best qualities of both parents and have become enormously popular. Somewhat hypoallergenic with non-shedding and low-dander coats, Labradoodles are highly intelligent, energetic and easily trainable while also exhibiting particularly good temperaments from their Poodle blood.
They are bred in three sizes: standard, medium or miniature.

Average height (inches)	Average weight (pounds)	Average life expectancy (years)
48	100+	16+
	80	14
36		
	60	12
24	40	10
	20	8
12		
	10	6

Common Coat Colors

AT A GLANCE

Ease of training	■ ■ ■ ■ ■
Affection	■ ■ ■ ■ ■
Playfulness	■ ■ ■ ■ ■
Good with children	■ ■ ■ ■ ■
Good with other dogs	■ ■ ■ ■ ■
Grooming required	■ ■ ■ ■

! Labradoodle coats (fleece and wool type) are more suitable for allergy sufferers, but they are not "non-allergenic."

+ Although generally healthy, some issues can include skin problems, ear problems, progressive retinal atrophy, epilepsy, diabetes, hip dysplasia, elbow dysplasia, and hypothyroidism.

HISTORY

The Labradoodle was developed by Wally Cochran of the Royal Guide Dogs in Victoria, Australia in the late twentieth century. Cochran was approached by a blind woman from Hawaii who sought a hypoallergenic seeing-eye dog as her husband was allergic to dogs. Cochran's breeding program was enormously successful, and a large percentage of his dogs became guide dogs. Ensuing media coverage saw the breed rapidly becoming hugely popular.

Longdog

UNITED STATES

Longdog puppy

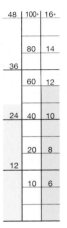

Average height (inches)	Average weight (pounds)	Average life expectancy (years)
48	100+	16+
	80	14
36		
	60	12
24	40	10
	20	8
12		
	10	6

Common Coat Colors

AT A GLANCE

Ease of training	■■■
Affection	■■■
Playfulness	■■■
Good with children	■■■
Good with other dogs	■■■
Grooming required	■

! Longdogs are instinctively hunting dogs and have very high stamina and agility. Longdogs are often used for hunting rabbits, hares, foxes, deer, and coyotes, but are happy to be a companion to a loving family.

+ Generally healthy breed. Prone to gastric torsion, cardiomyopathy, muscle injuries

The longdog is a cross between any two sighthounds (compared with a Lurcher, which is a cross between a Sighthound and any other dog). Most common are crosses between the Greyhound and other sighthounds including the Saluki, Scottish Deerhound, and Whippet. The Longdog is a highly versatile and active breed that exhibits typical sighthound qualities such as strong hunting instincts and boundless energy. They are very active and love to run, and as a result require much physical and mental activity to ensure proper development.

Mal-Shi
MaltiZu / Malt-Tzui

AUSTRALIA / UNITED STATES / ENGLAND

Mal-Shi puppy

Exercise required

48	100+	16+
	80	14
36		
	60	12
24	40	10
	20	8
12		
	10	6

Average height (inches)
Average weight (pounds)
Average life expectancy (years)

Common Coat Colors

AT A GLANCE

Ease of training	■ ■ ■
Affection	■ ■ ■ ■ ■
Playfulness	■ ■ ■ ■
Good with children	■ ■ ■ ■
Good with other dogs	■ ■ ■
Grooming required	■ ■ ■ ■

! The Mal-Shi is one of the most popular hybrids in Australia.

 Patellar luxation, kidney problems, eye problems, liver problems, hip dysplasia

The Mal-Shi is one of the few more popular designer breeds that does not feature the Poodle in its mix. Also known as the Malti-Zu and Malt Tzu, they are a cross between the Maltese and Shih Tzu. The Mal-Shi was bred in the late twentieth century as a low-shedding companion breed. These dogs are generally gregarious, intelligent and affectionate dogs that are highly suitable as family dogs, as they make vigilant watchdogs and loving companions. If left alone they can be prone to barking.

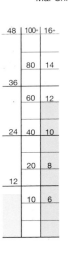

Maltipoo

UNITED STATES

Exercise required

Maltipoo puppy

Common Coat Colors

	48	100+	16+
		80	14
	36		
		60	12
Average height (inches) Average weight (pounds) Average life expectancy (years)	24	40	10
		20	8
	12		
		10	6

AT A GLANCE

Ease of training	■■■■■
Affection	■■■■■■
Playfulness	■■■■
Good with children	■■■■
Good with other dogs	■■■
Grooming required	■■■■

! Maltipoo puppies are difficult to distinguish from adult dogs, as they retain their "puppyish" looks throughout their lives.

+ Generally healthy, but they can suffer from epilepsy, progressive retinal atrophy, shaker syndrome, and patellar luxation.

A cross between a Maltese and a Miniature or Toy Poodle, the Maltese is an adorable, affectionate dog. They are devoted to their families but need much attention and adoration. As a result, if they are left alone they become very prone to barking and become unsettled. Maltipoos can take a long time to adapt and be accustomed to strangers, and have a tendency to be aloof, demanding proper socialization and considerable patience. It is worth the effort though, as these delightful little dogs are enormously loyal and loving to their families.

HISTORY

The Maltipoo was developed as small companion dog with a low-shedding coat, making this breed partially hypoallergenic and therefore a more suitable companion dog for allergy sufferers than most other breeds.

DESIGNER

Puggle

Bug / Buggle

UNITED STATES

Puggle puppy

Exercise required

■ ■■ ■

48	100+	16+
	80	14
36		
	60	12
24	40	10
	20	8
12		
	10	6

Average height (inches)
Average weight (pounds)
Average life expectancy (years)

Common Coat Colors

AT A GLANCE

Ease of training	■■ ■■
Affection	■■ ■■ ■■
Playfulness	■■ ■■ ■■ ■■
Good with children	■■ ■■ ■■ ■■
Good with other dogs	■■ ■■ ■■
Grooming required	■■

! Pugs love to get on furniture and the Puggle may well expect similar comforts.

+ Although generally healthy, issues can include brachycephalic airway obstruction syndrome, back problems, eye problems.

HISTORY

The Puggle was developed in the United States about 40 years ago as breeders began to experiment in creating new breeds. Like many designer dogs, the Puggle may have initially been created accidentally, but maintained as a breed due to their endearing qualities. By the twenty-first century, Puggles were sold commercially to pet owners looking for a new distinctive breed.

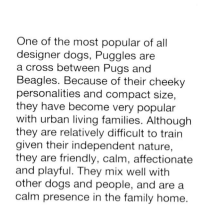

One of the most popular of all designer dogs, Puggles are a cross between Pugs and Beagles. Because of their cheeky personalities and compact size, they have become very popular with urban living families. Although they are relatively difficult to train given their independent nature, they are friendly, calm, affectionate and playful. They mix well with other dogs and people, and are a calm presence in the family home.

Schnoodle

UNITED STATES / ENGLAND

Schnoodle puppy

48	100+	16+
	80	14
36		
	60	12
24	40	10
	20	8
12		
	10	6

Average height (inches)
Average weight (pounds)
Average life expectancy (years)

Common Coat Colors

AT A GLANCE

Ease of training	■ ■ ■ ■
Affection	■ ■ ■ ■
Playfulness	■ ■ ■ ■
Good with children	■ ■ ■ ■ ■
Good with other dogs	■ ■ ■ ■
Grooming required	■ ■ ■ ■

! Schnoodles are highly intelligent and agile, making them a good choice for agility and obedience contests.

+ Large amount of in-ear hair leads to ear infections, progressive retinal atrophy, cataracts, Legg-Calve-Perthes disease

The Schnoodle is a cross between the Poodle and the Schnauzer. As both parent breeds come in three or four sizes, the Schnoodle's size varies greatly too. For example, the Giant Schnoodle which weighs up to 70 pounds is bred from the Standard Poodle and Giant Schnauzer, whereas the Miniature Schnoodle can weigh as little as 15 pounds. Generally, they are highly intelligent, affectionate, playful dogs that enjoy lots of activity. Although they are compatible with other dogs and people, and make great family dogs, they do have a tendency to bark—the upside of which is they make vigilant watchdogs.

Shih-Poo
UNITED STATES

DESIGNER

Shih-Poo puppy

Exercise required
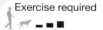

Common Coat Colors

	48	100+	16+
		80	14
	36		
		60	12
	24	40	10
		20	8
	12		
		10	6

Average height (inches)
Average weight (pounds)
Average life expectancy (years)

AT A GLANCE

Ease of training	▬▬ ▬▬ ▬▬ ▬▬
Affection	▬▬ ▬▬ ▬▬ ▬▬ ▬▬
Playfulness	▬▬ ▬▬ ▬▬ ▬▬ ▬▬
Good with children	▬▬ ▬▬ ▬▬ ▬▬
Good with other dogs	▬▬ ▬▬ ▬▬
Grooming required	▬▬ ▬▬ ▬▬ ▬▬

! Shih-Poos are companion dogs and are great for those living in a small home.

Like many of the poodle hybrids, the Shih-Poo was developed to create an intelligent breed with a low-shed coat. As a cross between the Shih Tzu and the Poodle, their coats may either have the straight long coat of a Shih Tzu or the curly coat of a Poodle, or a combination of the two. The size also varies depending on the size of the parent Poodle—normally a Toy or Miniature. Regardless of their coat and size, the Shih-Poo is alert, affectionate and easy to train.

 Entropion, patellar luxation, hip dysplasia, cataracts.

531

INDEX & CREDITS

INDEX